James H. Fraser

Publishing and Book Design
in Latvia 1919–1940: a Re-discovery

James H. Fraser

Publishing and Book Design in Latvia 1919–1940: a Re-discovery

For Sibylle

Contents

PART 4   GERMAN-LANGUAGE PUBLISHING

As this work was being finalized for publication, the author died of a terminal illness which prevented him from applying his characteristic editorial acuity to the final polishing of this manuscript.

Consequently, others close to the author have had to review the final proofs and undertake any necessary revisions. They have done so to the best of their abilities.

This work is a labor of love reflecting the author's longtime interest in and appreciation for the creativity and richness of Latvian publishing and book design between 1919 and 1940. We trust that the reader will see it as such and will overlook any errors or infelicities that may remain in the text.

Acknowledgments

Note: All earned and honorary degrees as well as titles have been excluded from names of individuals acknowledged.

This project could not have been undertaken without loyal supporters: my wife, Sibylle von Holstein Fraser, without whose constant support, tireless research, and steady encouragement I would not have been able to develop my original vision or bring it to conclusion. I am also so grateful to Elfrida Melbārzde, Jānis Borgs, Mara Vishniac Kohn, and Marina Hoff.

Singled out for a special word of appreciation is Dace Pamata, an untiring reference librarian at the National Library of Latvia, who has maintained her good humor throughout this project. Her amazing biblio-detective talents have been crucial to carrying this project forward. Without her consistent help and encouragement, to say nothing of her valued editorial comments and corrections, this work could not have reached its present state.

Guna Zelmene spent many hours reading, looking for errors, and improving many a rough spot. When titles important to the narrative could not be found for examination, she found them through her efficient network.

Raimonds Briedis subsequently read the text, checked statements for accuracy, expanded sentences for clarification, standardized Latvian and Russian spellings, and made overall improvements. His foreword and summary have greatly enhanced the presentation and without his continuing help and encouragement, together with that of Guna Zelmene, this work would likely have languished in a desk drawer.

Deborah Hussey read, edited, and greatly improved the flow of the text.

None of these individuals, however, is responsible for any of my observations or interpretations of data.

Booksellers deserve special mention. Without their continuing support and the many items they provided, this project would have been greatly diminished. Christian Bartsch, Konstantin Beloglazov, Tom Congalton, Laimdota Degro, Frank Deodene (d.), Jeffrey Eger, Henrik Einarsson, Virginia Faulkner, Robert Fleck, Leila Geižna, Ari and Taisa Kamenkowitsch, Preston McMann (d.), Jesse Mann, Heiko Schmidt, Guna Šmite (d.), Vidmantas Staniulis, Michael Weintraub, Chris Wolf, Guna Zelmene.

The following have assisted in a variety of other creative ways: Galena Anshelevich, Anita Batarags, Ināra Beļinkaja, Ilgonis Bērsons, Rita Bogdonova, Māris Brancis, Ingrīda Burāne, Brigid Burke, Aija Čakste, Ruta Čaupova, Emma Linen Dana, Susanne Hagen Delaney, Mary Donnelly, Tom Freudenheim, Eleanor Friedl, Ella Gankin, Irra Schlossberg Gelin (d.), Andrejs Ģērmanis, Agita Grants, Māra Grudule, Jürgen Holstein, Michiyo Honjo, Aivars Kalējs, Ieva Kalniņa, Gregoriĭ Kasovskiĭ, Naomichi Kawahata, Velga Kince, Ingrida Korsakaitė, Maija Kreibina, Jānis Krēsliņš, Vladimir Kuznetsov, Ruta Shats-Mariash, Gertrude Michelson, Judith Bagg Neumann (d.), Jāzeps Osmanis, Rudīte Ozoliņa, Mai Pähn, Igor Palley, Maria Palley, Aubrey Pomerance, Lia Poorvu, Guntars Pupa, Renate Raecke-Hauswedell, Anatoliĭ Rakitianskiĭ, Jānis Rapa (d.), Rasma Rapa, Laima Reihmane, Vladimir Rezhetov, Ainars Roze, Neil Salzman, Elizabeth Sandor, Leonard Seastone, Gregoriĭ Smirin, Astrīda Stahnke, Vidmantas Staniulis, Tatjana Suta (d.),

Silvija Tretjakova, Fay Unschuld (d.), Marģers Vestermanis, Valdis Villerušs, Velga Vīlipa, Luta Bagg Vishniac (d.), Maria Webb, Barbara Wind, Dmitrijs Zinovjevs.

The research phase of this project has been carried forward without institutional support. The "foundation support" has been the collective helpfulness of the individuals named above. It is regrettable that six of the informants and three booksellers died before seeing the result of their contribution. Their names are followed with a (d.).

The institutional collections consulted, among which the National Library of Latvia is pre-eminent: the Jewish Museum in Riga, the New York Public Library (NYPL) Slavic Division (closed in 2009 after nearly 100 years), and the Library of Congress in Washington, D.C. The online library catalogs of Harvard University, Yale University, and the New York Public Library have all been invaluable in the bibliographical verification process.

Transliteration notes and abbreviations

Regarding the transliteration of Russian and Yiddish, the Library of Congress scheme has been followed with some variation, e.g., Gorky rather than Gorkiĭ, Mayakovsky rather than Maiakovskiĭ. This practice has also been followed with the names of other, widely translated authors known particularly to the Anglo-American community. The transliteration of Yiddish words and titles follows that of the Library of Congress scheme most of the time. The issue of the Latvianization of personal and family names is a vexing one, to say the least. The choice to use the Latvianized form of German family and personal names has been followed only where the individual was a Baltic-German known by the Latvianized form, thus Kārlis Mīlenbahs, rather than the compromised form of Kārlis Mülenbachs and not the name on his birth certificate, Karl Mühlenbach. For other German writers whose works were translated into Latvian together with the Latvianization of their names, the generally accepted spelling among Anglophone readers and in Western online catalogs has been used. For example: Johann Wolfgang von Goethe, rather than Johans Volfgangs fon Gēte; Friedrich Schiller, rather than Frīdrihs Šillers. The birth certificate name for many Jewish, Latvian-born citizens has been retained in the text, e.g., Friedman instead of Frīdmanis. In the instance of a Russianized form, the spelling used is that of the author's mother language, e.g., the English writer Olivia Wadsley, rather than Oliviĭa Uedsli.

Book titles, including those in Latvia's pre-reform orthography, are given as they appear on the title page.

Preface

During the years 2002-2004, I read, interviewed, and looked for fragments in English-language texts of what seemed to be a rapidly vanishing chapter in 20th century publishing history and book culture: Latvia's Interwar period. I wanted to know how that book culture "looked". My subsequent "field survey" meant simply browsing through a significant sample of books and periodicals and looking at covers.

The initial objective was personal satisfaction. If what was found proved to be of wider interest, I gave a thought to preparing a summary journal article for English readers. As I spoke to colleagues about the project, it seemed that an expanded summary of findings highlighting a sample of publishers, authors, and designers might be helpful. Perhaps then some future researcher might undertake a scholarly exploration of Latvia's Interwar book scene, which seemed to be rapidly receding from the memory of many of the Latvian informants contacted.

Neither my idea nor approach was new, only the choice of country. A number of book historians have conducted similar inquiries and established various guidelines for similar undertakings in other countries.

Alan Powers, a leading English historian of "how books look", calls attention to a categorization of book covers that guided him and others who have collected, written, or made observations about this integral part of books published since the mid 19th century. [1] In his essay, Powers cites the Baku-born industrial designer Sir Misha Black and his three categories: "1. conventional picture-jacket [that] carries a good or bad drawing; 2. carefully planned, inexpensive jacket, usually typographical; 3. expensive self-indulgence on the part of the publisher."[2] (Here Black refers to illustrated jackets where an artist or designer has been commissioned to produce something likely to attract a potential buyer.)

In the following pages, this last category will dominate the presentation of the "look". In Latvia, however, it is not usually a jacket as such but rather an illustrated paper wrapper of varying weight and surface texture that serves as the book's case, instead of a cloth- or paper-over-board binding. This does not mean the case-bound book was an anomaly in Latvia in those years. The larger publishing houses often brought out titles in both binding types. The smaller, short-lived publishing houses usually published their books sewn or stapled in paper. For such covers, an artist was commissioned or volunteered to create an illustration.

It is with these illustrated covers or wrappers for books (and, for comparison, covers of selected periodicals, sheet music, and a few posters) that this investigation is concerned. Again, the objective is to provide a glimpse of the look of the Latvian book during the Independence—late 1919 to the summer of 1940—with reference to other mediums competing for the reader's attention.

There will be abundant opportunity for second-guessing among the Latvian book design cognoscenti as to the choice of this book cover or another, why there is no representation of this or that artist or author. Often based on available or existing resource materials, the choices made offer but one approach in making better known that vibrant era's publishing and book design life.

---

1 "From promotion to protection: the uses of the book jacket" in *Books for Sale: The advertising and promotion of print since the fifteenth century* edited by Robin Myers, Michael Harris and Giles Mandelbrote (New Castle, DE and London: Oak Knoll Press and The British Library, 2009), p. 127.
2 Black's writing in *Typography* (London) vol. 4, Autumn 1937, p. 4.

One evening in Riga, in the autumn of 1996, I was looking at photo albums belonging to several acquaintances, two or three of whom had been young children during the period from the late 1920s to the end of the 1930s. All this looking was tinged with melancholy, as those fading images of family groups, business enterprises, street scenes, and summer beach outings evoked a life abruptly terminated a half century before.

Allowing a decade to pass before being stirred into action meant a loss of the last remaining opportunity to sit and listen to the few still-living, prime movers in the general professional areas to which I had some connection: book design, printing, and publishing. In those intervening years, two major Latvian publishing figures died: Miķelis Goppers (1908-1996) and Helmārs Rudzītis (1903-2001).

In spite of these and other important losses among writers and illustrators, I decided to disregard the advice of a few individuals who implied, "Curiosity isn't sufficient motivation for such a serious matter," or, "It's past the time to venture out on such a project."

I skirted this well-meaning advice and instead began regular browsing in Baltic print resources and English-, German-, Russian-, and Baltic-language articles and monographs.

As indicated, the initial plan had been to satisfy my curiosity and perhaps provide a brief overview in a simple sketch for book design aficionados who might lack a clear (or any) image of "the Latvian book".

Since the intended audience was viewed as being generally conversant with book design trends and history, most commentary on influences or derivations seemed superfluous and therefore it was decided to keep such commentary to a minimum. Unfamiliarity among English-language readers of the historic book culture in the three Baltic States necessitated some comment on aspects of Latvian publishing history and authors, as well as notes on designers, in order to give some context to what is essentially a visual overview.

To keep the project to a manageable size, the mix of forms has been limited to representative works.

It is hoped that the Latvian reader will overlook any shortcomings in a commentary that has so often meant reliance on others to confirm the meaning of some original texts. Some conclusions are undoubtedly open to challenge. This challenge is unavoidable, not because of a Latvian-reading acquaintance's interpreted account, but because of the hit-and-sometimes-miss process through which meaning was teased from texts when no period informant was available for precise confirmation. With but three exceptions, all translation and interpretive assistance was given by individuals born in the final years of Latvia's Interwar period.

Introduction

This exploration of Latvia's print culture calls attention in a more expanded way to the book and periodical in European graphic design history undertaken by a number of scholars over the past 30 years, but not necessarily resulting in English-language publications. For examples of such activity, one need only examine the bibliographies of works compiled by Steven Mansbach,[3] Inese Riņķe,[4] Alla Rosenfeld,[5] Dace Lamberga,[6] and Irēna Bužinska.[7]

A landmark compilation preceding these is *Unerwartete Begegnung: Lettische Avantgarde, 1910-1935; Der Beitrag Lettlands zur Kunst der Europäischen Moderne* (Unexpected Encounter: The Latvian Avantgarde 1910-1935; The Contribution of Latvia to the Art of European Modernism).[8]

The endeavors cited owe a certain debt to the legendary Swedish impresario of vanguard art and design movements in Europe, the late Pontus Hulten, with his exhibitions and accompanying catalogs for the Pompidou Center's staging of *Paris–New York* (1977); *Paris–Berlin* (1978); *Paris–Moscou* (1979); and *Paris–Paris* (1981).

Nearly all of the preceding publications cite the work of Latvian studio artists who were engaged in book illustration or design in addition to their studio work, e.g., Kārlis Padegs, Uga Skulme, Sigismunds Vidbergs, Hilda Vīka, and others. But the Latvian book or periodical as a dynamic medium does not have a presence in the overall discussion represented by the above exhibition/monograph efforts, except for the mention of Vidbergs' *Les Chansons de Bilitis* (The Songs of Bilitis, Riga, 1926), Arnolds Dzirkalis' journal *Laikmets* (The Era, Potsdam, 1923), and a few other passing references in several of the cited exhibition catalogs.

---

3   *Modern Art in Eastern Europe: From the Baltic to the Balkans, ca. 1890-1939* (Cambridge: Cambridge University Press, 1999).

4   *Mākslinieki Skulmes: 20. gadsimts, Latvija; Artists Skulmes: 20th Century, Latvia; Khudozhniki Skulme: XX vek, Latviïa* (Riga: Tretiakov Gallery Moscow and State Art Museum Riga, 2000) and *Aleksandra Belcova, 1892-1981* (Riga: Rīgas galerija, 2002).

5   Background chapters by various contributors to her collaboration with Norton T. Dodge in *Art of the Baltics: The Struggle for Freedom of Artistic Expression under the Soviets, 1945-1991* (New Brunswick, NJ: Rutgers University Press, 2002).

6   *Rīgas mākslinieku grupa* (Riga: Neputns, 2001); *Kubisms Latvijas mākslā; Cubism in Latvian Art.* (Riga: Neputns, 2002); *Klasiskais modernisms: Latvijas glezniecība 20. gadsimta sākumā* (Riga: Neputns, 2004); *Reālisms: Jaunā lietišķība 20. gs. 20.-30. gadi; Realism. New Objectivity, 1920s-1930s* (Riga: Latvian State Museum and Neputns, 2004).

7   *Theoretical Writings and Manifestoes by Latvian Artists* (Riga: Neputns, 2002).

8   An effort by Leons Balodis, Indulis Bilzēns, Mārtiņš Būmanis, Ilze Gulēns, Peter Hielscher, Jāzeps Kukulis-Baltinavietis, Edvīns Paas, Maruta Schmidt, Dorina Ting, Andrejs Toše, Catharina Wackes, published by the Neue Gesellschaft für Bildende Kunst e.V., accompanying an exhibition in the Staatliche Kunsthalle, Berlin, Sept. 18-Oct. 28, 1990.

Books and ethnic communities in Latvia before 1914

The Republic of Latvia proclaimed its independence on November 18, 1918. Three former provinces of the Russian Empire with ethnic Latvian majorities united to form the new nation: Vidzeme (*Liefland, Livland* in German), Kurzeme (*Kurland, Courland*), and Latgale (*Inflanty*). Each of these regions of Latvia, however, had a different history. In addition to Latvians, all three regions were also home to other ethnic groups, such as Germans, Jews, Russians, Poles, Lithuanians, Estonians, and others, all of whom received citizenship in the new democratic nation. The Law on Citizenship of 1919 did away with the social, ethnic, and religious inequality of previous centuries. The law defined a citizen of Latvia as any former citizen of the Russian Empire, regardless of ethnic origin or religious affiliation, who lived in, had been born in, or was a citizen of what became the territory of Latvia on or before August 1, 1914, and had not accepted the citizenship of another country.

Religion. Since antiquity, various cultures and religions have intersected in the Baltic region. The ancient Amber Road linked the shores of the Baltic Sea with the Mediterranean Sea, and the Vikings travelled through the Baltic region on their way east. The arrival of Christianity in the Baltic region in the 13th century drew the local pagan tribes (Livonians, Latgalians, Couronians, Semigallians) into the rest of Europe. The spread of Christianity also introduced the first books into this region. The most famous of these books was the Bible of the Livonian leader Kaupo, who had received the book in Rome in 1204 as a gift from Pope Innocent III. The Kaupo Bible survived in the Riga Cathedral (*Rīgas doms*) until the riots of the Reformation. Protestantism took hold in Livonia in the 16th century during the Reformation, and what was left of the ravaged monastery libraries became the beginnings of the now oldest library in Riga (now known as the Academic Library of the University of Latvia, established in 1524). Catholicism, however, retained its influence in Latgale and Kurzeme alongside Lutheranism. The Eastern Orthodox Church arrived in the Baltic region along with the arrival of Russian merchants in Riga. Old Believers of the Orthodox Church, in turn, began settling in Latgale in the late 17th century as the result of the persecution they experienced in Russia following the reforms introduced by Patriarch Nikon. Likewise, Jewish merchants encountering restrictions elsewhere began settling first in Kurzeme, later in Latgale and Vidzeme, and opened the first synagogues in the region. Even though Orthodoxy was declared the state religion after Vidzeme, Latgale, and Kurzeme were ceded to the Russian Empire in the 18th century, the Baltic region's special status within the empire allowed Lutheranism to remain dominant in Kurzeme and Vidzeme and Catholicism in Latgale. The presence of various religions thus encouraged the existence and development of separate ethnic and religious communities and cultures, which over time came into contact with each other but also preserved their separate identities.

Rights. The majority of the population of Livonia consisted of the Livonian, Latgalian, Couronian, and Semigallian tribes, who were subjugated by the German knights, gradually lost their independence, and became dependent on the conquerors. The descendants of these tribes, however, still formed the majority of the local population in the 16th and 17th centuries and eventually merged into a more or less unified population that would go on to form the base of the Latvian nation and language. The German land-owning classes controlled most of the political, economic, and cultural forces in the Baltic region until the 19th century, regardless of the fact that the area was actually administratively a part of the Polish-Lithuanian Commonwealth and Sweden and, later, the Russian Empire. Reforms in the Russian Empire freed Latvian peasants from serfdom only in the early 19th century, and the gradual diminishing of rights for the land-owning classes and urban trade guilds in the 19th century offered former serfs more opportunities in the cities and towns. Concurrent with this evolution in 19th century Latvian culture, the social and religious side of the Jewish community was also evolving, as were Russian, Polish, Lithuanian, and Estonian communities, societies, and cultural activities. The acceleration of these economic, political, and cultural processes in the early 20th century led to the Baltic provinces becoming the most developed provinces and Riga the most modern and European city in the Russian Empire, where various social and cultural strata existed that had traditional cultural ties with Europe but administrative ties with Russia.

Ethnic groups

Germans. The first German merchants arrived in the territory that was to later become Latvia around the year 1180. Meinhard, a canon of the Segeberg monastery in Schleswig-Holstein (Germany), arrived along with the merchants to preach Christianity to the local tribes, and he established the first German colony in Ikšķile (Uexküll). In 1186 the Archbishop of Bremen ordained Meinhard as the first bishop of Livonia. After encountering resistance from the Livonian tribes, crusaders arrived in the Baltic lands in 1201 and began building the city of Riga with a fortified castle.

The aggressive colonization of the local tribes was continued by the Livonian Order, a branch of the Teutonic Order. By 1290 the Livonian Order had subdued the tribes and created a Livonian confederation consisting of the state of the Livonian Order, the free city of Riga, and the Bishopric of Courland. The descendants of the German bishoprics and the vassals of the Livonian Order later became the German land-owning classes. The Livonian state existed until November 28, 1561, when its last Master, Gotthard Kettler, signed a treaty in Vilnius (Vilna, Vilno) that ceded Livonian lands to the combined state of Poland and Lithuania (*Rzeczpospolita*). According to this treaty, however, the German land-owning classes retained their privileges and religious freedom. Gotthard Kettler became the first Duke of Courland and Semigallia, but Vidzeme, Latgale, and southern Estonia came under the direct rule of Sigismund II Augustus of Poland until 1629, when, as the result of the Truce of Altmark, Vidzeme became a part of Sweden and Latgale (*Inflanty*) came under Polish rule until 1772, when it was ceded to the Russian Empire as a part of the First Partition of Poland. Vidzeme (along with a part of modern-day Estonia) became a part of the Russian Empire in 1721. The Duchy of Courland and Semigallia was ceded to Russia in 1795. Despite rule by various powers, the Baltic-German minority retained its political status as a majority until the 19th century. The German land-owning classes and the Lutheran Church largely determined the economic and cultural processes in the Baltic region throughout the 19th century and the era of the Russian Empire.

Latvians. The Latvian nation took shape as the local indigenous tribes merged together. Even though they enjoyed a certain level of independence until the 16th century, the Latvian inhabitants of Riga gradually came to be considered non-Germans, who little by little were forced out of the more economically lucrative professions or became Germanized. As the result of warfare and famine, the rural inhabitants were gradually relegated to the status of serfs, a position that was officially established in the 17th century, and they remained a population deprived of rights until the early 19th century. Religious publications in the Latvian language in the 16th and 17th centuries promoted the development of a unified Latvian language, although in the 18th century schools and their encouragement of literacy actually played a larger role in this process. The abolishment of serfdom and economic reforms in the first half of the 19th century allowed a class of more prosperous Latvian peasants to emerge, from which the first Latvian businessmen and academically educated "farmers' sons" arose. In the mid 19th century these people took over the creation of Latvian culture from the German clergymen, who had up until then largely determined the range of Latvian peasant culture. This "New Latvian" (*Jaunlatvieši*) movement accelerated Latvian emancipation. The Riga Latvian Society was established in 1868 and soon became a template for a network of other societies that promoted the centralization of Latvians and a feeling of unity among them.

Jews. The first Jewish merchants arrived in Kurzeme in the 14th or 15th century and settled in Aizpute, where, thanks to the town's special status (Piltene district was under the direct rule of Denmark and later the King of Poland), the first Jewish community was established. Jews began settling in other parts of Kurzeme only in the late 17th century, although they continuously faced various restrictions and threats of expulsion. Only their importance to business transactions and their payments for the right to reside in Kurzeme protected the Jews from frequent efforts to expel them from the Duchy of Courland and Semigallia. As opposed to the Jews who had arrived in Latgale beginning in the second half of the 17th century and who mainly spoke Polish and Russian, most of the Jews in Kurzeme had arrived from Germany and used German as their main language. The few Jews who had settled in Vidzeme were expelled from there in 1743.

Jews began settling again in Vidzeme and Riga in 1785, when Russian Empress Catherine II (Catherine the Great) gave them permission to live in Sloka as "foreign citizens" without religious, ethnic, or class restrictions and to trade in Riga as so-called "citizens of Sloka". In 1813 these citizens of Sloka were allowed to live in the suburbs of Riga, and by 1829 they were allowed to settle permanently in Riga proper. Following several subsequent attempts by the Russian state to restrict the arrival of Jews in Riga, in 1841 the Jews were granted provisions that allowed them to register their residence in Riga, although these provisions did not give them the right to vote or own property. A Jewish community complete with religious and economic organizations began forming in Riga in the 1840s. The community maintained the first Jewish school in the Russian Empire with German as the language of instruction. During the first part of the 19th century the Jews of Riga mainly strove to assimilate with the local German culture. In 1851 they received permission to build the first synagogue in Riga. Jews received the right to own property and the right to permanently settle in all of Riga only in 1858, but a number of other restrictions remained in place until 1918. Jewish assimilation into German society was replaced by the Russian Empire's policy of Russification in the 1860s and 1870s. In 1888 Jewish schools were forced to switch to Russian as the language of instruction, even though most of the students spoke German or Yiddish. The first and only 19th-century Jewish periodical in Riga was the journal *Yevreyskie zapiski* (Jewish Notes), published in Russian beginning in 1881-1882 by the rabbi of Riga, Aaron Pumpjanskiĭ (1835-1893). Pumpjanskii's journal was the only Jewish publication in Riga until 1907. By the end of the century, a wave of antiJewish pogroms in Russia along with growing Russian nationalism curbed further assimilation. Alongside the establishment in 1893 of the Jewish Education Society, whose goal was to encourage the integration of Jews into Russian culture, Zionism and socialism found fertile ground in Riga.

Russians. The first Russians to arrive in Riga were merchants who settled in the so-called *Russische Dorf* and built a church and cemetery there, both destroyed during the Livonian War. A Muscovite House (*Maskaviešu nams*), where merchants from Pskov and Novgorod settled, was established in the 17th century just outside the city. The Russian population in the Baltic region grew during the 18th century, when Vidzeme, Latgale, and Kurzeme were ceded to Russia (in 1719, 1772, and 1795, respectively). Russian government officials and merchants moved to the Baltic region, Russian land-owners moved their serfs to their newly acquired estates, and eventually Russian factory workers also settled in the region. Due to the proximity of Prussia and Poland, Russia established army garrisons in the Baltic provinces. But a difference in religion—between the official Orthodoxy and the Old Believers persecuted in the 19th century—preserved a unique schism in the Russian environment. In order to strengthen the position of Russia and the Russian population in the Baltic provinces, former rights of property owners (*namnieku tiesības*) were abolished in Riga. In 1785 Russians were given the right to join guilds and work in the traditional trades, and the first Russian-language school in Riga was established in 1789. More Russian schools were established alongside German secondary schools during the 19th century. But Russian became the dominant language in the second half of the 19th century when, following the Russian administration's policy of Russification, non-Russian schools were forced to switch to Russian as the language of instruction. In addition, a law making Russian the official language at government offices went into effect in 1885. In 1877, according to the Russian Municipal Statute, a city council elected by all Rigans who owned property and payed taxes to the city replaced the German city council (*Rat*), which had existed since the 13th century.

The continual competition between the Russian and German cultures not only encouraged the assimilation of Baltic-Germans into the Russian culture, but also the assimilation of Baltic-Russians into the German culture. In the early 19th century many Germans of Baltic descent—government officials and scientists—began their careers in the capitals of the Russian Empire, and by the end of that century Russian-speaking Baltic-Germans were encouraging greater awareness of Russian culture among Germans. Russian government officials, in turn, often used the German language in daily life.

A local Russian community began developing in the early 19th century with the establishment of several welfare societies (including Old Believers). In 1816 August Albanus, a Lutheran clergyman and rector of the Dom School (*Domskola*), published Riga's first newspaper in the Russian language: *Rossijskoje ezhedenel'noje izdan'ie* (53 issues). In 1852 the official newspapers *Liflyandskiye gubernskiye vedomosti / Livländische Gouvernementszeitung* (until 1917) and *Kurlyandskiye gubernskiye vedomosti / Kurländische*

Gouvernements-Zeitung (Jelgava, until 1915) began to be published in both Russian and German.

A swift transformation of the Russian community began in the 1860s and 1870s, when several Russian merchants', welfare, and cultural societies were established. The Russian Club was established in 1863 (active until World War I), which in 1868 assisted in setting up two secondary schools (gymnasiums) with Russian as the language of instruction. The daily newspaper *Rizhskij Vestnik*, edited by Yevgraf Cheshikhin, began to be published in 1869 and ran until 1917. The Russian literary group *Russkij literaturnyj kruzhok v Rige* was established in 1874; its first leader was Nikolai Gamburtsev and secretary was Yevgraf Cheshikhin.

In the late 19th and early 20th centuries Riga, with its very diverse population, became the social and cultural center of the three Baltic provinces of the Russian Empire. In 1779 Riga's total population of 19,463 included 8965 (46%) Germans, 6260 (32.2%) Latvians, 2578 (13.2%) Russians, and 1649 (8.5%) Poles. By 1897 the proportion of ethnic groups in Riga had changed, namely, to 127,046 (45%) Latvians, 67,286 (24%) Germans, 43,300 (16%) Russians, and 21,962 (6%) Jews. Each of these communities had its own social organizations; there were Russian, German, and Latvian theaters in Riga. In 1897/1898 there were seven weekly and two daily newspapers as well as three journals in Latvian, seven weekly and two daily newspapers and five journals in German, two weekly and one daily newspaper as well as one journal in Russian, eight advertisement publications in three languages and two official newspapers. Only the Jewish community did not have a periodical at this time.

Books

Up until the 16th century and beyond, all books for readers in Riga (calendars, hymnals, homages, etc.) were printed outside of Livonia, mainly in the German towns of Rostock, Wittenberg, and Königsberg (which had a printing house since 1551). Vilnius became the center of Catholic book printing in 1522. The very first books in the Latvian language are associated with Lübeck. In 1525, customs in Lübeck detained a barrel of books *in vulgari livonico lettico ac estonico* intended for Lutherans in Riga.

The first printing of books in Riga can be traced to 1558, when the typesetter Nikolai Mollyn (~1550-1625) of Amsterdam arrived in Riga by invitation of the city council and set up a printing house. A printing house was set up in Tartu (Tērbata) considerably later, in 1631, and in Reval (Tallinn) in 1633. The first book to be printed in Riga was Anselmus Boccius' homage to Polish king Sigismund III Vasa and chancellor Jan Zamoyski titled *Carmen gratulatorium de Sigismundi III Reg. Pol. felici in Regn. Pol. ingressu et subsequente inauguratione et coronatione, scriptum ad Joh. Samoiscium* (1588).

Mollyn's first printed books already contained illustrations, which may have been made locally in Riga. The first panorama of Riga—perhaps created by Mollyn himself or another local engraver—was published on the title page of Johann Nicolaus Arboreus' calendar *Schryff Calender vp dat Jaer na der Gebordt vnses Heren vnd Heylandes Jesu Christi, M.D.XC*, published in 1589. An engraving of the Riga coat of arms appeared in the book *Eines Erbarn Raths der Koeninglichen Stadt Riga* (published in 1591) and was also used in later publications. Heinrich Thum, an engraver employed at Mollyn's printing house, created the first *ex libris* (for the von Hof family) as well as a copper engraving of a panorama of Riga (1612), of which three parts have been preserved. In its 37 years of operation Mollyn's printing house published over 160 items—hymnals, sermons, calendars, treatises, announcements—mainly in Latin and German. Mollyn's only publication in Latvian, a handbook for Riga Lutherans containing fragments of the Gospels and Epistles as well as translations of hymns and the Catechism, was published in 1615. Mollyn's publications started a tradition of design that continued to be used in Riga's publications, for example, the use of *Fraktur* for religious texts and *Roman* typefaces for scientific publications, the use of two colors for book title pages, abundant use of typographical ornamentation, and woodcut illustrations interspersed in texts. The illustration stereotype plates in Mollyn's publications were used over and over throughout the 17th century.

In 1626 the Riga city council granted Christian Rittau the right to sell books. Rittau had formerly printed books in Lübeck. The work of typesetters in Riga depended on book publishing and selling privileges (Mollyn received privileges from the King of Poland in 1590 and from the King of Sweden in 1621), and a second printing house in Riga was created only at the end of the 17th century. After Mollyn's death, Gerhard Schroeder married his widow, thus becoming the typesetter of Riga and receiving his privileges in 1631.

Schroeder continued publishing books until 1657 and was succeeded by Albrecht Hackelmann (1658-1659) of Lübeck, Heinrich Bessemesser (1660-1683), and Georg Matthias Nöller (1684-1712), who was in turn succeeded by his son-in-law Samuel Lorenz Frölich (1713-1762), who passed his business on to his son, Gottlob Christian Frölich (1763-1765; 1786). The printing business was then inherited by Frölich's son-in-law Julius Conrad Daniel Müller, who lost his royal typesetter's privileges in 1806 to a man named Häcker. From 1857 onward the printing house was run by Müller's grandson, Adolf Müller, who sold it to Johann Adolf Kröger in 1877.

The second printing house in Riga operated only from 1675 to 1713. Its permit to operate had been issued by the general superintendent of Vidzeme Johann Fischer, who had received privileges from the King of Sweden to open the Royal Printing House on Monētu iela (Monētu Street) in Riga. Johann Georg Wilcken became the typesetter at this house. The house's largest publication was a translation of the Bible into Latvian, a 2500-page quarto prepared from 1685 to 1694. 1500 copies of this Bible were published.

Another publishing house, which operated almost until the middle of the 20th century, was established in Riga in the late 18th century. This printing house was set up in 1777 by Georg Friedrich Keil, an assistant to G. C. Frölich. In 1804 Keil sold the business to Wilhelm Ferdinand Häcker (1774-1842), who received "royal" printing privileges in 1806. His work was continued by his sons Ferdinand Eduard Häcker (1812-1877) and Woldemar Magnus Häcker (1818-1888). The printing house belonged to descendants of the Häcker family until 1944; the last Häcker descendant to direct the printing house was Fritz Woldemar Häcker, from 1927-1939 and again from 1941-1944. The Häcker's longest running publication was *Vidzemes kalendārs* (Vidzeme Calendar), published from 1812-1918.

This system of two printing houses in Riga lasted until the beginning of the 19th century. The businesses were most often passed down as inheritances or as granted privileges. Due to lower prices, books (including more ornate publications) were also printed outside of the Baltic region; books for the Riga market were also printed in Western Europe.

After Riga, Jelgava (Mitau, the capital of the Duchy of Courland and Semigallia) became the Baltic region's second capital of book printing. The first printing house in Jelgava was established in 1666-1667. The Duke's printing house mainly printed the Duke's own placards and publications for the local market. The first typesetter was Michael Karnall, and a couple of years after his death, in 1684, Georg Radecki (1684-1724) became the chief of the printing house in Jelgava. When Radecki died, Johann Heinrich Köster married his widow and thus inherited the privileges bestowed by the Duke. Christian Liedtke (1733-1766) became the typesetter at the Duke's printing house in 1761 and, with a loan from the Duke, obtained more modern fonts and was the only person to receive privileges to publish books in German and Latvian in Courland. Together with Johann Kanter, a book merchant from Königsberg and the owner of Jelgava's book store, Liedtke established Jelgava's first newspaper, the *Mitauische Nachrichten von Staats-Gelehrten und Einheimischen Sachen*, which continued to be published into the 19th century, albeit under different names.

Around the year 1763 Johann Friedrich Hartknoch (1740-1789) arrived in Jelgava from Königsberg to direct a branch of Kanter's book store. Soon he and the merchant Jakob Friedrich Hinz became the owners of the store and began publishing books. Then Hartknoch moved to Riga, where he opened another book store and became by the end of the 18th century the director of the largest publishing house in the Baltic region (Hartknoch, though, did not manage to receive privileges to set up his own printing office). Having studied at the university in Königsberg and having made the acquaintance there of the German philosophers Immanuel Kant, Johann Georg Hamann, and Johann Gottfried Herder, Hartknoch became the first publisher of their works.

After moving to Riga, Hartknoch printed the scientific works of local German authors and German authors abroad as well as translations in German of the works of Russian scientists. Hartknoch published almost no books in the Latvian language. Hinz, on the other hand, continued publishing books in Jelgava and Aizpute (Hasenpoth), among which were a collection of poetry titled *Gedichte von einem pohlnischen Juden* (1772) by the first modern Jewish poet writing in German, Isaschar Falkensohn Behr, as well as Gotthard Friedrich Stender's encyclopedic publication *Augstās gudrības grāmata* (1774), intended for Latvian farmers. The cover of Stender's book features an engraving by the Leipzig artist Gustav Georg Endner (1754-1824) in which a father shows his son the beauty of God's world. After Hartknoch's death, his son, Johann Friedrich Hartknoch Jr. (1768-1819) took over publishing operations in Riga. The business published approximately 580 books between the years of 1762 and 1789. Unhappy with the restrictions and censorship imposed by the Russian Empire, Hartknoch Jr. left Riga (his publishing house operated in Leipzig until 1879) and the store was bought in 1800 by Carl Johann Gottfried Hartmann (1770-1828), who also continued publishing books. The store was later bought by Eduard Frentzen, who in turn sold it to Nikolai Kymmel in 1841. Kymmel established the "N. Kymmel" business, which sold books until the 1920s.

In 1769 Jelgava printer Christian Liedtke's widow married Johann Friedrich Steffenhagen (1744-1812), who thus took over the Duke's privileges and went on to create the largest book printing office in the Baltic region. The Steffenhagen family of publishers continued to publish books in Jelgava until 1919, when part of the destroyed business was bought by the Riga company Valters un Rapa. The Steffenhagen publishing house published books in German, Russian, French, Estonian, Lithuanian, Latin, Greek, and Hebrew; these books were distributed in other provinces of the Russian Empire as well. The Steffenhagens decorated their books with Rococo vignettes and woodcuts. In 1787 they published *Bildu ābice* (ABC with Pictures), a Latvian reading primer intended for the rural Latvian population with a text and illustrations by Gotthard Friedrich Stender. Influenced by the Enlightenment, Steffenhagen published the first journal in the Latvian language, titled *Latviska Gada Grāmata* (Latvian Yearbook, 1797-1798) decorated with a medallion on its title page. A book of Georg Manzel's (Mancelius) sermons was adorned with a portrait of the publisher himself, drawn by Kārlis Krauklings, who was at the time a journalist in Dresden, and a copper engraving by Johann Gottfried Scheffner in Jelgava. From 1825 onward, the J. F. Steffenhagen und Sohn publishing house began using lithographs. In 1822 the house began publishing the first newspaper in the Latvian language, *Latviešu Avīzes* (until 1915). Its publication in Jelgava of collections of articles by the Latvian Literary Society, titled *Magazin, herausgegeben von der Lettisch-Literärischen Gesellschaft*, began in 1827 and continued until 1936. Steffenhagen's descendants studied the art of typesetting and printing in Leipzig, Berlin, and Hamburg, and from 1858 onward their business was privately owned. In 1840 the Steffenhagen business introduced the high-speed printing press and set up their own type foundry, which made 30 different typefaces.

Smaller printing offices were established outside Riga and Jelgava after the *ukaz* (decree) of Catherine II in 1783 regarding independent printing offices, which allowed private persons to set up printing offices. This decree was in effect until 1796, when such printing offices were outlawed in Russia. The clergyman Gustav von Bergmann and Christoph Harder published small runs of publications in Rūjiena and Rubene, respectively.

Alongside Steffenhagen's publishing business, Gustav Adolf Reyher (1794-1864) opened a book store in Jelgava in 1826 and also began printing books. Reyher mostly published scientific publications (many of his publications were printed in Leipzig) and paid much attention to book design. One of his most ornate publications was *Genera plantarum oder die Pflanzengattungen der in der Ostseeprovinzen Est-, Liv- und Curland wildwachsenden Pflanzen*, a work containing many illustrations and written by Christoph Wilhelm Engelmann, the science and mathematics teacher at the Jelgava Gymnasium. In 1860 Reyher published Rev. Heinrich Kawall's book *Dieva radījumi pasaulē* (God's Creatures in the World) with color illustrations; in 1861 he published the first illustrated book for children in the Latvian language, Ernests Dinsberg's book of poetry titled *Māte* (Mother) with 12 illustrations; and in 1862 he published *Piecdesmit pasaciņas ar bildēm* (Fifty Fairy Tales with Picture). Contrary to the tradition of illustrating a book with "one picture", Reyher's publications stood out for the diversity of their illustrations.

In the early 19th century book publishers continued in the tradition established in the previous century, printing books in their own printing houses for both the local market in the local languages as well as books for the Russian and Western European book markets. As the demand for books in Latvian grew, a large part of the publications were inexpensive books with a very simple design that were within the financial reach of farmers. Publications in German tended to be more ornate and printed on better quality paper. Religious publications received more attention than others; church hymnals and Bibles continued to be printed with woodcut or lithograph vignettes or lithograph images. Their design usually included an engraving on the frontispiece or separate illustrations within the text. Most often the ornateness of the book depended on its binding—from books bound in brown or black leather with brass bindings to various styles of paper binding. Scientific texts were often illustrated with portraits, landscapes, maps, diagrams, or technical drawings.

Changes in book design during the 19th century most affected book covers, no longer just copies of the title page. Book design thus became more diverse, although the dichotomy between ornate publications featuring black-and-white (and later, color) illustrations on separate pages or interspersed within the text and simple publications for the masses with an illustration only on the cover survived throughout the century. Such cover illustrations were most often purchased in Germany as stereotype plates and were not associated with the actual text, so they could be used repeatedly for several publications. The vast majority of books were published with printed covers made according to a traditional design using typographical ornaments around the border and a variety of lettering (bold, ornamented, or illusory letters). Page design included a frame and small vignettes.

Books began having more illustrations in the late 1850s and early 1860s, when the larger book companies (W. F. Häcker, Steffenhagen, and E. Plates) began illustrating their calendars. W. F. Häcker ordered illustrations from Germany made from photographs of Riga and portraits of prominent personalities to supplement his yearbook *Rigascher Almanach* (Almanac of Riga, 1858-1913/1915). A collection of 25 engravings titled *Album von Riga* (The Riga Album, compiled by Napoleon Asmuss, 1871) was published to celebrate the 15-year anniversary of the calendar. The inclusion of separate images in books was continued with Wilhelm Siegfried Stavenhagen's landscapes of Vidzeme, Kurzeme, and Estonia in the three-volume *Album baltischer Ansichten* (An Album of Baltic Landscapes, 1866-1867), an album of steel engravings that were also sold separately as single pages. Lithograph and woodcut portraits were also added to Latvian-language publications, such as Kristaps Kaktiņš' portrait in the book *Svētas patiesības liecinieks* (Witness of a Holy Truth, 1843) and woodcut portraits of Stenders and Friedrich I (Frederick the Great) in Krišjānis Valdemārs' *300 stāsti* (300 Stories, 1853). Illustrations were also included in the first calendar for a Latgalian audience, G. Manteuffel's *Inflantuzemes laikagrōmata aba kalenders* (Daybook or Calendar of Inflantia, 1861-1870). Alongside books, illustrated "picture pages" also became popular. In 1863 Steffenhagen's company published *Jelgavas bilžu lapas* (Picture Pages from Jelgava), a series of 15 pages with a lithograph image on one side and a text on the other side.

The number and activities of private printing offices increased in the mid 19th century. Alongside German publishers and printers, the first Latvian, Russian, and Jewish publishers also began establishing printing offices and publishing houses. However, the privileged typesetters in Riga and Jelgava continued to dominate printing traditions throughout the first half of the 19th century; these printers (Häcker and J. C. D. Müller in Riga, Steffenhagen in Jelgava) continued operating until the 20th century. The number of printing offices and publishing houses continued to grow in the second half of the 19th century: in 1868 there were seven private printing offices in Riga, but by 1883 the number of printing businesses (including lithographers) had already grown to 28, with an additional three printing offices in Jelgava, three in Liepāja, and nine in the smaller towns of Vidzeme and Kurzeme. By 1897 Vidzeme had 49 printing offices, typolithographers, and lithographers, Kurzeme had 22, and Latgale had five.

Printing and regular publishing of Russian-language publications was ensured by the establishment of the Vidzeme (1853) and Kurzeme (1854) provincial printing offices in Riga and Jelgava. The majority of works by Russian authors, however, were printed in German printing houses. Even in the second half of the century Russian-language publications were not known for their distinct design. The greatest attention to design can be observed in late 19th century advertisement publications (*Portovyj gorod Riga*, Port City of Riga, 1870) and guide books. Journals became pioneers in introducing illustrations; *Svet v kartinkah* (The World in Picture; from 1882 onward *Novij svet*, The New World), a Russian-language journal, began to be published in 1878. The first Latvian literary journals—*Pagalms* (The Backyard, 1881-1882) and *Rota* (Adornment, 1884-1888)—also began publishing illustrations in the 1880s.

The Latvian printing offices created more and more competition for German publishers. In 1851 Ernst Plates (1821-1887), a Germanized Latvian, set up his printing business and in 1858 he bought Ludwig Hartung's printing office. Like Häcker's company, Plates also paid much attention to illustrations in his calendars and books. Plates published the first newspaper edited by Latvians themselves, *Mājas Viesis* (1856), and at the end of the century, when his son Arnold Plates had inherited the business, the company published the journal *Mājas Viesa Mēnešraksts*, in which much attention was paid to the visual image of the journal. In 1898 Plates' company published an ornate edition of Johann Wolfgang von Goethe's *Faust* containing a number of illustrations purchased in Germany.

In the 1860s the Latvian publishers Heinrihs Alunāns and Johans Frīdrihs Šablovskis began operating in Jelgava and Kārlis Štālbergs in Riga. In the 1870s Klāvs Ukstiņš began operating in Liepāja and Eduards Zīslaks (*Sieslack*) in Jelgava. The limited partnership B. Dīriķis un biedri, which became one of the largest Latvian printing businesses, was established in 1877.

In 1864 Riga had only five printing businesses. But by 1868 the city had seven, in 1883 it had 28, in 1897 it had 44, and by 1910 it had 45 printing businesses. In the 1890s Jelgava had six printing businesses, 12 book stores, and 13 book printing offices. The first specialized type foundry, "Gutenberg", was established in Riga in 1898.

Latvian publishers were paying increasing attention to the design of their publications. As in German publications, Latvians added maps and engravings of prominent Latvian cultural figures to their books or sold the images separately; they paid more and more attention to book cover design. By the 1870s Latvian artists such as Augusts Daugulis, Kārlis Kronvalds, and Mārtiņš Bušs and the Estonian artist Eduard Magnus Jakobson were involved in creating book cover designs. National Romanticism entered book design with composer Baumaņu Kārlis' lithograph for the cover of his own collection of songs, *Līgo* (1874). By the 1890s academically educated Latvian artists were commissioned for book artwork: Rihards Zariņš (cover design for Jēkabs Purkalītis' collection of poetry *Dziesmu pazarītes* [Song Branches], published by Jānis Ozols, 1893) and Arturs Baumanis (covers for the journal *Austrums* and cover design for Eduards Zeibots' collection of poetry *Balādes un romances*, Ballades and Romances, 1896).

Already in the 1860s Kārlis Štālbergs' publications differed from the others in their varying formats (larger editions, small-format books); he paid particular attention to text composition and sometimes even used colored paper or printed text in several different colors. Štālbergs was also one of the first publishers to turn away from *Fraktur* and start using the new orthography. The covers on books published by Eduards Zīslaks differed from their title pages; his printing office made chromolithographs and paid special attention to fonts and the design of each page. Zīslaks began publishing the illustrated *Latviešu kalendārs* (The Latvian Calendar, 1876-1909), which included images and portraits. His most elaborate publication was Goethe's *Lapsa Kūmiņš* (*The Story of Reynard the Fox,* 1879) with 60 illustrations by the German artist Wilhelm Kaulbach. Eventually Jēkabs Dravnieks bought Zīslaks' printing house and published the journal *Austrums* and the first Latvian conversational dictionary, *Konversācijas vārdnīca* (Latvian Encyclopedia, 1891-1893), and also began publishing Krišjānis Barons' compilation of Latvian folk songs, *Latvju dainas,* with a cover design by Rihards Zariņš.

Photo albums began to be published at the very end of the 19th century. Some of the first were the photography album *Baltisches Album,* published in Riga in 1895 by Karl Maria Hebensperger's company, and *Sehenswürdigkeiten der Stadt Riga und Umgegend in Wort und Bild,* an album of Riga landscapes published by Plates in 1899. This tradition of picture albums continued into the early 20th century with *Malerische Ansichten aus Livland, Estland, Kurland* (1901) and Emanuel Eggert's album of original lithographs titled *Album von Riga* (1900) as well as the separately published portfolio *Zur 700 jährigen Jubiläums-Feier der Stadt Riga 1201-1901* (1901).

A broad network of publishers, publishing houses, and book stores developed in the second half of the 19th century. Publishers and printing businesses also established themselves in other parts of the province. Jugendstil (Art Nouveau) as well as the new possibilities offered by photomechanical reproduction in the early 20th century introduced new trends to book design, especially after Riga's 700-year anniversary exhibition in 1901. Jugendstil's dynamism and plasticity of form entered both Latvian and German publications. Publishers now began paying considerable attention to typefaces and the color and texture of paper in an effort to harmonize a book's design with its content. Books were sometimes even published in two editions (one plain, the other ornate) or different versions of the cover design were printed.

Alexander Grosset created Jugendstil-inspired book designs for Wilhelm Neumann's *Baltische Maler und Bildhauer des XIX. Jahrhunderts* (1902) and Lydia Tugan's collection of stories *Dve povest'i iz proshlogo Lifljandii* (Two Stories from Livonian History) with a cover by Margot Grosset (1912). Jonck & Poliewsky also employed the Jugendstil style in Constantin Mettig's book *Baltische Städte* (1905) and the travel guide *Illustrierter Führer durch Riga* (1914).

The Latvian publisher Zalktis was established in 1904. Zalktis' mission was to publish books of high printing and artistic quality and thus created its books as it would a piece of artwork. Zalktis engaged the most prominent Latvian artists, paid attention to details such as choice of paper and fonts, and created illustrations specially for its publications. In addition to individual books, Zalktis also published the almanac *Zalktis* (1906-1908). Original lithographs by Janis Rozentāls and etchings by Gustavs Šķilters were included as supplements to the almanac. Later, a journal titled *Zalktis,* with designs by Janis Rozentāls and Jūlijs Madernieks, was published until 1910. Jugendstil was also widely used in the diverse journals published by the new generation of Latvian literary figures: *Dzelme, Pret Sauli,* and *Stari,* which began to be published after changes in Russia's press law in 1905.

A new generation of publishers entered Latvian book publishing at the turn of the century, and this generation largely dictated book design up until World War I and into the 1920s and 1930s. Jānis Ozols began operating in Cēsis and Vecpiebalga in the 1890s; Jānis Brigaders began publishing books in 1894, and in 1912 his business was continued by the limited partnership A. Valters, J. Rapa un biedri; Dāvids Zeltiņš began publishing in 1897; Ansis Gulbis began his publishing business in St. Petersburg in 1903; Augusts Golts began publishing books at the beginning of the 20th century; Andrejs Jesens began his publishing business in 1910; and Jānis Roze opened his book store in 1912.

Up until the end of the 19th century Jewish publishing in the Baltic region was fragmentary. It was restricted by Russia's restrictions on Jewish publications; later, it was influenced by the lack of property rights and competition with larger Russian-Jewish publishing houses as well as the poor knowledge of Yiddish among Jewish intellectuals, who were mainly oriented towards Russian and German publications. Until the beginning of the 20th century book publishing in Hebrew and Yiddish mostly took place outside of the Baltic region (Vilnius, St. Petersburg, Warsaw, Odessa, and elsewhere) or books were imported from Europe. The establishment in Riga of the first Jewish book censorship committee in the Russia Empire in 1797 serves as evidence that Jewish books did flow through the Riga port. Significant Jewish publications were published in Jelgava (Hofmann und Johanson published Reuben Joseph Wunderbar's [1812-1868] essay *Geschichte der Juden in den Provinzen Liv und Kurland* in 1853) as well as in Riga (Nikolai Kymmel published Anton Buchholz's essay *Geschichte der Juden in Riga* in 1899, repr. in 1996 by Verlag Harro v. Hirschheydt).

Aaron J. Lipschütz's printing business operated in Riga in the second half of the 19th century. At the end of the century this printing office belonged to L. Gershelman. Eli Levin opened the first Yiddish and Hebrew printing office in Riga in 1909. Smaller businesses operated in other provincial towns: Bauska (Nachman Jankelovich) and Ludza (the Gutner brothers from Rēzekne in 1903, Wulf Suer in 1907, and Haim Shor with the only Jewish printing business in Latgale). Rabbi Ovchinsky established the first book printing office in Auce in 1911.

Nacional Caitung, the first Yiddish-language periodical, was published for a short time in 1907 (11 issues); its publisher was Alexander von Budberg and the editor was Hirsh Dovid Nombergn. The youth journal *Gehaver*, printed by Eli Levin and edited by Israel Haim Tavyev, became the first Hebrew-language publication. The newspaper *Di idische Stime*, edited by Bal-Makhshoves (Isidor Elyashov) and published by E. (or Z.) Levitas, began to be published in 1910 and ran for 51 issues.

Map of Interwar Europe (*P. Mantinieka paplašināts ģeogrāfijas atlants* [Enhanced Geographical Atlas by P. Mantinieks]. Riga: P. Mantinieka kartogrāfijas institūta izdevums, n.d.)

The first political map of Latvia. An edition of the Latvian National Assembly (1918).
Design: Burkards Dzenis

LATVIAN-LANGUAGE PUBLISHING   PART 1

L1

Historical sketch and bibliographical background

Numerous memoirs by Latvian survivors of the Latvian Republic's early years reiterate a similar Riga scene in late autumn 1919: the fighting was over, hospitals were slowly emptying, and debris was being cleared along the main thoroughfares leading out of the old town and northeast toward the newer districts. Here was a city, like much of the countryside around it, devastated but tentatively experiencing freedom at last.

Scores of personal accounts tell a tale of stunned, war-weary, yet determined Latvians restoring what had been destroyed in three years of fighting. The Russians, then the Germans, and then the Russians once again had left or were in the process of "going". The struggle that remained was simply one of being thrown on one's own resources. But for all of the hardships, this was a welcome challenge to most Latvians, to say nothing of the neighboring Baltic peoples.

The pieces of Latvia that needed picking up or stitching back together included a hungry, still bleeding population; ports choked with war materiel; and infrastructure stripped by the retreating Russians (a portent of future Russian-Soviet retreats). There were also 45,000 German troops still roaming the country. A photograph of central Riga with the Daugava River in the foreground partially illustrates this scene.[1] L1–L4 But the indomitable Latvians could now see beyond the wet, cold, snow, and hunger of the winter of 1918–19 and, for that matter, the winter to follow. Ādolfs Bļodnieks[2] described the situation thus:

"My thoughts go back to the indescribable misery into which the war had then plunged the Latvian country and people. Tens of thousands of young men had lost their lives or had become cripples at the front, hundreds of thousands had been worn down by the harsh life in exile, not to speak of the devastation of the countryside...burned-down farm houses and fields turned up by shells and furrowed by trenches.... It seemed it would take scores of years before the wounds are healed."[3]

1 *Izpostītā Latwija. I. Rīga* (Rīga: W. Olawa fonda izdevums, 1920)
2 Prime Minister of Latvia, 1933-1934.
3 See his autobiography, *The Undefeated Nation* (New York: Robert Speller & Sons, 1960), p. 138.

Skats us Karļa eeiu (no dselsszeļa tilta puses).
Vue sur la rue de Charles (du côté du pont de fer).   Charles Street (from the Railway Bridge).

8

L2

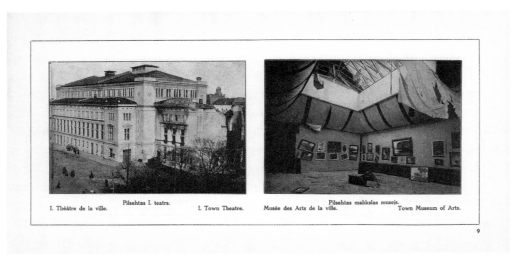

Pilsehtas I. teatrs.   Pilsehtas mahkslas musejs.
I. Théâtre de la ville.   I. Town Theatre.   Musée des Arts de la ville.   Town Museum of Arts.

9

L3

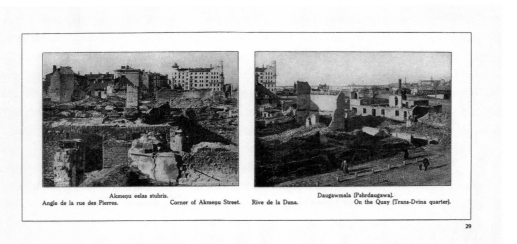

Akmeņu eelas stuhris.   Daugawmala (Pahrdaugawa).
Angle de la rue des Pierres.   Corner of Akmeņu Street.   Rive de la Duna.   On the Quay (Trans-Dvina quarter).

29

L4

The collapse of the German state with its long-standing hegemony over the Estonian-Latvian region of the Russian Empire together with the chaos to the east, where Bolshevik forces were busy blasting their way into "utopia", gave Latvians, Estonians, and, to a lesser degree, Lithuanians, the political opportunities for which they had long been waiting.

A hastily formed state council had already taken a collective deep breath and declared an independent Latvia with a provisional government on November 18, 1918. To show it meant business, the council summarily granted Latvian citizenship to everyone (well, almost everyone) living within what the council determined to be the borders of a now free Latvia. The council, however, also took this opportunity to disenfranchise members of a large political party thought to be a future threat: the German Unionist Party with its constituency of mainly nationalistic German landowners and businessmen under whom broad swaths of the Latvian peasant population had quailed for generations.

In addition to the German extremists, among the region's population were hardcore Bolsheviks and Bolshevik sympathizers who, regardless of ethnic background, were feared for their intent to destabilize any new government and thus were candidates, along with the German Unionists, for exclusion from the process of building a new Latvia.

Outsiders might construe this latter gesture as vindictive, but for most ethnic Latvians, it was time to eliminate the perceived troublesome elements from among the population of Germans who had for centuries confined the region's ethnic Latvian peasant population to a stratum one level above that of "hewers of wood and drawers of water".

As to the portion of the Russian-Latvian population in sympathy with—or actively engaged in—the "Soviet experiment" playing out to the east, the answer was a resounding "no" to citizenship. If contemporary diaries and reminiscences are accurate indicators, the prescient members of the fledgling government did not view this exclusionary law as an attempt to get even but, as with the German Unionists, it was applied as a protective measure.

These steps forward in the stirring saga of the creation of the first Latvian state, along with the story of the concurrent ethnic and political conflict, provide dramatic reading in a number of English-language sources. A worthy starting place is Andrejs Plakans' *The Latvians: A Short History.*[4]

As to what faced those seeking to build a distinctively Latvian publishing sector, once again Ādolfs Bļodnieks summarized the prospect in a line: "the war and the German occupation had reduced the Latvian press to a bare minimum."[5] The implication was that rebuilding a "book culture" would be long and arduous. A variety of mainly Latvian sources, including reminiscences, speak directly and indirectly to the role played by the writers, artists, and publishers who created this relatively free publishing culture in the two decades between 1919 and early summer 1940, that fateful year when once again life turned dark for so many Latvian citizens.

There are references and allusions that indirectly prepare the way—some even answer a few questions—in the forewords and introductions to studies of the post-1939 periods of occupation. A number of such sources are in Western European languages, e.g., English,

---

4 (Stanford, CA: Hoover Institution Press, 1995). Still relevant: Stanley Page, *Formation of the Baltic States* (Cambridge, MA: Harvard University Press, 1959), [reprint, Howard Fertig, 1970]; Georg v. Rauch, *The Baltic States: The Years of Independence, 1917-1940* (Berkeley: University of California Press, 1974); Inese Smith and Marita V. Grunts, *The Baltic States: Estonia, Latvia, Lithuania* (Oxford: Clio Press, 1993). Scores of journal articles are also accessible through online databases.

5 Bļodnieks, ibid., p. 155.

German, and Swedish. A growing number of Latvian-language sources touch tantalizingly on these subjects or are raised directly in the memoirs of editors, authors, and publishers. One notable example is the memoirs of Jānis Grīns, a long-time editor of Valters un Rapa.[6] A quite different work is the tendentious autobiographical memoir of that literary war-horse of Latvian communism, Andrejs Upīts.[7] These are just two figures, each with a wide circle of associates whose divergent and unyielding ideological views kept the circles they represented from intersecting.

Publishers' reminiscences are rare due to the fact that many publishers were shot either during the first Soviet occupation from July 1940 to July 1941 or the first years of the Nazi occupation from 1941 and 1942. Others died in exile without having written book-length reminiscences. One notable exception was the dashing Helmārs Rudzītis,[8] who fled to Germany in 1944 and ultimately to Brooklyn, New York, in 1949, where he set about publishing Latvian books for other Latvian émigrés.

As to publishing house histories spanning the years of the Interwar period, we have only one work that qualifies for the category, a work commissioned by the publishing house of Jānis Roze.[9] Although it consists of contributions by several researchers as well as family members and includes a comprehensive bibliography of all Latvian-language titles published by Roze, it is more celebration than monograph. Nonetheless, it is important for its content and serves as a model of layout and design for similar future undertakings.

One could only wish that a Vladas Žukas would appear on the Latvian scene to do what this thorough and energetic publishing historian did for Lithuanian publishing of the same period.[10]

There are exhibition catalogs and individual and collective monographs both of the period and of recent years that provide extensive information on the ethnic Latvian artists actively involved in book illustration as well as book design in the 1920-1930s. The single most useful non-monographic reference work is the uneven-in-treatment yet invaluable *Māksla un arhitektūra biogrāfijās* (Art and Architecture in Biographies) in four volumes, which appeared one volume at a time beginning in 1995 with the final volume and supplement published in 2003.

To the great credit of the Latvian National Museum of Art in Riga and its director Māra Lāce, the museum has been consistently exploring the Interwar era by means of major exhibitions and accompanying catalogs. One prime example is an exhibition of a leading family of artists and book illustrators, spanning three generations, published in 2000, *Mākslinieki Skulmes: 20. gadsimts, Latvija* (Artists Skulmes: 20th Century, Latvia). Another example is a thematic exhibition published in 2004 titled *Reālisms. Jaunā lietišķība* (Realism. The New Objectivity). There is also the museum's important but unfortunately short-lived series *Doma: Mākslas teorija, vēsture, kritika, hronika* (Thought: Art Theory, History, Criticism, Chronicle) published from 1991 through 2000.

---

6   *Jānis Grīns, Redaktora atmiņas* [Jānis Grīns: An Editor's Reminiscences] (Stockholm: Daugava, 1968), edited by his son, Ervīns Grīns.

7   *Atmiņas par Andreju Upīti* [Reminiscences of Andrejs Upīts] (Riga: Liesma, 1977); compiled by Jānis Upītis.

8   Rudzītis, Helmārs. *Manas dzīves dēkas* [My Life's Adventure] (Brooklyn, NY: Grāmatu Draugs, 1984).

9   *Grāmata par grāmatnieku Jāni Rozi* (A Book About the Bookman Jānis Roze), with contributions by Konstantīns Karulis, Jānis Roze, Vladislavs Urtāns, Aina Roze, Gunta Jaunmuktāne, Ieva Lejasmeijere, and Valdis Villeruišs (Riga: Jāņa Rozes apgāds, 1999).

10   See Vladas Žukas' histories of these publishing houses: *Dirvos, bendrovē knygoms leisti, 1918-1940* (Vilnius: Baltos Lankos, 1994); *Sakalo…1924-1940 ir 1943-1944* (Vilnius: Vilniaus universiteto leidykla, 1998); *Švyturio.. 1918-1931* (Vilnius: Vilniaus universiteto leidykla, 1998); *Bendrovēs..1918-1940* (Vilnius: Baltos Lankos, 1998).

The post-1991 publisher Neputns deserves much praise for its various monographs and periodicals furthering inquiry into the art and design of the Latvian past as well as present. Of particular note is its series (six volumes published to date) of thematic inquiries on Latvian art history, *Materiāli Latvijas mākslas vēsturei* (Materials for Latvian Art History). Neputns' editing, design, production, and high-quality English translations are remarkably consistent.

During the second Soviet occupation, from 1946 to 1991, a number of useful works for the book-oriented graphic design historian were published as monographs as well as general, collective works. Two notable titles are *Latviešu tēlotāja māksla, 1860–1940* (Latvian Fine Art, 1860–1940),[11] and a more specialized title, Velta Lapacinska's *Linogriezums latviešu tēlotājā mākslā* (Linocut in Latvian Fine Art),[12] an overview of linocut illustration from 1919 through the mid 1970s, which is confined to artists whose politics conformed to that of the second Soviet period.

Setting and circumstances of publishing in the early years

Try to visualize greater metropolitan Riga from the mid 19th century to World War I: a noise- and smoke-filled manufacturing center for everything from railroad rolling stock to electrical appliances, textiles, and a wide variety of other consumer goods. The Russian Empire, of which Riga was an integral part, was the prime market. As to be expected, considerable wealth accumulated in the capital city Riga, alongside the usual pockets of poverty and economic disparity one could expect to find in a smaller-scale St. Petersburg or Berlin, two centers to which Riga had close ties. The countryside and its productive farmland even supplied Berlin, London, and cities between with butter, eggs, and other agricultural commodities. The forests and the tree farms of Latvia supplied pulp logs for the paper mills of the Russian and German empires before World War I and continued to supply these same regions with similar products during Latvia's first period of independence.

It is generally recognized that the engineers, inventors, and industrial designers of Riga brought all manner of innovative appliances and equipment into the Russian Empire's domestic and foreign markets.

Throughout its independence in the 1920s and 1930s, Latvia began to once again produce such goods for its own population and for export. During the Interwar period and the post-WWII Soviet era, the VEF[13] research and manufacturing complex was a legend for quality and innovation throughout Eastern Europe and the Soviet Empire.

Today's first-time visitors to Riga are often amazed at the creativity of Latvia's architects working from the late 19th century into the first decade of the 20th century. Those local architectural interpreters of cultural trends farther west left a legacy of dramatic Jugendstil structures, which many claim to be the largest surviving aggregation of such buildings in Europe. Several of the architects who created these buildings also designed residential buildings in other European capitals before the formation of the Republic of Latvia.[14]

11   (Riga: Zinātne, 1986).
12   (Riga: Zinātne, 1975).
13   Established in 1919 on the framework of an earlier enterprise, the Valsts elektrotehniskā fabrika (State Electrotechnical Factory) declined with the coming of competition after 1991 and has since been broken into a number of small companies.
14   *Rīgas arhitektūras meistari, 1850–1940* (Riga's Architectural Masters: 1950–1940), by Jānis Krastiņš (Riga: Jumava, 2002).

L5

L6

The advantageous location of Riga on the Daugava River (formerly Düna) and the coastal all-weather ports of Liepāja (Libau) and Ventspils (Windau) served the resident, German commercial entrepreneurs for hundreds of years and continued to serve those interests and those of the Russian Empire from the late 18th century into the first years of World War I. All these elements gave Latvia and its cities, principally Riga, a crossroads position far greater in importance than the size of the country's modest population might indicate.

As to print culture, Riga's population of 482,500[15] in 1913 could count on 15 daily newspapers (eleven were Latvian-language publications) being delivered to the city's kiosks before dawn. As for books, it is estimated that 8,000 to 10,000 titles were published in the Latvian language alone between 1900 and 1917.[16] All this despite the fact that the publishing infrastructure had suffered along with the manufacturing and communication sectors.

Before considering the Interwar rebuilding process as it relates to press and book publishing, Riga experienced yet another setback that had a decided impact on the print culture to come.

Just when Rigensians thought they had seen the end of the Bolshevik specter with which they had been living for a number of months, it reappeared on New Year's Day in 1919, guided by the Latvian Communist and Bolshevik Party supporter Pēteris Stučka, who, with his Moscow apparat, lingered until May 22nd. During this time the only regular newspaper available was the Communist newspaper *Latwijas Sozialistiskās Padomju Waldibas Siņotajs* (Latvian Socialist Soviet Government Reporter). L5 While the final departure of these "spoilers" was welcomed by most Latvians, there were unwelcome accompanying losses aside from their selective murder of political opponents and intellectuals.

---

15   *Der Grosse Brockhaus*, vol. 15 (Leipzig, 1933), p. 740. The same source also cites the population as having dropped to 378,000 by 1930.

16   *Geschichte des Buchhandels in Russland und der Sowjetunion* by Iosif E. Barenbaum (Wiesbaden: Otto Harrassowitz, 1991), p. 133.

Attendant on their exodus went whatever moveable goods of substance that had been left by the previous withdrawal of the Bolshevik government troops. The Latvian leaders charged with the task of rebuilding watched helplessly as more loads of iron, steel, timber, and machine tools, to say nothing of printing presses and type—anything to satisfy the needs of the Soviet government's prolonged and debilitating civil war—were piled on ships, railroad cars, trucks, and horse carts and moved eastward.

Only gradually did newspaper and periodical publishing once again take hold and with it, book publishing. The appearance of what was printed in those first years tells us a great deal; for example, the general lack of color was indicative of the impoverishment of resources and the Herculean tasks that had to be overcome in such basic areas as paper and ink supply, properly functioning printing equipment, and adequately filled type cases. Notable among those publishers continuing from before the founding of an independent Latvia were Valters un Rapa, Ansis Gulbis, and Jānis Roze.

Valters un Rapa, established in 1912 by Arturs Valters and Jānis Rapa, and the publisher Ansis Gulbis managed to continue publishing through the turmoil, bringing out 61 titles in 1920 with a total of 336,000 copies.[17] By 1921 this production had more than doubled to 142 titles.[18]

The relatively somber appearance of a few examples of what even an established publisher with capital to draw upon managed to produce in such difficult years speaks for the situation: for example, the *Tautas kalendars, 1919* (People's Calendar 1919)[19] L6 with its cover illustration and design by the nationalist book and poster artist Vilhelms Krūmiņš. Another example is Jānis Veselis'[20] *Pasaules dārdos: Stāsti un fantazijas* (In the Roaring World: Stories and Fantasies)[21] L7 with a design possibly created by Jūlijs Madernieks, the celebrated creator of stylized graphic folk idioms. If the designer was indeed Madernieks, the choice was appropriate as a graphic interpreter, for Veselis' writings fit the larger movement of that time to "mythologize" Latvian legends. This movement included a group of like-minded intellectuals among whom Madernieks was one of two highly visible graphic designers before independence and whose commissions continued well into the Republican period.[22] Ansis Cīrulis, a student of Madernieks, was to outshine his teacher in a creative synthesis of folk elements—a William Morris-like figure who effortlessly transformed each decorative object he created. Rūta Rinka's study of Cīrulis leaves little doubt of his genius.[23]

The sober-appearing Valters un Rapa catalog L8 for 1921/1922 hints at the publishing constraints during those years.[24] The books clearly reflect the circumstances that forced

17 *Valtera un Rapas A/S 25 darba gadi* (Riga: Valters un Rapa, 1937), p. 28.

18 Ibid. [This same source states that by 1936 this production had increased to 270 titles per annum for a total of 806,100 copies.]

19 Printed and published in 1918.

20 Veselis immigrated to the United States from Germany in 1950 and died in Milwaukee, Wisconsin.

21 (Valters un Rapa, 1921).

22 Ināra Novadniece's monograph *Jūlijs Madernieks* (Riga: Zinātne, 1982) is the most thorough account of this teacher-designer who left his distinctive imprint on textiles, book covers, sheet music, wall coverings, and ex libris as well as devoting much time to his studio paintings.

23 *Ansis Cīrulis: Saules pagalmos* (Ansis Cīrulis: In the Sun's Courtyards) (Riga: Neputns, 2008).

24 This 36-page catalog of books published and distributed by Valters un Rapa signals the firm's future hopes with more than 200 titles published or distributed by them. The "Educational Book" section contains eighty-some novels and story collections—all Valters un Rapa titles—in addition to 33 titles of poetry. 86 titles are offered in the "Theater" section, although a number were distributed titles. Also listed are 47 titles for children and young people, 23 works on religion and philosophy, and 33 titles in the broad category of music. Concluding the catalog is an antiquarian section of 158 items dating from the 1860s onward. The most expensive title, a work by the Lutheran divine C.G.G. Croon, is listed at 25 lats.

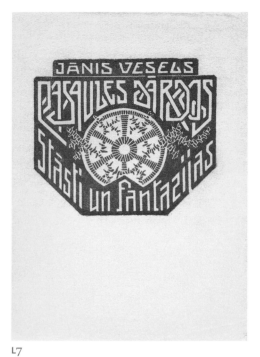

L7

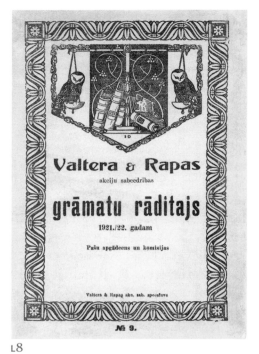

L8

L9

L10

publishers to rely on wit to give some element of graphic interest to their productions. This challenge of limited materials ran across the spectrum of publishing, including government publishers.

L11

Two such examples of early government publications are Jakov Abramovich Berlin's[25] *Darba ļaužu vēsture* (The History of Working People) L9 published by the Latvian Education Commission in 1919 and Vilis Plūdons'[26] *Mazā Anduļa pirmās bērnības atmiņas* (First Childhood Memories of Little Andulis), L10 also published in 1919, both with cover illustrations by designer-editor Alberts Prande. The typeface used in both of these government-sponsored titles maintains the soon-to-be discontinued use of the Latvian Fraktur. This was the typeface, in its various cuttings, used from the days before the spelling reform when German typography and printing dominated in the region and influenced the design of pre-independence Latvian type forms. It might also be added that type design and type founding in Latvia and Estonia were primarily in the hands of German or German-trained individuals from the closing decades of the 16th century until the early 20th century.[27]

Because of the depredations sustained in the printing and publishing industry during the years of transition, many printers used what was available throughout the 1920s despite a government decree effective July 1, 1921, stating that publications of government and official local bodies and schools be produced with "Latin letters...in place of Gothic letters". In 1922 the issue of spelling and orthographic reform was addressed as well, with a requirement that "the new orthography be used in schools and in government and local government agencies".[28] It is apparent when looking at the variety of printing produced in the early 1920s (books, pamphlets, periodicals, and official reports) that only gradually was Latvian Fraktur type melted down for scrap and more contemporary typefaces acquired, no doubt a matter of economics as well as resistance to change among the older generation.[29] Among other changes, this orthographic reform included the conversion of "h" to a macron as a lengthening mark, as in "spehkeem" to "spēkiem" (powers) ("tas ir pahri maneem spehkeem" after reform became "tas ir pāri maniem spēkiem" [that is beyond my powers]); the conversion of "w" to "v", as in "Awīse" to Avīse" (newspaper); the conversion of "ee" to "ie"; "sch" to "š"; etc. L11

---

25   There is uncertainty about his life dates (born either in 1880 or 1889; no year of death found). Berlin was a Russian historian and ethnographer who wrote primarily for young people.

26   The family name after spelling reforms were implemented.

27   See Arend Buchholtz, *Geschichte der Buchdruckerkunst in Riga 1588-1888* (Riga: Müllerische Buchdruckerei, 1890). Reprinted by B. De Graaf (Nieuwkoop, 1965).

28   See Pēteris Vanags, "Language policy and linguistics under Ulmanis" in *The Ethnic Dimension in Politics and Culture in the Baltic Countries 1920-1945*, edited by Baiba Metuzāle-Kangere (Huddinge, Sweden: Södertörn Högskola, 2004), p. 126.

29   Nearly 15 years after these edicts, most daily newspapers in the new Latvia continued to use the old orthography with notable exceptions being *Valdības Vēstnesis* (Government Herald, 1920-1940) and *Latvijas Kareivis* (Latvian Soldier, 1920-1940). The daily *Rīts* (Morning, 1934-1940) began publishing with only a Roman letterform.

L12

L13

Trade publishers ready at the Republic's founding:
Ansis Gulbis, Valters un Rapa, Jānis Roze

Relatively few publishers managed to endure the economic problems of the early years and carry on to the end of the Republic. Many, however, began and then faded after a few years. Profiles of these publishers ranging in size from the large and dominant to the small and economically vulnerable will be discussed, along with those whose political orientation ranged from the ideological left (social democrat to communist) to the right (intense Latvian nationalists and, later, supporters of the Ulmanis regime of the 1934–1940 period).

As implied at the outset, the number of publishers existing in the two decades of the Interwar period was too numerous to allow for more than a sampling. Excluded are those with a publishing plan and approach to design so similar to the included publishers that duplication was not warranted. What has been chosen for inclusion in this survey is based on what is revealed about the culture of the period in a given publisher's content and design choices.

Ansis Gulbis

Ansis Gulbis Publishing Co., like Valters un Rapa, was operating from the first days of the Republic, thanks to both publishing houses having been established before the close of World War I. Barenbaum asserts that Gulbis was the "most important Latvian publisher before the Russian Revolution of October 1917", having established his firm by 1903.[30]

Ansis Gulbis, an essayist and critic, not only had the foresight to choose young writers likely to become major literary figures, but also had the intuition to commission cover designers and illustrators, who in time became the leading artists of the era. One such cover designer was Romans Suta, who was to become the most versatile artist of the period—a ceramicist, studio painter, print maker, and set designer. One of Suta's early book cover designs was for *Vērojumi un sapņojumi* (Observations and Dreams, 1920). L12 This booklet was little more than an enthusiastic and lengthy comment about Italy and its centers of art by the essayist Angelika Gailīte. However, a critique of Suta's ability should not be passed on the basis of the tentative expressionist design for this cover. A more deftly handled approach was yet to come in the following year with Suta's design for a tragicomedy in three acts titled *Zeļa beedri* (Fellow Travelers, 1922) by Viktors Eglītis. L13

Gulbis followed this work that same year with a decorative typographic cover commission for Andrejs Kurcijs' *Vita nuova* (The New Life, 1921), L14 commissioning the young Sigismunds Vidbergs, who was ultimately to become the Latvian book artist and designer most recognized throughout Western Europe and North America.

Because of Gulbis' stature as a major figure in Latvian culture in general and book culture in specific, his life and accomplishments merit more than a footnote here. His personality and willpower come through clearly in his most often reproduced photo portrait. L15 His rise to a position of publishing giant in the Latvia was something of a Horatio Alger saga. Gulbis was a self-taught farm boy working his way through menial jobs in Riga, including a sales stint in a book shop. He found his way to the management of a regional branch of the Karl Jozes bookshops in Dünaburg (now Daugavpils). By 1900, Gulbis had moved to St. Petersburg as a sales representative for the S. Baechli wholesale company. In 1903, while still a clerk and a few months before establishing his own business there, Gulbis was already calling for reforms in the Latvian book trade. This energetic, reform-minded young publisher spoke regularly about the need for organization at an annual meeting of intellectuals, book people, publishers, and interested persons. His mission was to see that Latvian book publishing and book selling reforms be implemented through an association with enforceable regulations and a framework for establishing an apprenticeship program for "book workers". As the result of these annual conferences, and certainly with credit to the 30-year-old Gulbis, such an association was formed.[31] All of this activity took place while the Latvian-speaking area was still a part of the Russian Empire.

L14

L15

30 Ibid., p. 133.

31 Gulbis had come upon Hermann Weissbach's *Encyclopädie des gesamten buchhändlerischen Wissens*, Fascicles 1-7, all published (Weimar, 1887-88), outlining concepts and organizational structures for a well-run national book trade. The common sense appeal of its content inspired Gulbis to a lifetime cause. It should also be mentioned that the Bibliographische Institut (Leipzig) and particularly its director, Joseph Meyer, provided further inspiration and incentive to Gulbis. See *Das Lettische Buch* (Riga: Zelta Ābele, 1942), edited by Ziedonis Krastiņš et al., pp. 152-153.

L16

L17

L18

L19

A keystone of the Gulbis book publishing enterprise was his *Universālā Bibliotēka* (Universal Library), L16 initiated in 1911 and patterned after the highly successful *Reclams Universal Bibliothek* of Verlag Phillipp Reclam (Leipzig).[32] L17

It was in St. Petersburg that the prescient Gulbis first published the collected writings of Elza Rozenberga,[33] who under the pen name Aspazija[34] was to become the most talked-about Latvian woman writer of the Interwar period and likely the most widely read. She is among a select group of poets to arrive back from exile (in her case, the spring of 1920) and be greeted along avenues lined with well-wishers in the country's capital city of Riga. Her reception was shared equally, however, with her life companion, the social democratic revolutionary and Latvia's most widely recognized poet, Rainis, i.e., Jānis Pliekšāns. L18

Rightly speculating that an entrepreneurial life in the "New Russia" was likely to be somewhat uncertain, Gulbis returned to Riga in 1918 among the vanguard of those seeking the challenge of publishing in a country just coming into being. Already in the March 16, 1919, issue of *Uz Preekschu* (Forward!, with its subtitle in translation being "The Newspaper of Latvia's Revolutionary Socialist Party") Gulbis purchased a front page advertisement underneath the paper's banner announcing titles "just published" in his *Universāla Bibliotēka*,[35] a series of small-format booklets he continued as part of his goal to bring world literature in translation to the new republic. In this *Uz Preekschu* announcement was Gerhart Hauptmann's drama *Audeji* (The Weavers) with its working class theme, indicating a social concern and recognition of German literature—two continuing features of the Gulbis publishing program.

For the following two decades, translations, collected writings, and series were to be the foundation of Gulbis' publishing empire along with major reference works, e.g., the monumental *Latviešu konversācijas vārdnīca* (Latvian Encyclopedia) L19. For quite a long time this remained the most comprehensive general encyclopedia published in the Latvian language, thus providing a compendium of all-one-ever-wanted-to-know-about-Latvia and presenting "the world" to Latvian readers. Under the editorship of the historian and literary figure Arveds Švābe and modeled after the 14th edition of *Der*

---

32 Gulbis began this series with Goethe's *Faust* (translated by Rainis) in two volumes. The series was heavy with German and Russian translations among a number of contemporary Latvian and Scandinavian authors. Of the first 94 titles, 17 were German translations and 17 were Russian translations. Latvian authors included A. Deglavs, K. Skalbe, V. Plūdons, Rainis, and A. Upīts.

33 Despite a title implying previously published works, *Aspazijas Kopotie raksti* (Aspazija's Collected Writings) (St. Petersburg: A. Gulbis, 1904) marked the first appearance in print of her accumulated poetry and plays in 900 pages!

34 Ms. Rozenberga presumably saw herself as a latter-day embodiment of Aspasia (ffl 440 BCE), the allegedly beautiful and reputedly clever mistress of Pericles.

35 The series continued until 1927 with a total of 305 numbered titles.

Grosse Brockhaus,[36] this encyclopedia became the standard general-reference work in public and school libraries as well as the homes of many a Latvian family. Publication was supported by the Latvian Cultural Fund[37] (founded on November 18, 1920) and began appearing one volume at a time in 1927, with near-completion in 21 volumes in 1940.[38] The edition size of the first two volumes was 1,500 copies per volume, although the *Valsts bibliotēkas biļetens* (National Library Bulletin) for 1927 does not indicate the size of the edition in its two variant bindings.

Gulbis, ever the far-sighted businessman, knew that a government association with attendant publishing agreements could provide a sustained cash flow. At the beginning of the 1920s, he arranged for a contract with the Ministry of Justice to publish *Tieslietu Ministrijas Vēstnesis* (The Ministry of Justice Gazette), a publication that provided a record of all laws enacted and all official regulations guiding life in the new republic. Even the Gulbis catalog that appeared in July 1939 L20 has an in-print listing of every issue of *Tieslietu Ministrijas Vēstnesis* beginning with the first issue in 1920.[39] Although Gulbis had died by the time this catalog appeared, his firm continued and maintained its position as a publisher of government and government-supported publications.

Another Gulbis endeavor that enjoyed a Cultural Fund subsidy, although not so ambitious as the encyclopedia, was the single most important Latvian lexicographical work to appear up to that time, the *Lettisch-deutsches Wörterbuch* (Latvian-German Dictionary) L21 initiated by Kārlis Mīlenbahs.[40] Four volumes appeared between 1923 and 1932. Four supplementary volumes with many corrections and revisions compiled by the renowned philologist and lexicographer Jānis Endzelīns (with collaborator Edīte Hauzenberga-Šturma) were partly published in fascicles by Gulbis (1934-1946) but later gathered in volumes and published in Chicago (1953-1956).

Gulbis' cultural involvement was many-sided and included support of and participation in the founding of Dailes teātris (Art Theatre). For a time, he was even director of

L20

L21

36   The 14th edition of *Brockhaus Konversations-Lexicon* in 17 volumes (1908-1910) was reprinted in 1920.

37   The Latvian Cultural Fund's assistance to both book and journal publishers was akin to the Soros Foundation's similar assistance to the publishing sector in the 1990s.

38   Like most astute encyclopedia publishers, Gulbis brought out a less expensive edition in a modest binding and a more elaborate binding at a considerably higher price. Both editions were available by subscription. The onset of the first Soviet occupation and the subsequent upheaval brought publication to a close with volume 21, closing with an article on "Tiepolo". Švābe escaped to Germany in 1944 and emigrated to Sweden in 1949, where he continued his work, initiating a new encyclopedia titled *Latvju Enciklopēdija* in three volumes (Stockholm: Daugava, 1950-55) with material from the earlier work abridged but in many cases brought up to date. A 200+-page supplement was compiled by his wife, Lidija Švābe, and published by Daugava in 1962.

39   Cover designed by Niklāvs Strunke.

40   An etymological dictionary based partially on historical principles. It followed the model of Jacob and Wilhelm Grimms' *Deutsches Wörterbuch*, begun in 1854 and completed in 1957 in 16 volumes, establishing something of a record for delayed completion.

L22

L24

L26

L23

L27

L28

L29

L30

L22   *Peters Danga*
by Jānis Akuraters (1921)
Cover design: Vasyl Masjutyn

L23   *Vasara* (Summer)
by Jānis Jaunsudrabiņš (1923)
Cover design: Jānis Jaunsudrabiņš

L24   *Mušu ķēniņš*
(King of the Flies)
by Jānis Rainis (1923)
Cover design: Alexander Woldemar

L25   *Portrejas: Noveles*
(Portraits: Novellas)
by Pāvils Rozītis (1922)
Cover design: Kārlis Miesnieks

L26   *Lauku skatuve*
(Countryside Stage)
by Pēteris Ašaks and Rūdolfs Pīlādzis
(1937)
Cover design: Rūdolfs Pīlādzis

L27   *Balkāni* (Balkan Countries)
by Jānis Kārkliņš (1937)
Cover design: Unknown

L28   *Dziedošais gliemežvāks*
(The Singing Shell)
by Elza Ķezebere (1938)
Cover design: Kārlis Padegs

L29   *Zem vītola un citas pasakas*
(Under the Willow)
by Hans Christian Andersen,
trans. by Apsīšu Jēkabs (1938)
Cover design: Rūdolfs Pīlādzis

L30   *Lielās pasaules sākums*
(Creation of the Great World)
by Jānis Širmanis (1939)
Cover design and illus.:
Fridrihs Milts

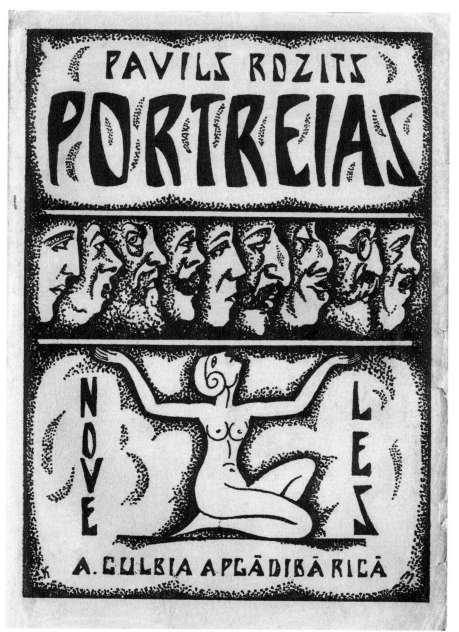

L25

L31

L32

L33

L34

L31 *Klusie ciemi: dzejoļi*
(The Quiet Villages: Poems, 1920)
by Arveds Švābe
Cover design: Jānis Jaunsudrabiņš

L32 *Nopūtas vējā*
(Sighs in the Wind, 1920)
by Antons Austriņš
Cover design: Niklāvs Strunke

L33 *Necilveks: poema*
(The Anti-man, 1920)
by Antons Austriņš
Cover design: Niklāvs Strunke

L34 *Zatirs un krusts*
(The Satyre and the Cross, 1922)
by Ādolfs Erss
Cover design: Uga Skulme

the National Opera—just two among many of the challenges he took upon himself, all the while maintaining his publishing activities.

Gulbis' books were distinguished by his concern for cover design, quality of paper, and clarity and care in setting of the internal typography—good leading, no broken letters or mixed fonts, and other aesthetic concerns that one often finds among smaller publishers. The examples on the previous pages give some hint as to Gulbis' interest in fostering Latvian literature with covers by well-known Latvian artists, along with his previously mentioned concern for bringing foreign literature to Latvia. In this small representation, the cover designers Kārlis Miesnieks, Kārlis Padegs, and Rūdolfs Pīlādzis went on to distinguish themselves in various areas from book to set design as well as studio work, as did Vasyl Masjutyn, who passed through Riga on his way to Berlin in the early years of the Republic.

L35

Valters un Rapa

A rival of Gulbis, Valters un Rapa is one of the two early publishers continuing to the present day.

In March 2003 I had the opportunity of visiting with Jānis Rapa (the son of Jānis Rapa, the firm's founder L35) in his office in the Valters un Rapa building across from Riga's opera house. L36, L37 Rapa recounted something of the years his father lived with their culturally influential relatives, the Brigaders family, and the salon-like events at their home crowded with the famous or soon-to-be-famous writers and artists of the time. Although the chance to mingle with writers and artists was important, equally important to the young Rapa was the opportunity to work in the bookshop of Jānis Brigaders, one of the first Latvian publishers.

My conversation with Jānis Rapa Jr. turned at length to the turbulent early years after the 1912 establishment of the Valters un Rapa firm through its purchase of the C. J. Sichmann publishing company (founded in 1881).[41] Rapa spoke wistfully of the "golden years" between the wars and the subsequent tragedy of family and members of the firm being deported or shot. The fortunate ones managed to escape to other countries during the years of the brief first Soviet occupation and the longer Nazi occupation. Aside from the personal loss and grief overshadowing our discussion of those years, particularly his father's suicide in 1941, Rapa bemoaned the never-to-be-retrieved business records, editorial files, the firm's library of publications, and formal and informal photographs lost through willful destruction on the part of the Soviet occupying forces or through collateral destruction during wartime battle and fires. The few mementos rescued by those who managed to escape with their lives are just that—mementos. What fragmentary records

---

41   By mid-1915, three years after the founding of the firm, Jānis Rapa evacuated many of the staff to a provisional office in Moscow, leaving his partner, Arturs Valters, in Riga. The situation in Riga deteriorated month by month with the bookshelves emptying and no prospect of replenishing because of dwindling paper supplies and limited production staff. Then, in 1917, when the Russian army retreated, it confiscated the contents of the Valters un Rapa shop on Marijas iela (Marijas Street). When the German army arrived, more problems were added in that only publishing of German school books was allowed and distribution was limited to Riga. Contact with Moscow was soon cut. By the time Rapa and the staff returned to Riga in 1918, publishing and book selling had come to a standstill. On January 3, 1918, the Bolsheviks arrived, took the owners' keys, and nationalized the company, putting Rapa and Valters out on the street. Within four months, the Bolshevik Educational Commissariat managed to squander all capital and what little stock remained. When the new government was formed under Kārlis Ulmanis in the summer of 1919, the only direction for a business to go was up. With capital sequestered abroad, Valters un Rapa bought what was left of the Sichmann school book publishing and school supply operation (acquired in 1912 but operated independently). With little more than enthusiasm and insight to guide them, they began reorganizing, rebuilding, issuing one million rubles of stock, and moving to their present location on Teātra iela.

L36

L39

L37

L40

L41

L38

did survive are mostly part of publishers' records in other countries where Valters un Rapa had business relations.

Between the first and subsequent interview the following year, Mr. Rapa and I met on occasion in antiquarian bookshops where he continued his search for Valters un Rapa catalogs, publishing ephemera, and the occasional publication from the 1920s and 1930s still missing from the currently-maintained archive. Mr. Rapa was even attempting to fill in his broken file of the primary journal of publishing from 1922 to 1931, *Latvju Grāmata* (The Latvians' Book), a chief source for study of Latvia's print culture in the early years and for which we shared a mutual admiration of its editor, Rūdolfs Egle. Such searching and meeting came to an end with Rapa's untimely death in June 2005.

For a period view of some aspects of Valters un Rapa's long history, there are several printed sources of importance not the least of which is a company *Festschrift* published in 1937 on the occasion of the firm's 25th anniversary. This volume, *Valtera un Rapas A/S 25 darba gadi, 1912-1937* (25 Years of Valters un Rapa: 1912-1937), L38 with its cover design by Niklāvs Strunke, is profusely illustrated with photographs of persons who made the firm the most successful publisher in the Baltic States during its time. An interior view of the retail operation gives some sense of the period. L39 One photo even gives a glimpse of the

L42

L43

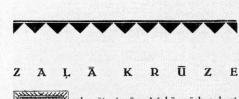

L44

Valters un Rapa approach to binding design in the bind-ing's cover art and typography for the Valters un Rapa house journal *Daugava* (an unbound issue and its cover is shown here). L40, L41

While ostensibly a company history, this publication is so much more because it provides a brief introduction to Latvian-language publishing in the Interwar era beginning with book historian Kārlis Egle's general essay on Lat-vian publishing history. This is followed by an essay by the founding Jānis Rapa Sr. on the firm's first 25 years. The longest and most detailed contribution is by the firm's longtime editor Jānis Grīns, whose primary role was estab-lishing and editing (1928-1938) the firm's cultural monthly *Daugava*,[42] published from 1928 to the spring of 1940, and the firm's quarterly *Grāmatnieks* (The Bookman, 1935-1939), the current-awareness journal for "book people". L42

How did Valters un Rapa books look? The images appended to this section show a small selection from approximately 3,500 titles published from the firm's inception in 1912 to the close of the First Republic in 1940.[43] This selection illustrates a mix of above-average quality design along with the mediocre and a few examples that must have made any design-perceptive clerk wince when placing such books in window displays.

The text pages in the works of fiction show a relatively consistent effort to achieve typographic clarity. Notice the page spread with a chapter opening from *Zaļā krūze* (Green Pitcher, 1935) by Ādolfs Erss. L43, L44

What incentive attracted writers to submit manuscripts to Valters un Rapa? It was not necessarily the prospect of stellar design and typography but more probably the anticipation of sales, possibly even the sale of translation rights. For every writer knew

42 Browsing through a file of *Daugava*, one sees Grīns' effort to bring the contemporary European and Anglo-American literary world to his readers. Thirty years later Grīns recounted his Valters un Rapa years in *Redaktora atmiņas* (An Editor's Reminiscences) (Stockholm: Daugava, 1968) edited by his son, Ervīns Grīns.

43 See "History," Valters un Rapa website posted 1/19/2008.

L45

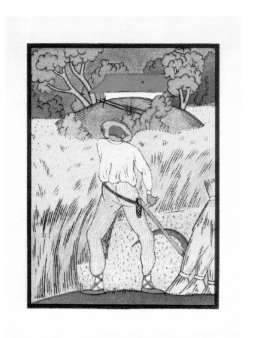

L46

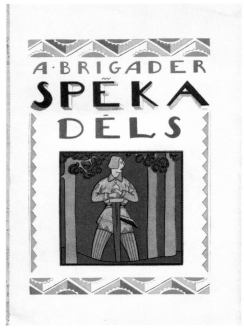

L47

L48

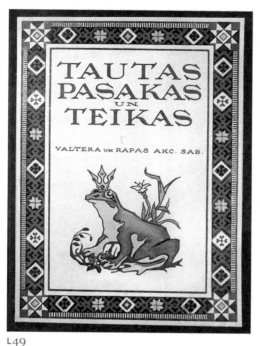

L49

L50

that Valters un Rapa was the biggest firm, had the best distribution network, *and* the most prominent book display windows in the heart of Riga. What more could an author want!

An area in which Valters un Rapa distinguished itself in both design and content was the children's picture book. Although there was a considerable range in quality among their children's books, those illustrated by Niklāvs Strunke beg for inclusion in histories of the 20th century European picture book for children. Two of the best-known of that time, and even today among elderly Latvians, are *Puķu lodziņš* (Flower Window, 1924) by Rainis L45, L46 and *Spēka dēls* (Strong Son, 1927) by Anna Brigadere. L47, L48 These stories by two of the best-known writers for adults in Latvia still keep young Latvian children fascinated to this day, according to staff at the Children's Literature Center of the National Library of Latvia.

For contrast, mention should be made of the illustrative work of Indriķis Zeberiņš included in another collection of stories edited by Brigadere, *Tautas pasakas un teikas* (Folk Tales and Legends, 1923). L49, L50 Zeberiņš' illustrations for children, like those of his countryman Eduards Brencēns, seem frozen in another, more bucolic time, so much so it is unlikely that any child today would give them a second look. Strunke's stylized pictures, by comparison, have a greater likelihood of getting a contemporary child's attention.

The following six panel groupings give some idea of the range in Valters un Rapa book cover designs from the early 1920s to the close of the era in 1940. Once again, the better-known artists then as well as now are Aleksandrs Apsītis, Uga Skulme, Niklāvs Strunke, Valdemārs Tone, Konrāds Ubāns, Sigismunds Vidbergs, and Hilda Vīka. (Tone[44] and Strunke[45] have received monographic treatment in the past decade and Skulme a "walk-on

---

44   *Valdemārs Tone* by Dace Lamberga (Riga: Neputns, 2010).
45   *Niklāvs Strunke* by Dzintra Andrušaite (Riga: Valters un Rapa, 2002).

L51

L52

L53

L54

L51 *Saules kapsēta*
(The Sun's Cemetery, 1921)
by Jānis Veselis
Cover design: Kārlis Ubāns

L52 *Nāves deja*
(Dance of Death, 1924)
by Jānis Jaunsudrabiņš
Cover design: Jānis Jaunsudrabiņš

L53 *Klusais karnevals: Dzejas*
(Silent Carnival: Poems, 1924)
by Valdemārs Dambergs
Cover design: Valdemārs Tone

L54 Printer's proof, Valters un
Rapa publications catalog for 1924,
cover by Aleksandrs Apsītis

L55 *Staru spārni pār dūmainu
upurtrauku*
(Smoke Plumes Rising from the Altar
of Sacrifice, 1925)
by Biruta Skujeniece
Cover design: not credited

L56 *Juris Mancelis*
edited by Aleksandrs Dauge and
Vilis Plūdons for the series
Rakstnieku sejas
(The Faces of Writers, 1927)
Introduction for students to writings
of Lutheran pastor and scholar
Georg Mancelius
Cover design: not credited

L57 *Izdzisuši ziedokļi: stāsti*
(Burned Out Altars: Stories, 1927)
by Augusts Laiviņš
Cover design: Burkards Dzenis

L58 *Raksti*
(Ornaments, 1930)
by Jānis Madernieks
Cover design: Jānis Madernieks

L55

L56

L57

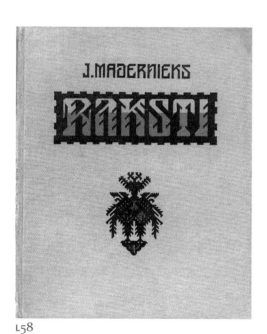

L58

L59

L59 *Modernā Amerika*
(Modern America, 1930)
by Anna Grēviņa
Cover design: Niklāvs Strunke

L60 *Spožie ūdeņi: dzejas*
(Bright Water: Poems, 1932)
by Hilda Vīka
Cover design: Hilda Vīka

L61 *Mīlas kontrabanda*
(Contraband Love, 1931)
by Lūcija Zamaiča
Cover design: Mihails Jo

L62 *Zvejnieka dēls*
(The Fisherman's Son, 1934)
by Vilis Lācis
Cover design: Jānis Šternbergs
One of the most popular books, even
into the second Soviet era; made
into Latvia's first full-length feature
film (released in 1939) with Pēteris
Lūcis and Nina Melbārde in the lead
roles. A poster by Egils Hermanovskis
promoting showings of the film in
the early 1940s was a high point for
Latvian film posters. L63

L64 *Tobago*
(a novel set on the Caribbean
island, 1934)
by Aleksandrs Grīns
Cover design: Niklāvs Strunke

L65 *Zemgales stāsti*
(Zemgale Stories, 1938)
by Oskar Grosberg
Cover design: Erna Geistaute

L66 *Ludis dodas pasaulē*
(Ludis Strikes Out into the World,
1937)
by Lidija Perlbaha
Cover design: Margarita Kovaļevska

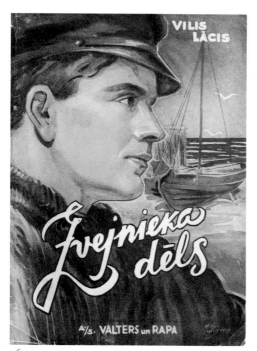

L62

L60

L61

L63

L64

L65

L66

L67

L68

L69

L70

L67   *Lidmašīna*
(Airplane, 1933)[46]
by Rūdolfs Drillis
Cover design:
attributed to Niklāvs Strunke

L68   *No avīžpuikas par miljonāru*
(From Newsboy to Millionaire,
1934) by Hans Dominik
Cover design: Niklāvs Strunke
Illustrations: O. Veize (Oswald
Weise)
Adaptation and translation
by "J. G." (Jānis Grīns) of *John
Workman der Zeitungsboy:
Vom Zeitungsboy zum Dollar-
millionär* (Leipzig, 1925?)

L69   *Jaunā virtuve*
(The New Kitchen, 3rd ed., 1938)
by Marija Feldmane
Cover design: not credited

L70   *Lācītis Miks ceļ māju*
(Little Bear Miks Builds a House,
1938)[47]
by A. A. Milne,
trans. by Austra Zaļā
Cover design: not credited, but
after an Ernest Shepard design

---

46   This "New Scientist" series, begun in 1927, was priced at one lats for the benefit of the school and adult
education audience.
47   Currently in-print in Latvia under the title *Vinnijs Pūks* (Winnie-the-Pooh).

part" in a monograph on the Skulme family.[48]) Meriting a major monograph for their extensive creative work in several areas are the poet, painter, and graphic designer Hilda Vīka; the set designer, graphic artist, and painter Mihails Jo; and the still-celebrated book illustrator, porcelain artist, and poster designer Sigismunds Vidbergs.

L71

Jānis Roze

The Roze firm's contribution to book design in Interwar Latvia was rooted in tradition and from the beginning set a high standard in the quality of its production. In the editorial sense, the firm's founder, Jānis Roze, L71 never wavered in his long-range plan of bringing Latvian writers with a strong national identity to a waiting public. As the "quintessential bookman", Roze demonstrated his commitment to publishing the first "book about books" in the new republic.[49] This work certainly set the tone for a high standard of quality in content and production in the Latvian publishing scene. Sponsored by the Graphic Arts Commission of the Latvian Association of Book Workers, this work was envisioned as an annual publication but was the only volume published. As the one such work to appear in Latvia at that time, its content merits mention as a period document in Latvia's publishing and printing history. Contributions include a capsule history of Latvian printing and publishing by the bookman-collector Jānis Misiņš, a profusely illustrated overview of Latvian applied graphic design (book illustration, ex libris, posters, logos, certificates, candy wrappers, letterhead, security paper) by the critic Visvaldis Peņģerots,[50] graphic design education in various countries by Herberts Haušilds, books as art by Jānis Albrehts, and technical innovations in the book industry by Artur Kupfer. Included throughout are illustrations in black and white and color.

The Roze publishing firm and bookshops, in spite of the vicissitudes of three occupations, have remained a core element in Latvian publishing life since not long after the firm's founding in the inauspicious year of 1915. The firm's first bookshop was established three years later, the same year the Republic was founded. Through several moves of the bookselling operation to the present site of its main shop on K. Barona iela (K. Barona Street), a few meters from the doors of the National Library of Latvia, the Roze name has remained a major presence in the book culture of Riga and all of Latvia.[51]

Like other publishers and writers of the time, Jānis Roze died for his publishing cause. His distinguished career, which began well before the establishment of Latvia, continued without cessation in the 1920-1930s. When the Soviets occupied Latvia in 1940, his company was nationalized. Roze and his wife, Emma, and daughter, Aina, were loaded onto a cattle car with scores of others and deported to Siberia on June 14, 1941. Roze died in a concentration camp in Solikamsk on May 10, 1942.[52] Such was an all-too-common fate with only differences in detail in the centuries-long saga of tyrants fearing press freedom and fearing publishers who, like Roze, were determined to nurture national aspirations.

48 *Mākslinieki Skulmes: 20.gadsimts, Latvija*, compiled and edited by Inese Riņķe (Riga: Jumava, 2000).
49 *Grāmata par grāmatu* (A Book about Books), edited by Jānis Grīnbergs (Riga: J. Roze, 1925).
50 Appended to Peņģerots' contribution is a brief biographical directory of 41 active graphic designers.
51 Roze has three separate shops in Riga, three sizeable shops in other towns, 18 smaller locations in various shopping malls and trade stores.
52 Roze's wife, Emma Henrieta, and daughter, Aina, returned to Latvia in 1948, although Emma was forced to live there illegally, which she did until 1956, when she informed the authorities. But she was not sent back to Siberia. She died in 1985 at the age of 93. The sons, Ilmārs and Jānis, remained in Latvia and later fled to Germany, where Ilmārs died in 1963. Jānis died in 1988. His son, Ainārs, now serves as the firm's director.

L72

L73

L74

As mentioned elsewhere in the text, the large publisher Roze and a much smaller publisher, Zelta Ābele, are the only two publishing houses for which we have a publishing history[53] together with a complete bibliography for the Interwar period. Both histories draw on personal and family-related accounts, and both give a textual and visual insight into the life of the respective firms along with the revelations of editorial purpose that only a detailed bibliography can provide.

For our concern here and for the curiosity of the cultural or book historian, a trip to the Jānis Roze shop in Riga or a visit to the Jānis Roze website to purchase copies of the company history[54] makes much additional commentary here unnecessary. This Roze *Festschrift* with its consummate editing, design,[55] and printing leaves little to add, although one could have wished for a more substantial English-language summary. Nonetheless, this work is an exemplary demonstration of the conservative and refined design of a publisher devoted to Latvian tradition and its developing literature throughout nearly a century.

In conclusion, browsing through the Roze bibliography one readily sees that the firm remained in the middle of the Latvian literary road. The solid, non-causist (with a few exceptions) writers that an educated, middle-class person might want to read are cited here: Jānis Akuraters, Augusts Deglavs, Jānis Ezeriņš, Jānis Poruks, Augusts Saulietis, and Kārlis Skalbe among others. School books and children's books are also present and with good reason: they were a large part of the Roze business. Calendars for various audiences were a definite mainstay of the business as well. Thanks to Gunta Jaunmuktāne's detailed bibliography, there are few questions left unanswered.[56] Even edition size is cited where known.

53   *Apgāda Zelta Ābele ilustrēts bibliogrāfiskais rādītājs ar papildinājumiem un pielikumiem*, ed. by Laimonis Osis and Guntars Pupa (Riga: Literatūra un Māksla, 1993).

54   Jaunmuktāne, Gunta, "Bibliogrāfiskie rādītāji", in *Grāmata par grāmatnieku Jāni Rozi* (Riga: J. Roze, 1999).

55   Layout and typography by Prof. Valdis Villerušs.

56   Jaunmuktāne, Gunta, ibid., pp. 149-187.

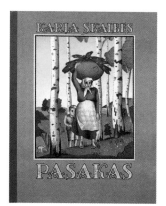

L75

L76

L77

This true bibliographer went a step further and provided a 57-item checklist of writings about the Roze establishment from its beginnings up to 2004, the year of the *Festschrift*'s publication.

The illustration and cover designers of Roze books were quite properly attuned to the conservative reading tastes of the intended audiences. With Indriķis Zeberiņš as a *de facto* house designer and illustrator, a certain "countryside" tone was set. L72 When Zeberiņš had too much work on his desk, his comrade-in-aesthetic-sensibility, Eduards Brencēns, was called in to further expand the "look of the land" among Roze titles. L73 A few covers and illustrations were provided by more original designer-illustrators of the time, e.g., Sigismunds Vidbergs' cover design and three illustrations for Elisa Rais' *Duara meita* (Daughter of Duara, 1926; translated by R. Kroders) L74 and Niklāvs Strunke's cover and eight illustrations for Kārlis Skalbe's *Pasakas* (Fairy Tales, 1934). L75–L77 On one occasion even the father of Latvian landscape painting, Vilhelms Purvītis, was given a commission or simply volunteered (no record survives) to create a book cover illustration for Augusts Saulietis' *Tālas vēstis: Liriska dzeja* (Future Portents: Lyrical Poems, 1924). L78

Roze, like its major competitor, Valters un Rapa, provided its readership with a monthly literary journal, *Piesaule* (The Sunny Side, 1928-1935), which included portions of yet-to-be-published works by Roze as well as original poetry and prose. The journal covers had two designs by the graphic artist Pēteris Upītis. L79–L81

In spite of the dark memories that still crowd around when the history of the few surviving publishing houses are discussed, there is that reaffirming, inviting light coming at dusk from the present-day windows of the Roze and the Valters un Rapa retail shops. Among the surviving Riga publishers/booksellers, Roze has a coveted location on K. Barona iela where several thousand passing pedestrians and tram riders are reminded daily that Latvia's book culture is alive and well.

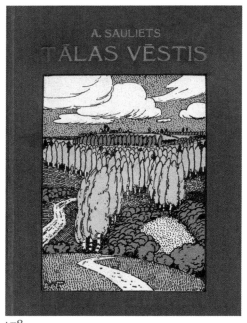

L78

L79

L80

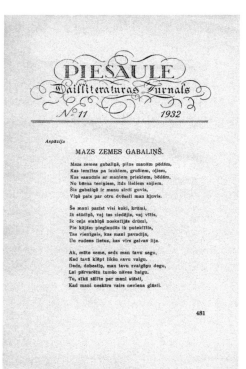

L81

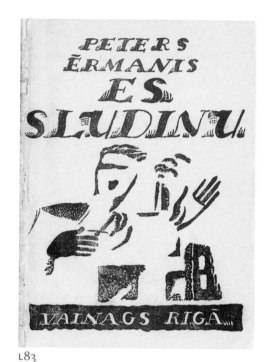

L82

L83

Vaiņags

The Vaiņags (Wreath) publishing house provides a stark contrast in size to the large, financially stable houses of A. Gulbis, Valters un Rapa, and Jānis Roze. From what is known, Vaiņags operated throughout its relatively brief life from modest quarters on the second floor of Troņmantnieka bulvāris 25 (Thornfolger-Boulevard; from 1920 Raiņa bulvāris).

From the content and design points of view, Vaiņags attempted a forward look and tried to reflect, in a cautious way, trends in graphic design observable elsewhere in Europe. During the Interwar period, a number of publishers—both large and small—were inclined to look backward, following examples that stylistically show a tentative continuation of elements from an earlier Art Nouveau style or a Latvian folk idiom. One need only examine a sample of Latvian trade books from the period for corroboration.

The publisher and editor Augusts Mežsēts made an effort to bring distinction to his publishing house in book design and content from its founding in 1919 to its liquidation in 1923. Part of this plan meant featuring translations from English, French, Russian, and American literature, e.g., Theodore Dreiser, Upton Sinclair, and others as well as original work by new Latvian writers. Mežsēts' eye for the gifted artist/illustrator could be readily seen in the cover designs by such young artists as Konrāds Ubāns, Sigismunds Vidbergs, and Romans Suta as well as older artists such as Jūlijs Madernieks.

In the first year of the new decade, Suta was chosen to illustrate the cover of Aleksandrs Plensners' story *Antica fiamma* (Ancient Flame, 1920). L82 Vaiņags also published "the father of Latvian [literary] Expressionism"[57] Pēteris Ērmanis and his collection of

---

57   A designation by Jānis Rudzītis in "Die in der Emigration entstandene lettische Literatur", *Acta Baltica* [Königstein im Taunus], vol. 6, 1966, p. 161.

L85

L86

L84

prose poems titled *Es sludinu* (I Preach, 1920), L83 with a cover design by Alberts Prande. Valdis Villerušs, a leading Latvian book historian, categorized the design as part of Prande's moment of "modernism" before returning to "traditional realism". ("Modern" it may be, but if Prande's design attempt was to convey an "expressionist feel", its graphic uncertainty falls somewhat short of the mark.)

Looking at another Vaiņags title for 1920, one sees a surer design hand at work. Linards Laicens' *Karavane*, L84 a collection of "socially engaged" poems written between 1913 and 1919 by this intense, left-leaning poet-propagandist, is of particular interest.[58] It was Laicens' first collection of poetry to be published in the new Latvia. A previous collection of his poems, *Kvēle* (Fervor), was published in 1908, the year of his illegal return to Riga from Pskov, Russia, where he was also living illegally. Living "on the run" was explained by the negative way in which Russian Imperial authorities viewed his politics. A slender volume, *Kvēle* had been no help to his reputation. As the result of its publication, he was convicted of "revolutionary activities" and put in prison in 1909. His imprisonment was a counter-productive step on the part of the government and only gave Laicens time to write more radical poetry.

Problems aside, Laicens was a writer with an intuitive sense of design who took great interest in the look of his publications.[59] Strunke undoubtedly received suggestions from Laicens, who was known to work with each of his publishers and their in-house designers in order to give the "right visual impression" to the work at hand.[60] Strunke provided five lithographic illustrations for these poems. L85, L86 The images reflect the spare, angular style seen in the contributions to any number of contemporary vanguard

58 The year and place of Laicens' death has been a source of debate. Various sources give August 3, 1937, and December 14, 1938. His granddaughter, Anna Laicena, maintains he died in 1942 in Moscow's Lubianka Prison, according to documents released since 1991 (see her article in *Latvija Amerika* (Toronto), Jan. 6, 1996, p. 7).
59 Interview with Anna Laicena, Feb. 2010.
60 Interview with Anna Laicena, Feb. 2010.

L88   L89   L90

L87

art-literary periodicals spreading an expressionist style throughout other countries, e.g., *Der Ararat* (Berlin, 1919-1921) or the earlier *Die Aktion* (Berlin, 1911-1918). In light of the general level of German-language literacy among intellectuals in Riga and the Baltic area, such periodicals were likely known and circulated among artists. This late expressionism and its manifestation can certainly be seen for a brief period in the book designs of Strunke and his Estonian contemporary Märt Laarman among others.[61]

One might easily pass over the unassuming cover of Arveds Švābe's book of poems *Gong Gong* (1922), L87 but the illustrations by Vidbergs convey a sophistication looking beyond the problems of the day—precisely what readers needed in those years—with the exception of the illustrations for the first poems, collected under the titling "Japaniete". These are designed with a stylization common to books of the time that were illustrated by Westerners attempting to interpret Japan. L88 The book's title page for a few poems on ancient peoples headed "Paleaziati" (Paleo-Asians) carries a more imaginative style of illustration. L89 The last section of the book takes the reader on an erratic, lyrical trip around the rest of the globe with the customary stopover in Paris. L90 A more interesting Vaiņags cover approach is seen in the calligraphic titling by Konrāds Ubāns for Jānis Akuraters' poems *Saules valgos* (Tethered by the Sun, 1921).[62] L91

Last but not least among Vaiņags book titles is *Ho-Taï* (1922),[63] a diminutive[64] book of poems from the romantic side of Linards Laicens' brain. The book may even reflect a "heart search" for some sort of transcendent experience, indicated by the author's evocation of a faint Buddhist element in several of these love poems.[65] Laicens' inspiration, aside from Ho-Taï, seems to have been the compelling actress Anna Lāce, also known as Anna Lācis or Asja Lācis;[66] at least the poems are dedicated to her in 14 point type. But

L91

---

61   A recent survey of the Estonian expressionist phenomenon has been treated in *Expressionismus* by Ene Lamp (Tallinn: Eesti Kunstiakadeemie, 2004).
62   The concluding poem is dated [Summer] 1920, although the title page carries no date of publication.
63   Ho-Taï usually depicted laughing in Chinese art.
64   14x11 cm.
65   Ho-Taï, the Buddhist god of good fortune.
66   Legend has it that the title Ho-Taï was a combination of Honolulu and Tahiti, the code names of Anna Lācis and Linards Laicens in illegal correspondence circulating in the prison.

L92

L93

who could blame him? One only hopes that he fared better with this lyrical offering than the wordy Walter Benjamin, one of many admirers Lāce left in her wake. Niklāvs Strunke designed the cover. L92

Mežsēts' short-lived journal, also titled *Vaiņags*, L93 of "*belles lettres*, art, and politics" with a cover design by the versatile writer-painter Jānis Jaunsudrabiņš[67] lasted for but three issues—January through March 1920. It was preceded by the slightly longer-lived journal *Latvijas Rīts* (Latvia's Morning, September-December 1919). Both publications were brave efforts in attempting to bring "literature and discourse on the arts" to the small audiences shared by other struggling journals. Judging by the authors published, both of Mežsēts' journals might be classed as somewhat conservative in style and literary content when compared to competing publications. Having no great financial backing, coupled with an insistence on publishing works of quality and appealing to a small audience, the Vaiņags journal and book publishing effort was doomed.

Discouraged but not daunted by his publishing misfortunes, Mežsēts eliminated any opportunity for further losses by taking his considerable translating abilities and putting them to work with two burgeoning publishing enterprises. First he turned to LETA, the Latvian Telegraph Agency's book publishing division,[68] which provided opportunities for a gifted translator in its popular and serious literature translation program as well as its periodical division, primarily with the illustrated monthly *Ilustrēts Žurnāls* (Illustrated Journal, 1920-1929).

Mežsēts later joined the young and able Helmārs Rudzītis, one of the most dynamic publishers of that time, who shared Mežsēts' publishing interest in seeing quality literature translated from Western European countries as well as the Anglo-American community.

Mežsēts worked as translator, proofreader, and copy editor for both LETA and Rudzītis. He worked for Rudzītis' publishing house Grāmatu Draugs until the first Soviet occupation in 1940 and survived the German occupation and second Soviet occupation, translating and writing until his death.

Other early publishers and their designs, including Zalktis and Golts un Zeltiņš

Although Ansis Gulbis and his cover artists and designers were mentioned earlier, one important commission of his has relevance to a smaller publisher commented upon here, namely, the cover illustration for a book of poems by the most widely known 20th century Latvian poet, Rainis. According to the art historian Inta Pujāte, Rainis asked his friend Vilhelms Purvītis, the greatest of Latvia's early 20th century landscape painters, to illustrate a collection of poems and presumably to create the overall cover design for this paper-bound collection with its three sections, each having designs on the titled, dividing pages.[69] Pujāte states, "Purvītis produced the cover art for each of the [three]

67 Jaunsudrabiņš was one of the era's most creative personalities. He wrote poetry, short stories, novels, and dramas; translated from German and French; and also designed book covers, including the titling calligraphy. Jaunsudrabiņš studied painting under Lovis Corinth in Berlin in 1909 and died in Körbecke, Germany, in 1962.
68 LETA's publishing program, judging from its extensive catalog for 1925, emphasized popular literature of both domestic and foreign (in translation) origin as well as a subscription service for Latvian newspapers and magazines (in Latvian, Russian, German, and English). 49 newspapers and 66 journals are listed in this catalog alone.
69 "Vilhelms Purvītis and Art Nouveau" in *Vilhelms Purvītis 1872-1945*, edited by the Latvian National Museum of Art staff (Riga: Neputns, 2000), p. 171.

publications individually as well as for a publication of all three sketches together." This collection, published by Gulbis in 1920 under the gathering title *Treji loki* (Three Circles), L94 was not the first appearance of book cover design by Purvītis. In 1904 he created the cover art for *Mazā pasaule* (Small World), a work by the nature-symbolist poet and teacher Augusts Saulietis. This leads to Zalktis (Grass Snake), a publishing house Saulietis founded that same year with his friends the poet Atis Ķeniņš and the artist Janis Rozentāls.[70] But before discussing what became of the Zalktis publishing house during the Interwar period, a few more words are in order about *Mazā pasaule* and the cover artist Purvītis in order to demonstrate that publishing and book cover design were discussed as much in that time as in subsequent periods.

L94

There is no doubt that Purvītis was the leading Latvian landscape painter of his time. But his being drawn into book cover design points to the fact that one's primary ability does not necessarily transfer easily into another. One is inclined to agree with the assessment of Visvaldis Peņģerots that Purvītis' cover design could be put on any book.[71]

Although Purvītis was decidedly of another generation and his involvement in the book arts in the Republican years was modest, Pujāte considers him to be "at the forefront of Russian and Western European artists" and a teaching influence and "presence" throughout much of the 1920s.[72] An indication of Purvītis' recognition by the European art community, particularly in the pre-World War I period, can be seen in the commentary on his work in art periodicals from that period, e.g., *Apollon* (St. Petersburg), *Die Kunst* (Munich), *The Studio* (London), and *Ver Sacrum* (Vienna) among others. Steven Mansbach, a major English-language chronicler of Eastern European art history, speaks of Purvītis in his role as the founder and first rector (1919-1934) of the Art Academy of Latvia and the first director (1919-1944) of the Latvian National Museum of Art, crediting him with being an "educator of a great wave of avant-gardists in the 1920s".[73]

L95

Returning to printing circumstances in the early 1920s, one can also find examples of innovation resulting in a remarkable display of design and technical know-how. In a relatively unusual step, the publishing-printing house of Augusts Golts and Dāvids Zeltiņš turned to Alise Dmitrijeva,[74] an accomplished Baltic-German woodcut and linocut graphic artist and painter.[75] She was given the challenge of creating a cover design for a collection of poems titled *No nakts līdz rītam* (From Nightfall to Dawn) by Vilis Plūdons, written between 1906 and 1919 for publication in 1921. Dmitrijeva's design L95 required a lithographic

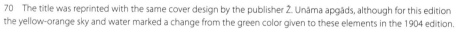

---

70 The title was reprinted with the same cover design by the publisher Ž. Unāma apgāds, although for this edition the yellow-orange sky and water marked a change from the green color given to these elements in the 1904 edition.

71 See his critical overview of illustrative and typographic book cover design in "Grāmatu grafika" in *Latvju Grāmata*, Nr. 2 (1925), pp. 136-140. Here he criticizes the publishers Freināts and Valters un Rapa and the artist-designers Suta, Madernieks, Vidbergs, and Ubāns.

72 See her "Vilhelms Purvītis and Art Nouveau" in *Vilhelms Purvītis 1872-1945*, edited by Latvian National Museum of Art staff (Riga: Neputns, 2000), p. 170.

73 See his *Modern Art in Eastern Europe: From the Baltic to the Balkans, ca. 1890-1939* (Cambridge: Cambridge University Press, 1999), p. 146.

74 According to Valdis Villerušs, "Latvian publishers seldom commissioned Baltic-German artists" for book cover designs or illustrations in the Interwar years. While Villerušs has suggested Dmitrijeva as being "A. D.", it has also been suggested that the signet could have been that of Arturs Duburs (until 1940, Arturs Drekslers), although the image quality points to Dmitrijeva.

75 According to Villerušs, this was possibly the only book design commission Dmitrijeva received in her Riga years. But she was also a landscape painter and created a "Latvian-Jugend" style in needlework. According to Kuno Hagen's *Lexikon deutschbaltischer bildender Künstler. 20. Jahrhundert* (Köln, 1983), she "worked in Berlin from time to time in the 1920s with Susa Walter in her design studio" and in 1939 left Berlin for Poznan and from there to a Displaced Persons camp in Alten-Treptow in Mecklenburg, where she died.

L96

L97

process that could skillfully lay down subtle green with white, gold, and black on a porous slate-gray cover stock—no small feat. Contemporary opinion about the success of her design, however, was mixed with one critic calling it downright "ugly".[76]

It should be mentioned that in the production of this work Zeltiņš and Golts had already moved away from the use of *Fraktur* type and the old orthography in favor of the new letter forms and reformed spelling. Both men were experienced in business, including printing and publishing. Augusts Golts had a printing business from before the beginning of the Republic and continued printing and publishing throughout the Republican period. Together with Ansis Gulbis he was also involved in publishing the illustrated political-literary journal *Rigas Ziņas* (1924-1927). Zeltiņš and Golts went on to publish some 300 titles by the close of 1939.[77]

Periodicals in the early 1920s: *Taurētājs* and *Kolektīvs*

Before commenting on other publishers of the 1920s—their books and their designers—three periodical cover designs from the first years of the Republican era allow an opportunity for design comparisons, supporting the contention that resources were stretched thin at that time and periodical publishers faced limitations similar to those of book publishers.

Taurētājs (The Trumpeter) was the short-lived creation of the indefatigable writer-editor Kārlis Freinbergs who, with his strong interest in culture and particularly the performing arts, went on to initiate other journals. A far-left, cultural-political journal with much promise, *Taurētājs* managed to survive, albeit on a somewhat erratic schedule, through the turbulent years from May 1916 to March 1919 in Moscow. Following a break, it then continued with two numbers in 1920 in Riga. Its two covers designed in the 1910s and signed "P. K." were the work of the poster artist-painter Pēteris Kundziņš but give little indication of his skill as a set designer.[78] Kundziņš was involved with the National Opera in the early years, mainly 1919-1921. Ernsts Stenders followed Kundziņš with the cover designs for the next issues. In his brief life Stenders managed to produce a modest body of expressionist linocuts for proletarian themed publications. For the final two issues of *Taurētājs*, published in 1920, Freinbergs commissioned Oto Skulme to create a cover design, L96 reflecting what was termed a Latvian cubist style, which made a brief appearance in Riga's graphic and plastic arts.[79]

Another periodical with an even shorter life was the single-issue *Kolektīvs* (The Collective, September 1920), L97 a social-democratic art and literature effort edited by Kārlis Dzelzītis, a lawyer, parliamentary deputy, and veteran of the Russian Imperial Army. The Strunke-designed cover image appears to be a version of yet another example of Latvian graphic cubism appearing as an illustration for the previously cited *Karavane*.

---

76 In a review in *Latvijas Kareivis*, Nr. 115 (May 27, 1921) and continued in Nr. 116 (May 28), Viktors Eglītis wrote that the cover reminded him of a carry-over from the time of Alexander III and must be considered "among the worst book covers [of the time]". Eglītis apparently did not know the identity of the artist, simply stating that "the unknown artist has signed with A.D."

77 See entry for Golts in *Es viņu pazīstu* (Riga: Biografiskā arhīva apgāds, 1939).

78 See *Kārlis Freinbergs, Taurētāja aicinājumi* by Ilgonis Bērsons (Riga: Liesma, 1985) p. 88. Bērsons' monograph is a primary document on Freinbergs' work in *Taurētājs*.

79 Extensive commentary on Freinbergs as an editor and critic is provided by Ilgonis Bērsons in *Kārlis Freinbergs, Taurētāja aicinājumi* (Riga: Liesma, 1985).

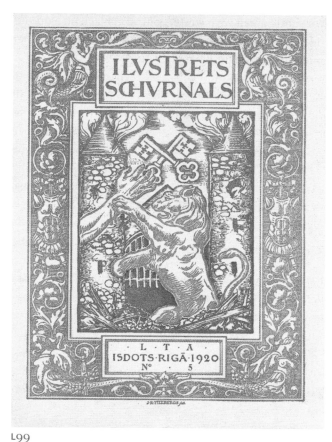

L99

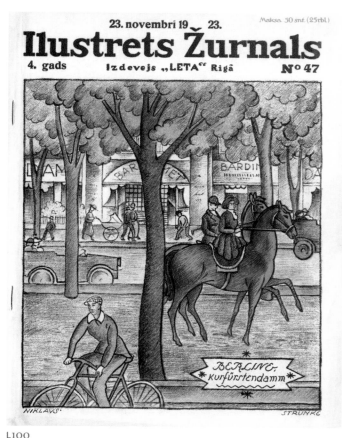

L100

Ilustrēts Žurnāls and the Latvian Telegraph Agency

Even some journals and newspapers with relatively strong financial backing looked drab in this early period. One example, launched in the spring of 1920, was the Latvian Telegraph Agency's (LETA) art and literary monthly *Ilustrēts Žurnāls* (Illustrated Journal). A poster announcing the journal with a cover design by Aleksandrs Apsītis was indicative of how the agency perceived its readership. L98 The September 1920 cover was created by renowned artist Jānis Tillbergs. While strong in symbols, this cover was perhaps more fitting for a Latvian folklore journal than for an illustrated monthly aimed at the growing middle class. L99 By 1923 an editorial decision was made to move away from the staid cover designs and instead commission younger artists who seemed more in tune with graphic design trends in other countries. Improvement was immediate. One example is Niklāvs Strunke's cover for the November 1923 issue. L100

L98

In its time, leading conservative and middle-of-the-road writers and artists contributed to *Ilustrēts Žurnāls*. Browsing through the first twelve issues for 1921 gives some idea of what the journal offered its eager readers at the outset. The lead article for January of that year on Beethoven is followed by photographs of a rather relaxed-appearing Soviet Russian Commission meeting in Riga to deal with the matter of war reparations. The task: returning four million rubles of the estimated nine million rubles owed to accounts held by

Sigizmunda Vidberga grafisko darbu izstāde L. T. A. Mākslas Zalonā (Suvorova eelā № 4),

kura darbu reprodukcijas še eevcetojam, tika slēgta 13. nov. Vidbergs peeder pee mūsu labakajeem grafiķeem. Izstādē bij sakopoti triju gadu darbi, kopskaitā ap simts gab. Kā no darbeem redzejām, tad mākslineeks, sevišķi pēdejos ir ipatnejs un pilnīgi izveidojees, bet viņa atiprā puse tomēr technika. No izstādes 10 darbus eeguva Nacionalais muzejs.

Pilsēta. (Ārleetu ministrijas ipašums)

Uz kafejnīcu. (H. Alberta kga ipašums)

Iz „Revolucija." (Ārleetu ministrijas ipašums)

Eela.

L101

private citizens in the Latvian State Bank.[80] This, in turn, is followed by a scene in which gold rubles are counted by serious-looking men in white coats. Another photo shows the weighing process. The young Soviet Union returning gold rubles as an act of reparation to a portion of the population of the equally young Latvia was likely the first and last such event of its kind in Latvian history.

The art section of this same issue features paintings by Otomārs Nemme, Jūlijs Madernieks (designs, not paintings), Janis Rozentāls (died in 1916), and Konrāds Ubāns. Also shown is an installation photo of the "L.T.A. Mākslas salons" at Suvorova iela 4 (from 1923, K. Barona iela) with works by Latvian artists who, in time, would figure among the most important of that period: Aleksandra Beļcova, Burkards Dzenis, Jēkabs Kazaks, Marta Skulme, Oto Skulme, Romans Suta, Valdemārs Tone, Konrāds Ubāns, and Sigismunds Vidbergs. L101 It is an appealing idea that a state telegraph agency in any country should take such a stand for the arts to the point of encouraging local artists by providing exhibition space—and with weekday hours from 11:00 a.m. to 5:00 p.m.! It is also worth noting that LETA's commitment to fostering the arts is exemplified in its publishing of *Latvju māksla: Īss pārskats* (Latvian Art: A Brief Overview, 1927), considered one of the more important essays on Latvian art of the time by Russian art critic Boriss Vipers.

Poetry is a regular feature in each number of *Ilustrēts Žurnāls* along with reportage on theatre, opera, politics, and the social issues of concern in this new society. A spirit of national pride is apparent throughout the coverage. As the decade progressed and more and more general news publications appeared, *Ilustrēts Žurnāls* increasingly concentrated on art and featured cover stories on an individual artist or extended literary contributions, with general news being relegated to a secondary position. For example, the October 1925 issue features two Latvian artists, Aleksandrs Romans and Pēteris Krastiņš, with more than 15 reproductions each. Krastiņš merited a color tip-in cover illustration. L102

Some of the journal's most memorable covers were original designs by Niklāvs Strunke and Sigismunds Vidbergs. L103, L104

Without question, the Latvian Telegraph Agency occupied a special place in Latvian publishing history, although some might raise eyebrows today at the idea of a parliamentary decree giving a government agency the right to publish books and periodicals in competition with trade publishers in addition to enjoying the privilege of being the prime press vendor in railroad stations and at newspaper kiosks. On the positive side, this monopoly allowed the agency to pay its workers well, which was not necessarily the case with other publishers and booksellers.

80   See Aivars Stranga, *Latvijas-padomju Krievijas miera līgums 1920. gada 11. augustā* (Riga: Fonds "Latvijas vēsture," 2000), for a discussion of how the Soviet Union disregarded debt owed to the new Latvian state and only reluctantly repaid individuals carrying letters of credit.

L104

L102

L103

Under Rihards Bērziņš'[81] dynamic direction the Latvian Telegraph Agency became a modern agency in every respect, working in cooperation with more than 20 international news agencies. Its primary periodical, *Ilustrēts Žurnāls*, remained editorially serious, conservative, and well-printed and maintained a successful and rising circulation until 1928, when it began to decline. Increased competition and a withdrawal of government support presumably resulted in the periodical's suspension with the May/June 1929 issue.

The Latvian Telegraph Agency as a book publisher

The physical appearance of the books issued by the Latvian Telegraph Agency's publishing arm LETA and the diversity of the authors it published varied in the extreme. The Latvian Telegraph Agency was a big business—a monopoly, as was the publisher LETA—and it offered something for everyone among its publications. By 1922 LETA had already become an autonomous commercial enterprise under the supervision of the State Chancellery yet continued to hold its government-granted prime railway station shop and kiosk sites.[82]

Like that of other large publishers,[83] the 1925 LETA book catalog[84] L105 contained titles originating with LETA as well as those distributed for other publishers. A selected list of the authors offered in translation allows some insight into the mind of LETA's editorial board as it formulated standards for translation into Latvian and inclusion among its offerings. Only the translated author's last name is provided unless the given name is necessary for differentiation: D'Annunzio, Baden-Powell, Balzac, Boccacio, Dante, Fénelon,

L105

---

81   Like so many of the talented editors of his generation, Bērziņš was arrested by the NKVD in 1941 and died in the Usol'lag camp in Perm, Russia, in 1942.

82   The surviving LETA archives are held in the Latvian State Historical Archives.

83   One example is the Gulbis catalog published in 1926 with 312 pages offering its own and other publishers' works and published under the sponsorship of the Latvian Book Trade and Publisher's Association.

84   Cover design by Alberts Prande.

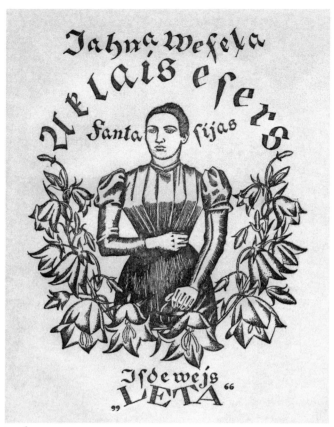

L106

Flaubert, France, Gjellerup, Goldoni, Haggard, Hamsun, Thea v. Harbou, Hebbel, Hedin, E.T.A. Hoffmann, Ibsen, Lagerlöf, Jack London, Longfellow, Merezhovskiĭ, Méri-mée, Poe, Shakespeare, Upton Sinclair, Hjalmar Söderberg, Tagore, Vildrac, von Wildenbruch, and Zola. While most of the authors in translation were considered at that time as "mainstream", LETA's list of Latvian authors ranges from the conservative to the far left.

The artists commissioned to illustrate book covers as well as internal illustrations run the gamut from the uninspired work of Alberts Prande (a LETA staff artist)[85] or the sentimental images of Aleksandrs Apsītis and the less-than-the-best efforts of Uga Skulme to the contributions of the perennially able duo of Niklāvs Strunke and Sigismunds Vidbergs, also a staff artist. Uga Skulme was capable of so much more than is indicated by any of his examined book covers. To see the range of his ability one need only look at a selection of his cubist-phase paintings and drawings, e.g., his "Cūku bēres" (Hog Butchering) done in 1921 at the same time as his "Aklais ezers" (Blind Lake, 1921) by J. Veselis L106 and "Lieldienas" (Easter).[86]

An examination of more than 90 LETA titles reveals the majority of cover designs to be mediocre by any acceptable design standard. This opinion was also given by the period editor and book critic Visvaldis Peņģerots, who maintained in a "Grāmatu grafika" article that the books published by LETA were, in their design, of less than high quality and not unlike the design of books published by Atis Freināts and that both publishers, in Peņģerots' opinion, addressed their cover designs to the "potential reader's lack of sophistication".[87]

There were, of course, exceptions. If one were to select two LETA titles notable for design and illustration, the honors would quite likely be given to *Melnās pasakas* (Black Tales, 1926), transcribed and translated from the oral tales of various cultures[88] by Linards Laicens and illustrated with six color tipped-in plates by Niklāvs Strunke, L107, L108 and the Strunke-illustrated edition of *Tūkstots un viena nakts (Alf laila wa-laila): Arabiešu pasakas* (A Thousand and One Nights, 4 vol., 1924-1929), LETA's last major work of *belles lettres*.

LETA's book publishing operation had been stumbling financially for several months around this time.[89] A governmental investigation of LETA's warehousing and management practices in 1928 and 1929 found irregularities, which resulted in the liquidation of its bookshops in Riga, Liepāja, and Daugavpils, leaving only the shops in Vecgulbene and Rēzekne. By the end of 1929, the shops in the latter two towns were also sold.

85   Prande's contributions to LETA publications and other illustrated journals of the period lack graphic distinction. Yet he must have been adept at political survival, having remained director of the Art Academy of Latvia from 1939 to 1944, when he left Latvia for Germany and then later for the United States in 1951.

86   *Mākslinieki Skulmes: 20. gadsimts, Latvija.* p. 76, 79.

87   See *Latvju Grāmata*, ibid.

88   Primarily a Polynesian and Australian selection with some sub-Saharan African representation.

89   Some 240 titles had been published under the LETA imprint by the time the operation ceased.

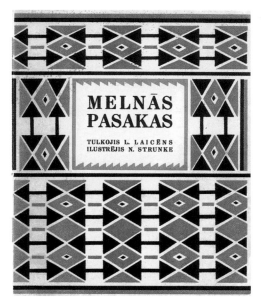

L107

L108

L109

Yet among all this tumult, one more title appeared: Claude Farrère's *Noslēpumains kreisers 1914* (Mysterious Cruiser 1914),[90] translated by Rihards Bērziņš and published in late 1929 or the beginning of 1930 under the imprint of J. Altbergs, the business manager of LETA. Vidbergs designed the cover. L109 From 1930 onward, LETA's activities were apparently limited to the production of ledgers and stationery for its kiosk trade. A train timetable schedule for the Latvian Soviet Socialist Republic was issued by LETA sometime after July 1940, a metaphor in content, perhaps, for the conclusion of its publishing years.

Latvian Cultural Fund

But how did independent[91] publishers of books and periodicals in these first few years find the capital to begin or, if existing earlier, continue within the general economic situation?

The answer is in the unanimity of the young government's parliament and its commitment to the arts and literature, certainly a model in its time. The Latvian Cultural Fund was established by the government at the beginning of the Republic to fund the publication of *belles lettres* as well as to support theatre performances, renovate theatres, give grants to literary periodicals, provide artists and writers with travel grants to study abroad, and support participation of artists in exhibitions outside of Latvia as well as to support exhibitions of foreign artists in Latvia.

This governmental fostering of artistic activity had an understandably positive effect, from the founding of various publishing enterprises to the establishment of sound standards of content and quality to which publishers could turn to and insist upon for submitted book and periodical ideas.

90 Translation of *Combats et batailles sur mer [Septembre 1914-Décembre 1914]*, (Paris, 1925).
91 Not aligned with Latvian political parties or subsidized by political or other groups outside of Latvia.

L110

L111

L112

L113

L114

L110   *Stāsts par Tristanu un Izoti*
(The Romance of Tristan and Iseult,
1922)
by Joseph Bédier,
trans. by Elza Stērste
Cover design: Alberts Prande

L111   *Svētā Antonija kārdinašana*
(Temptation of St. Anthony, 1924)
by Gustav Flaubert,
trans. by Edvarts Virza
Cover design: possibly Alberts
Silzemnieks

L112   *Praktiska latviešu gramatika:*
Pamatkurss
(Practical Latvian Grammar:
A Basic Course, 1922)
by Augusts Ģiezens
Cover design: Ansis Cīrulis

L113   *Pasaka par glupo brali*
(Tale of the Silly Brother, 1921)
Cover design: Niklāvs Strunke

L114   *Aizejošie: Stāsti*
(Bygone: Stories, 1927)
by Augusts Mežsēts
Cover design: Sigismunds Vidbergs (?)

One direct result of the Cultural Fund's sponsorship of publishing was an increase in the involvement of trained artists in book and periodical cover design.[92] Thus, a professional look began to appear in the print culture. To be sure, there were models to follow. Students returning from abroad, intellectuals, visitors, and press entrepreneurs brought periodicals and newspapers from the major capitals both west and east of Riga. German publications from Berlin, Leipzig, and München; English and French publications from London and Paris; and certainly all manner of publications from St. Petersburg up to the winter of 1917 found their way to the kiosks and into the hands of the intelligentsia of Riga and other Latvian cities and towns. Non-Latvian literature could also be found at kiosks catering to the Polish, Lithuanian, and Yiddish reading sectors of the population. In addition to the domestic Yiddish-language press, these kiosks offered a variety of Yiddish periodicals from Warsaw, Kaunas, and other centers.

These book kiosks as well as bookshops were in business again even before the rubble of war had been cleared away. Contemporary accounts and latter day informants indicate that by 1920 reasonably well-stocked shops were offering a number of Western European journals for graphic designers and would-be publishers eagerly looking for ideas.

One partially government-subsidized group that was intellectually primed and ready for participation in publishing and in a position to have a far-reaching effect on the arts was the Rīgas mākslinieku grupa (Rīga Art Group). The initial core of 16 men and two women, the majority in their 20s, was considered relatively naïve[93] but with solid artistic ambitions. Only two of the artists had been born outside of Latvia. All, however, had studied abroad before 1919. Most had their art training in Russia at either the well-endowed Stieglitz Central School of Technical Drawing in St. Petersburg with its emphasis on the decorative arts or at the Penza School of Art. Three members of the group—Jāzeps Grosvalds,[94] Ģederts Eliass, and Erasts Šveics[95]—had studied art in Germany. Grosvalds and Eliass had also studied in Paris. Their formative years as artists largely coincided with those of the new republic and its budding cultural infrastructure. With energy and a spirit of cultural volunteerism, younger artists were taking every imaginable design commission—packaging, book, poster, theater set, periodical illustration, porcelain decoration—and much of this while also maintaining a studio work schedule.

Three artists were to become the most noted in Latvia and abroad for their ability and productivity, especially in book and periodical cover design as well as illustration: Niklāvs Strunke, Romans Suta, and Sigismunds Vidbergs. Looking at their work 80 years later, one sees a freshness and distinctiveness that, had it been created in Berlin, Paris, Leningrad, or New York, would have assuredly found representation in the canon of 20th century art and thus been included in standard art histories. Until recently, however, the general tendency among Western art historians was to all but ignore the contribution

92 There was no shortage of trained artists from which to draw. Numerous promising artists (young men, mostly) had found their way to art schools in various parts of the Russian Empire before the October Revolution. The famed Stieglitz Central School of Technical Drawing in St. Petersburg was one among several choices available to potential students, including schools in Moscow, Kazan, Penza, and other centers. Berlin, among other Western European cities, beckoned talented students wishing to study art. "Away" was preferred over staying "at home" and enrolling in Riga's conservative Blum Drawing and Painting School.

93 One of their own, Jāzeps Grosvalds, even suggested the group change its name to "Ekspresionisti". Grosvalds stated, "There have never been such groups as 'impressionists', 'cubists', and so on. They were given these names later." *Rīgas mākslinieku grupa: Izstādes katalogs*, edited by Dace Lamberga (Riga: Latvian National Museum of Art, 2001), p. 51.

94 See *Džo. Jāzepa Grosvalda dzīve un māksla*, by Eduards Kļaviņš (Riga: Neputns, 2006).

95 *Erasts Šveics, 1895-1992: Valsts mākslas muzeja kolekcijas katalogs* (Riga: Latvian National Museum of Art, 1995).

of the world's small-language areas, and these names and most of the other names mentioned in the following chapters will likely bring little or no recognition among non-Baltic readers. Not even the stream of titillating exhibitions or monographic series treating the arts in Interwar Eastern Europe, including most avant-garde shows at museums and libraries in the last three decades, has shown an appreciation of the arts in Estonia, Latvia, and Lithuania during that period.[96] Even at the beginning of the 21st century, the compilers[97] of *Between Worlds: A Sourcebook of Central European Avant-Gardes, 1910-1930* remained with the now-dated geographic circumscription that has traditionally ignored Estonia, Latvia, and Lithuania. Notable exceptions have been the writings and compilations of Steven Mansbach,[98] Alla Rosenfeld,[99] and a very few others, although these two authors do call attention to Strunke, Suta, and Vidbergs. With that said, the range of book and periodical design from that long-ago print culture remains the era's own best witness to its publishing and design vitality.

Daile un Darbs

The publishing houses Daile un Darbs (Beauty and Work)[100] and Valters un Rapa were at opposite ends of the publishing spectrum in both purpose and graphic style. The first fostered close ties with the world communist movement and its "prime mover" to the east; the other was committed to a democratic Latvia. As to appearance, Valters un Rapa's books were conservative and, with few exceptions, reflected the utilitarian book design of most trade publishers throughout Europe at that time. The same was true of the appearance of most Daile un Darbs titles. Most of their cover designs were undistinguished, not unlike most leftist publications of the time. But a few Daile un Darbs titles were obviously designed by an individual in tune with an aesthetic approaching the contemporary trend for asymmetrical cover typography and sparse layout. These few Daile un Darbs titles could have easily fit among works issued by vanguard, design-savvy publishers on the ideological left in Czechoslovakia, Germany, and Poland before the mid 1930s or in the USSR before 1929. The work of many such publishers and their designers and typographers in these countries is so well known today that little comment is necessary. As the German book design historian Jürgen Holstein famously said, "The left often had the best designers... We may disagree with the content... [still books of the left] are often more interesting in appearance; were a primary force in the development of the new graphics." [101]

Before looking at the few, comparatively interesting-in-appearance Daile un Darbs titles, a note on this publisher's ideology for context.

---

96   Failure to acknowledge a print culture in the Baltic States or explore the possibilities might be attributed to curatorial ignorance of artistic and cultural life in the area. A contributing problem has been limited availability of resources in Western and Anglo-American research collections or, if the books are present, they have often been bound without the illustrated covers in the case of soft-cover books or the dust jackets have been removed from the hard cover volumes, if originally present. A notable institutional exception is the now-dissolved Slavic and Baltic Division of the New York Public Library, which has had exchange arrangements with the National Library of Latvia and other Baltic institutions since the beginning of the 1920s and whose staff left the covers intact.

97   Timothy O. Benson and Éva Forgács (Los Angeles County Museum of Art and MIT Press, 2002).

98   *Modern Art in Eastern Europe: From the Baltic to the Balkans, ca. 1890-1939* (Cambridge University Press, 1999).

99   *Art of the Baltics: The Struggle for Freedom of Artistic Expression Under the Soviets, 1945-1991*, edited by Alla Rosenfeld and Norton T. Dodge (New Brunswick, NJ: Rutgers and the Jane Voorhees Zimmerli Art Museum, 2001). Despite the title, the contributors treat the art of the Interwar period.

100   The name was chosen by the famed social democrat and poet Rainis.

101   From the question-and-answer session following the acceptance speech at the Antiquaria-Preis zur Förderung der Buchkultur, Feb. 23, 2006.

Daile un Darbs was given a head start, so to speak, as a "front" for various propaganda and other activities in that festering revolutionary experiment on Latvia's eastern border that was to become the USSR. According to Indulis Ronis,[102] Pauls Betlers, a political activist on the left wing of the Latvian Social Democratic movement, was given the task by the Latvian Communist Party (LCP) in 1919 to initiate the necessary licensing paperwork for founding a "legal publishing house in Riga". That publishing house was given the disarming name of "Daile un Darbs" (Beauty[103] and Work). Funding was provided by the LCP and other like-minded sources. The celebrated poet Rainis and the lesser-known civil engineer Alfrēds Razums were chosen to be co-directors. The account of intrigues at every level—financial, editorial direction, management—has been delineated by Ronis.

L115

For our account here it is sufficient to say that the murky funding scenario ascribed to Daile un Darbs was not unlike that of Lawrence and Wishart (London)[104] or International Publishers (New York).[105]

It is a sobering exercise to even recite a list of the titles and authors connected with Daile un Darbs. In most cases, they stood for so much sorrow experienced by those individuals unsympathetic to the publisher's aims, so much blood on the ground for the others.

It is all so long ago now that one is reluctant to revive painful memories of those past battles. Yet Daile un Darbs remains part of the Latvian 1920s publishing lore and notes on this firm's publishing agenda provide a necessary point of comparison with other publishing houses—those with a democratic orientation in contrast to the goals of Daile un Darbs, its circle of participants, and dedicated customers.

When first coming upon this publisher's titles in antiquarian bookshops in the mid 1990s and noticing the publisher's logo[106] L115 along with the dreary titles, I looked out of curiosity and then moved on in sadness for what most of the titles evoked.

In time, a friend gave me a copy of *Grāmatas un grāmatnieki* (Books and Book People)[107] and pointed out Jūlijs Ķipers' chapter titled "Komunistiskā izdevniecība 'Daile un Darbs'" (The Communist Publisher "Daile un Darbs"), in which Ķipers conveniently listed all the titles published by the house from its inception in 1920, including dates, edition size, and even the quantity unsold when the publishing house was closed in November 1929. It was clear from this tabulation that Daile un Darbs was not in the business of producing best-sellers. But before there was time to absorb this revealing table, another friend gave me a copy of *Cīņas balsis* (Voices of Struggle),[108] a collection of essays edited by the same Ķipers and with his own chapter containing much of the same text as the previously cited work. But this work, which preceded *Grāmatas un grāmatnieki*, included photos—

102   Details in this paragraph have been taken from an online account on April 7, 2011, by Dr. Ronis, "Latvija un Rainis: Noklusētas sensācijas un jauni fakti par 20. gadu Latviju!" (Latvia and Rainis: Hidden Sensation and New Facts about 20th Century Latvia), appearing in *Nedēļa* on December 8, 2003. No pagination.

103   "Daile" conveys a type of beauty transcending that of physical, human beauty. In the ideological sense employed by the Daile un Darbs editors, it implies the "beauty of completeness" attainable only through "socialist intervention" striving to perfect existing society and the physical environment.

104   "Lawrence" was for "Martin Lawrence", the publishing arm of the Communist Party of the UK up to 1936, when it merged with Wishart Ltd. The funding history for both entities is a matter for speculation.

105   Founded in 1924 by American Communist Party member Alexander Trachtenberg. Initial funding from Abraham Heller, a businessman, was later supplemented through channels that, like Daile un Darbs, pointed to the USSR. International Publishers (IP) worked together with Lawrence and Wishart as well as Foreign Languages Publishing House (Moscow). Today, IP is the official publishing arm of the Communist Party USA.

106   Designed by the illustrator of adult and children's books Indriķis Zeberiņš.

107   Riga: Zinātne, 1986.

108   Riga: Latvijas Valsts izdevniecība, 1959.

L116

L117

grim looking Kämpfer, reproductions of book covers—and more tables and statistics. This work's many chapters provide a veritable history of Latvian publishing "designed for revolution"—all written by surviving participants of the "struggles of the 1920s and 1930s".

Looking out from page 426 in the Daile un Darbs chapter in *Cīņas balsis*, the reader can see the determined face of Mārtiņš Ozols, the leader of the Latvian Communist Party. L116 On the facing page is a grainy photograph of the shop windows of the Daile un Darbs retail outlet at Brīvības iela 11, where management oversight was part of Ozols' responsibility. L117

If a group photo had been made of the principals assisting Ozols, one would have seen a grim lot: Pauls Betlers, Linards Laicens, Ernestīne Niedra, Leons Paegle, Andrejs Upīts—all politically calculating individuals on a revolutionary mission with no time for smiles and no time in their poems and stories for much "daile", humor or "grateful expressions for life".

This thoroughly Marxist publishing initiative was called into being in October 1920, hardly giving Latvia and Latvians a chance to savor even a full year of freedom from the heavy-hitting ideology of the Stučka regime of 1919. But then, who could fear a firm publishing under the banner "beauty" and "work"?

The individuals behind Daile un Darbs had their own vision of "beauty" and it certainly showed in the driving ideology of the *belles lettres* published. "Work" was assuredly the unintentional effort it must have taken all but the most committed ideologues to struggle through the content of the titles published.

At this distance it is difficult to do more than speculate on the poor sales figures, though slow sales may at least point toward more interesting reading offered by the competition. In the eight years of its existence there appear to be only two authors whose projected sales matched demand: the first two volumes of the collected writings (1921) of the dour theorist Janis Jansons-Brauns, with 3,000 copies published and only one set remaining at the operation's closing in 1929; and the collected writings (1922/1923) of the educator and prolific children's book author Ernests Birznieks-Upītis, with 2,000 copies published and only four copies of volume one remaining in 1929. The later volumes of Jansons-Brauns' collected writings (seven volumes in all) were a small disaster in publishing terms with less than one third of the edition sold by the time the firm closed. The remaining Daile un Darbs list—poetry, prose, theoretical works—all seemed to suffer from editorial miscalculation regarding the likely number of eager buyers. For example: from April 1922 to November 1929, 874 copies of Friedrich Engels' treatise on Ludwig Feuerbach and German classical philosophy were sold of the 1,560 copies printed. Even Jānis Rainis' *Klusā grāmata* (The Quiet Book, 1921)[109] L118 over a period of eight years sold only 3,420 copies of the 10,000 printed! From the standpoint of potential market appeal, Aspazija's *Atriebēja* (The Avenger, 1921), a romantic drama of Latvians fighting against German barons, did better in percentage of sales than the book of poems by her life's companion, Rainis. Aspazija's sales were 1,098 of an edition of 2,896 during the same eight-year period.

L118

In its nine years, Daile un Darbs remained more of a "front" than a conventional publisher, if output is a meaningful criterion, for only 49 Latvian titles appeared (several in multiple volumes) and a revolutionary tract in Yiddish.[110] The genres represented were: politics (15 titles, including Marx,[111] Engels,[112] Plekhanov,[113] Janis Jansons-Brauns[114]), *belles lettres* (26 titles by Linards Laicens, Leons Paegle, Rainis, Andrejs Upīts, and others), school and children's books (five titles), one dictionary, and two other reference books. L119, L120 Part of its role as a publishing front was having a license to acquire paper, which in turn was diverted for printing the illegal communist paper *Cīņa* (Struggle). The paper carried on, presumably with another supplier after 1927, until it also ceased publication in 1931.[115]

L119

That a publishing house with such a revolutionary agenda could exist for nearly a decade tells us a great deal about press freedom in the fledgling republic with its initial constitutional goal of ridding the country of "oppressive yokes". The theme of shaking off "chains" was explicit in several Daile un Darbs titles and implicit in others.

Similarly, it is bewildering to this outsider, who thought that the constitutional ban on books coming into Latvia from the Soviet Union was a ban linked to enforcement. From 1924 onwards the publisher (and bookshop) also represented Prometejs, the Moscow-based Latvian-language publishing house for Latvians in the USSR whose books and periodicals were banned in Latvia.[116] Beginning in 1925, Daile un Darbs was also the representative in Latvia of the Soviet Union's central publishing agency, Gosizdat, i.e. Gosudarstvennoe Izdatelstvo. All those "foxes in the henhouse" at Brīvības iela 11 must have been a continuing source of concern to those democratic parliamentarians, many of whom undoubtedly stopped by this prominent location on "Freedom Street" (Brīvības iela)[117]

L120

109 First published in 1909 when he was in exile.

110 *Jung-Sturem*, edited by Iciks Kanders (pseudonym?). As this title is not held by the Misiņš Library (Misiņa bibliotēka) or the National Library of Latvia, it is not possible to determine if the content was the work of Kanders or only edited by him. It is known that by decision of the Criminal Court the title was censored and prohibited. See *Valdibas Vestnesis* Nr. 22 (Jan. 28, 1929), which also mentions "I. Sandlers" as the editor-publisher.

111 *Lui Bonaparta astoņpadsmitais brimers* (1922).

112 *Ludvigs Feierbahs un vācu klasiskās filozofijas liktenis* (1922).

113 *Marksisma pamatjautājumi* (1920).

114 His collected writings with volumes appearing in 1921, 1923, 1927, and 1928.

115 *Cīņa* resumed publication underground in 1934 and continued until 1940.

116 The publishing house Prometejs will be treated in its own section.

117 The shop was moved from its original location at Jumāras iela 8 (now E. Birznieka-Upīša iela) only in 1935.

L121

L122

L123

L124

to check the literary production not only of Daile un Darbs but also other politically left publishers who were invited to add their periodicals and newspapers to the store's shelves.

L125

On weekends in the 1920s, when one went looking for mild-to-violent revolutionary reading in Yiddish, German, Russian, Lithuanian, Estonian, and Polish as well as Latvian, one set out for the Daile un Darbs bookshop. For certain, on most Saturday mornings it was the place to visit, "talk left", and possibly plot a little while browsing through the unsold stacks of Georgiĭ Plekhanov's *Marksisma pamatjautājumi* (Basic Questions of Marxism), a very slow seller.[118] There was also *Audzināšana sociālismam* (Education Toward Socialism, 1920) by the charismatic German radical educator, Otto Rűhle, with its shorter stacks of unsold copies, having sold nearly 3,500 copies of its print run of 5,000 copies in the same eight-year period from April 1922 to November 1929.

In general, *belles lettres* and books about other countries seem to have sold better, an impression gained from what was piled on the book tables simply by citing from the tabular information mentioned. Thus, on almost any given weekend between the snowy Christmas season of 1920, and mid October of 1929, browsers could expect to find piles of such titles as Linards Laicens' *Skaistā Itālija* (Beautiful Italy, 1925), Kārlis Dzelzītis' *Gājienā uz nākotni* (Procession Toward the Future, 1928), Heinrich Mann's *Nabagee* (Der Untertan, i.e. The Supplicant [English titles: The Patrioteer or Man of Straw], 1921), and Upton Sinclair's *Amerikas miljonāra dzīves stāsts* (The Life of an American Millionaire, 1925). L121

L126

It is difficult to know if there was a single art director or design overseer at Daile un Darbs, but credit should be given for cover design variety ranging from the reserved folkloric design by Ansis Cīrulis for Leons Paegle's *Vālodzīte: Bilžu ābece* (Little Oriole: Picture ABC Book, 1920) L122 to the unimaginatively austere style of Rainis' *Klusā grāmata* (The Quiet Book) or the rough-hewn proletarian design of Andrejs Kurcijs' *Pasaules klajumā* (The Wide World, 1921). L123 Note as well Niklāvs Strunke's cover design for Paegle's translation of Samuil G. Lozinskiĭ's *Darba vēsture* (The History of Work, 1921). L124

A few titles also hinted at the typographic experimentation that was taking place in Moscow and Leningrad, particularly the typographic work of the Moscow designer Solomon Telingater. At least a shadow of such influence could be seen in the work of Linards Laicens and the cover of his travel accounts *Skaistā Itālija* (Beautiful Italy) and *69 dienas socialistisko padomju republiku savienībā* (69 days in the Union of Socialist Soviet Republics, 1928). L125 Laicens, as mentioned previously, took a great interest in how his books looked and, according to his granddaughter,[119] made an effort to sketch his design ideas for execution by the in-house designer, whenever there was one. At least these two Daile un Darbs titles would hold their own in any representation of the better-designed European books of the time, as would Jānis Liepiņš' cover for Laicens' *Mēbelīgā Rīga un peelikumi* (Furnished Riga and Supplements, 1923). L126

As to Daile un Darbs' influence on Latvian book culture in the 1920s, a simple conclusion can be extrapolated from reviewing the authors and titles published. If nothing else, the content of Daile un Darbs' titles gave color to the spectrum of 1920s political life, even though for many Latvians the color was a threatening "red".

118 It took eight years to sell less than half of the 5,000 copies published.
119 Interview with Anna Laicena, Feb. 2010.

L127

L129

L128

Atis Freināts

Named for its idiosyncratic founder-director, this publishing house is memorable for de-sign reasons as well as Atis Freināts' autobiographical account.[120]

Colophons and publishers' signets are often chosen at the beginning of a publisher's adventure rather than after success is achieved or, more likely, before the publisher ap-points an art director. Thus, early logo or signet choices may tell us more about a publisher's personality than the polished designs created or re-designed later on. Atis Freināts stayed with his first design. No one can argue against the impression it conveys: "I'm an unusual publisher. This is my brand!"

Several years ago, while browsing the sole book shelf in a Riga antique store, one title immediately caught my attention because of its cover design—a church with flames as a backdrop. The flames even seemed to leap out of the cartouche illustration and onto the matte black background of the cover design. The black appeared to be screened onto the burnt-orange colored covers through some imaginative printing process, although it was likely no more than the well-crafted offset lithography of the time. The 1926 title: *Tukums 1905. gadā* (Tukums in 1905). The author, Freināts, was also listed as the publisher. L127 The book's subtitle indicated that the stories dealt with the revolutionary echo in the Latvian town of Tukums and of St. Petersburg's 1905 "Bloody Sunday", a turning point in the lives of "those without voices" in both countries. While in Russia "1905" was a prelude to further revolution, for Latvians the year "1905" marked rebellion against and the ultimate loosen-ing of the German and Russian imperial yokes.

The publisher's curious signet on the back cover of this book as well as the title page showed a violin-carrying man of athletic build, full length and in profile. L128 There

120   *Grāmatnieki pa mājām, tirgiem un pilsētām* [Booksellers Door-to-Door, at Fairs, and in Towns] (Riga: Ata Freināta izdevniecība, 1939).

was an immediate interest in both the man behind the book and the "spark in Tukums" that was to light much more than the regional night sky at the beginning of the 20th century.

Little did I then know that the author-publisher was one of the more colorful publishers to appear on the Latvian publishing scene or, for that matter, the broader Baltic book scene between World Wars I and II.

Freināts came to publishing relatively late. He was born in Tukums. After finishing school in Riga's German trade school, where he learned bricklaying and stone masonry, he went off to Kaunas and Vilnius and then traveled to various German cities and later on to Zürich to seek his fortune, or at least to find work. He returned to Riga in 1910 and worked for a time with the social democrat welfare society "Laboremus". Freināts was in St. Petersburg at the outbreak of World War I and was drafted into the Russian army in 1916, serving during the period of 1917-18 and spending time as a German prisoner of war. After returning to Riga, he worked at odd jobs, including a stint as colporteur with Ansis Gulbis, who allowed him to take books on credit. This was the beginning of Freināts' lifelong attachment to peripatetic bookselling that at the outset meant heading into the countryside with mainly Gulbis' easy-to-carry *Universālā Bibliotēka* (Universal Library) in his rucksack along with the ever-popular "dream books" of the time and Robinsonaden for farm boys.

L130

By the mid 1920s Freināts had saved enough capital to begin publishing and settled at Brīvības iela 70 with his bookshop and publishing office. Between 1919 and 1940 he published 106 titles, concentrating on popular fiction and specializing in contemporary and earlier translations.

During his active years, Freināts' sense of adventure and social conscience were apparent in the choice of titles published. L129 Jack London's writings were a favorite, and a collected edition of London in twelve volumes was one of Freināts' early series in translation. The composer and music critic Jānis Cīrulis provided the translations with illustrations mainly by Freināts' friend Eduards Melbārzdis. A few titles in the London series had already appeared by 1925 with *Spehle* (The Game) as No. 9. L130 The cover for this title by Melbārzdis was one of the artist's more successful designs in an oeuvre often suffering from mediocrity. His stylization, however, was a much stronger interpretation of the content than that of the uncredited designer for the cover of the first English edition.[121] L131

Freināts apparently acted as his own art director much of the time and showed a concern for design, first with an unconventional format for the time, as in the size of *Spehle* (22x16 cm) or the 1932 edition of London's *Aļaska* (Alaska) L132 and his own 1926

L131

121 Published by Heinemann (London, 1919). The first American edition appeared in 1905.

L132

title (21.5x17 cm) on the Tukums revolution of 1905.[122] Another fictionalized account of the broader events stemming from the Tukums revolt by a participant and one of the "grand old men" of Latvian letters was Roberts Sēlis' *Leišmalē: 1905.g. tēlojums* (Along the Lithuanian Border: A Portrayal of 1905), published in 1927. (The colloquial term Leišmale is applied to the Latvian region bordering Lithuania.) These titles all have what might be considered "creative" trim sizes, giving an overall design appeal but at the expense of a higher paper cost.

Business concerns, rather than ideology, likely played a part in Freināts choosing Knut Hamsun and Jack London as the only authors to be represented with multiple titles.[123] Both writers were already popular in Latvia, Hamsun having been published in Latvian translation as early as 1904.

With his collected edition of London's works, in 1926 Freināts commissioned Jānis Jaunsudrabiņš, Teodors Lejas-Krūmiņš, Milda Ruzel, and Lizete Skalbe to each translate a Knut Hamsun novel. The multi-talented Jaunsudrabiņš was given a further commission to design the cover and chapter headings for Hamsun's *Pans* (Pan, 1926). L133 Freināts commissioned Nikolajs Puzirevskis to illustrate three titles: *Sem rudens swaigsnēm* (Under Autumn Stars, 1927), *Klaidoņu gaitās* (The Ways of Wanderers, 1927), and *Mihlas wergi* (Slaves of Love, 1928). L134 A 100-copy limited edition of *Mihlas wergi* was also announced in addition to the trade edition. Jānis Zegners was commissioned to illustrate *Viktorija* (Victoria, 1927) and Gvido Dīcmanis to illustrate the first in the series *Jauna seme* (The New Earth, 1926), translated by Milda Ruzel. But without question, among all these illustrators Puzirevskis provided the most memorable and skillfully executed illustrations. L135

The size of the Freināts' editions was modest but in keeping with press-run sizes for many publishers in those years—2,500 copies of Hamsun's *Sem rudens swaigsnēm* and 2,000 copies of his *Viktorija* published the same year. For comparison, Gulbis, a much larger publishing house, published Hamsun's novel *Misterijas* (Mysteries) in an edition of 6,000 copies that same year. We will never know if sales were brisk, thus warranting the large edition size. If it did sell well, its success cannot be attributed to Alberts Prande's clumsy illustrations.

122   The 1905 revolution in Latvia, continuing sporadically into 1907, while coinciding with the 1905 revolutions in Russia, was, as Leo Dribins and Ojārs Spārītis point out on p. 259 of *Vācieši Latvijā* (Germans in Latvia) (Riga: Latvijas universitātes Filozofijas un socioloģijas institūts, 2000), "actually a civil war between the Baltic-German gentry and the Latvian working class, supported by peasants. Russia organized bloody reprisals and suppressed the revolution. The Baltic-German gentry played an active role in the counter-revolution, which repeatedly damaged relations between Baltic-Germans and Latvians."

123   Both were concerned with the plight of the underclass in their fiction. Both held strong racist views—Hamsun harbored a negative attitude toward the Sami, Jews, and most "foreigners"; London was antipathetic toward Asians. From mid-life on, they were in thrall to antithetical causes: Hamsun with National Socialism and London with Socialism and a contradictory touch of syndicalism.

L133

L134

L135

Other authors of adventure tales translated and published by Freināts throughout the two decades of his career included R. M. Ballantyne, Louis Gallet (more of his wild animal tales than his adventure stories), Bruno Traven, Jules Verne, and others. Freināts did not employ just any translators; in most cases he commissioned well-known Latvian authors whose multiple language abilities fit them for the task of providing felicitous, literary translations. In addition to those already involved with translating Hamsun's works were Jānis Cīrulis (English), Rainis (French), Emīls Skujenieks (English and Russian), Andrejs Upīts (French and Italian), and the two previously mentioned Hamsun translators, Jānis Jaunsudrabiņš (German) and Teodors Lejas-Krūmiņš (Norwegian).

As already stated, the sophistication of Freināts' choice of illustrators was somewhat beneath the level of his gifted translators. The artists chosen tended toward the sensational in their styles and included Eduards Melbārzdis and Aleksandrs Apsītis. The Apsītis cover for Rainis' translation of Alexandre Dumas' *Grafs Monte Kristo* (The Count of Monte Cristo, 1926) is a good example, L136 as are the covers illustrated by Oskars Norītis and Aleksandrs Šutka for other titles.

L136

From time to time Freināts' offerings included original works by Latvian writers as well as non-fiction titles. Among the former were such best-sellers of the time as Jānis Grīziņš' popular *Vārnu eelas republika* (The Republic of Vārnu Street, 1929),[124] L137 a fictionalized, somewhat autobiographical account of growing up in a working class district of Riga. Of particular interest is this work's sympathetic way of portraying Jewish characters, specifically, a Jewish doctor caring for poor families without charge.

From a book history standpoint, perhaps the most interesting title in this publisher's list is the previously cited work by Freināts, *Grāmatnieki pa mājām, tirgiem un*

L137

124   First serialized in the cultural journal *Domas*, Nos. 8-10. The two contributions were later combined in book form and published in 1929 with illustrations by Kārlis Krauze.

L138

L139

pilsētām with its quaint cover design by Kārlis Krauze L138 and text illustrations by many who had illustrated Freināts' books throughout the years as well as a few others. Illustrators for this work included: Aleksandrs Apsītis, Margarita Kovaļevska, Voldemārs Krastiņš, Kārlis Krauze, Rūdolfs Kronbergs, Oskars Norītis, Nikolajs Puzirevskis, Aleksandrs Šutka, and Indriķis Zeberiņš. Freināts would have been better served by commissioning Puzirevskis or Kronbergs to illustrate the entire work, L139 as the majority of the illustrators chosen seemed to have given little inspired effort.

This work served as a celebration of "Freināts-as-bookseller/publisher" beginning with his house-to-house and farm-to-farm bookselling adventures back when road sign distances were still given in versts.[125] While not containing many specifics, there is a good deal of local color as he describes the country bookshops with "more flies than books". Freināts does mention that in one month after the advent of regular bus service to the smaller towns he logged 5,902 kilometers! In the book he also speaks of bookselling in Riga and makes comparisons between Zürich and the great variety of books in the Swiss shops compared with Riga's German-language bookshops in the "Old Town". Also described are the Zeltiņš bookshops with books "stacked in the windows—little books, big books, Bebel and Marx, and, for contrast, on the top of the pile, works by the renowned late 18th and early 19th century educator Garlībs Merķelis."[126]

Freināts also recounts stopping by Bergs' Bazaar (Berga bazārs), where, while not mentioning the year or season, he passes the Jewish shops of ready-made clothes, where in between is a shop with many Latvian books, such as Anna Brigadere's *Sprīdītis*, but

---

125 Before conversion of the Russian system of distance measurement to kilometers.

126 Garlieb Merkel, a Baltic-German who fostered concern for the plight of ethnic Latvians and Estonians under German baronial rule. Because of his writings and activism, Merkel was forced into exile but later returned to Riga in 1816, continuing in causes on behalf of Latvians and Estonians.

also offering books that qualify it as a quasi-legal shop because of the display of works written by Latvians abroad as well as writings by the Marxist Jānis Asars and copies of August Bebel's *Die Frau und der Sozialismus* (The Woman and Socialism) in a Latvian translation.

If only Freināts had described more of the bookshops visited through the years and left us his observations along with a few dates!

A final note about this memorable publisher: at the beginning of his publishing business he walked, took buses, and later drove his second-hand car into the countryside and sold from his backpack or car trunk. It was a "personalized" business—visiting shop owners in small towns as well as stopping by the small paper goods shops in towns that had no local bookshop. Freināts was the epitome of a dedicated publisher with modest aspirations and, as his reminiscences make clear, he took greater pleasure in putting a book in the hands of a schoolboy or a farmer than mixing with other publishers at national or international book fairs.

L140

When the ill-fated summer of 1940 arrived, Freināts spent more time working in his personal library in his mansard-roofed flat on Grēcinieku iela "in Šēnfeld's house", where he had lived since 1927 with his wife. This venerable house along with Freināts' 10,000-volume library was destroyed by Russian military action in October 1944, forcing Freināts and his wife to seek provisional refuge in his bookshop with its boarded windows, also the result of bombing. There, by candlelight, he began an autobiographical manuscript. Freināts survived occupation and war and concluded his bookselling life in sharply reduced circumstances by selling new and used books from a small shop on what is now Brīvības iela (then Ļeņina iela, or, Lenin Street) at number 64/66 almost until his death in 1955.

In the autumn of 2006, Andris Kolbergs organized and presided over a mini-symposium in Riga to honor Freināts. Kolbergs took this opportunity to present his distillation of the manuscript Freināts left behind in which he recounted his World War II experiences in Riga. Some of the details presented here were provided by Kolbergs during that presentation.

Kultūras Balss

With the slogan "Forward, forward to the sun!" the publishing cooperative Kultūras Balss (Voice of Culture; KB) was launched in the border town of Valka on January 6, 1918, by individuals driven by political and social conviction rather than business intent. Considering the prevailing tumult in a region that was not yet independent, this was a courageous effort.

The initial KB team consisted of two brothers—the literary researcher Antons Birkerts and writer Pēteris Birkerts—the lawyer Vilis Holcmanis, A. Krieviņš, Teodors Līventāls, and Kārlis D. Ozoliņš.

In 1923, this social democratic project looked back at the first five years with a 246-page report cum catalog L140 so impressive that one could not help but be in awe of what had been organized and produced in the face of political and economic odds.

From a beginning with little more than an idea of bringing "education to the people", while emphasizing a social democratic viewpoint, this undertaking grew rapidly and stabilized by 1923, with 20 regional outlets for its literature and educational materials.

L141

L142

L143

L144

With the concept of a paid-membership publishing cooperative, it prospered and was able to form a foundation for advancing its program of establishing libraries, providing stipends for students, and initiating a child health and welfare investigative program, among other activities.

Through its bookshops that sold stationery, schoolbooks, and other educational materials, KB also maintained continuing education programs for adults. L141, L142 Although its publishing program was decidedly more open than that of Daile un Darbs, the other publisher with a socio-political agenda, the design of most KB publications was similarly utilitarian with only a smattering of creativity shown on covers and internal illustrations.

KB's short-lived monthly *Kulturas Balss Apskats* (Kultūras Balss Review, 1920-1921) was clearly not aiming for any cover design competition nor was its more substantial compilation of proceedings *Kulturas Balss Sabeedrisku un zinatnisku rakstu krājums* (The Kultūras Balss Collection of Articles on Social and Scientific Topics, 1921).[127] Although originally intended for regular publication, it ceased after one issue without explanation. L143 There was an effort by KB in that same year to have more appealing *belles lettres* offerings. A collection of somewhat tendentious lyrics by Linards Laicens in *Attaisnotee* (The Exonerated, 1920), L144–L152 with a cover design appropriate to the content's grating rhythm (illustrations by Niklāvs Strunke), showed as much graphic design harshness as did the uncredited cover design for *Mans klusais brīdis* (My Quiet Moment, 1921), a collection of poems by Apsesdēls (pseudonym of Augusts Apsītis). L153

Cover design and internal illustration for KB books gradually improved throughout the 1920s. In 1924 Uga Skulme was commissioned to design the cover L154 for a collection of war poems titled *Nāves laukos* (In the Fields of Death), which were quite varied in their political intensity.[128] Included were translations of poems by Martin Andersen-Nexö, Aleksandr Blok, Ilya Ērenburg, Ivan Goll, Walter Hasenclever, Henry Wadsworth Longfellow, Alfons Petzold, Bruno Schönlank, Ernst Toller, and Walt Whitman. Also included were poems by Latvian writers such as Aspazija, Valdis Grēviņš, Vilis Plūdons, Rainis, Pāvils Rozītis, and Kārlis Skalbe—an imaginative assemblage of literary and political bedfellows, to say the least.

While this list of writers typified the diversity of *belles lettres* offered by KB, such a compilation represented something of a departure from offerings in more orthodox social democratic publications in other countries. The Kultūras Balss editorial board seemed to

---

127   The content gives some insight into what the KB editorial board deemed important with such contributions as "(The possibility of) everlasting life in light of microbiology", "Sex education", "Digestion of food in an organism", "Essays on the theory of justice," etc.

128   Edited by Kārlis Dziļleja.

ATtAISNOTeE

Linarda Laicena
Stāsti 1917*
1920

N.
StRuNnEs
ilustracijas

KULTURAS BALSs

L145

L146

L147

L148

L149

L150

L151

L152

L153

L154

L155

L157

32

Vienīgais, kas var justies šogad mierīgs

Civis zīm.

Jo viņa pilnvaras beidzas tikai pēc diviem gadiem.

L156

have few qualms about publishing hard-core communist writers on its general trade list. For example, in its 1925 catalog, Clara Zetkin and Karl Liebknecht share space with individuals committed to democratic means of revolution.

In 1928 the editorial board decided it was time to add a calendar to its publications and thus the *KB Satiriskais Kalendars* (Kultūras Balss Satirical Calendar) L155 was born under the editorship of the author-journalist Valdis Grēviņš writing under the pseudonym Dr. Orientācijs. In addition to the usual calendar content, such as day-by-day sunrise and sunset information, readers were reminded of "Latvia's curious history" in year-by-year notes facing each month's days, with a page of "Greek Orthodox and Roman Catholic holidays" and "Jewish festivals" for the year. There are epigrams, satirical cartoons by Civinskis-Civis, L156 and 46 pages of book advertising—mainly for publishers other than KB. A revealing insight into Latvian life of the time is provided in six pages (closely printed) of all the year's market days in the major cities and towns throughout the country. Evidently the calendar was not in great demand or production costs were too high, or both, for it had no sequel. The close of the 1920s saw titles in KB's popular "one and a half lats series" by well-known Latvian writers such as Aspazija, Kārlis Dziļleja, Kārlis Egle, Jānis Grots, and Rainis as well as Andrejs Kurcijs' *Cilvēciskie lopi* (The Humane Brutes, 1929) L157 with its cover design by Romans Suta leaving little question about its content.

L158

L159

L160

How did the KB schoolbooks and children's picture books look? Perhaps they should be judged by other standards. If the following example is characteristic, one can only say the young Latvians deserved better, and "better" was certainly available, if one looks at the professional quality of paintings and graphics being shown in galleries and the national museum in the mid 1920s. One would like to think that the title shown here was not characteristic, in spite of its presumed school adoption. The work is from a series titled *Mazajiem draugiem skolā un mājā* (For Little Friends at School and Home), presented here in two volumes titled *Daiņu, mīklu un sakāmvārdu pūriņš* (The Little Dowry of Folk Songs, Riddles, and Proverbs, 1926; 1927) L158 and compiled by the pedagogue Millija Ošiņa with illustrations by Arvīds Vinegrs. But if these two schoolbooks and his other illustration work for Valters un Rapa reflect his abilities, it is understand-able why he was not included in *Māksla un arhitektūra* (Art and Architecture, 1995-2003), although he compiled a manual on "how to draw", also published by Valters un Rapa

In 1923, KB had an attention-getting offering in its physical dimensions alone (34.3x 24.3 cm) when it commissioned the painter and decorative artist Ernests Brastiņš to design and illustrate one of its first picture books, the folk tale *Kalejpuika* (Blacksmith Boy, 1921) L159, L160 with its theme of a Golem-like creature created by a blacksmith. By the close of 1931 KB had run its course and folded after publishing *Konspiratora piezīmes* (A Secret Agent's Notes) by librarian-journalist Voldemārs Caune and *Kā izcēlās kristīgā ticība un baznīca?* (What is the Origin of the Christian Faith and Church?) by Kristaps Eliass, a journalist, art critic, and one-time editor of *Socialdemokrats* (The Social Democrat).

Unfortunately, this publishing cooperative apparently lacked a sufficiently skilled management staff and, as time went on, found itself in court-ordered bankruptcy on March 16, 1932. It was taken over by the Latvian Credit Bank in 1937 for liquidation.[129]

129　See *Valdības Vēstnesis* No. 187, 1937.

Kaija

Like many before them, the individuals who set out to establish new publishing houses in the mid 1930s saw a reasonable future by publishing collected works of foreign authors, select Latvian authors, and books for children and young people. These three categories were features of the Kaija (Seagull) venture throughout the few years of its existence, from 1936 to 1940. In fact, one of the publishing house's most popular series was the *Jaunatnes literatūra* (Youth Literature) series, which by mid 1939 numbered 23 titles with a few titles having reached multiple editions, such as Jack London's *Mazā vīra lielais varoņdarbs* (The Heroic Deed of a Small Man), L161 already in its third edition by 1939. The modestly talented painter-illustrator Ģirts Ārvaldis provided the cover design for this wrapped title as he had done for other Kaija titles, including three of Mark Twain's works that were not in the Youth Literature series. Kaija[130] editors continued this successful series and possibly appropriated other publishing ideas from the editors at Orient (founded in 1925), the publishing house to which it could be considered a successor.

L161

This was the same Orient that published Russian books under the directorship of Oto Grobiņš, who had caused several financial problems for himself and his Russian-language publishing house that resulted in Grobiņš contemplating his misdeeds in the Riga city prison from 1933 to 1936. (We will meet him again in the chapter on Russian-language publishing.) Perhaps it was Oto's wife, Anna (the "A" in "A. Grobiņš" cited as proprietor of the Kaija offices at Ģertrūdes iela 49), who was acting on behalf of her husband, who wished to stay in publishing and perhaps for legal reasons had to use his wife as a surrogate during his prison stay. Adding to the question of what was *really* going on "behind the doors" at the Kaija publishing house, Laima Muktupāvela makes an allusion or two in her novel.[131] Sergei Karachevtsev, Oto Grobiņš' partner in Russian publishing and who evidently lived in the same apartment building as the Grobiņš couple, may have suggested to Anna that there was money to be made in the publishing of pornographic books—in Latvian.

L162

But why draw attention to such a small publishing house as Kaija in the first place? Although other publishers underwent change and even closed after the restrictions imposed by the Ulmanis regime in 1934, transformation of a Russian publishing house such as Orient into the Latvian publisher Kaija is one of the few instances where such a transition was more or less successful. Recognition should also be given to the individual charged with design and content organization at Kaija. This was most likely Valdis Grēviņš, who commissioned the illustrators Oskars Norītis and Aleksandrs Apsītis to enliven projected titles and arrange for the design of the Estonian book designer Ernst Kollom to be used for the Jack London collected edition cited. Developing a focus for the list and finding young writers in such a short time were assuredly major challenges for Valdis Grēviņš, who was the editorial "glue" attempting to hold Kaija together. One of his many interests was already shown with title No. 17, Grēviņš' own compilation titled *Lielēdājs: Latvju tautas pasakas* (The Big Eater: Latvian Folk Tales, ca. 1936) in the steadily selling young people's series called Youth Literature, L162 which consisted of abridged versions of popular novels taken over from the Orient back list. Grēviņš and his translator-wife, Anna, were ideal for taking on the problems of a small publishing house in need of multiple talents.

---

130   This "Kaija" seems to be unrelated to another but short-lived "Kaija" publishing house that announced a book-in-parts in weekly installments, Rūdolfs Krafts' *Zihna par Indijas karaļkroni* (The Struggle for India's Crown). This "Kaija" seems to have failed almost before it got started, as no other titles are recorded.

131   *Mīla. Benjamiņa.* (Riga: Daugava, 2005).

L163

L164

L165

Grēviņš was not a new face in publishing. He had been managing editor of the newspaper *Socialdemokrats* from 1918 to 1924 and, as mentioned previously, edited the one-time publication *Kultūras Balss Satiriskais Kalendars*. These were but two publications of the 1920s with which he was associated. He wrote, translated, and dramatized the works of others throughout much of his life, and when he arrived at Kaija he seemed ready to do everything from writing and translating three children's books to translating the six volumes of the collected works of Lev Tolstoi.

Although Kaija records showing the actual publishing successes are apparently no longer extant, the collected works of Jack London, which were published in various subseries, must have been something of a success for the series had already reached 28 titles by 1939 with two titles appearing in two volumes. London's adventure stories with a social concern were sufficiently popular among Latvian readers to warrant this collected edition, following the Freināts collected edition of London's works appearing a decade earlier.

The Kaija series was highly visible on bookshop shelves because of Kollom's distinctive silver-colored paper binding with rectangular rules in black and red. L163 It may be of some interest that Kollom had created this design for the Tartu publisher Loodus for its collected editions of Knut Hamsun and Jack London, L164 among other writers. According to his daughter, Velga Vīlipa, Pāvils Vīlips had close ties with the Estonian literary scene and made the necessary connection between the Loodus publishing house and Kaija so that this sophisticated design could be used in the Latvian edition.[132]

The London series certainly must have been a full-employment undertaking for the English-reading individuals among the circle of friends and family of Kaija. Grēviņš was involved as a translation editor for at least three of the titles and likely approved the English translations by the other translators of London: Elizabete Kauliņa, Roberts Kroders, Zelma Krodere, Sigurds Melnalksnis, Velta Ozola, and Jānis Zariņš. Credit should be given to Grēviņš for bringing much of Jack London's oeuvre into a Latvian translation, although one well-read informant of several of the translations commented that literary quality varies considerably from translator to translator.[133]

Hugh Lofting's Doctor Doolittle books first began appearing with the Kaija imprint in 1936 of *Doktors Dolitls un viņa zvēri* (The Story of Doctor Doolittle) with an appreciative introduction by Jānis Jaunsudrabiņš. The titles retained the original Lofting illustrations but relied on uncredited local illustrators for new cover designs. The *Doktora Dolitla peldoša sala* (Doctor Doolittle's Floating Island, 1937) cover with the initials "A. R. A."[134] L165 was translated by the indefatigable Grēviņš, who went on to translate the remaining five Lofting titles published by Kaija.

When the first Soviet occupation began in July 1940, with its turmoil and terror, Kaija editors may have unconsciously been preparing themselves against political criticism—if that were even possible—by having already released in 1939 two collections of stories by Vilis Lācis, whose writings fit comfortably into the socialist-realist aesthetic. This was also the year of the firm's publication of several titles by Mark Twain. Determining whether or not Kaija ended with its bills paid is a detail for which we will have to wait until the discovery of at least a fragment of its business archive.

132   Conversation with Velga Vīlipa, Mar. 2004.
133   Jānis Borgs commented that the "silver" Jack London series was "read to pieces" by many young boys of his generation growing up in post-WWII Latvia. Interview, Jan. 2007.
134   Possibly Arturs Apinis.

For two generations after ceasing publication, a portion of the Kaija legacy lived on in the surviving copies that were carried by refugees into exile: books from the unmistakable "silver" Jack London collected edition, the Doctor Doolittle translations, and a number of its *Jaunatnes literatūra* titles. Some much-thumbed copies of Kaija's translations of foreign literature can still be found on the shelves of Riga's antiquarian bookshops.

Zelta Grauds

L166

Augusts Pētersons represents a classic case of an idealist going into publishing to foster his causes to the extent of turning his modest salary back into the business. Ideological classifications become complicated when looking back at an era in which social democrats, communist sympathizers, and acratists were known to work amicably side by side and have their writings published by one house, such as Zelta Grauds (Golden Grain). Given such a mélange, it is difficult to be precise about Pētersons' causes other than to call his list "progressive". Andrejs Upīts considered Pētersons a "work fanatic", fearless in his publishing choices and therefore not shy about publishing "me (a known communist) as well as Maksim Gorky".[135] From Pēterson's list we know he published young revolutionaries and commissioned illustrators and designers who ranged in their thinking from the center to the far left. He also gave commissions to a few illustrators who, for their obvious lack of skill, were unlikely to have found work elsewhere.

For some individuals, another criterion for certifying the contention that Pētersons was an idealist was his consistently losing more money than he made.

By all accounts, Pētersons was a hands-on publisher involved in all aspects of the business, from manuscript acquisition and manuscript editing to supervising typographic design and even filling in as compositor. The collected writings in eleven volumes of Ivande Kaija (pseudonym of Antonija Lūkina) L166 gave Pētersons' publishing house its start. Heading the list of available titles at the back of volume eight of these writings is one explanation of the need for publishing, "as her writings were no longer available". Publishing her writings was a perceptive choice for other reasons as well. Ivande Kaija already had visibility as an author and known friend of Rainis and Aspazija from their years in Switzerland. Thus, there was built-in publicity for almost any of her books.

For those familiar with Kaija's remarkable life, there was decided appeal, to say nothing of general curiosity. She was certainly a true European by most definitions—studying in Bern, Leipzig, and Paris and traveling widely throughout other countries of Europe as well as Russia. She settled in Latvia and continued to receive recognition throughout her life. Some of Kaija's fiction bordered on the ephemeral and sold well, as such fiction often does. When asked to characterize her fiction in general terms, one informant responded somewhat uncharitably, "Well, [her writing] was on the order of Barbara Cartland's[136] romances... maybe the novels of Courths-Mahler[137]... I guess that's why she was so popular." Unlike the two writers with whom she was compared, Kaija's collected writings would fit on a small shelf and none of her works appear to have been translated, although a few titles have been reprinted and are still in-print in Latvia.

135 *Atmiņas par Andreju Upīti* (Riga: Liesma, 1977), p. 218.
136 English author of the "Harlequin" romances and step-grandmother of Princess Diana.
137 Hedwig Courths-Mahler, one of the most widely read German novelists of the first half of the 20th century, with some 200 popular novels to her name and more than 40 million copies sold.

L167

L168

L169

L173

Other than the widely traveled Kārlis Eliass, author of *Madonnas pēdās* (In the Madonna's Footsteps, 1928), Ivande Kaija was the only other well-known author, at least in Latvia, to be published by Zelta Grauds in its first year, 1928. That year saw nine out of eleven volumes of her collected writings published; the tenth and eleventh volumes were published in 1931.

Probably the best-known Zelta Grauds titles remembered for content and format are two books by the "exceptional modernist...and urban poet"[138] Aleksandrs Čaks: *Poēma par ormani* (Poem About a Cab Driver, 1930) L167 with illustrations by Romans Suta[139] L168, L169 and a narrative poem called *Umur-Kumurs*[140] (1932) L170–L172 with illustrations by Niklāvs Strunke. In text and illustration both titles support the appellation given to Čaks as the quintessential city-scene poet, and both titles brought positive attention to the fledgling publishing house. The film and stage actress Elvīra Bramberga L173 likely provided financial support for part of the production costs of both books,[141] possibly accounting for their impressive format.[142] In addition, the illustrations for *Umur-Kumurs* were printed directly from the lithographic plates onto a better quality paper than the text stock. The copy of *Umur-Kumurs* examined is signed by both the author and illustrator and contains a printed list of 62 subscribers, suggesting a limited edition. The subscriber

138 As W. K. Matthews categorizes this ebullient social democrat, born Aleksandrs Čadarainis. See W. K. Matthews' *A Century of Latvian Poetry* (London: John Calder, 1957), p. 12.

139 The copy examined is inscribed from Čaks to Elvīra Bramberga: "Please, Elvīra, consider this book a token of appreciation for the beauty that I experience in your hospitality, Sasha, 17.11.30."

140 Now spelled "Umurkumurs". A folk construction derived from the German phrase "Das Hunger-Kummer Fest" originating in the 17th century when war forced many peasants to flee to Riga, where they lived in camps. The medium of communication in these camps consisted of a flagpole where messages were tacked by those who brought news from the region or village of the camp dwellers. When a messenger returned from a peasant's native place with good news, the messenger climbed the post, tore off the flag, and received a present for his efforts. Later, this became a festivity tradition with individuals attempting to climb a greased pole to retrieve a prize hanging from the top. The festivity became passé by the beginning of the 20th century, although it is occasionally incorporated into regional summer events. In Čaks' poem an unlucky boy dreaming of a life-changing prize climbs the pole, falls, and dies while the indifferent onlookers sing a nonsense tune "Cumtinglingling, cumtinglingling..."

141 Interview with Bramberga's daughter, Velga Vilipa, May 13, 2004.

142 Measuring 22.4x19.5 cm and 23.5x20.2 cm, respectively.

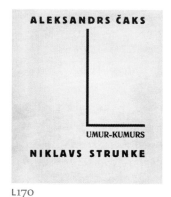

L170

L171

L172

list is an interesting document in its own right, indicating likely supporters of Pētersons as well as individuals interested in the content.[143] Both titles are distinctive in their clear but austere typography.

Although Pētersons continued to use known and talented cover designers, their work for Pētersons was not necessarily distinctive except for Kārlis Padegs' cover design for Elza Ķezbere's collection of poems *Profils stiklā* (Profile in the Glass Mirror, 1936), L174 the first published collection in book form of this young poet who fled Latvia for Germany in 1944. She left for the United States in 1950, continuing to write and publish.

Looking at this book's cover design by Padegs, together with his book illustrations,[144] posters, and studio work, one can well imagine the intense design—at times bitingly sarcastic, at times erotic—being at odds with the dominant, conservative aesthetic of the Ulmanis regime. Shown here is an example of his stark poster design for a 1936 exhibition of his painting and graphics. L175 Unquestionably, Padegs remains one of the greatest socially engaged caricaturists in Europe of the Interwar period. Unfortunately, his greatness is virtually unknown outside the Baltic region, except for modest representation in regional group shows, if citation in contemporary indexes is an indication. His style and imagery were akin to those of such Weimar era contemporaries as the satirists George Grosz, Karl Hubbuch, and Rudolf Schlichter. Padegs' work, previously unknown in Berlin, created interest among the attendees at the exhibition "Unerwartete Begegnung: Lettische Avantgarde, 1910-1935" (Unexpected Encounter: Latvian Avantgarde, 1910-1935) mounted in Berlin's Staatliche Kunsthalle in the autumn of 1990.[145] Today, a bronze likeness of this remarkable eccentric is seated by the Merķeļa iela entrance to Vērmanes dārzs (Vērmanes Park) in Riga and is invariably decorated with a fresh flower

L174

L175

143   To list a few: Pēteris Aigars, Rūdolfs and Kārlis Egle, Arvīds Grigulis, Jānis Grots, Pāvils Rozītis, Jānis Siliņš, Emīls Skujenieks, Ādolfs Talcis.
144   In addition to numerous periodical illustrations, Padegs contributed illustrations to 16 books or booklets in his brief lifetime. The most recent study of his work is *Rīgas dendijs un autsaiders Kārlis Padegs* by Jānis Kalnačs (Riga: Neputns, 2012).

L176

L177

L178

L179

or two, an oddly delicate form of remembrance for one whose most memorable works are such gritty satirizations.[146]

The cover for Viktors Eglītis'[147] *Meitenes stāsti* (A Girl's Stories, 1936) L176 with its design by Hilda Vīka, another gifted eccentric, should be included in the more sophisticated cover designs of the Zelta Grauds list of those years.

Pētersons also commissioned Aleksandra Beļcova, a leading Latvian cubist painter and pottery designer, to illustrate the covers of Indriķis Lēmanis' *Cietās rokas* (Rough Hands, 1938) L177 and *Tālais rīts* (Distant Morning, 1937). L178 Other artists of note who received design commissions from Zelta Grauds but produced work in a manner inconsistent with their usual high creative standards include the all-purpose designer-illustrator Sigismunds Vidbergs with his cover for Edvīns Mednis' travel account *Saules viesos* (Visiting the Sun, 1933) L179 and the collection of stories *Jūtu dārzos* (In the Gardens of Emotion, 1936) L180 or the stiff design he produced for Vilis Lesiņš' stories in *Laimes untumi* (Capriciousness of Happiness, 1930). L181 Also working below his usual level of ability was the woodcut illustrator and poster maker of the revolutionary left, Augusts Pupa, with his cover for *Nomales vējos* (In Suburban Winds, 1940) L182 written by Indriķis Lēmanis. This was one of a half dozen books by Lēmanis that Pētersons published in the fatal, final year of republican Latvia's freedom, when many publishers had informers in their editorial departments and it was considered wise to subtly curry favor with the hovering Soviet neighbors.

Andrejs Grigelis, best known for his constructivist-style cover illustrations for the social democratic journal *Signāls*, created both the cover design and illustrations for *Gājiens pret nāvi* (Procession Toward Death, 1932) L183 written by the editor of *Signāls* and his colleague Voldemārs Branks who, according to Rolfs Ekmanis,[148] earned a portion of his living as a gold appraiser. The cover design for Branks' collection of stories of the Latvian Riflemen[149] was also illustrated with woodcut vignettes and full-page illustrations by Grigelis. Another work by Branks about Latvian Riflemen, *Kauju negaisos* (In the Storm of Battle, 1936), was published without illustrations and no credit given for the linocut-illustrated cover. L184

145 Interview with Jürgen Holstein, Oct. 2009. The accompanying monograph for the exhibition contains a 14-page contribution by Jānis Kalnačs with 16 illustrations, two in color.

146 The late Tatjana Suta spurred a revival of interest in Padegs with "Dialogs ar sevi" in *Māksla* No. 3, pp. 8-13 (1981). This was followed by Jānis Kalnačs' bio-critical monograph titled *..arī sapņu zīmētājs Kārlis Padegs* (Riga: Liesma, 1993) as well as his editing *Variācijas par Kārļa Padega tēmu* (Riga: Jāņa sēta, 1996), a compilation of 25 contributors' reminiscences and comments on Padegs.

147 Eglītis belongs in the pantheon of Latvian modernist writers working in the first quarter of the 20th century. Sufficiently out of step with Soviet literary ideology, he was scheduled for death by KGB torture at the outset of the second Soviet occupation, according to Jānis Krēsliņš, interview, Apr. 2004.

148 http://www.zagarins.net/jg/jg66/JG66-68_Ekmanis.htm.

149 A Latvian defense force formed before the establishment of Latvian independence in 1918.

L180

L181

L183

L182

L184

A summary of the scope of Zelta Grauds' 12 years of publishing: slightly out of editorial focus. But it should be given credit for diversity and there is no doubt about Pētersons' support of young revolutionary writers, e.g., Lēmanis and Kārlis Fimbers. Pētersons chose to publish the work of that older revolutionary, the prickly Andrejs Upīts, in the final years of the Ulmanis regime when no other publisher wanted to take risks with his manuscripts. Upīts' novel *Smaidošā lapa* (Smiling Leaf) appeared in 1937.

Out of the total number of works published by Zelta Grauds, some 24 were translations, including works by Edward FitzGerald, C. S. Forester, Victor Hugo, Ernst Juenger, Carlo Lorenzini, and E. Phillips Oppenheim. Such a roster taken together with the Latvian writers published unquestionably demonstrates a remarkable diversity!

Add to the above translations and non-fiction titles three titles by the diet and nutrition gurus of the era, the Swiss Dr. Max Otto Bircher-Benner and his brother, Max Edwin Bircher, of the famed breakfast cereal formulation "Bircher Muesli". One could only guess that these three treatises[150] must have been well-received among those identified with the "don't forget the land" enthusiasm of Ulmanis[151] and his regime or the general health

150   Translations of *Revolution der Ernährung, die neue vollwertige Ernährung der Menschen; Früchtspeisen und Rohgemüse*; and *Säuglings Ernährung mit Fruchtmilch*.
151   Kārlis Ulmanis studied and received degrees in agriculture, including one in 1909 from the University of Nebraska in the United States.

L185

L186

reform movements among German-speaking populations. Given the social policy emphasis of the government, it may also have been a politically wise decision for Pētersons to undertake publication of a three-volume popular encyclopedia of agriculture in 1937/1938 as a counterweight to some of his ideologically leftist titles.[152]

Overall, the Latvian writers on the Zelta Grauds list ranged from the well-known figures already mentioned as well as the popular novelist Kārlis Fimbers, the poet Elza Ķezbere, and the Soviet-oriented Indriķis Lēmanis to several marginal figures in the era's literary canon, e.g., Jānis Grīvnieks (pseudonym of botanist Nikolajs Malta).

As to cover design and illustration, it has already been shown in the examples reproduced that the work ranged from sophisticated, e.g., Padegs, Beļcova, and Strunke, to less-than-the-best work of such talented illustrators as Sigismunds Vidbergs or the sculptor and painter Emīls Melderis and his cover for Jānis Ošs' novel *Zelta drudzī* (Gold Rush, 1931). L185

Questions of financing remain about the concluding years of Zelta Grauds and Augusts Pētersons, questions that will likely go unanswered unless archival materials are discovered.

Andrejs Jesens and Latvian children's book publishing

Before considering the contribution of Andrejs Jesens,[153] it should be mentioned that from the beginning of this undertaking, the plan had been to incorporate a sampling of trade children's books and periodicals from the main Latvian publishers into the commentary on their respective publishing houses. Instead, such commentary has been included here, following mention of the non-Latvian-language children's book inclusions.

Because of relatively little in the way of children's book publishing by the minority language publishers, mention of these books has been incorporated along with adult works in the Russian and Yiddish language chapters. In the instance of German-language publishing, discussion of children's books was left out altogether, because after Latvian independence in 1918 the German-speaking population tended to buy children's books from importers and distributors such as Jonck & Poliewsky, E. Bruhns, and Academia, all of which carried extensive stock from publishers in Germany, as can be seen in their respective catalogs. However, one pre-1918 example of a German-language children's picture book, *Geschichte von der Krabbetasche: Ein Märchen mit vielen bunten Bildern* (The Story of the Krabbetasche: A Fairytale with Many Colored Pictures), is of particular interest because of the importance of the author.[154] Although neither author nor illustrator is credited, the work is known to have been written by the Baltic-German folklorist and physician Georg Julius von Schultz.[155] L186 Much commentary on the pre-1918 children's literature written by Baltic-Germans and published in the Latvian and Estonian region rests quietly in the general histories of literary development and education of this Baltic area. These

---

152   Jānis Apsīts, ed. *Lauksaimniecības leksikons.*

153   Surname spelled "Jessens" during his publishing years.

154   (Riga: Druck und Verlag W. F. Häcker, 1895). *Krabbetasche* is the sack into which a socially concerned fairy stuffs bad children, taking them away for discipline. Reprinted as *Martha Marzibill oder der Traum im Ulmenbaum: Eine livländische Geschichte für artige Kinder* (Michelstadt: Neuthor Verlag, 1988).

155   Georg Julius von Schultz was a colleague of the Estonian folklorist and educator Friedrich Reinhold Kreutzwald who reputedly suggested to him in 1839 the concept for what became the *Kalevipoeg* (1861), the Estonian national epic. See Kristi Metste and Marin Laak's *Kreutzwald. Missioon. Tegelikkus* (Tartu: Eesti Kirjandusmuuseum j. k., 2003), p. 28.

references show this children's literature as more often than not the work of Baltic-German educators, pastors, and pastors' wives.

A general note on Latvian-language children's books

While what follows is but a brief sketch of Latvian children's literature before Latvian independence, it is followed by extended comment on the remarkable idealist-entrepreneur Andrejs Jesens, who spent the better part of his life energetically devoted to editing, translating, writing, and publishing books and periodicals for children and young people. For the 200 years before Jesens appeared on the scene—until the beginning of the 20th century—children's literature was limited to a scattering of titles by pioneering authors in this genre. There are those who would minimize the contribution of the forerunners. As indicated, they were usually pastors or educators whose first efforts were didactic and thus lacking in interest to all but the more objective researcher who saw these tentative beginnings as documents that portrayed the world view of the time.

Their offerings were clearly designed to touch the cerebral element in their intended audience, as clumsy as their respective approaches may have been. For the most part, though, their names and their little books are largely lost to memory. These enlightened individuals prepared the way in a language that was still in the process of being codified in written form.

To give a brief historical background sketch before moving on to Andrejs Jesens' efforts in the decades of the Interwar period, a name and date recitation should be made of a few individuals of this vanguard: Georg Mancelius (1593-1654, credited with establishing a basis of Latvian prose style thus influencing children's literature), Gotthard Friedrich Stender (1714-1796, whose *Pasakas un stāsti* [Tales and Stories, 1789] is considered the first work of *belles lettres* in the Latvian language), Christoph Reinhold Gürgensohn (1752-1814, who gave Latvians the first translation of *Robinson Crusoe*, 1824), Karl Gotthard Elverfeld (1756-1819, who composed the first original Latvian-language drama *Tā dzimšanas diena* [The Birthday, 1804]), and Garlieb Merkel (1769-1850). One can deduct from the family names that these individuals were German or of German heritage. Not until the mid 19th century were ethnic Latvians or at least individuals whose primary language was Latvian creating an authentically Latvian children's literature: Ansis Līventāls (1803-1878), Krišjānis Valdemārs (1825-1891), and Jēkabs Zvaigznīte (1833-1867), who brought Latvian children a retelling of the Brothers Grimm's stories as well as the tales of Hans Christian Andersen. *Uncle Tom's Cabin* came into the Latvian language thanks to the teacher-author Ernests Dinsbergs (1816-1902), who also had time to translate Goethe's *Reineke Fuchs* and many other works into Latvian.

The first children's periodical in Latvian, *Behrnu Pastineeks* (Children's Postman, 1866-1869; supplement of the journal *Draugs un Biedris*), appears through the initiation of pastor Johann Julius Hugo Braunschweig. An online search for any of the preceding names should satisfy any lingering curiosity about the contribution of these individuals.

Regrettably, this list gives short shrift to these literary pioneers, to say nothing of the criticism that may be precipitated for omitting an entire roster of the great names of later Latvian writers. What must be said, however, is that both early and later writers made little distinction between writing for children and writing for adults—a common phenomenon among nation-building writers. Elsewhere in this text, for most of the

L187

L188

L189

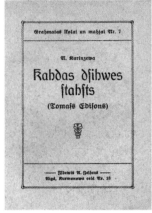

L190

later literary figures writing for children but known primarily as writers for adults, e.g., Aspazija, Rūdolfs Blaumanis, Anna Brigadere, and Vilis Plūdons, emphasis is given to their adult writings. Credit is certainly due to the architects of the young Latvian Republic's educational system, who ensured support for the larger trade publishers to initiate series of collateral reading for children and young people. Again, it was frequently the authors of adult fiction to whom educators and publishers turned for rewritten or abridged works for various series. Among the better-known numbered series were *Jaunatnes literatūra* launched in 1924 by J. Roze and *Rakstnieku sejas* (Faces of the Authors) and *Skolai un jaunatnei* (For Schools and Youth) initiated by Valters un Rapa in 1926 as well as their series *Latvju klasiķi skolai* (Latvian Classics for School) begun a few years later. Gulbis created the series *Jaunības apcirkņi* (Coffers of Youth) in 1937. The Latvian School Cooperative Publishing House also published collateral reading titles both in- and out-of-series, as did the Latvian Evangelical Lutheran Church Publishing Office.

We now turn to Andrejs Jesens as the epitome of a children's book publisher of the early 20th century. Jesens owed much to the 19th century heritage for the beginnings of Latvian children's literature. With his friend Dāvids Zeltiņš he began the *Jaunības bibliotēka* (Youth's Library) series in 1908. They published this series together until 1910, when Zeltiņš moved on to other efforts and Jesens made *Jaunības bibliotēka* the foundation of his publishing business. By 1931, when the series was discontinued, it had published 136 titles. This remarkable series brought selections by world writers into Latvia for an audience of the newly literate as well as young people. As a teacher whose own life had been inspired by teachers and the periodical literature of the time, it was not unusual for Jesens to come to the idea of starting a journal for young people in 1910. His *Jaunības Tekas* (Youth's Pathways) continued until the beginning of the political and economic upheaval in 1915. He resumed publication in a different format in 1920, continuing publication until 1930. Latvia's most renowned writers contributed to the journal, including Aspazija, Jānis Jaunsudrabiņš, Rainis, and Augusts Saulietis. In 1924, Jesens launched a monthly for young children titled *Mazās Jaunības Tekas* (Small Pathways of Youth), which continued until 1935. L187, L188 Cover illustrations for many other issues were created by Alberts Kronenbergs, a prolific illustrator of children's books and periodicals throughout the First Republic.[156]

Jesens' progressive concept of "availability to all" seems to have been foremost in his comparatively low pricing philosophy for books as well as periodical subscriptions. But this may also have led to his recurring business problems. Typical of his inexpensive

---

156   See *Alberts Kronenbergs* by Romis Bēms (Riga: Latvijas Valsts izdevniecība, 1961).

L191

L192

L193

series was *Jaunības bibliotēka*, which ran from 1928 to 1931 with a total of 108 titles in the *Jaunais kovbojs* (Young Cowboy, 1931) format.[157] L189

Jesens' broad outlook can be seen in his publishing of numerous full translations that included fiction and non-fiction from German, Russian, French, English, and other languages that followed his first series of translated selections and stories. He also understood the psychology of publishing titles in series[158]—an assured method for keeping teachers, parents, and booksellers checking regularly for "the next title". One of his earliest series was *Grāmatas skolai un mājai* (Books for School and Home), which began in 1914 and through which he also introduced fiction and non-fiction translations from other languages. One such non-fiction example was *Kahdas dsihwes stahsts: Tomass Edisons* (The Story of a Life: Thomas Edison, ca. 1915) by Nikolaĭ Aleksandrovich Karinzews. L190 In this same series one finds Edmondo De Amicis sharing space with Aspazija, L191 Harriet Beecher-Stowe alongside Jānis Jaunsudrabiņš, Rudyard Kipling with Sudrabu Edžus, and Jack London with Andrejs Upīts, among many more. When the series ceased publication in 1931, 83 titles had appeared.

What is referred to in the Anglo-American community as the *Twins* series by the American author Lucy Fitch-Perkins was an author series in which Jesens published only seven titles. L192, L193 In Latvia, the titles were changed to "Little" followed by an ethnic designation, thus *Mazie japāņi* (Little Japanese, 1924). Jesens also published Fitch-Perkins' Dutch, Eskimo, Irish, Swedish, and Italian "Twins" books together with her story of children in prehistoric times, *Mazie alinieki: Stāsti par aizvēsturisko bērnu dzīvi* (Little

157   By "T. Hukera" cited as "T. Hooker" in the Latvian National Library catalog but with no translator indicated. A likely author of such a work named Hooker with a given name beginning with "T" could not be found in an extensive search through English-language sources.

158   Other series included *Popular Science Library* 1921-1930 (43 titles), *Foreign Lands* 1924-1931 (eight titles), and The *Lives and Works of Famous Men* 1924-1931 (13 titles). In this last series, along with Diogenes, Christopher Columbus, and Helen Keller, he acquaints his young readers with those early contributors to Latvian youth (and adult) literature mentioned at the outset.

L194

Cave Dwellers: Stories about Children's Lives in Prehistoric Times) and announced her *Mazie filipiņi* (Little Filipinos) in his 1931 catalog titled *A. Jessena izdotās grāmatas* (Books Published by A. Jessen). L194

Jesens' illustrators and cover designers were of varied ability. The best-known seemed to have remained with him throughout his First Republic period and included Alberts Kronenbergs, Eduards Brencēns, and Indriķis Zeberiņš, with Kronenbergs leading in the number of commissions. Many of the illustrated works Jesens published in translation appeared with the original illustrations. Unfortunately, Jesens' publishing venture had incurred so much debt by the early 1930s that even with the strictest of economic measures he was unable to stay in business and ceased publishing in 1935. Jesens' life and contribution have yet to receive the attention deserved. One pamphlet-sized monograph was published in the Soviet era, Antons Birkerts' *Jaunatnes audzinātājs Andrejs Jesens* (Educator of the Young, Andrejs Jesens),[159] as well as a few articles. The information condensed herein has been drawn from public websites as well as Jesens' own catalogs, the indispensable *Latviešu rakstniecība biogrāfijās* (Latvian Writing in Biographies) (Riga: Zinātne, 2003), and last, but not least, Jāzeps Osmanis' *Saules akmens: Latviešu bērnu literatūras gadu gaita* (Sun Stone: Latvian Children's Literature Through the Years).[160]

While brief overviews of Latvian children's literature do exist in Latvian and Russian, Osmanis' history, *Saules akmens*, remains the most exhaustive. Although constrained by the politics of the era, Osmanis did his best to touch on adult literature appropriated for children down to that literature expressly written for children from the outset, from the time of the first Republic, through the occupations of the early 1940s, and up to the period in which he concluded, the waning years of the Brezhnev era. Osmanis is understandably cautious about the first Soviet occupation of Latvia with its end of "free children's literature" and only gives a passing glance at the years of Nazi occupation. He does, however, give as full a story as politically possible up to the second period of Soviet occupation. Except for a few passing references, he did not include for political reasons the category of children's literature produced by Latvians in exile—from the Displaced Persons camps to the countries of ultimate residence. To his great credit, however, Osmanis gives considerable information on illustrators of all periods discussed.

While we wait for a new publication extending Osmanis' work and a more detailed account of the past three decades, Silvija Tretjakova[161] has given us *A Horse that Sings at Night: Children's Literature in Latvia*,[162] a tantalizing illustrated summary of 20th century Latvian children's literature—all in 38 pages.

During the past five years of gathering examples for this project, it was a surprise to find few remnants of children's literature from the Interwar period in the antiquarian bookshops and flea markets of Latvia. Of course, one must consider the destructive forces of war and occupation—factors militating against survival. The titles that were eventually discovered in this shop-to-shop search had endured many young and not necessarily clean hands, thus leaving much to be desired from the standpoint of condition.

159   (Riga: Latvijas valsts izdevniecība, 1958), 52 pages. This is a disappointing publication, providing no precise statistical data about Jesens' enterprise or substantive bio-bibliographical data not already available in other sources.
160   (Riga: Liesma, 1977).
161   Silvija Tretjakova is the director of the Children's and Youth Book Division of the National Library of Latvia.
162   Tretjakova, S., ed. with Ilze Stikāne and Inese Zandere (Riga: Latvian Literature Center and Latvian Board on Books for Young People, 2006).

L195 *Pastariņš dzīvē*
(Pastariņš' Life, 1924)
by Ernests Birznieks-Upītis
Cover design: Alberts Kronenbergs

L196 *Leišu svētbilžu griezējs*
(The Carver of Lithuanian Icons,
1928) by Jānis Purapuķe
Cover design: Aleksandrs Apsītis

L197 *Darbi bērniem*
(Crafts for Children, 1928)
by Antonija Āre
Cover design: Zina Āre

L198 *Mazā māsiņa*
(Little Sister, 1931)
[with cover art unrelated to the
stories, "little sister" is a "girl nurse"]
Cover design: Jānis Jaunsudrabiņš

L195

L196

L197

L198

L199

L200

In the years before independence, it was the Latvian Educational Association that on one occasion took the lead in producing a children's book appearing to foster identification with Latvian culture, e.g., *Misiņbahrdis un stiprais kalps: Latweeschu tautas pasaka* (Brass-Beard and the Mighty Servant: A Latvian Folk Tale, 1913),[163] a collaboration of two major figures of both literature and art, author Anna Brigadere and painter-illustrator Jānis Roberts Tillbergs. L199 The full-page design shown here L200 reflects Zaiga Kuple's assertion of the Russian influence in this remarkable book in its large, horizontal format common among turn-of-the-century Russian picture book artists. More importantly, she calls attention to Tillbergs' style, which vaguely echoes that of the books of Ivan Bilibin and Yelena Polenova.[164]

In the Interwar period, it is estimated that at least 880 children's book titles were published, 65 of which were non-fiction in character.[165] Some 450 of these titles were published by Jesens. This total estimate excludes school books and, according to the various accounts, appears to be concerned only with Latvian fiction and picture books for children and young people. Publishing for children in Russian, German, and Yiddish has not been included in these statistics. With the exception of Jesens and to lesser degrees Valters un Rapa and Jānis Roze, most publishers were content to bring out a relatively small number of titles over the course of their existence. From time to time the larger publishers would take the work of an idealistic pedagogue on commission and distribute it, as opposed to handling the work as a conventional trade title.

In 1928 Valters un Rapa initiated a series for the public school market that concentrated on works by Latvia's leading writers of *belles lettres*. The works chosen could be read and appreciated by 12- to 16-year-olds and included such authors as Rūdolfs Blaumanis, Anna Brigadere, Juris Neikens, Vilis Plūdons, and Sudrabu Edžus. By 1936 the series had reached No. 15 with a collection of Birznieks-Upītis' stories, *Pelēkā akmens stāsti* (Stories of the Grey Rock), and then apparently ended that same year.

---

163   Publisher: Latvian Education Council in association with the Latvian Art Promotion Society.

164   See Zaiga Kuple's "Latviešu bērnu grāmatas pirmsākumi Eiropas mākslas ierosmēs" in *Latvijas māksla starptautisko sakaru kontekstā*, edited by Silvija Grosa (Riga: Neputns, 2000), p. 109.

165   See I. Janovska's Master's degree thesis, *Latviešu bērnu un jaunatnes literatūra 20.gs. 20.-30. gados: Grāmatu sērijas* (Riga: Faculty of Philology, University of Latvia, 2000).

L201

L202

In the Republican era, educational bodies and non-governmental organizations with an idealistic agenda would, from time to time, produce a book. An example of a one-time effort (in 1933) was the Baltic State Mother and Child Protection Committee in Riga with its noble goal of nurturing a pan-Baltic view through its trilingual—Latvian, Estonian, and Lithuanian—book *Bērnu draudzība. Laste sõprus. Vaikų draugavimas* (Friendship Among Children, in the Latvian, Estonian, and Lithuanian languages). L201 From the mid 1920s to the close of the decade, the Latvian School Cooperative Publishing house produced collateral or recreational reading for children and young people in addition to their main purpose of publishing school books.

Another children's book publisher, the Latvian Secondary School Cooperative with its primary role in publishing administrative monographs and schoolbooks, released a title that became quite popular among its audience: Valts Grēviņš' *Nams Raiņa bulvārī* (The House on Rainis Boulevard, 1938), illustrated by Gunārs Hermanovskis. L202

The larger religious denominations produced literature for children and young people with Lutheran-oriented material being the most widely available to a general audience, the periodical and children's calendar predominating. Of note was the Evangelical Lutheran Church's journal for children, *Bitīte* (Little Bee), beginning in 1926 and continuing through 1939. Its 64-page[166] contributions of fiction, non-fiction, and poetry were often signed and included translations from Lutheran children's publications in other countries, primarily German-speaking. *Bitīte* was illustrated throughout with drawings and photographs. Other religious and secular children's serials had shorter lives, although the total number of issues were greater, e.g., *Bērnu Atpūta* (Children's Leisure, 1927-1931), *Bērnu Dārzs* (Children's Garden, 1926-1928), *Bērnu Draugs* (Children's Friend, 1923-1931), and *Bērnu Prieks* (Children's Pleasure, 1928-1931).

---

166 It maintained a 64-page publication through most of the 1930s.

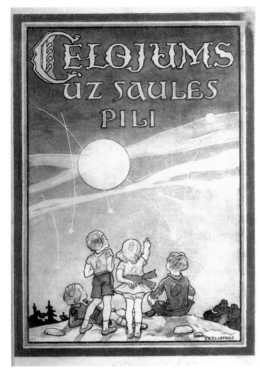

L203

6

L204

A minor category of children's books was the self-published effort, in which a book of some interest appeared on occasion. In many countries, books appearing under this banner often slip between the bibliographical cracks because they are either insipid or lacking any redeeming quality and thus not kept by the libraries to which their eager authors send them. In countries with loose or unenforced deposit regulations, tracking down such books is often futile. But in Latvia, all printers were required to send such books to the deposit libraries. One self-published book of interest was a large picture book[167] written and illustrated by well-known figures: *Ceļojums uz Saulespili* (A Trip to the Palace of the Sun, 1934) featuring Atis Ķeniņš' fairy tales in lyric form, illustrations by the magisterial Jānis Roberts Tillbergs L203, L204, and Emīlija Benjamiņa as editor.[168] One wonders why a book by such a team had to be "self-published". Benjamiņa, a publisher in her own right, was the wife of Antons Benjamiņš, the most prominent publisher in Interwar Latvia who in turn was also a noted journalist and publisher of the long-lived *Jaunākās Ziņas* (1911-1940), the newspaper with the largest circulation (200,000) of any paper in the Baltic countries.[169] Benjamiņa's understanding of distribution networks assured her book of finding its way to the intended readers, a favorable circumstance for the self-published book and as rare then as today.

167 Measuring 34.5x24.5 cm

168 Emīlija Benjamiņa was closely involved with the editing and publishing of *Atpūta* (1924-1940), the most widely read Latvian weekly periodical of its time. Benjamiņa's life ended abruptly at age 60, following her being captured by a Soviet NKVD detail when leaving a party in June 1941. Wearing only evening clothes, she was loaded into a railway car with other hapless individuals, deported to Siberia, and died from exposure shortly thereafter.

169 A "fact-filled", poorly documented compilation: Jānis Kārkliņš' *Latvijas preses karalis: Atmiņas par Jaunāko Ziņu laikiem* (Latvia's Press King: Memories of the Times of *Jaunākās Ziņas*) (2nd ed.; Riga: Karoga bibliotēka, 1990).

Not to be overlooked is the enterprising printer-as-publisher taking advantage of seasonal opportunities, primarily Christmas, in order to bring out a fitting title. One such printer, Kārlis Dūnis, with printing and publishing offices in Valmiera and Cēsis, brought out a booklet of Plūdons' works for children, *Kad Ziemas svētki pievārtē* (Christmas at the Gate), just in time for the 1930 Christmas season. L205 This productive publisher, already established by the end of the 19th century, was among those publishers who saw the opportunity in publishing for both the adult and the school markets.

L205

Children's periodicals

When one thinks of the children's periodicals of this era, those of Andrejs Jesens come to mind, even though such publishing was certainly not limited to Jesens. Browsing through the 1920-1940 volume of *Latviešu periodika* (Latvian Periodicals),[170] one readily sees that publishing children's periodicals or children's supplements in newspapers in all four of the major publishing languages of Latvia was a common although rarely successful enterprise. Some titles were secular, some religious, some political; a few were inspired in content while a comparable number appear to have exhibited a certain lack of children's reading interests. All such views were expressed by informants having experienced reading such publications during their childhoods in Latvia's early years.

The consensus has been that most editors meant well, with perhaps the exception of those with a communist political agenda.[171] Surviving for more than three years was unusual for these papers unless they happened to be connected to a major publisher such as Valters un Rapa, a well-financed political party such as the Latvian Communist Party, a religious group, or an international organization such the Junior Red Cross, publisher of *Latvijas Jaunatne* (Latvia's Youth) which, like its counterparts in other countries, appeared throughout the school year and, in the case of Latvia, was published from 1924 to 1940. Its emphasis was decidedly on Latvian culture and history with only a modest international emphasis. L206

L206

Grāmatu Draugs

On a raw March day in 1978 I left the Hotel Latvija (now Radisson Blue Hotel Latvia) and walked down Kirova iela (now Elizabetes iela). I was out to have a look around on my first visit to Riga. I turned left after one block and walked up Pētera Stučkas iela (now Tērbatas iela). Part way along the street, an age-darkened sign above a shop spelled out *Grāmatu Draugs* (Friend of Books)—a good omen, despite the dreary jumble of Latvian Sovietica in the window. I walked into the over-heated shop, smiled, and cheerily greeted one of the three saleswomen. I was answered with stoney frowns all around. For a moment I thought of asking if there was a connection between the shop's name and a publishing office I had visited several times in Brooklyn, New York, a decade earlier. A flash of common sense prevented me from asking the question. The air inside the shop remained socially frosty as I browsed and, since I was the only customer, all attention was on this

---

170   (Riga: Zinātne, 1988).
171   *Jauni Ceļi* (New Roads, 1925-1928), *Darba Bērni* (Children at Work, 1929-1937), *Mazais Kolektīvists* (Little Collectivist, 1931-1937), among others.

L207

L208

outof-place American. I saw but one title[172] with some design interest and two names I vaguely recognized as important in Latvian literature: Rainis and Aspazija. L207 I purchased the two-volume work and, despite the shop's name, thought it best to hurry out.

Out on the street I looked up again at that 40-year-old sign stretching the length of the shop and thought back to another day in the early spring of 1968, when I first visited a publishing office in Brooklyn, with the same inviting "Friend of Books" text in its sign. That visit and the couple encountered provided a dramatic contrast to the defeated and unhelpful staff in the shop I visited on that March day in Riga.

The Brooklyn office and the couple in charge of it evoked the courage of the survivors in that era of geopolitical change between 1944 and 1968. The charming, dapper fellow in his mid 60s and his equally well-dressed and pleasant wife who greeted and welcomed me into the *new* Grāmatu Draugs had started their publishing lives in the vibrant period of Interwar Riga. But at the time I entered the Brooklyn Grāmatu Draugs (GD) office I did not know that this couple, Helmārs and Austra Rudzītis, represented Latvia's "golden years" of publishing history. Nor did I know that now, some 40 years later, I would be regretting not having gone back repeatedly to ask the questions I have now, questions only they could answer.

Instead, on that day in 1968, I selected a carton of in-print titles with their distinctive book jackets designed by Veronika Janelsiņa, chose a few antiquarian items that appealed to me, then paid and left.[173] I returned a few months later, bought a few more books, and chatted a bit but continued to wander in ignorance of being in the presence of legendary figures in Latvian history.

Now on the 40th anniversary of meeting Helmārs Rudzītis and his wife, I am trying to conjure a picture of his Latvian publishing years from a few surviving GD catalogs of the late 1920s and 1930s together with some odds and ends included in the scrapbook of an employee, "R. Veinbergs", along with comments from Rudzītis' conversational autobiography, *Manas dzīves dēkas* (My Life's Adventures).[174] A glimpse of his canny business approach is provided in the chapter on Russian-language publishing in the Interwar period.

It was clear that Rudzītis had ideas percolating continuously from the day he opened his publishing business at the age of 23 in 1926 to the last years of his life. He was even an audio innovator, having established the Latvia's (and the whole region's) most successful record company, Bellacord, L208 recently revived and producing music CDs.[175]

By the time of Rudzītis' second biennium (1928/1929) in publishing, he had not only established and increased a Russian list to 43 titles, but had also organized a sufficient number of highly competent translators to fulfill his goal of bringing world literature, mainly Anglo-European, into the Latvian-language market. Like his local competition, he relied on established, saleable authors for translation and only tentatively ventured into the untested Latvian market for American writers. That meant for every book by André Maurois, Romain Rolland, Arthur Schnitzler, Hermann Sudermann, and Stefan Zweig, he advertised one American author. Sinclair Lewis was chosen in this second publishing season and his

172   *Rainis un Aspazija dzīvē un mākslā: Sarakstīšanās* (Rainis and Aspazija in Life and in Art: Correspondence), 2 volumes, (Riga: Kultūras Draugs, 1937). Cover design by Sigismunds Vidbergs.

173   A student at the time writing about foreign-language publishing for children in the United States, I was simultaneously scouting for books published by émigré publishers.

174   (Brooklyn, NY: Grāmatu Draugs, 1984).

175   With the success of his Bellacord enterprise, Rudzītis began to lose interest in the Russian publishing side of his business, according to a telephone interview with Iuriĭ Abyzov in October 2004, conducted through Konstantin Beloglazov.

L209

L211

L212

L210

Doktors Arausmits (Arrowsmith) was announced in 1926, although there is no record of a Grāmatu Draugs publication. For Christmas 1930, Rudzītis continued his introduction of American writers by publishing Theodore Dreiser's *Amerikāņu traģēdija* (An American Tragedy),[176] translated by Lizete Skalbe, L209 who must have been ready for a vacation by the time she finished, considering both the book's length and tedious English prose.

The designer of the book certainly put color in the GD display window that Christmas season. Although no record survives, a veteran Latvian bibliographer speculated that the designer could possibly have been Niklāvs Strunke, a deduction made from the design for Anna Grēviņa's *Modernā Amerika* (see illustration of this Strunke-designed work in the Valters un Rapa section). Photographs of Manhattan skylines, from which the stylized *Amerikāņu traģēdija* design could have been derived, were as ubiquitous as Mickey Mouse images in the world press of the time. An additional clue to the possibility of Strunke having been the designer is the confident use of bold colors. Whoever the artist may have been, the design is a refreshing contrast to the uninspired design of the first American edition in 1925 L210 or the design of the mid 1930s Czech edition by the surrealist Toyen, i.e., Marie Čerminová. Her approach focused on the book's human tragedy, rather than the physical setting. In doing so, her covers for the book are not readily identifiable as being her work. L211, L212 But these cover designs pale in comparison with the graphic sophistication of the later-appearing first Lithuanian edition, *Amerikoniška tragedija*,[177] with its crisp Art Deco style for volume one and tortured human figure for volume two, both by the Lithuanian modernist Telesforas Kulakauskas. L213, L214

Rudzītis, like many of his competitors, made the "one lats" book a decided part of his business plan,[178] a revolutionary idea for Latvian publishing at the time and soon

176   Edition size: 4,000.
177   (Kaunas: Spaudos fondas, 1937).
178   For an extended discussion of this program see Jānis Zālītis' article "Grāmatas par velti", *Karogs*, No. 11 (Nov. 2005), pp. 66-72.

L213

L214

L215

L216

L217

L218

L2194

followed by Riga's Russian-language publishers. Just consider what that meant when an average day's wages ranged from 3.50 to 5.75 lats. The negative aspect of titles selling for one lats is that to reduce production costs, numerous works were cut in length regardless of textual continuity, to say nothing of authorial approval.

One writer already on the GD "one lats" list by this time was the best-selling Bernhard Kellermann, who enjoyed having each of his ten titles available at this bargain price, all ten being listed in the 1929/1930 GD prospectus as part of a collected edition. Number eight in this edition was Kellermann's Japanese travel account titled as *Krizantēmu zeme* (Land of Chrysanthemums, 1928; translated by Z. Krodere) with a cover design by Strunke that seems to have been created on one of his "off" days. L215 But because Latvia was still nearly a decade away from joining the Bern Copyright Convention, one is unsure whether Kellermann or any of the translated authors of Rudzītis' first years of publishing were consulted about condensing text or enjoyed receiving royalty checks from his firm.

A decade later, Grāmatu Draugs' list of translated authors boasted representation from 13 countries. English writers included Elinor Glyn, W. Somerset Maugham, and H. G. Wells added to a long list of previously published English writers including Edgar Wallace, the perennial money-maker for any publisher. At one time, GD had 32 Wallace titles in print.

The cover designs for the books of American writers published by Rudzītis provide some interesting comparisons with covers from other contemporary European editions as well as the dust wrappers covering the original American editions. These writers included Upton Sinclair and his *Nafta* (Oil, 1933), translated by Augusts Mežsēts. L216 The cover designer is not credited but it is clear the design was boldly "lifted" from John Heartfield's front cover design for the Malik-Verlag's German translation of Sinclair's *Mountain City*,[179] L217 surely one of Sinclair's weakest works having nothing to do with oil or Wall Street, as the Heartfield design would indicate.[180] The GD designer would have done better plagiarizing Heartfield's Malik edition cover of *Petroleum*. L218 The uncredited GD designer might also have given cover design emphasis to the rough romance aspect of the novel similar to that of the Estonian edition published in the Loodus "1 Kroon" series in 1932. L219

Books by other American writers of the time similarly received uneven attention by the GD design department, for example, the austere design for Pearl Buck's *Labā zeme* (The Good Earth, 1936). L220 The Rudzītis designer might have shown more imagination in light of the competition in other countries. Note the subtle symbolism of the first German edition L221 with its uncredited design or Antanas Gudaitis' more stylized design for the Lithuanian edition.[181] L222 Pearl Buck's *Patriots* was also published by GD in the spring of 1940 just as Latvia's independence was coming to a close. L223

L220

L221

L222

L223

The widely translated Vicki Baum led the Grāmatu Draugs German list with five titles, along with other successful German writers such as Hans Fallada, Irmgard Keun, Thomas Mann, and Ludwig Renn. In these years Rudzītis certainly did not miss the opportunity presented by such a popular writer as Erich Maria Remarque, whose *Rietumu frontē bez pārmaiņām* (All Quiet on the Western Front, translated by Aleksandrs Grīns) may have been published shortly after its first appearance in Germany in 1929, although the GD edition is not dated. Assuming this was the first Remarque title published, Rudzītis followed it with *Sapņu būda* (The Dream Room) in 1930 and Remarque's widely translated *Trīs draugi* (Three Comrades) L224 in 1937, the former translated by Roberts Kroders, the latter by Valdemārs Kārkliņš. The first London translation L225 also appeared in 1937. One Remarque title that appears to have been distributed rather than published by GD was *Atgriešanās* (The Road Back, 1931). L226

Orbis, a short-lived Russian-language publisher possibly with a connection to GD, had brought out the Russian edition earlier in 1931 with the same cover art. GD arranged

179   The Malik translation was published as *So macht man Dollars* (Berlin, 1930).
180   Instead, it is an account of a small-town Colorado newspaper publisher.
181   Translated by Kazys Boruta (Kaunas: Sakalas, 1935).

Ne kaŗa grāmata, bet meistarisks
mīlas un draudzības romāns

L224

THREE COMRADES

"One of the most poignant love stories that
have been told in our time." — J. Donald
Adams in the New York Times Book Review.

ERICH MARIA REMARQUE

L225

L226

L227

L228

for translation by E. Feldmanis into Latvian. L227 Vidbergs's design is in strong contrast to Karel Teige's[182] photomontage design for the Czech edition of 1931. L228

Sure-selling French authors also appeared on the GD list in the 1930s, such as the 19th century writers Honoré de Balzac, Alexandre Dumas, Victor Hugo, and Émile Zola. 20th century authors on the list included Maurice Bedel, Georges Duhamel, André Maurois, and Claude Farrère. The Latvian translation of Farrère's *Kauja* (The Battle, 1936),[183] L229 with its typographic cover design, missed a design opportunity taken by the Czech publisher[184] who used Jaroslav Šváb's emotionally charged cover design for the Czech translation of this title that same year. L230

Books for children and youth were not a significant part of the GD list, yet they kept in print a number of cheaply produced picture books not credited as to compiler or illustrator. In addition, the firm showed in its 1937/1938 catalog such standard titles

182 Teige's legendary contacts in vanguard design circles of the 1920s and 1930s and people with whom he corresponded or met in travels between Prague and Amsterdam, Berlin, Moscow, and Paris included Gerd Arntz, Gustav Klucis (Klutsis), John Heartfield, El Lissitzky, and Piet Zwart. Confirmation of a Riga visit has yet to be confirmed.
183 Published as *La Bataille* (Paris, 1923).
184 Kvasnička A. Hampl.

in Latvian translation as A. A. Milne's *Winnie the Pooh*, Lewis Carroll's *Alice's Adventures in Wonderland*, James Barrie's *Peter Pan*, and Selma Lagerlöf's *Wonderful Adventures of Nils Holgersson*, L231 which carried the Wilhelm Schulz design of the German edition of 1923 but with a variant color.[185] There were also a number of titles on the various GD adult lists that were appropriated by adolescents, e.g., Edgar Rice Burroughs' *Tarzans un skudru cilvēki* (Tarzan and the Ant Men, 1936).[186] The GD edition carries the original cover art by James Allen St. John. L232

It would be helpful if we knew more about GD's use of designers and illustrators. We do know the firm began an economically cautious approach to design by using mainly typographic covers and relatively subdued colors for the covers of bound books with jackets as well as soft cover titles. A decided improvement in cover appearance is noticeable by the early to mid-1930s, with the increasing awareness among many Latvian publishers that a cover illustration with professional design and typography *does* sell books. Among those receiving design commissions during the second decade of GD's operation were Nikolajs Puzirevskis, Niklāvs Strunke, and Hilda Vīka, who often provided the cover art and design for her own books.

The following panels of covers from 1929 to 1940 give additional indication of GD design variety: A testimony to Rudzītis' ability to maintain his publishing vision in spite of having to abandon his flourishing Riga business in 1944, is that he continued publishing in a Displaced Persons camp in Esslingen, West Germany, from 1944 to 1949. He began publishing again almost from the time of his arrival in New York City in 1949 and continued until his death in 2001. The editorial file of his American imprints is held by the New York Public Library, thanks to Jānis Krēsliņš, a long-time bibliographer and librarian at the Council on Foreign Relations in New York City.

Rudzītis' life as a publisher was one of continuing success; he did not leave a trail of bankruptcies. It is to his credit that in the upheaval of exile and re-establishing his book publishing he also founded and edited, together with his wife and others, the only long-term successful Latvian-language newspaper of the exile community, *Laiks* (Brooklyn, 1949 to date). An English-language biography of this remarkable publisher begs to be written.

L229

L230

L231

L232

185   This German edition was in fact the 111-115th printing of the first German edition.

186   Although number one in *Romānu sērija* (Series of Novels), this title does not appear in GD catalogs. It appears to have been published by a possible front, "Populāra lektīra", which had the same address as GD and printed in the GD printing plant. Five titles are recorded for this series, all translated by Valdis Bāliņš. A speculation about this seeming "front": Latvia had joined the Bern Convention in 1937, so Rudzītis likely decided not to risk a suit against the main GD firm by Burroughs' army of lawyers. Rudzītis seems to have toyed with this idea earlier by fronting with a firm called Dzintarzeme in 1934 for publishing Karl May's *Sudrabezera dzelmes noslēpums* (Secret of the Silver Lake's Depths), printed by GD. N. B.: Karl May also had good lawyers.

L233

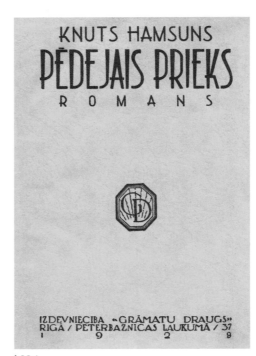

L234

L235

L236

L233   *Budenbroki*
(Buddenbrooks, 1929)
by Thomas Mann,
transl. by L. Skalbe,
K. Štrāls and Z. Krodere
Cover design: not credited

L234   *Pēdejais prieks*
(The Last Joy, 1929)
by Knut Hamsun,
transl. by L. Skalbe
Cover design: not credited

L235   Kultūras un tikumu vēsture
(History of Culture and Custom, 1931)
by Aleksandrs Grīns, 2 vols.
Cover design: Niklāvs Strunke

L236   Atdzimšanas dziesma
(Song of Regeneration, 1934)
by Roberts Kroders
Cover design: Niklāvs Strunke

L237   *Latvju modernas dzejas
antoloģija*
(An Anthology of Modern Latvian
Poetry, 1930),
edited by Aleksandrs Čaks and
Pēteris Ķikuts
Cover design: not credited

L238   Skaistā Skandinavija
(Beautiful Scandinavia, 1940)
by Karel Čapek,
transl. by V. Grēviņš
Cover design: possibly a Latvian artist's
reworking of an internal illustration by
Karel Čapek's brother, Josef

L239   *Amerikas brīnumi*
(The Miracle of America, 1940)
by Jānis Plaudis
Cover design: Nikolajs Puzirevskis

L240   *Lielā slāpe: Stāsti*
(Great Thirst: Stories, 1940)
by Hilda Vīka
Cover design: Hilda Vīka

L241   Cover of GD 1934/1935 catalog

L242   Cover of GD 1939/1940 catalog

L237

L238

L241

L239

L240

L242

Zelta Ābele

An early 17th century Dutch printer-publisher recognized a market in the latent longing among book lovers for small, well-printed books in sturdy bindings.[187] The clever response was to give the book world of his time a series of just that—small, uniform-format, well-designed, and illustrated books at a reasonable price. Since the appearance of these "Elsevier", as they came to be known, the publishing world has seen many a subsequent venture. For example, the Aldine series of small books on English poets begun in the second quarter of the 19th century by William Pickering may readily come to the minds of many elderly book collectors.

Less than a century later, Insel Verlag's uniform series of translations and original texts bound in decorated paper-over boards began appearing in 1912 and continue to be published to the present day. Examples of this *Insel-Bücherei* series were to be found on the shelves of numerous German-reading Baltic families in Latvia, if contemporary antiquarian bookshop evidence is any indication. These *Insel Bücher* spawned any number of similarly styled series (often identical in size) even in Germany.[188]

It is not surprising that a Latvian bookman influenced by German publishing should make his way onto the book scene with the concept of a small, well-printed, well-designed, and illustrated book at a reasonable price. The early 1930s provided a particularly auspicious moment because the physical quality of the Latvian book began to decline markedly in the 1932/1933 period. The worldwide depression was forcing publishers throughout the industrialized world, including Latvia, to conserve resources.

In the case of the man behind the Zelta Ābele (Golden Apple Tree) imprint, the concept of good design was taken to a much higher level in production quality, size variation, and adventurous content in some instances.

Unlike his forerunners in the fine, small-sized book tradition, the bookman founding the Zelta Ābele imprint, Miķelis Goppers (also Gopers), *did* vary the sizes somewhat, although in the minds of many the pre-war titles (1935-1940) were remembered for their approximate 14x10 cm size. Ask any book-oriented Latvian 60 years of age and older to characterize a Goppers book, and more often than not they will use their hands to illustrate a size in the range mentioned, along with comments about uniformly conservative typography, fine printing and illustration, and "texts that were our first encounter with a particular author".

Like Rudzītis before him, Goppers was a born publisher and certainly a survivor. His firm was the second longest in existence (1935-1985), after Grāmatu Draugs. Also, like Rudzītis, Goppers survived the first Soviet occupation and most of the Nazi occupation. But rather than go to America, as did Rudzītis, he chose to continue his inspired publishing program in Sweden.

Unlike Rudzītis and *his* publishing venture, for which we have no bibliography or extensive period reminiscences by others, we do have Laimonis Osis and Guntars Pupa to thank for their invaluable compilation *Apgāda Zelta Ābele ilustrēts bibliogrāfiskais*

---

187 In 1629 the Dutch printing-publishing family Elsevier began a series of 32mo books with engraved title page, narrow margins, and high-quality paper—solid in text and binding. Content ranged from Greek and Roman classics to more contemporary works. Because of their pleasant appearance, although difficult to read without magnification, they were readily collected by bibliophiles up to the mid 20th century.

188 Two examples: the Russian-language Berlin publisher Argonavty, active in 1921/1922 with its fiction and non-fiction titles, and Salman Schocken's *Bücherei des Schocken Verlags* in 1933-1938.

rādītājs ar papildinājumiem un pielikumiem (Zelta Ābele Publishing House: An Illustrated Bibliographic Index with Supplement and Appendix),[189] which serves as the basis for this section.

The Osis-Pupa collaboration is a model for a publishing house bibliography and is one of only two such works to be published to date for Latvia's Interwar period. The detailed bibliographic description in the Anglo-American tradition that the compilers provide, together with title page illustration in black and white for each title is augmented by supplementary and appendix information, which includes bibliographic descriptions for prospectuses and postcards. The appendix even provides content notes for the Latvian National Library's boxes of Zelta Ābele manuscript materials for the period 1935 to 1944. Appended to the text are accounts and commentaries on Goppers, the publishing house, and a few of its authors and artists. If one were to comment on a fundamental lacuna, it is the lack of a brief, introductory sketch on the day-to-day running of the business under two occupations and exile.

A few works are singled out here for comment and illustration. Although not necessarily the most famous of the total production, they do illustrate something of the character of the publishing house's output. One departure from the previous Latvian publishers discussed is the inclusion of a few works from the Nazi occupation production.

The first title Goppers announced, *Žanina un viņas lielais draugs* (Jeannine and her Great Friend, 1935), was certainly not the most applauded book of the once popular French writer Louis-Frédéric Rouquette, who was best known for the book translated and published by Goppers three years later, *Lielais baltais klusums: Aļaskā piedzīvots romāns* (The Great White Silence: A Novel Experienced in Alaska, 1938).[190] It might be a puzzle to some why Goppers did not choose a more auspicious title or a more renowned international author with which to announce his publishing house to the world, or at least to the Latvian-speaking world. One explanation may be that the selection was made by his founding partner, Alma Gobniece, a French-educated, professional translator. Still, Rouquette seems an odd choice for launching a literary publishing venture. But Goppers was to redeem himself by selecting such authors as Jānis Akuraters (1936), Aspazija (1940), Rūdolfs Blaumanis (1937), Anšlavs Eglītis (1940), E. T. A. Hoffmann (1939), Aleksandr Kuprin (1937), Selma Lagerlöf (1937), Jānis Poruks (1939), Aleksandr Pushkin (1936), Rainer Maria Rilke (1939), Kārlis Skalbe (1936, 1939, 1940), and Oscar Wilde (1936, 1939) among others—48 titles in all during the brief period from the publishing house's founding until 1940.

The artists chosen to illustrate these carefully produced books were in nearly all cases the best artists of the time: Jānis Plēpis (a leading modernist found drowned in the summer of 1947 and likely murdered for political reasons), Romāns Suta (a stellar figure in Latvian art who fled to Soviet Georgia hoping to escape the long arm of the NKVD but met an equally ignominious death there in 1944), Ludolfs Liberts (a major set designer and studio painter who happily escaped to New York and died just short of his 64th birthday), and Oskars Norītis (a painter and graphic artist whose dark and somewhat melancholy illustrations graced numerous books, periodicals, and a few posters,

---

189 (Riga: Literatūra un Māksla, 1993).

190 This novel of a Frenchman who settled in Alaska, originally titled *Le grand silence blanc: Roman vécu d'Alaska* (Paris: Férenczi, 1921), was the most widely read and translated (English, German, Latvian, Romanian, Slovenian) of Rouquette's twenty-some books.

L243

L244

L246

L245

L247

including one commission by the Nazi occupying force warning against helping Soviet partisans in any way, produced the year of his death in the autumn of 1942).

Two Zelta Ābele works from the pre-WWII period show the high quality of book illustration and typography of Goppers' books: *Poem pa kulšen: Ventiņ valde rakstits peršs* (A Poem about Grain Threshing: Doggerel Written in the Ventiņi Dialect, 1939) by Alant Vils (Fricis Dziesma) and illustrated with lithographs by Roman Suta. L243, L244 The trade edition was issued in 1,000 copies and a limited edition on Zander paper of six copies. The second title, a poem by Edvarts Virza titled *Karals Nameitis* (King Nameitis, 1939),[191] was illustrated with original lithographs by Voldemārs Krastiņš, L245 who also designed the endsheets and binding. L246, L247 An eight-copy limited edition on mould-made paper preceded the 1,200-copy trade edition.

Of the few small books so many WWII Latvian refugees carried to the various stopping places in their exile odyssey, Zelta Ābele books were often a first choice. They almost seemed designed to fit into luggage corners for just such extremity. The last Zelta Ābele books to grab before leaving in those turbulent years of 1943/1944 were more often than not those titles just recently published. An example with the right tone of encouragement

191   Nameitis was the last king of the Semigallian nation, one of the "tribal" nations into which Latvian lands were divided. All these nations, except for the Semigallians, had been subdued and then slaughtered by the German order of Livonian Knights by the close of the 13th century. Nameitis died after 1281, when the tribe left the castle of Tērvete. Virza's poem celebrates this valiant king's battle against overwhelming odds.

L248

L249

L250

to "fight on" and with a surprise "happy ending" is *Kara dainas* (War Poems)[192] edited by literary critic Jānis Rudzītis with woodcut illustrations by Jānis Plēpis. The text's implicit goal: return to a homeland without war. L248–L250

Goppers even had something for the children in wartime: *Tētis karavīrs: Vēstule no Volchovas* (My Dad the Soldier: Letter from Volkhov)[193] L251 and *Apses bērni* (The Aspen Children),[194] L252 both telling documents of the German occupation. While Vilis Ciesnieks, the illustrator of the former book, is credited under his actual name, the author given as Milda Grīnfelde[195] is in fact a pseudonym for the renowned poet Aleksandrs Čaks, who wished to keep a low profile in this period. As to the second book, Klāvs Sarma is the pseudonym of the social-democratic poet Pāvils Vīlips,[196] who likely had much more to risk from the Nazi administration than Čaks. It is a puzzle to this outsider how two such individuals generally known as leftist ideologues and with such known publishing records in the Republic of Latvia could survive undetected with only a pseudonym during the entire German occupation. And just as puzzling, with the advent of the Soviet re-occupation at the end of WWII, how could they then not be considered "collaborators" and be allowed to continue writing and publishing?

About the content of the books themselves, in the case of "Letters from Volkhov", a marsh area near Leningrad, there is not even a mention of the Germans. Did the Nazi censors also "look the other way" or not notice the Latvian symbols along with audacious appearances of the Latvian flag on the book's cover and in illustrations? Another puzzle: if the anti-Soviet subtlety of the text brought the author and the book "through" the Nazi occupation, how did Vīlips reconcile this with his beliefs and why was this particular book's content overlooked by the literary *apparat* during the second Soviet occupation?

The Latvian flag flutters in only one location in the second book. Of particular interest is the skillful use of photomontage, combined with Zina Āre's drawings, in this story of match manufacture from the wood of the aspen tree.

L251

L252

192   50,000 copies printed in 1943; measuring 13.5x8.5 cm.
193   50,000 copies printed in 1943; measuring 19x17 cm.
194   8,000 copies printed in 1943; measuring 21.5x15.5 cm.
195   Milda Grīnfelde was a translator and friend of Čaks; Čaks used her name as a pseudonym.
196   In contrast, Vīlips' artist-colleague and friend on the left, Kārlis Bušs, was arrested and confined to the Salaspils Concentration Camp for a time, according to Jānis Kalnačs (see *Tēlotājas mākslas dzīve nacistiskās Vācijas okupētajā Latvijā, 1941-1945* [Riga: Neputns, 2005], p. 287).

While some questions about this publishing venture have been answered in the last two decades from reminiscenses about Goppers and his Zelta Ābele, other questions still remain, not the least of which is the matter of how Goppers managed relations with the Soviet occupying force in 1940/1941, although his two titles published (although Zelta Ābele did not feature as the publisher) at that time apparently fell within the "acceptable" range.[197] The question of his relationship with the Nazi publishing supervisors in the years before his emigration to Sweden also remains unanswered.

Publishing on the political left

The publishing history of the Latvian political left, from mild social democratic strains in various left-oriented organizations to that of the hardest core within the Latvian Communist Party, has been told, in part, in many an article from the mid 1950s to the close of the second Soviet occupation in 1991. Alas, most of these publications are in Latvian and thus lost to many readers. Commentary on the social democrats of that era written between 1946 and 1990 consist of highly colored accounts and brief biographical sketches, sometimes little more than footnotes. In contrast, and as to be expected, the straight-arrow communist publishers of the Interwar period—plus the authors, editors, illustrators, and publications—received continuing attention throughout the four decades of the second Soviet era. One work of that period essential for the study of the far-left and non-social democratic press has already been referred to in several instances: Jūlijs Ķipers' *Cīņas balsis: Apceŗējumu un atmiņu krājums par revolucionāro presi latviešu nacionālistiskās buržuāzijas kundzības laikā, 1920-1940* (Voices of Struggle: An Anthology of Treatises and Recollections of the Revolutionary Press During the Time of Domination by the Latvian Nationalist Bourgeoisie 1920-1940).[198] It is clear from the title that a tendentious "read" awaits. But it is thanks to the compiler that interviews of the activists directly engaged in the day-to-day work of writing, editing, printing, and publishing were done while there were survivors who could be interviewed or contribute to the work. Although the book suffers from grainy photos and poor-quality reproductions, it provides the best contemporary starting place for the publishing and printing historian concerned with the far-left's efforts in Interwar Latvia. One could only wish that it had an index.

But an index of the periodical press of the Interwar period *does* exist and what an index it is! One can only marvel at this undertaking being produced without the computerized ease with which such a work could be compiled today. The team engaged in compiling the *Latviešu periodika* exhaustive work merits far more than the customary round of applause. Deserving of thanks are those largely unsung bibliographers[199] for their efforts in this monumental five-volume bibliographical performance.[200] A special word of acknowledgment should be given to Ērika Flīgere, who seems to have been the force that kept this operation together over many years.

---

197 Benvenuto Cellini's *Life* and Rainis' famed drama *Uguns un nakts* (Fire and Night), designed and illustrated by Oskars Norītis.

198 (Riga: Latvijas Valsts izdevniecība, 1959).

199 Listed on the title pages of the volumes to which they contributed.

200 *Latviešu periodika* is the general title for 4 volumes published over a period of years and spanning the last years of the Soviet occupation and into the present period. Vol. 1: 1768-1919 (1977); vol. 2: left periodicals cited above (1976); vol. 3: part one—Interwar period, 1920-1940 (1988); vol. 3: part two—index to vol. 3, part one (1989); vol. 4: 1940-1945 and title index to all volumes (1995).

L253

L254

L255

L256

L257

L258

L259

L260

The first volume to be completed holds the answers to the basic bibliographic questions about the far-left, non-social democratic press, *Latviešu periodika, 2. sējums: 1920-1940, Revolucionārā un padomju periodika.*[201] After 421 pages one has a fairly good sense of the intensity with which this sector of the Latvian left was working to change the nature of Latvian society, along with Baltic history. What doesn't appear in this work regarding the revolutionary left's serials, editors, frequency of publication, physical size, and edition size, probably cannot be known. Even the non-Latvian language press fitting this sector is cited: Russian, Yiddish, and German, although citations for titles in these languages are abbreviated. For the same level of exhaustive detail for social democratic periodicals one must search through a later volume in the aforementioned set, namely, volume 3, part 1: 1920-1940. This volume includes serials in all categories published in that period.

Since beginning with a mention of guides to the press of the left, continuing with comments on examples of the periodicals themselves seems in order before considering the *book* publishers of the left. Discussion is limited only to those journals having some design interest, a category with less than a dozen examples. The revolutionary, far-left journals having the appearance of a professional designer at work are mainly the following: *Jaunā Gvarde* [Riga] (The New Guard, 1928; 10 issues), made interesting by Ernests Kālis' covers and Samuils Haskins' cartoons; L253–L260 *Informators* (The Informer, 1932;

201   (Riga: Zinātne, 1976).

123

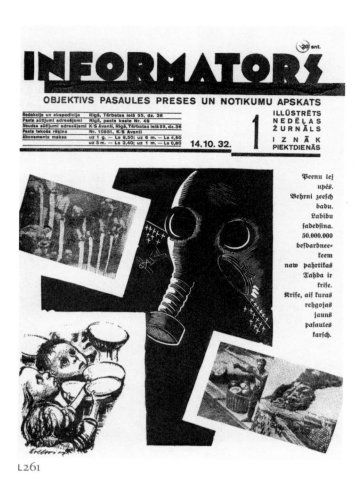

L261

11 issues) with covers and illustrations by Kārlis Bušs, Samuils Haskins, Augusts Pupa, and Alfrēds Žurgins; L261 *Nord-Ost* (Northeast, see discussion in Russian-language publishing chapter); and, lastly, *Kreisā Fronte* (The Left Front, 1928-30; 17 issues) with cover designs by Ernests Kālis and design guidance by the editor, Linards Laicens. *Kreisā Fronte* has been singled out for an extended comment as well as for several of its covers because it was the longest-lived journal and considered the most influential of the graphically interesting revolutionary periodicals.

As already mentioned, Laicens was hardly just another revolutionary editor with design aspirations. And *Kreisā Fronte* by no means marked the beginning of his life as causist or editor. By the time he and his wife, Olga Eiženija Laicena (an experienced Russian-language translator), initiated the journal in the spring of 1928, he had more than a decade of agitation, writing, and editing behind him.

Some hint of Laicens' life has been provided previously and implied that he did not begin his adult years as a hard-edged communist. In his student years, Laicens was aligned with what might be termed "social democratic nationalism", that is, he was a Latvian first and a proponent of Latvian independence but with social democracy as a goal for a country not yet in existence. With his publication in 1917 of a 16-page brochure titled *Latvijas valsts* (The Latvian State)[202] he called for full independence of the Latvian lands. In this "call" Laicens is credited as the first nationalist to make such a courageous, printed demand.

A prolific writer[203] throughout his lifetime, Laicens contributed numerous articles of a literary-critical nature (but with social democratic overtones) to newspapers and journals from the time of his student years before World War I and continuing into the early 1920s. By the mid 1920s he had become increasingly radicalized and sympathetic toward the aims of an international communist revolution and the Soviet "experiment". There is no question about the seriousness of his idealism.

By several definitions there was no substantial leftist Latvian-language journal with international aspirations until the launching of *Kreisā Fronte* in 1928 by a team of young revolutionaries including Laicens' friend Leons Paegle. Laicens' initial plan was to take his idea to Mārtiņš Ozols, a member of the Central Committee of the Latvian Communist Party, and get support.[204] At a meeting of the Central Committee of the Latvian Communist Party (LCP) the suggestion was floated as was the proposal to involve "independent writers, even bourgeois writers... and further, that the language should be easy enough for the masses..."[205] The LCP was clearly in charge of the journal at the beginning stage

---

202 Published in Moscow by the Moscow Group of Latvian National Democratic Party.
203 See *Linards Laicens: Biobibliogrāfiskais rādītājs* (Riga: 1989).
204 *Cīņas balsis*, p. 350.
205 Ibid., p. 351.

L262

L263

L264

and provided the editorial guidelines. In an account of their reminiscences of the *Kreisā Fronte* days,[206] Olga Laicena and Jūlijs Ķipers recall a meeting in the Laicens' apartment, choosing the name of the journal and following the concept of Vladimir Mayakovsky's *LEF* (1923-1925). Although by the time that *Kreisā Fronte* L262 began, it was more likely inspired by the design and content of *Novyĭ Lef* (The New Left, 1927-1928), L263 copies of which in all probability were in "careful" circulation in Riga. One can only speculate that the cover designs by Ernests Kālis for *Kreisā Fronte* and Mayakovsky's covers for *Novyĭ Lef* moved across borders to also influence the Lithuanian designer Telesforas Kulakauskas in his cover designs for the Lithuanian vanguard journal *Trečias Frontas* (The Third Front, Kaunas, 1930-31). L264

Under the literary editorship of Emīls Rozenbahs (pseudonym of E. Fross), the content of *Kreisā Fronte* followed along lines more cultural than political. This direction appears to have been more or less consistent, although the "culture" was surely political in the choice of books reviewed, literary essays commissioned, movies recommended, and individuals highlighted in biographical notes. The same could be said for the illustrations. A few examples include the photomontage in No. 4 (1930), with its phrase "Mēs augam" (We're progressing) L265 and the *Kurpnieki* (Shoemakers) woodcut by E. Lielcepure in No. 4 (1929), L266 to which could be added the illustrations and captions on facing pages in No. 2 (1930), L267 under the George Grosz caricature of the businessman blowing a bubble that reads "Never again war", which faces a New Year's card cliché image with the caption "Collapse of the bourgeois ideological mystiques".

According to Olga Laicena and Jūlijs Ķipers, the Latvian Communist Party provided 500 lats for start-up support (likely from Moscow) with other funds coming privately

206   Ibid., pp. 349-367.

L265

Ziepju burbuļi. Georga Grosz'a karikatura

L267

Kurpnieki. Ē. Lieicepures zīmējums

L266

from Laicens. The 200 lats production costs of each issue were paid for by Laicens until he was arrested at the close of 1928 for "producing a journal with the implicit goal of overthrowing the state". But the continued production of the 1,000 to 1,200 copies per issue was done on credit extended by the printer. Laicens was eventually freed, but by 1931 the journal was shut down only to reappear in May 1931 under the new name *Tribīne* (The Rostrum, 1931-1933; 12 issues) L268 with Laicens as publisher and Jānis Bušs as editor. It is reasonable to assume that Laicens continued as a behind-the-scenes editor.

In addition to designing all the covers for *Kreisā Fronte*, Ernests Kālis also produced the cover design for *Tribīne*, which remained the same into its second year, when the design was altered somewhat as seen here for No. 1 (June 1933). L269 Samuils Haskins produced several internal linocut illustrations. Two examples are a title page image for No. 2 (1932), and a linocut portrait of Karl Marx L270 inside the Kālis-designed front cover for No. 1 (June 1933), which was confiscated and destroyed upon publication.[207] L271

The authorities had lost all patience by this second time around. *Tribīne* was shut down in July 1933, but not without warnings. The history of confiscation of certain issues, e.g., No. 1 (1932) and Nos. 1 and 2 (1933) has been carefully documented.[208] The ruse of changing the editorial involvement in order to confuse the authorities did not work. Jānis Bušs was given the opportunity to reflect during two sessions in prison for his choosing to publish two anti-war articles.

207 This issue also had two trim sizes: 22x14.7 cm and 23.2x16.2 cm, the latter being less common.
208 See *Latviešu periodika, 2. sējums; 1920-1940, Revolucionārā un padomju periodika* (Riga: Zinātne, 1976), pp. 212-213.

Tribīne lacked not only color covers for most issues of its short life, but also the professional photographs contributed by Laicens to its forerunner, *Kreisā Fronte*.[209]

As a designer, Kālis was as obsessed about his work as Laicens was about being an editor. During the period from the mid 1920s to the time of his fleeing to the Soviet Union in 1935, Kālis produced covers for the legal as well as underground leftist press: book jacket designs, posters, L272 and paintings. A fragmentary record is documented in the introductory text of a 1956 exhibition catalog,[210] containing 201 entries and 32 illustrations. A year later, a small monograph appeared with a slightly longer text than in the exhibition catalog and with 55 sepia illustrations and a tipped-in color frontispiece.[211] With these two publications, Kālis was posthumously rehabilitated after having been arrested and executed in the USSR and subsequently declared a nonperson for 17 years.

Although a cast of revolutionaries was involved in writing many of the articles in both *Kreisā Fronte* and *Tribīne*, Laicens and his wife bore the responsibility for rewriting, editing, and translating (Czech and Russian). Laicens had the additional burden of supervising the typesetting and typography in the cramped quarters of their second-floor courtyard flat on Marijas iela (Marijas Street).[212]

Manuscripts were submitted, usually handwritten, and awaited Laicens' hand-corrections or a complete rewrite in longhand, as he worked without a typewriter. Still this was not his full-time job but instead an activity carried

L268

L269

L270

L271

out along with his social work (attempting to alleviate problems among workers and poorer party members), participation in Latvian Communist Party meetings, and attendance at meetings of the Saeima (Parliament) as a regular parliamentarian as well as meetings of the Riga City Council. Clearly he was not a skulking revolutionary editor coming out only at night. What remains an enigma, however: in light of what the authorities knew about Laicens and his publishing, why did it take so many years before the crackdown in the summer of 1933 on these ostensibly clandestine periodicals?

Laicens intuitively knew his days in Latvia were numbered and in mid summer 1932 he cleared his desk, left production of the remaining issues of *Tribīne* to his colleagues, and under the party's pressure fled to Moscow. There he continued to be involved in Latvian-language publishing until, like so many other Latvian communists exiled in the USSR, he found a common fate in the purges that swept through their exile communities beginning in 1937. The date and circumstances of his death vary, although his granddaughter,

L272

209   In an interview in February 2010, Anna Laicena supported previous contentions that Linards Laicens was a competent photographer and provided photographs for *Kreisā Fronte*.

210   *Ernesta Kāļa (1904-1939) saglabāto darbu izstādes katalogs*, ed. by V. Valdmanis (Riga: Latvijas PSR Valsts revolūcijas muzejs, 1956). Cover design and typography by Samuils Haskins.

211   *Ernests Kālis* ed. by Arturs Lapiņš (Riga: Latvijas Valsts izdevniecība, 1957).

212   According to Anna Laicena, Feb. 2010.

L273

Anna Laicena,[213] claims that he died much later than 1938 and in fact lived until 1941, when he was shot in Lubianka Prison during a wartime purge.

Olga Laicena survived the purges but endured nine years of prison, returning empty-handed[214] to Latvia in 1946. Forbidden by the Soviet occupiers to go back to Riga, she lived out most of her remaining life in Valmiera, about 65 miles northeast of the capital city, and died in Riga in 1993.

The scattering of Latvian communists who chose to live in the Soviet Union after 1920 had some of their Latvian-language reading needs met by their own publishing ventures. The production of these various Latvian-language regional printing operations were closely supervised by the Soviet state as were the books and periodicals produced by the larger Latvian publishing houses Spartaks and Prometejs in Leningrad and Moscow, respectively, where the largest number of exiles tended to congregate. L273

Design distinctiveness did not characterize the majority of publications—book and periodical—issuing from these USSR-based Latvian-language publishing offices, large or small. This may have been a protective cover in the early to mid 1930s, when Soviet graphic design had lost scores of its more innovative designers to various purges or exile. Caution had become the byword for Soviet as well as Latvian designers and illustrators at that time. Prometejs, the best-known and most productive house, is singled out for comment in the following section.

Latvian-language publishing in the USSR in the 1920s and 1930s: Prometejs Publishing House and the periodical *Celtne*

L274

For "right-thinking", left-leaning Latvians in the USSR of the 1920s and 1930s Prometejs published a range of literature, from children's books and school books to a general cultural periodical called *Celtne* (Structure, 1929-1937). L274–L278 *Celtne* experienced six changes of cover design and as many speculations about the designers, although it is likely that the individuals credited with overall design responsibilities, e.g., Jānis Aižens, Kārlis Veidemans, and Linards Laicens, took their hand to cover design creation. A case might even be made for a Klucis influence in the electrical power line design on a number of the early 1932 issues, given Klucis' early and continuing obsession with electrification in the USSR.

The subtitle of *Celtne* clarifies its content: "proletarian history, literature, art, and theory". Poetry, short stories, translations from contemporary European literature, book reviews, and "political news" (local and foreign) were part of the regular fare offered. Given the time, place, and general climate of fear, readers could rest assured that interesting deviation among the contributors' viewpoints would never lighten its pages. There

---

213   In "Pa rakstnieka Linarda Laicena pēdām" (On the trail of the writer Linards Laicens) in *Latvija Amerikā*, 6:7 (Jan. 1996), Anna Laicena recounts circumstances as reported by her mother some years later. However, data confirming a 1941 death year is somewhat vague.

214   At the time of her arrest and deportation from the USSR, the authorities confiscated from her Moscow apartment all of Laicens' papers, photographs, sketches, books—even the family Bible—according to Anna Laicena in an interview with the author in February 2010.

L275

L276

L277

L278

L280

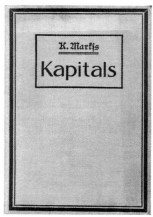

was strict adherence among editors (Laicens was one, following his Moscow arrival) to the party line *de jour*. Beginning in 1932, it was perhaps Laicens who also contributed to the choices of more appealing cover designs. Anna Laicena confirmed that Laicens provided much of the photographic content.[215] The *Celtne* edition sizes ranged from 1,000 to 3,000 copies.

In addition to publishing, Prometejs operated its own Moscow retail bookshop for a time at Ul. Maroseĭka 8.[216] It is not clear whether this was also the address of its own printing plant. Pēteris Stučka was the director and Jūlijs Daniševskis the co-director. Among Prometejs' more important translation and publishing efforts was Marx's *Das Kapital* (2 volumes, 1924), L279 translated by Pēteris Stučka with an appropriately severe cover design. Multi-volume selected writings of Lenin came out in more than one edition with editorial and translation teams involved. Another important original photo document shown here: Latvians who had lost their lives in the Latvian 1905[217] revolution (cover design by Kārlis Veidemans). L280

L279

With continuing financial assistance from the Soviet government, Prometejs published some 300 book titles in its 14 years of existence with edition sizes ranging from 500 to 1,500 copies.

215   Interview with Anna Laicena, Feb. 2010.
216   There were two Prometejs retail shops in Leningrad, at Ul. Nekrasova 10 and 3-go liulia 32.
217   (Moscow: Prometejs, 1925).

L281

L283

L284

L282

For design and illustration, Prometejs could call upon any number of Latvian exile artists in the USSR, including Jānis Aižens, Voldemārs Andersons, Jānis Birzgals, Aleksandrs Drēviņš, Ernests Grīnvalds, Pauls Irbīts, Voldemārs Jakubs, Ernsts Kālis, Gustavs Klucis, Kārlis Rinkuss, and Kārlis Veidemans. All of these artists except Birzgals died at the hands of the NKVD.[218] This pool of artists was drawn upon to provide illustrations and cover designs for *Celtne* and the periodical for youth titled *Mazais Kolektīvists* (The Little Collectivist, 1931-1937).[219] L281 The stylized cover designs for 1932 and 1933 are specifically credited to "JA-AI" (Jānis Aižens).[220]

Typical of the unappealing appearance of the school and children's books published by Prometejs are: a translation of *Fizika uz katra soļa* (Physics at Every Step, 1936) for the middle grades by the noted Russian science popularizer Yakov Perelman with its cover design by Iuriĭ Skaldin, L282 a title by Konrāds Jokums in the Prometejs literary series *Maise* (Bread),[221] L283 and a children's book of Latvian folk tales compiled by M. Endziņa and illustrated by Ernests Grīnvalds.[222] L284 The Prometejs children's book publishing activity was anything but a sideline, for translations of Charles Dickens, Mark Twain, Jules Verne, and Russian writers such as Agniya Barto, Maksim Gorky, and Aleksandr Pushkin were provided, usually with new illustrations by artists from the aforementioned group.

A characteristic adult publication in brochure format—in this case poetry—is Voldemārs Jākobsons' *Gaitas* (Motion) L285 with its Favorskiĭ-style,[223] wood-engraved cover illustration by Kārlis Rinkuss. Other examples of *belles lettres* are Jānis Eiduks' *Strēlnieki*

---

218   A similar fate—shot by the NKVD—befell the Prometejs authors as well as the editors of those years.
219   Published in Leningrad by *Latviešu Pedagoģiskā tehnikuma saiknes komisijas izdevums* (Latvian Pedagogical Technical College Union Commission Publishing House).
220   Interview with Jāzeps Osmanis, Nov. 2006.
221   Edition size: 2,000.
222   Edition size: 1,800.

L285

L286

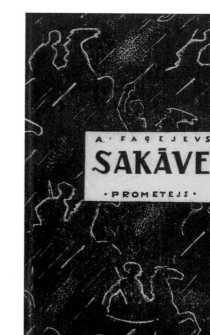

L289

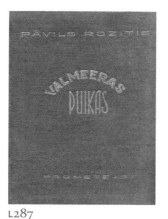

L287

L288

pagrież stobrus (Riflemen Turn their Guns, 1934) with an uncredited cover design, L286 Pāvils Rozītis' novel *Valmieras puikas* (Valmiera's Boys, 1937) with its cover design by V. Samsonov, L287 and Augusts Brūklenājs' *Stāsti un dzejoļi* (Stories and Poems, 1937) with a cover design also by Samsonov. L288 Soviet authors were also published, e.g, Aleksandr Fadeyev's *Razgróm* (The Rout), translated by Kārlis Pelēkais as *Sakāve* (The Rout, 1933) with a somber cover design by Nikolaĭ Alekseev. L289 A yearbook, titled *Latvju kolektivista gada grāmata* (The Latvian Collectivists' Yearbook) and edited by Konrāds Jokums, was also published in 1932 and 1933. L290 Prometejs operated from 1923 until 1937, the year Stalin ordered it shut down and the NKVD began pursuing and shooting the majority of its board of directors.

While Latvian exile publishing in the USSR is admittedly a publishing sidestream, it is nonetheless of interest. Not only because so many of its principals were "eaten by the revolution", but also (despite proscriptions against importing Prometejs' works into Latvia) because a surprising degree of contact was maintained and copies of most Prometejs titles found their way to Riga and beyond in varying quantities.

As yet there is no monographic, bibliographic history of the Latvian publishing houses established by Latvian exiles, although journal articles and online contributions

L290

223　Vladimir Favorskiĭ, a leading wood engraver in favor throughout the Stalinist era.

L291

L292

L293

L294

with publishing history details do exist. It may be some time before such a history is pieced together. In the case of the two publishing houses, Prometejs and Spartaks, archives are not known to have survived in their entirety. The Latvian State Archives, however, do hold a group of Prometejs records from the period 1922 to 1924. Records for the years 1925 to the firm's closing in 1937 have yet to be discovered.

Other publishers on the political left

When one sets out on a highly focused bibliographic excursion, a proper, well-informed guide is crucial. In the introduction, reference is made to the Latvian graphic design historian and collector Prof. Valdis Villerušs and his role in my quest. Discouraging as it was to listen to his comments about the historic destruction of materials and records as well as the absence of a current, highly developed antiquarian book trade, this phase of the project was undertaken nonetheless. There was hope that chance encounters just might lead to finding a few examples of the quite remarkable book design examples that Prof. Villerušs spread before me in that autumn of 2004. A number of the examples shown tentatively confirmed a working hypothesis that much of the "best design" in Interwar Latvia was "on the left", as alluded to in the following chapters on Russian and Yiddish publishing.

My initial acquisitions reaffirmed this hypothesis when, on one of my first bookshop visits, an understanding and helpful antiquarian dealer handed me three poetry titles—all from the same publisher, Tagadne (Our Time), and shown here. L292–L294

The poetry in the three books was probably considered vanguard at that time. The authors, Pāvils Vīlips and Jānis Plaudis, were philosophically left-minded social democrats; both were previously involved with social democratic-oriented periodicals and both survived into the second Soviet era.

Tagadne's *Jauno Trauksme* (Anxiety of the Young, 1930-1931; 6 issues) L291 was a venture that served as the publishing front for these and other young (and sometimes relatively unknown) writers meeting and talking under the bold banner *Trauksme* (Anxiety, 1928-1929; 5 issues), although the content of the Tagadne poems and that of the journal seem more self-conscious than alarming. Possibly the element of social democratic concerns running throughout their various publications may have seemed frightening to some individuals. Plaudis used his own money for this publishing venture and received additional support from Vīlips' wife, Elvīra Bramberga,[224] who also contributed to the initial

224   Interview with Velga Vīlipa, Nov. 2006.
225   Six issues were produced (1928-1929) by Plaudis and his like-minded colleagues Jānis Grots and Pēteris Ķikuts.

cost of publishing Plaudis's short-lived *Trauksme*.[225] The cover designs of all three of the first Tagadne titles were certainly vanguard for Latvia and would have been noticed in any design competition of "late-flowering, constructivist design" appearing at that time in Moscow, Prague, or Berlin. The credited cover designer of the two Vīlips' titles, *21 dzeja* (21 Poems, 1930) L292 and *Romantika autobusā* (Romance on the Bus, 1930), L293 and quite likely the stated designer[226] of the third, Plaudis' *Panama galvā* (Panama Hat, 1930), L294 was one and the same individual, Ernests Kālis, who was certifiably on the political left, as already indicated in the preceding commentary on the periodical *Kreisā Fronte*.

L295

The initial burst of activity for the Tagadne publishing operation existed for a little more than one year, just long enough to publish two more titles. The fourth title, *Imitācija un sirds* (Imitation and the Heart, 1931), was a collection of poems by the communist-oriented Arvīds Grigulis. A true-to-the-party-line writer, Grigulis survived the changing political winds longer than Vīlips and Plaudis, living nearly until the end of the second Soviet occupation and even collecting a number of honors for his ideological loyalty. Mihails Jo was commissioned for the cover design. The fifth and final title in the initial period of Tagadne[227] was *Vīrs ar basām kājām: Naturalas dzejas* (Barefoot Man: Naturalistic Poetry, 1931) L295 by Meinhards Rudzītis, who lived out his life quite successfully in the service of the second Soviet regime. The cover gives no credit to its designer.[228]

At the outset of this undertaking, one hypothesis more or less in line with that of graphic design historians, was that many designers on the political left in most countries tended to maintain at least rudimentary connections[229] with some of the design leaders in greater direct contact, as presented in Matthew S. Witkovsky's compilation, *Avant-Garde Art in Everyday Life: Early-Twentieth-Century European Modernism*.[230] Such contact has been repeatedly demonstrated in the writings and exhibitions referred to in the chapter on Russian publishing. Streams of influence from Moscow-Leningrad, Berlin, Prague, and several other capitals were crossing and recrossing as the result of travel, regional exhibitions, and the official (and unofficial) book trade.

Even a cursory survey of book and periodical publications shows a similar *penchant* among politically left Latvian designers for flat colors, bold shapes, stark geometrical elements, sans-serif typography, and photomontage. The design of these few Tagadne titles and several issues of *Kreisā Fronte* are easily comparable to almost any showing of graphic vanguard work from Poland, Czechoslovakia, the USSR, and other European countries, thereby indicating to some degree that Riga's left designers were in touch with design innovation and trends beyond Latvia's borders.

Signāls (Signal, 1928-1930),[231] a journal styled as a social democratic student journal and quasi-official journal of the Riga People's College had a shifting team of editors and contributors self-identified as Marxist, including Voldemārs Branks, Kārlis Dēķens, Arvīds Grigulis, Fricis Rokpelnis, Arnolds Serdants, Edgars Šillers, and Ādolfs Talcis among others. All of those named except Dēķens and Šillers survived and even thrived

226 Although credited to "G. Stuba", this is likely a pseudonym. The design and typography point to Ernests Kālis.
227 Tagadne was revived in 1934 for the publication of more poems by Grigulis, *Nogurušo namā* (The House of the Tired) with cover design and illustrations by Niklāvs Strunke.
228 A second book of poems by Plaudis, *Bada dziesmas* (Hunger Songs), was announced by Tagadne in 1932 but a search for a copy to examine has so far been unsuccessful.
229 Interviews with Steven Heller and Jürgen Holstein, Dec. 2006.
230 (Chicago and New Haven: Art Institute of Chicago and Yale University Press, 2011)
231 There appear to be 17 issues all told before it expired.

L296

L297

L298

L299

L300

L301

L302

L303

L304

in the various political occupations of Latvia, living out relatively normal life spans. The contributions to *Signāls* ranged from theoretical ramblings to poetry, reports from other countries, cultural criticism, book reviews, and from time to time even humor, something not found in *Kreisā Fronte*.

The first two years of *Signāls* were characterized by plodding content but out-of-the-ordinary covers by different hands, e.g., V. Leimanis L296, Alfrēds Rentovics, and Elza Zandersone, L297 who were perhaps students at the College.[232] Zandersone's color linocut design for the first issue echoed the Czech Devětsil-style in its linocut typography—a commendable start toward introducing a fresh, although short-lived, design concept. Of the two linocut covers by part-time set designer Jānis Aižens, his design for the April 1929 issue was decidedly more of an attention-getter than Zandersone's design. L298 By February 1929 the 24-year-old Andrejs Grigelis began designing covers, bringing some degree of mainstream European vanguard style to these issues. But as these covers are unsigned, this is only speculation based on characteristics typical of his work.[233] For an idea of Grigelis' signed work, three covers are shown here. L299–L301

Grigelis seemed to have more time to spend with the journal in 1929 and possibly began serving as *de facto* art director, judging from the regular appearance of his friends' original wood- and linocut illustrations, which were not necessarily commissioned for the journal. Illustrators whose work was shown included Jānis Aižens, who also wrote for the journal as well as contributed poetry and the above-mentioned cover;[234] Ernests Akolovs; Ādolfs Girdvoins;[235] Andrejs Grigelis; Aleksandrs Junkers; Vilis Mednis, the only artist mentioned of the covers examined who contributed a wood engraving rather than linocut; and Pauls Šterns. As to the quality of the linocut illustrations, the majority appear to be works by those self-taught in the medium with the exception of Girdvoins, although his one illustration was a linocut reprinted from *Dumpīgā grāmata* (The Rebellious Book), a series of stories by Ādolfs Talcis. In the final months of publication, the typographer and graphic designer Jānis Šneiders was asked to provide a photomontage cover for the next to the last issue commemorating the 1905 revolution and establishment of the Riga Social Democratic Committee. L304

For positive comparison with Grigelis' *Signāls* covers and the covers by E. Kālis for *Kreisā Fronte,* one needs to look at another journal of the period, *Domas* (Thoughts). This journal, also with a social-democratic orientation, drew the *Signāls* readers, although many were probably already among its readership. *Domas* was a cultural journal more sophisticated in tone and appearance than *Signāls.* Its editorial group consistently sought a wider range of political and literary thought and from writers working in a less tendentious style than those appearing in *Signāls.* There had been cross contributions, however, between the journals from a number of writers.

Although the majority of the contributions to *Domas* were by Latvians, from time to time there were translations from various non-Baltic writers. For example, selections from

---

232 It is only speculation that the designers were students as they do not appear in standard reference works of period artists.

233 The design for Sept. 1929 is credited to Grigelis; Nov. 1929 is not, but shows his hand; Feb. 1930 is credited to him while May 1930 is not, yet the design appears to be his style. The July 1930 issue L302 bears similarity to Grigelis, yet is credited to Arvēds Segliņš. No. 3 1930 is not identified, L303 yet has the late-constructivist style of Grigelis and Segliņš.

234 *Signāls*, No. 2, Oct. 1929, p. 50.

235 One linocut illustration reprinted in No. 2, Nov. 1930, from Ā. Talcis' *Dumpīgā grāmata*.

L305

L306

L307

the writings of Sergei Tretiakov and Henri Barbusse (both in 1932), Mikhail Sholokhov (in 1933), and even a selection from Michael Gold's celebrated account of Jewish life among the poor in New York City, *Jews Without Money*.[236] There were also four poems by Langston Hughes, the leading poet of the Harlem Renaissance.[237] Both the Gold and Hughes titles from which selections had been excerpted had recently been published, a further indication of cultural interconnections in that era. Although it is surprising that Gold's *Jews without Money*[238] was not published in book form in at least one of the major languages of Latvia, in light of its being available in the USSR and Germany already by 1931,[239] among other European countries. The overtly Marxist contributors to *Domas*—and the fact that the journal was a voice for social democracy—undoubtedly had something to do with its close by the Ulmanis regime in May 1934.

For a brief period at the end of its publication (1931/1932), *Domas* covers were typographically bold with late-constructivist imagery in flat color, exhibiting a diffuse tie to contemporary European vanguard design movements. L305, L306 While the designers for the covers prior to 1931 are not specifically cited, Niklāvs Strunke is credited for the two styles used for the 1931 covers,[240] yet his text illustrations in these issues are not credited while Aleksandrs Junkers' woodcut illustrations are.

It is possible that Kārlis Bušs designed the covers for the 1932 issues, although the crediting terminology is vague. In 1933 the policy returned to uncredited cover design. L307

While the number of short-lived, left-oriented publishers is as daunting as the number of self-published left-oriented writers, unusually interesting or notable designs turned out to be less frequent than the auspicious discoveries at the beginning of this search led one to expect. In discussing the early years of the 1920s, we have already introduced two publishers on the political left—one communist, Daile un Darbs, and one social democratic, Kultūras Balss. Citing these two and commenting on their programs and the look of their books allowed preliminary indication of design variety and content attached to a movement and time period. The relative size and publishing programs of these two houses deserved such an approach.

For a production sampling from the smaller, left-oriented publishing houses, a sequence of representative titles with brief comment will be sufficient to give some indication of content and design.

Once again we begin at the beginning, in the year 1919. The "hard" Latvian left, waiting in the wings in Moscow and eager to push its way to the forefront of discussion in a soon-to-be-established Latvian state, chose a publication genre on which most households in the Latvian lands depended—the calendar.[241] What better means of propaganda when a dearth of books exists! Thus, *Strahdneeku kalendars, 1919* (Workers' Calendar, 1919)[242] was

---

236   No. 6, 1931, pp. 442-448 (translated by Jānis Plaudis) as well as in Russian in *Nord-Ost* No. 7, 1932 (translated by A. Makov).

237   No. 10, 1933.

238   First published in New York in 1930 by Horace Liveright with illustrations by Howard Simon.

239   Published by Gos. izd. khudozh. lit. (Moscow, 1931) and Neuer Deutscher Verlag (Berlin, 1931).

240   A reviewer in *Latvijas Grāmatrūpniecības Apskats* (No. 36, 1931, p. 139) did not share our view, giving Strunke's design a backhanded compliment indicating its being "loud enough.. [but] such an accordion of abstractions would fit better on a poster for a paint factory than [the cover of] a literary journal."

241   The book-calendar has been a form with particular appeal to Latvians. An incontrovertible indication is a bibliographical project identifying all *kalendāri* published since the first one appeared in Latvia in 1758 up to 1919. Published as *Latviešu kalendāri*, editor-in-chief Līga Krūmiņa, assisted by Māra Kadiķe, Gunita Štāle, and Dzintra Zaķe, 3 vols. (Riga: Latvijas Akadēmiskā bibliotēka, 2004).

242   (Maskava: Latviešu Nacionālo lietu komisariāta Kultūras un izglītības nodaļas izdevums, 1918). pp. 172, [3].

L308

L309

conceived as a means of spreading and keeping the idea of revolution alive with birthdays and death years of revolutionary forerunners or events that, as the cover's heading enjoins, would lead the "Proletariat of the World, [to] Unite!" L308 The publisher—the Culture and Education Department of the Commission of Latvian National Affairs—was based in Moscow but staffed by Latvian activists. The content of 175 pages opens with portraits of Lenin and Marx facing each other, followed by a title page and Latvian lyrics for the *Internationale*. The calendar portion follows with "name days" and dates and events each month that the editors thought to be of possible interest to the "proletariat". If one is interested in a thumbnail sketch of revolutionary events with a Baltic emphasis before 1919 (*caveat lector*), this might be one place to look.

Following the "Russian Socialist Federative Soviet Republic's Constitution (Basic Law)", the reader could choose among articles by the communist Pēteris Stučka, the social democrat activist Fricis Roziņš, or biographical sketches of Marx and Engels, many words from Lenin (16½ pages), or many words *about* Lenin (16½ pages). If the reader made it that far, sketches about Karl Liebknecht and Stučka awaited and then, before turning in for the night, a sure soporific: Latvian workers' cultural organizations in Russia dispersed throughout the central part of the country. The back wrapper offered 13 in-print titles by, among others, the Dutch sociologist and socialist poet Henriette Roland Holst van der Schalk together with titles by Nikolai Bukharin and the Latvian journalist Pauls Vīksne. Titles in preparation ranged from writings by Rainis to Karl Kautsky.

This *Strahdneeku kalendars*, with its lack of inviting external and internal typography, offers a sharp contrast to another close-in-time publication that the present-day art critic Jānis Borgs referred to as "one of Latvia's few contributions to political Dadaism dressed in drama",[243] namely, Linards Laicens and Leons Paegle's *Panama*,[244] L309 the title of which

---

243   Interview, May 2008.
244   Printed in 1922 by Progress Printers; no publisher given.

L310

L311

is a Latvian term for a "hodge-podge" rather than a reference to the country of the famous isthmus. The slogans around the cover give some hint about "life as it is" to the potential audience of these cinematically presented chapters, summarizing the world view of the authors. Here limned for the reader are criminal speculators and government officials, political partisans, and prison escapees—"Cinema events from countries small, young, and sick", as the cover announces. The work in seven parts with 197 scenes plus intermissions gives some indication that it may have been planned on the order of a *Sprechchor*, a dramatic style popular with the German-speaking left of the Weimar era. This ephemeral document contains a sizeable dollop of tongue-in-cheek wit appropriate to the time and a fair amount of Dada-esque prose, as Borgs indicated. The "10,000 meters, only 30 rubles" (titling on the cover) is, like much of the content, an allusion lost in history, at least likely lost to many present-day readers.

Was this publication a "hit"? At the time of publication, Kārlis Zariņš reviewed the work in the literary journal *Ritums*[245] and concluded: "Unfortunately, nothing notable happens [in the drama]." But that could be confidently said of much European performance art of the period's vanguard. Zariņš at least gives Laicens credit for being a "serious poet". The censor assigned to pass judgment on its suitability for the general public apparently had less enthusiasm for the work declaring that "the aim of Laicens and Paegle [is] to propagate socialism... the work [is] a direct attack on the civic order."[246] The typographer who laid out the cover and the text pages is under debate. Some have suggested Niklāvs Strunke; others have suggested that Laicens worked directly with the compositor.

While the political left's production of pamphlets, books, and periodicals between 1922 and 1927 has been represented by the publishers and designers in the preceding pages, there are, of course, others. Three additional titles are shown here as they are from a design standpoint in the "too good to miss" category. All were designed by an artist for multiple mediums, Jānis Liepiņš, who not only studied at the major Imperial Russian schools in Kazan and St. Petersburg but also traveled and studied widely in Germany and France. Regardless of medium, his surviving work is a clear demonstration of his ability to creatively synthesize elements from various sources, resulting in a fresh concept, whether in the decorative arts, painting, or graphic design. Solidly residing within the small circle of Latvian cubists working in oil, his strength in this medium can be seen in *Kubisms Latvijas māksla* (Cubism in Latvian Art).[247] An example of his style in linocut is a print from 1920—heavy but cubist nonetheless—selected by Velta Lapacinska for her survey of Latvian linocut. L310, L311 The "Left Workers and Farmers" parliamentary election posters selected by Anšlavs Eglītis for illustration in an essay[248] provide a better indication of Liepiņš graphic style and artistic strength. No catalogue of his book cover designs has been made but one can see the promise in three book cover designs: Laicens' *Mebeliga Riga un peelikumi* (Furnished Riga and a Supplement), illustrated earlier in the section on Daile un Darbs publishing house; Laicens' *Laimes putns* (Firebird)[249] L312; and the cover for the Leons Paegle translation into Latvian of Aleksandr Blok's poem *The Twelve*,[250] reproduced in the Russian-language chapter. R18

245   No. 10, 1922, p. 788.
246   See Paeglis, J. *Kas bija liegts pirmās republikas lasītājiem?* (Riga: Zinātne, 1996), p. 44.
247   Essays: Māra Lāce, Dace Lamberga, Laila Bremša, and Zigurds Konstants (Riga: Neputns, 2002), pp. 94–95.
248   "Latviešu revolucionāri demokratiskā karikatūra" in *Latviešu tēlotāja māksla*, vol. 4 (Riga: Latvijas Valsts izdevniecība, 1962), p. 107.
249   (Riga: Rīgas mākslinieku grupa, 1924).
250   (Riga: Gulbis, 1923).

L313

L312

1927 witnessed the inaugural exhibition of book design and book production in the First Republic. The orga-
nizing committee was drawn from members of the Latvian
Book Publishers' Association, the Book Industry Association, Printing Industry Association, and the Booksellers Association.[251] The exhibition handbook gives a reasonably
clear indication of the selecting committee's aesthetic sensibilities, politics, and prejudices. The show was obviously
not about "the 50 most beautiful books" or a demonstration
of language diversity in Latvia's book publishing culture.
Primarily an industry exposition, it was a show for Latvian
and regional book industry partners and producers to exhibit what had been accomplished since independence.

Small publishers were obviously not considered part
of the picture. The catalog shows no representation of
small publishers of *belles lettres* nor small publishers on the political left. Judging from
an examination of the titles listed in the catalog, there did not seem to be well-designed
or otherwise distinguished examples of self-published works. Yiddish- and Russian-language publishers were excluded, even though Russian-language publishers already had
a respectable number of titles on the market by "show time" and Yiddish-language publishers certainly had produced several books of design and typographic note. In short, it
was an exposition for mainstream publishers, producers, and distributors and possibly
held in the Grāmatrūpnieku zāle (Book-printers' Hall), which also served for general
public gatherings and social events such as the "Grandiose Ball" advertised in a hastily
printed, mid 1920s poster designed by D. Bods. L313

There was, however, one outside-the-mainstream publisher represented in this exposition, namely, Nākotnes Kultūra, presented as printer and publisher. Of the five books
in its display and examples printed for others, two of its titles had a slight, left-of-center
slant: *Mūsu revolūcijas varoņi* (The Heroes of our Revolution) by Pēteris Birkerts and
Kārlis Dziļleja's *Tiesa un taisnība* (Justice and Truth). But neither of these two titles had
distinguished typography or illustrated covers, although another, (*Dumpīgā grāmata*,

251   *Vadonis: Izstāde Lietišķā grafika Latvijā, 1927* (Riga: 1928).

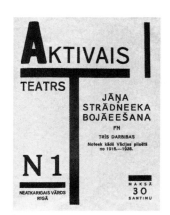

L314

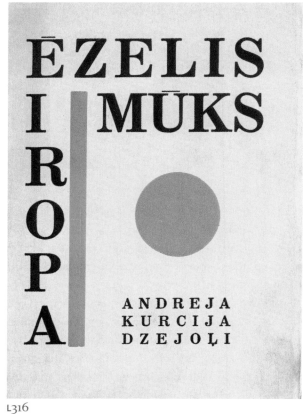

L316

discussed) does have a cover and illustrated content of more than passing graphic interest. One might imagine that the prime source of income for Nākotnes Kultūra was from its role as the printing-publishing arm of the cooperative movement in Latvia and its journal *Kooperators* (1926-1934). Nākotnes Kultūra also exhibited another journal that it published, *Lāčplēsis*.[252]

Two additional 1920s titles—both from another publisher on the left—deserve comment not only because of cover design interest, but also their content and relative scarcity. The publisher, Neatkarīgais Vārds (Independent Word), did not issue many titles; what it did publish, for one reason or another, resulted in confiscation. Its short-lived series *Aktivais Teatrs* (Activist Theater),[253] L314 with cover designs echoing Ivan Kliun's design for the MAF[254] poetry series pamphlets, L315 began publication with *Jāņa Strādnieka bojāeešana* (The Destruction of John the Worker), a brief political drama bound to irritate politically conservative citizens. This was followed by yet another title to irritate them even more, *Baņķeera rīkojums* (Banker's Order), three one-act plays by Osip Brik, Linards Laicens, and Vladimir Mayakovsky. The publisher's plan was to continue with works by Laicens, Ivan Goll, Andrejs Kurcijs, Ernst Toller, and others, add to their program, and sponsor performers traveling around to small performance spaces in towns and improvised stages in the country-side. The idea was to present "contemporary themes", not realistic themes in the Stanislavsky sense but more artistic as in the Meyerhold tradition.[255] The confiscation experience was discouraging and the series ended shortly after the titles appeared. The publisher, however, did follow with *Ēzelis, mūks, Eiropa* (Donkey, Monk, Europe). L316 Kurcijs' effort at what might be called "free verse" did not wear well with the years and lacked the felicitous

L315

---

252   A *Kalevala*-like poem published in 1888 giving the Latvian people a distinctive national epic. Lāčplēsis, a mythic bear-slaying, larger-than-life figure is the central element in Andrejs Pumpurs' poem and Rainis' drama *Fire and Night*.
253   In an interview in October 2005, Velga Vīlipa stated that it was an "activist theatre traveling one step ahead of the authorities" for a brief period. Antonija Āboliņa, one of the traveling performers with Aktivais Teatrs, had brought the publication to Velga Vīlipa's mother.
254   Moscow Association of Futurists was initiated in 1922 by V. Mayakovsky, Nikolaï Aseev, and others.
255   Interview with Velga Vīlipa, October 2005.

L317

L318

style often encountered in some of his earlier works.[256] This title suffered a confiscation fate like that of the publisher's other titles. No designer is given, although it has an "Ernests Kālis look".

A short poem from the collection, "Sakko un Vancetti piemiņai" (Remembering Sacco and Vanzetti), in an approximate translation without comment, follows:[257]

Poor friends
Sitting down courageously in the executioner's electric-chair!
About the future, no one need mourn.
Know
In your hearts there's a stronger current;
Millions and millions of volts
Of future tensions
See!
It will destroy the countries of the world;
But by workers' hands
The world will be built anew!

The 1930s saw many more leftist publications in Latvia and certainly some of the more memorable designs, beginning with the Nākotnes Kultūra title *Dumpīgā grāmata: Stāsti un feļetoni*[258] (The Rebellious Book: Stories and Feuilletons) by Ādolfs Talcis L317 with linocut illustrations L318 and possibly the cover design by Ādolfs Girdvoins.[259] One

256 Read out loud in translation to this writer (Jan. 2007).
257 Two Italian laborers and anarchists convicted of murder and payroll theft in 1920 and subsequently executed in 1927, resulting in a *cause célèbre* and inspiring songs, poems, and essays for two generations of the European and American left. Latter-day re-examination of evidence points to a miscarriage of justice.
258 (Riga: Nākotnes Kultūra, 1930).
259 Ādolfs Girdvoins remains an elusive figure. Little biographical information is available other than a birth date of January 22, 1908, and that he studied design and painting at the People's College of Riga. See Lapacinska's *Linogriezums latviešu tēlotājā māksla*, p. 252. Girdvoins was expelled from the Zaļā Vārna artists' group in 1932 for being "passive" and not participating in an exhibition in Jelgava.

L319

L320

L321

L322

L323

L324

L325

might wonder if Girdvoins, or whoever designed the cover, had drawn inspiration from the design for Mayakovsky's *Stikhi o Revoliutsiĭ* (Poems on Revolution),[260] published seven years earlier and likely circulated in Riga. L319 In this compilation Talcis[261] is at his vitriolic best in tirades against the established church, corrupt civil servants, crooked politicians, and other targets appealing to a left-oriented reader.

1930 was also the year that saw publication of the First Republic's most refined example of what surely could be called "Latvian vanguard book design", Linards Laicens' *Kliedzošie korpusi* (The Walls Cry Out, fotomontage by E. Kālis), a fictionalized account of the 1905 revolution in Latvian lands during which a number of participants were jailed and executed. First appearing in serial form in *Kreisā Fronte* (1927), it was translated into Russian and first published in book form in the USSR with a cover design by Boris Tatarinov.[262] L320 The Latvian edition in book form was designed by Ernests Kālis, the inhouse designer for *Kreisā Fronte*, which was also the book's publisher, and was one of

260   (Moscow: Krasnaia Nov', 1923).
261   Talcis served in the Soviet Army, was believed killed by German forces but survived, spent time as a prisoner, and was repressed during the second Soviet occupation until agreeing to collaborate by traveling abroad to convince Latvian exiles to return to Soviet Latvia. He lived a political balancing act until his death in 1983.
262   Published by Priboi in Leningrad (1929 and 1930) in two parts as volume three of *Izbrannie Proizvedenia*.

at least two titles published with the journal's imprint.[263] L321 Another *Kreisā Fronte* title worth mentioning for the austerity of its cover and title page design is *Kameras* (Prison Cells, 1929). This little book with its two stories on a political-prisoner theme, again by Laicens, was likely designed by Kālis but with Laicens as art director, given Laicens' penchant for understated design. L322

Two titles from 1931 with quite different covers of interest were both published by the Darba Muzejs (Museum of Labor), a short-lived institution and a victim of changes in public policy taking place with the coming of the Ulmanis regime. The Museum of Labor was decidedly social democratic in outlook and took its educational role seriously, as indicated by the titles of works shown here: Ansis Cielavs' *Racionālizācija un strādniecība* (Rationalization and Labor) L324 and Andrejs Jablonskis' *Arodkustība Latvijā* (Latvia's Trade Union Movement).[264] L325 Unfortunately, the cover designers are not credited, which does not speak well for a museum ostensibly celebrating the worker and a labor movement with presumed interest in recognizing a laborer's work. The Workers' Temperance Association, however, did credit Ernests Kālis for his photomontage cover for its 1931 annual. L326

L326

Distinctly different examples of leftist design appeared in 1932 on three titles and also merit inclusion for their content. The illustrative forms are wood-engraved and woodcut social realism, austere typography, and a dense typographic design. All three design approaches were employed by leftist designers throughout the era.

The woodcut realism of Kārlis Bušs' cover and internal illustrations for Pāvils Vīlips' *Poēma par Annu Lazdu un melno runci* (A Long Poem about Anna Lazda and the Black Tomcat) is a somewhat eccentric inclusion, being a "bourgeois concept", i.e., a limited edition. Other than its interesting cover design, the qualification for inclusion is the general political view of the collaborators. Bušs was a Communist Party member who spent the Ulmanis years in prison; Vīlips was a far-left social democrat. This work also qualifies for inclusion by virtue of its publisher, Avanti, the publisher of the banned, communist, illustrated periodical *Informators*, L327 to which Bušs contributed. The cover shown appropriates a John Heartfield photomontage from a 1932 issue of the *Arbeiter Illustrierte Zeitung* (Worker's Illustrated Newspaper).[265]

Poēma par Annu Lazdu un melno runci appeared with two cover designs: one with the author and title framed around a single-color printing of the illustration facing right. (The

L327

---

263 A second title by Laicens, *Aziats: dzejoļi, saucieni, dialogi* (The Asian: Poems, Cries, Dialogues, 1930), was advertised in *Kreisā Fronte* at the same time as Laicens' *Kameras* and carried the imprint of Latvju Kultūra. L323
264 Jablonskis, a known communist, was head of the Latvian health insurance organization and, for a time, one of the editors of the journal *Latvijas Grāmatrūpnieks* (Latvian Book-printers, 1920-1934).
265 The issue for August 28, 1932, with the caption: "Wollt ihr wieder fallen, damit die Aktien steigen?!" (Do you want to be killed again so that stocks can rise?!)

L328

L329

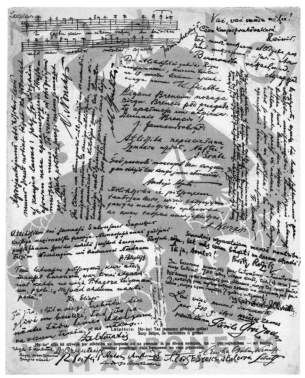

L330

L332

cover text is printed letterpress while the text and internal illustrations seem to have been printed by offset.) L328, L329 A second version of the cover is of a three-color illustration printed directly from the linocuts with no frame and no titling and with the cover illustration reversed. L330 No edition size is provided although it was likely small, given the high quality of the text paper and the manner of printing for the second cover.

L331

In the chapter on Russian-language publishing mention is made of a Russian-language journal for young Russian writers in Latvia, *Nord-Ost*. This special-audience journal on the political left also published a pamphlet or two, including this third title from 1932. Note that this publication appears in Latvian, unlike the publishing company's periodical. The reason was probably the publisher's hope of reaching a larger audience with its important, anti-war theme. The title in English translation, *Kira Wants to Play War*, leads one directly into the sobering but sarcastic tone of the drama. L331 Notice the anti-war slogans incorporated into the wrappers' running bands of text.[266]

The author's eccentric life and sad end are part of Latvian literary legend. Austra Ozoliņa-Krauze was educated as a lawyer at the university in Bern. While living in Switzerland, she became involved with the small Latvian community in exile there, her most notable association being with Latvia's renowned writer Rainis.

Back in Riga, Ozoliņa-Krauze found work writing for various publications, including the literary-satirical paper *Ho-Ho* to which, in an early issue,[267] she contributed the poem "Imantas pēcniekiem" (To the Descendents of Imanta [a Latvian hero]). L332 She also contributed to the periodicals *Domas* and *Nord-Ost*. The editors of the latter thought her previously mentioned play was in keeping with their editorial plan even though they decided to publish it in Latvian rather than Russian. She also collaborated with the renowned activist actress Marija Leiko[268] in writing the play "Marija Vaļevska" (1934), which was censored.

L333

Ozoliņa-Krauze's tendency toward personal theatricality may have had something to do with her trying her hand at being a double agent and then taking the even riskier step up (or down) to "triple-agenthood", so the story goes. But circumstances closed in on her and, in 1941, she took her life when the German Army moved into Latvia.

Another leftist writer of considerable energy, Pēters Zars, i.e., Indriķis Lēmanis, was a protégé of Linards Laicens and an uncompromising proletarian writer and storyteller. He could count on his books being confiscated almost upon publication because of the explicit and implied goals in his writing, for example, "victory of the proletariat over the bourgeois culture". Lēmanis wrote under the "Pēters Zars" pseudonym until the Ulmanis regime came to power, although it is hard to imagine that anyone in the government censorship offices had any doubt about his identity.[269] Three of his books of stories, published one after the other, all carry the same basic theme. The Semafors imprint for the first title, *Strādnieku dzīve* (A Worker's Life, 1932), L333 and the second, *Mašīnas*

---

266 An uncredited design, although likely one of the several *Nord-Ost* designers. Looking at design styles in the two *Nord-Ost* formats, a Romans Suta and Isaak Sherman collaboration seems plausible.
267 The cover of issue No. 5 shows Austra Ozoliņa's signature (lower right).
268 With censorship of the play and a ban on its being staged, Leiko left for Moscow and became yet another one of the ill-fated Latvian exiles in the USSR. She hung herself in Moscow's Butirku prison in 1938 rather than face execution.
269 At age 18, Lēmanis was involved in *Jaunais Komunārs*, an underground organization, and he paid for this adventure by sitting in prison from 1924 to 1928 for his illegal activities. After prison he worked for a time as a colporteur for the leftist bookshop "Laikmets". He was involved with the illegal Society of Revolutionary Writers and Artists and spent World War II in the Soviet Army. During the second Soviet occupation he enjoyed some 15 years in the Latvian Radio and Television organization.

L334

L335

L338

L336

L337

(Machines, 1933), L334 with its foreword by Laicens, were part of a three-title effort concluding with *Māte* (Mother, 1934), L335 which he published himself with a loan from the "Laikmets" bookshop.[270] The designer of the first title is unknown or at least uncredited. The revolutionary graphic designer Augusts Pupa (who contributed linocut illustrations to such journals as *Domas*, *Tribīne*, *Vienotā Fronte*, and *Informators*) produced the cover designs for the other two titles. Pupa's clean and subdued "proletarian-constructivist" approach compares favorably with Romans Suta's approach to the cover design for the lyrics of Pēteris Ķikuts' *Mašīna: Poēma* (The Machine: A Poem).[271] L336

"Laikmets" (The Age [as in "epoch" or "era"]) was, understandably, a popular name for periodicals and book publishers in the First Republic. One book publisher operating under the name Laikmets may have had a slight sympathy towards the political left within its editorial staff, if one considers that among the 21 titles it published between 1925 and 1936, five were by the decidedly leftist poet Andrejs Kurcijs, including one of his several excursions into art theory *Par mākslu* (On Art; Berlin, 1932) L337 with its uncredited cover design. Another example of a Laikmets title, *Darba tempi PSRS smagajā industrijā* (The Pace of Work in the USSR's Heavy Industry, 1933), L338 is indicated as number two in the series "Sabiedriski zinātniskā bibliotēka" (Social Science Library). The author Kārlis Ozoliņš (of the several writers by this name, possibly the social democratic

270   See Ingrīda Sokolova's introduction to Lēmanis' *Selected Works* in 2 volumes, vol. 1 (Riga: Liesma, 1967), p. 9.
271   (Riga: Jaunās Sliedes, 1930).

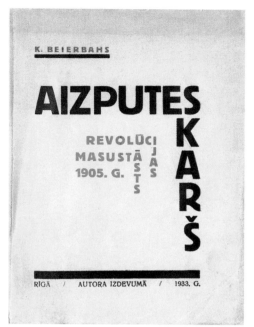

L339

L340

editor Ozoliņš) and Kurcijs add a bit of color among the other authors with their relatively innocuous-sounding Laikmets books. The Ozoliņš title does not appear in the National Library of Latvia catalog. It is therefore difficult to know if it might have been grouped with other such Laikmets titles or if further bibliographical research might show it to be yet another publisher using the same name. The subject matter and the style of the uncredited linocut cover illustration is more in keeping with a left-of-center publisher's list. Of course, there is the possibility it might have been a late-appearing title from the pamphlet-publishing division of the illegal newspaper *Laikmets* published in 1928.[272]

One additional title with a left-oriented theme and tied to Laikmets through commission is Kārlis Beierbahs'[273] *Aizputes karš: Revolūcijas masu stāsts 1905. g.* (The Aizpute[274] War: The Revolution Story of the Masses, 1905; 1933), L339 published privately by Beierbahs, who wrote three other books, two of which were also published privately and one appearing under the Daile un Darbs imprint. The cover designer for the title shown here is not credited.

The most interesting (and earliest) *Laikmets* item has been left until last.[275] An important feature of this journal[276] L340 is its clear demonstration of Riga's artists moving about in other European capitals and absorbing trends, while at the same time bringing members of the art community of Riga into productive contact with Western Europeans, in this case, those living in Berlin. The editorial group that initiated the journal evidently reached out to the progressive Berlin-Potsdam publisher Gustav Kiepenheuer and his

272   Only four issues published under that title and four additional issues in the same year with modified titling, presumably to confuse would-be censors.
273   Also spelled "Beierbachs."
274   A Latvian town (formerly Hasenpoth) in the Liepāja region.
275   Three of this periodical's four issues include contributions by Kurcijs, demonstrating that his writings were of general importance, not just of interest to the left-oriented reader.
276   All issues were published in 1923.

L341

connections for its needed production funds and a distribution network. For the first issue, managing editor Arnolds Dzirkalis together with Kārlis Zāle provided Europeans a tantalizing glimpse of "Latvian culture", for example, the vitality of Jēkabs Kazaks' poster (1920). L341 For Latvians at home, the journal provided a chance to see reproductions of the work of Juan Gris, Fernand Léger, and Georges Braque. From an art history standpoint perhaps the most important contribution in the first issue is Kurcijs' essay "Aktīvisms" (Activism), which Janet Zmoroczek considers to be "one of the few articulated Latvian modernist manifestos" in which Kurcijs "derived the terminology of 'activism'... from the German literary trend and complemented it with the artistic principles of Léger".[277] A contribution by the Berlin art historian Carl Einstein on Léger was included in this same issue.

The second issue continues in the direction of introducing Western European ideas in art to Latvians with an illustrated article by Ivan Goll on cubism, while the Berlin art critic Paul Westheim comments on the art of Kārlis Zālītis. The mystical "sound and color" poet and novelist Andrei Bely contributed a piece on the "Theory of Words", and concluding this issue is a poem by Laicens. Photos of works by Aleksandr Archipenko, Rudolf Belling, Jacques Lipchitz, and Picasso, among others, are included. The third and fourth issues continued this heady fare with several of the same writers but adding the German expressionist architect Hans Poelzig's contribution on the "New Architecture in Germany", Charlie Chaplin writing about his brand of humor, another article by Kurcijs titled "Activism and Kantianism", and a review by Ivan Puni. More reproductions show work by the Latvians Ludolfs Liberts, Jūlijs Madernieks, Voldemārs Matvejs (i.e., Vladimir Markov), and Konrāds Ubāns together with Amédée Ozenfant and Enrico Prampolini, among others. *Laikmets* is a solid candidate, with all the right "look" in design and content, for inclusion in any catalog of First Republic vanguard journals. It is regrettable that a file does not seem to have found its way into the major art reference libraries of Western Europe or America or, if so, has not been recognized and appropriately cataloged.

Now for a clutch of middle- and far-left publications, some of which have cover and internal design of considerable interest. We begin with Marksistu Klubs (Marxist Club), a social democratic rather than revolutionary organization. When *Signāls* was discontinued, the publishing program of the Marxist Club carried on with Edgars Šillers as guide, who moved from his editorial role at *Signāls* into that of publications editor for the Club with its primary concern of making available Latvian translations of publications by Marx as well as writings on Marxist theory. While not the house designer, Romans Suta designed at least two titles noteworthy for their appearance, particularly when the covers are viewed as a whole. These titles are also among the few from the First Republic to receive a full-cover treatment, i.e., more than a simple wrap-around line. The best-known and often reproduced (but unfortunately without showing the full cover) is Kārlis Ozoliņš' *Divas revolūcijas: Kā muižniecību: Kā Latvija cēlās, 1917-1920* (Two Revolutions: War with the Nobility: The Origins of Latvia, 1917-1920; 1934). L342

Requiring similar display for seeing Suta's full-cover treatment is volume one of *Kapitālisms un sociālisms pēc pasaules kara* (Capitalism and Socialism after the World War), L343 subtitled *Pareiza un nepareiza racionālizācija* (Rationalization and Faulty Rationalization, 1933).[278] Another title designed by Romans Suta, also published in 1933, was not

277 See her "Baltic States" in Stephen Bury, ed. *Breaking the Rules* (London: British Library, 2007), p. 69.
278 This appears to be the only Latvian translation of Otto Bauer's larger commentary on socialism and capitalism and World War I. Dr. Bauer was a leading Austrian social democrat and prolific Marxist ideologue. The translator, Fricis Menders (1885-1971), was a prominent Latvian social democrat.

L342

L343

quite so successful from a design standpoint. *Markss un marksisms: rakstu krājums* (Marx and Marxism: A Collection of Articles) L344 was given a curiously lyrical, calligraphic cover possibly to put the potential reader into a good mood for reading this cornucopia of articles on just about every subject a dedicated Marxist might, should, or possibly even want to read on the weekend. (The pieces are mercifully short—all 21 of them.) Many of the contributors once wrote for *Signāls*.

L344

The publishing efforts of Šillers (and most social democratic publishers on the far left of the movement) came to an end with the Kārlis Ulmanis government takeover in the spring of 1934. A telling public speech reprinted in the March 5, 1934, issue of *International Press Correspondence*[279] by a spokesman for the Latvian Communist Party gives some hint as to the tension between the LCP and the social democratic "left", to say nothing of the revealing, public utterances by the Communist "left":

"In face of the growing revolutionary movement in town and village the Latvian bourgeoisie, which has gone completely bankrupt in the struggle against the results of the crisis and is filled with frenzied hatred against the USSR, is forgetting its historic antagonism to the German barons and is throwing itself into the arms of fascist Germany. For the toilers of Latvia, a bloody fascist dictatorship and a war against the USSR have become a real menace for the near future. This menace is increased by the fact that the Latvian bourgeoisie still has a very strong social basis in the form of social democracy. Latvian social democracy belongs to the so-called left wing of the Second International. Utilizing cunning left maneuvers, it has succeeded in preserving its influence among considerable sections of the Latvian proletariat. Our party intensified the struggle against social fascism, exposing its 'left' maneuvers."

Another publication further to the left than *Signāls* was the almanac *Virziens* (Direction),[280] which had the original intent of being a cultural yearbook providing "young

---

279   The spokesman for *Inprecor*, the then weekly voice of the Third International, was an individual who signed simply "Comrade Krause".
280   Published by the General Commission of Jaunā Kultūra.

L345

L346

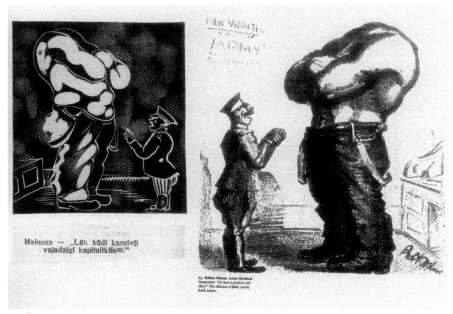

L348

L349

workers" with literature, art, and some idea of the cultural activities engaged in by "young workers" in other countries, i.e., the groups of radicalized young people on the left in other industrialized nations. The first issue (1933) L345, L346 in annual format contains reports on leftist political activity in Lithuania, Finland, Poland, The Netherlands, Japan, China, and Germany, with the longest report on the "successes" taking place in the USSR.

The linocut illustrations and the cover design were the work of Voldemārs Meija, L347 who seems to have been overlooked by the editors of fundamental art reference works. Meija's woodcut illustration with a translation of the original English caption "At last, a perfect soldier!" shown here was an uncredited derivation of an often-reproduced lithograph by Robert Minor, first appearing in the American communist periodical *The Masses*.[281] L348 One thousand copies of this issue of *Virziens* were produced.

The following year, 1934, *Virziens* was transformed into a more frequently appearing periodical, increasing the number of copies published from 1,000 to 1,200 and publishing a combined issue in January, with a new cover L349 and text linocut illustrations by Voldemārs Meija. A third issue appeared in March with a feature on Austrian proletarian literature and translations of poems by Ferdinand Freiligrath, Alfons Petzold, Stefan Zweig, and others. A glimpse of the journal's layout graphics can be seen on page 17 of the third issue, showing illustrations by the Latvian artist Edgars Bauze L350 who, like his colleague Meija, failed to find recognition in the last two decades by the editors of standard art reference works. These were not tranquil months for the editors of far-left journals, considering the rising sentiments culminating in the Ulmanis coup. The fourth (and last) issue of *Virziens* was seized at the printer and burned.[282]

It is only supposition, but from the first issue *Virziens* seemed to have attempted to camouflage itself as a social-democratic publication, thus contriving to avoid close

281   July 8, 1916.
282   See *Latviešu periodika, 1920-1940, Revolucionārā un padomju periodika*, p. 233.

Ed. Bauzes grafika -- Vīne februāra dienās

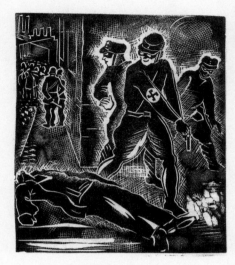

Fašisti slepkavo strādniekus

L347   L350

scrutiny. For example, the 1933 issue carried a bold full-page advertisement for *Social-demokrats* on its back page. In the combined issue at the beginning of 1934 it featured (inside the front cover) an advertisement by Atis Freināts, the eccentric, ideologically diffuse social-democratic publisher. The back cover had an advertisement for the social-democratic Marxist Club's publications. But leafing through the issue, it becomes clear that its editors' allegiance was firmly to the USSR. An initial editorial reflecting solidarity with Soviet authors further supports this contention. Although not all of the following writers were committed or "true to the party line", they are mentioned here to give a feeling for the sympathies of the *Virziens* editors: Isaac Babel, Sergei Esenin, Fedor Gladkov, Maxim Gorky, Vsevolod Ivanov, Leonid Leonov, Vladimir Mayakovsky, Nikolai Tichonov, Mikhail Zoshchenko, etc. and a scattering of Latvian writers such as Arvīds Borincs, Kārlis Fimbers, Olga Forša, Alberts Kalnleja, Jānis Niedre, and Marģers Tanks.

After the Ulmanis regime came to power, most publishers on the political left, both large and small, considered it the better part of wisdom to go underground or leave the country. Those who stayed resorted out of necessity to ephemeral forms of publishing (pamphlets, broadsides, or newsletter-sized folders) to continue their propaganda efforts due to the limited access to paper stock, printing services, etc. A number of such publications were produced in the apartment of Augusts Pupa on Dzirnavu iela, in rooms that he made available to fellow revolutionaries Kārlis Bušs and Samuils Haskins. There, working into the

L352

L353

L351

night, such fliers as the one shown L351 were produced and posted before dawn in public places or dropped through mail slots in working-class areas.[283]

In concluding this section it should be asked whether the left had any residual influence on overall book and periodical design in the remaining years of the 1930s? The short answer: it does not appear so. If one characterizes left-oriented Latvian book design as a synthesis of constructivist rectilinear style with bold, sans-serif titling and generous use of red and terra cotta in geometric forms, then one must look long and hard among trade book titles produced from the mid 1930s to the end of the decade. Outstanding Latvian-language book and periodical designs of the Ulmanis era in any quantity wait for discovery.

Among the few noteworthy exceptions appearing a year after Ulmanis came to power is *Grāmata par lakām, krāsām un politurām* (The Book about Lacquers, Paints, and Polishes) by the construction industry journalist Kārlis Upesleja.[284] L352 Its modernist cover was designed by the Baltic-German graphic designer Arturs Tims, who had several posters to his credit by the middle of the decade, including a winter tourism poster in 1937. L353 Tims' Baltic States promotional brochure for the 1937 Paris International Exposition won first prize for its cover. Unfortunately, his designs were not harbingers of better days on the design scene.

In the latter years of the 1930s, commissions for design leaders from the Republic's early years, e.g., Strunke and Vidbergs, could be seen with some regularity among the offerings of the publishers who could afford them or small publishers and private persons

---

283　See S. Haskins, "Revolucionārā grafika buržuāziskajā Latvijā", in Jūlijs Ķipers, *Cīņas balsis* (Riga: Latvijas Valsts izdevniecība, 1959), pp. 408-424. The practice of pushing such publications through mail slots in areas with some possibility of finding sympathetic readers was related to me by Ari Kamenkowitsch who, as a small boy, recalls his father quickly stuffing such material directly into the fire on receipt to avoid the appearance of sympathy.

284　(Riga: Zemnieka Domas, 1935) The publisher's name, translated as "Peasant Thoughts", was a major, well-funded Interwar-era publisher whose founding director was Kārlis Ulmanis.

with whom such artists had a personal connection. Studio artists with hard-to-catego-rize but nonetheless distinctive styles, e.g., Kārlis Padegs with his decadent treats or Hilda Vīka with her voluptuous painted forms, produced several memorable book cover designs as shown in the examples already provided as well as those mentioned. The work of Vīka and Padegs would surely have attracted attention in any international book cover design competition had they been entered along with their compatriots Strunke and Vidbergs.

The same design situation existed among the non-left periodical press, that is, com-petent, speaking-to-the-masses design as could be found in any Western or Northern European country of the time. The design exceptions in Latvia were usually those single periodical issues that carried designs by Strunke and Vidbergs. There were exceptional cases in which a celebrated studio artist such as Ludolfs Liberts or a sophisticated, deco-rative artist such as Jūlijs Madernieks was commissioned for a cover design. But looking at the panorama of periodical cover design reflected in the more than 1,400 periodical titles published during the Interwar years, one is hard-pressed to find more than a few examples that stood out from the commonplace. More commentary on the periodicals of the time is yet to come following the introduction of a selection of smaller publishers.

L354

Miscellanea: non-fiction, *belles lettres* from small publishers and self-publishers, exhibition and trade catalogs, and a few titles from provincial publishers

This concluding sample of works with all its eccentricity in design and style shows that the varied areas of publishing in Latvia were little different in content from that found in any small, industrialized European country of the time. The choice to show these ex-amples in gallery format rather than with text interspersed by illustrations seemed ap-propriate due to the fact that little data is available on a number of the publishers and designers.

L355

Non-fiction

Latvju prese: 1797-1822-1922 (The Latvian Press: 1797-1822-1922) [no specific edi-tor is given other than "Published by the Exhibition's Committee"]. L354

Published on the occasion of an exhibition celebrating 100 years of the Latvian Press held in the Riga City Museum of Art, Feb. 26—Mar. 12, 1922, the first such exhibition to be mounted in the new republic. Individuals with by-lines for various sections of the catalog and thus presumed to be part of the "Committee": Pēteris Ērmanis, Āronu Matīss, Jānis Misiņš. Contents: historical background, checklist of titles covering the period, alphabeti-cal and subject index, and brief biographical information on editors from the first news-papers published in the Latvian lands up to 1922. 140 pages. Cover design: reputedly Sigis-munds Vidbergs.

Poster of Press Exhibition by Ansis Cīrulis. L355

Ansis Cīrulis was a student of Madernieks whose ideological aesthetic, creativity, and productivity paralleled that of his teacher. These two masters of the decorative arts demonstrated beyond doubt that a national aesthetic could be derived from traditional ethnic symbols and an artist's imagination and appear as though they had existed for

L356

L357

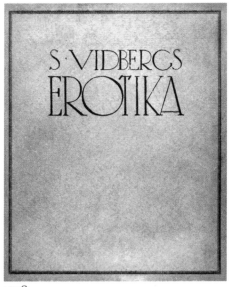

L358

L359

L360

L361

centuries. An example of a Cīrulis design for one in a series of postcards from 1918, published on the eve of the establishment of the country.[285] L356

Internazionalais schihds (The International Jew) by Henry Ford, trans. by Alfreds Bērzlaps (Riga: Kurzemneeka apgāds, 1924), 171 pages. L357

Translation of a notorious anti-Semitic tract by the American automobile tycoon; first appeared as a series in the Michigan newspaper *Dearborn Independent*. Articles gathered and published by Ford in 1920; translated into German in 1922 and published by the anti-Semitic Hammer Verlag (Leipzig, 1930?). Other editions include one in Portuguese (Porto Alegre, Brazil, 1933) and a Danish extract titled *Uddrag af Henry Ford's Bog "The International Jew"* (Copenhagen: Den Ny Tid, 1940). Cover design: Jānis Saukums.

Erotika: 24 zīmējumi (Erotica: 24 Pen-and-Ink Drawings) by Sigismunds Vidbergs with a foreword by Visvaldis Peņģerots (Riga: Saule, 1926). L358, L359

Twenty-four illustrations produced between 1917 and 1926 and published in this form in an edition of 1,500 copies (200 signed by the artist). With title page and captions (at back) in French and Latvian, it is assumed the publisher was looking for a market beyond Latvia. This was the first of three published compilations of erotic drawings by Vidbergs during the Interwar period. His *16 Bilitis dziesmas* (16 Songs of Bilitis, 1928) and *Kama Sutra* (1931), together with this title, are not erotic by today's standards but undoubtedly were high on desiderata lists of many Latvian book collectors. All printed on fine quality paper.

Jūlijs 14 (July 14) by Emil Ludwig, trans. by Emīls Feldmanis (Riga: Zalktis, 1929). L360, L361

---

285   The remarkable scope of Ansis Cīrulis' work can be seen in Rūta Rinka's monograph *Ansis Cīrulis: Saules pagalmos* (Riga: Neputns, 2008) with refreshing contributions, in addition to Rinka's, by the noted art historians Modris Esserts, Alīda Krēsliņa, Zaiga Kuple, Dace Lamberga, and Santa Podgaiska.

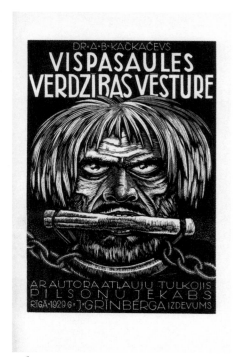

Ar pārtiku nebija labāk. Gaļu citi diendeņi nedabūja nekad, bet daži vairāk gadus no vietas tika ēdināti vienīgi ar maizi un ūdeni; piem., viņa puisis Ivans Tjeplovs dzīvoja pie maizes un ūdens nepārtraukti 15 gadus, amatnieks Andrējs Medvedjevs, 62 g. vecs sirmgalvis — 13 gadus, tāpat visa viņa ģimene u. t. t.
Dažiem muižas diendeņiem nebij pat ierādītas dzīvojamās telpas un tie mitinājās kur pagadījās »pie svešiem ļaudim«.
Strādāt visiem šiem ļaudim vajadzēja rokas nenolaižot, kā saka, līdz septītiem sviedriem. Ne gadi, ne dzimums netika ņemts vērā. Strādāja netikai darbdienās, bet arī svētdienās. Baznīcā iet tie nedrīkstēja, to ģenerālis bij uz stingrāko aizliedzis.

173

L362

L363

Translated and published the same year as the original German edition and with the same, slightly modified, uncredited cover design.

Vispasaules verdzības vēsture (World History of Slavery) by Aleksandr Kachkachev, trans. by Pilsoņu Jēkabs (pseud. of J. Birgers) (Riga: J. Grīnbergs, 1929). L362

A presumptuously titled work of only 188 pages and scarcity of sources. Nikolajs Puzirevskis L363 provided the grim title page and equally grim wood-engraved illustrations.

Skaistuma iegūšana dabīgiem līdzēkļiem: Praktisks padomdevējs sievietes veselības un skaistuma kopšanā (Acquiring Beauty by Natural Methods: Practical Advice for Women's Health and Beauty Care), ed. and trans. by Z. Meneks (Riga: Jaunatnes Vārds, 1931). Cover design: not credited. L364

Plakāts un sienas avīze (Poster and Wall Newspaper) by Arnolds Serdants (Riga: Latvijas Ārpusskolas izglītības padome, 1933). Cover design: Arvēds Segliņš. L365, L366

Serdants, a journalist and contributor to the social democratic journal *Signāls,* wrote on film and the poster as a communications medium.

Morgans, pasaules nekronētais karalis (Morgan, the Uncrowned King of the World) by Fritz Schwarz, trans. by "A. L." (Riga: Tautsaimniecības pētīšanas biedrība, 1934). L367

This translation of the best-known work by the Swiss free-trade polemicist Fritz Schwarz is yet another document of Latvia's book trade interconnections. Schwarz's attempted exposé[286] of the early 20th century American financier J. P. Morgan went through four printings in its first year of publication, 1932, and remains in print in Germany through Synergia Verlag in Darmstadt. Design not credited.

286   (Bern: Genossenschaftsverlag, Freiwirtschaftliche Schriften).

155

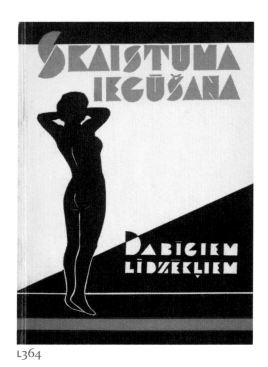

L364

L365

L366

L367

L368

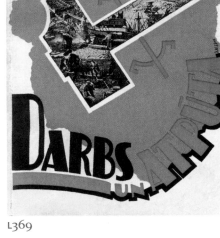

L369

L370

L371

Operas neredzamā dzīve (The Secret Life of the Opera) by Oto Krolls (Riga: Praktiskās bibliotēkas ģenerālkomisijā, 1934). L368

The title promises more than the National Opera "inspektors" Krolls delivered in this relatively conventional "background" pamphlet. Cover design not credited.

Darbs un atpūta: rakstu krājums darba dzīves jautājumiem (Work and Relaxation: Collected Writings on Working Condition Issues) by Rūdolfs Veidemanis (b. 1887) (Riga: Veselības veicināšanas biedrība, 1939). L369

This confidence-raising Health Promotion Association publication appeared just when war clouds hovered. Design not credited.

4. Latvijas skautu lielās nometnes ABC (4th Latvian Scouts Great Camp ABC), compiled and published by Latvijas Skautu centrālā organizācija "LSCO" (Latvian Scouting Association) L370 and poster in 1938. L371

This title was the next-to-the-last of the First Republic scouting camp handbooks; the last was published in 1939. The cover design of the handbook as well as the poster were by Oskars Norītis. According to National Library of Latvia holdings, the LSCO director issued a series of guidelines on single sheets as late as July 19, 1940. The scouting movement began in the Latvian lands with the formation of the first troop in April 1917, although the official scouting organization was not established until 1921. With the Soviet occupation in early summer 1940, the organization was officially abolished, whereupon it went underground. In 1941 the Soviets ordered the capture and assassination of the Latvian Scout's founder, the WWI military hero General Kārlis Goppers.

L372

L373

L375

Trade catalogs

Trade catalog publishing and trade catalog design history in Latvia was little different from that of any industrialized country in the Interwar decades. While an occasional Latvian manufacturer might use a novel shape such as the pre-World War I die-cut catalog issued by the A. G. Ruthenberg Tobacco Co.,[287] L372 trade catalogs in Latvia were generally straightforward in design such as those shown, e.g., the State Paper Printing and Publishing Co., or attempted to attract consumers through a more timely cover such as the radio parts catalog shown. While these two are Latvian in origin, German companies still played a part in the Latvian economy and, more often than not, used their trade catalogs produced in Germany without translation, such as the Rosenthal Porcelain Company catalog shown here.

Rosenthal Porzellan, J. Jaksch & Ko., ca. 1930, 56 pages. L373

Produced in 1930, shortly after the 50th anniversary of the company's founding in 1879. Printed throughout in sepia tone except for eight color pages. Aside from the Riga distributor's name, J. Jaksch & Ko.,[288] on the cover, it is the same catalog distributed in Germany.

Valstspapīru spiestuves izdevumu ilūstrēts katalogs (Illustrated Catalog of Publications by the Government Printing Office), ca. 1930, 31 pages. L374

Offerings of services and publications by this government printing operation, including lithographic and gravure portraits of presidents (past and present), state-sponsored books on the country's regions, portraits of historic figures, and patterned paper (4 samples tipped-on).

---

287   A trade catalog as "Jubilee Exhibition" memento for this major tobacco (cigars, cigarettes, and pipe mixtures) firm with headquarters in Vienna. Text: Russian and German. Illustrated with products as well as photos of scenic Riga, e.g., the Dom, "Kaiser Nikolai I Gymnasium", Polytechnic, National Theatre, etc.

288   Located at Svērtuves iela 11.

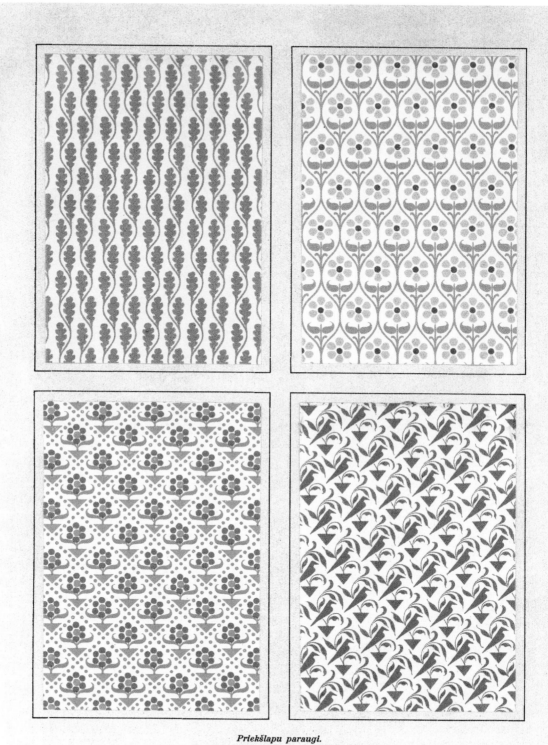

Priekšlapu paraugi.
Dabūjami Valstspapīru spiestuvē.

31

ᴸ374

L377

L378

L376

Ilustrēts radio katalogs (Illustrated Radio Catalog), 1931, 60 pages. L375

A catalog for the do-it-yourself radio enthusiast documents the manner in which firms such as Philips, Telefunken, Valvo, and other component manufacturers in radio's early years supported local distributors by advertising parts as well as assembled units. In addition, a list of 50 European stations with operating frequencies is given. Arnold Witt, the local distributor, maintained a shop at Vaļņu iela 8 in Riga.

Mūsu mēbeles (Our Furniture), Mēbeļu tirdzniecības un rūpniecības nama Rūdolfs Vītols, Rīga, katalogs, (Riga: Golts un Jurjāns, n.d.), 116 [1] pages. L376

This profusely illustrated catalog shows what could be found in any German or Austrian furniture store of the period catering to the middle class. L377, L378

Seed catalog of the Kārlis Ūdris Company, 48 pages. L379

Flower and vegetable seeds with line-drawing illustrations in the manner of seed catalogs published in other industrialized countries.

Forda-Vairoga preču automobiļa rokas grāmata (Ford-Vairogs Automobile Handbook), 1938, 64 [1] pages. L380

L379

L380

L381

A handbook/catalog marking the brief life of the Ford-licensed Vairogs (Shield) automobile in Latvia. According to Edvīns Liepiņš,[289] "The first new Ford-Vairogs... the FordVairogs Junior, rolled off the production line in the summer of 1938... a variation of Europe's Ford Junior Ten." The following year production began for a five-passenger model and a "seven-passenger... for state institution and taxicab needs". The Soviets nationalized the plant in the summer of 1940. Total production of the automobile division according to Liepiņš: "300 light automobiles, more than 1,000 Ford-Vairogs trucks, and a few hundred buses". The author points out that Vairogs, Inc. "was the largest auto manufacturing plant in the Baltics".

Lauksaimniecības mašinu, lokomobiļu, traktoru un motoru eļļas un eļļošana (Agricultural Machinery, Traction Engine, Tractor, and Engine Oil and Lubrication), published by Degviela, a quasi-governmental fuel company, 1939, Degviela Co., 63 pages. L381

Calendars and yearbooks

As mentioned earlier, the calendar and yearbook have had a venerable tradition in the Latvian region through all periods: Russian Empire, independence, Soviet and German occupations, and once again independence. Latvian yearbook cover design was as varied as the contents' themes and occasionally created by well-known designers. More common in appearance throughout Latvia were those relying on sentimental images, e.g., the 1928 household calendar, or those with a quasi-heraldic design such as the 1933 general calendar. Color covers became common from the late 1920s until the end of the era. The examples shown here give some indication of the range of designs. For contrast, the section concludes with the only general calendar published during the first Soviet occupation.

289   *Rīgas auto* (Riga: Baltika., 1997), p. 96.

L382

L383

L384

L385

L386

1927

Preses kalendars, 1927 (Press Calendar, 1927). L382

Neither editor nor publisher is cited although the title page indicates that the calendar has been combined with "Preses Balles Vēstnesis". Cover design: Sigismunds Vidbergs.

Mahjturibas kalendars 1928. gadam (Home Calendar 1928) (Riga: L. Audze, 1928). L383

The cover design by Reinholds Kasparsons is typical of his illustration and poster imagery.

1933

Zaļās Vārnas gada grāmata, 1933. g. (Zaļā Vārna Yearbook, 1933), ed. by Fricis Gulbis, Alfons Francis, Ēriks Raisters (Riga: Zaļā Vārna, 1933). Design: Aleksandrs Pētersons. L384

The artists' group *Zaļā Vārna* (Green Crow), formed in 1925, began publishing a bi-monthly journal titled *Zaļā Vārna* in January 1929 and lasting until December 1929. Another issue appeared in April 1931. In 1933 it published the annual shown here, the last of its publications. Aleksandrs Pētersons designed the cover in addition to making other contributions. Also shown is a Green Crow exhibition poster announcing a collaborative international woodcut show in 1935. L385

Latvijas kalendars, 1933 (Calendar of Latvia, 1933) (Riga: J. Roze, 1933). L386

The Vilis Krūmiņš cover is typical of his stylized book cover and poster designs. Internal designs for this and previous Roze calendars were the work of the Roze house designer Indriķis Zeberiņš.

1936

Dailes gada grāmata (Daile Yearbook) (Riga: Literatūra, 1936) L387 (Cover was-hown earlier in Russian-language publishing chapter R46).

L387

Although the editor is not named, M. Grass is credited with the cover design. The calendar includes the usual information with name days, holidays, festivals, etc., followed by contributions signed and unsigned on various subjects, including book culture with notes on authors and their writings. Of special interest are two sections of reproductions by the photographers Valdemārs Upītis (landscapes but with one exterior and one interior photo of a hotel in Ķemeri) and Arturs Grapmanis (portraits of theatre personalities).

1938

Latvijas Preses biedrības gada grāmata, 1938 (Latvian Press Association Yearbook, 1938), ed. by Jūlijs Druva, editor-in-chief; with editorial contributions by Artūrs Kroders, Līgotņu Jēkabs, Oto Nonācs (Riga: LPB izd., 1938). L388

Initiated in 1935 and continuing through 1939, the regime-subservient editors treated ideology, history, literature, humor, etc. Cover design and text caricatures by Sigismunds Vidbergs.

Termiņu kalendars, 1940 (Datebook, 1940) (Riga: Directorate of the City Government of Riga, 1940). L389

L388

No cover designer is credited for this poignant last official general calendar published by the last Riga city government of Latvia's Interwar period. The introduction by President Ulmanis and the afterword by City Supervisor Roberts Liepiņš give little hint of the darkening future that must have been on their minds.

Provincial publishing

Printing offices for the production of local newspapers and periodicals as well as books have existed in towns and cities outside of Riga for more than 300 years. A number of sources treat the history of printing and publishing in the Latvian lands, but nearly all those published in the 20th and 21st centuries are in Latvian. Several of these histories have had summaries in German, Russian, or English. Most are illustrated and provide some insight into book and periodical design. Some include references to publishing outside the center of Riga. Several of these titles have been referred to in this and other chapters. The most notable work among them and a model for the continuation of the theme is *Latviešu grāmatu grafika: 17. gadsimts, ilustrācijas un vinjetes* (Latvian Book Graphics: 17th century, Illustrations and Vignettes) edited by Valdis Villerušs.[290] An extensive Russian and German summary accompanies each chapter. One could only hope that the team that prepared this work would continue its collaboration into the 21 century with such "century surveys".

L389

290   (Riga: Liesma, 1988). Contributions by Valdis Villerušs, Silvija Šiško, and Elita Grosmane.

L390

L391

L394

L392

L393

More often than not, printing and publishing outside of Riga was utilitarian with design concerns having second place or no place at all. One notable exception was the publishing and printing office of Oskars Jēpe in Cēsis, the historic center of Latvian culture and also a town noted for Jēpe's worthy predecessor, Jānis Ozols.[291] School books and school supplies were a mainstay of Jēpe's business but *belles lettres* titles were an important part of his list. Whether school books or literary works, full attention was given to such details as typographic design and paper quality. According to the statistical tables in the 1926 Jēpe catalog, 132 titles were published between 1920 and 1926, including school books and calendars. Two early works from the beginning of the 1920s, when times were difficult, reflect Jēpe's attention to design: Arveds Smilga's *Siluetes: Mazi tehlojumi* (Silhouettes: Short Sketches, 1920) with its calligraphic cover design by Jānis Jaunsudrabiņš (linocut cover design and typography) and Eduards Tūters' *Laika soļi: dzejoļi* (The Steps of Time: Poems, 1922). L390

Zelta vabole: Stāsts (The Gold Bug: A Story) by Edgar Allan Poe, trans. by Vitolds Žībelis (Jelgava: Brāļu Hānu izd., 1925). L391

291   In his years of publishing, from the mid-1880s to 1906, Ozols paid particular attention to the appearance of his books, commissioning original designs for both cloth and paper editions. His work was the subject of an exhibition at the Cēsis Museum in 1989 drawn from the museum's holdings. Sarma Ruska compiled an illustrated catalog in which more than 90 titles are described.

L395

L396

An appended catalog of the publisher's *Foreign Literature Library* listed 40 titles, including works by Jacques Casanova, Jack London, and the Baroness Orczy.[292] Cover design by the painter and art teacher Kārlis Celmiņš.

Dievs, pērkons un velns: Tautas teikas un pasakas (God, Thunder, and the Devil: Folk Tales and Stories) (Valka: J. Rauska, ca. 1924). Design: Jānis Saukums. L392

Skumjie ceļinieki: Stāsti (The Sorrowful Wanderers: Stories) by Jānis Ķelpe (Valka: J. Rauska, 1932). L393

Rauska was both a printer and publisher in Valka, a northern Latvian town bordering Estonia. Cover design by Aleksandrs Junkers.

Kad gailis dzied (When the Rooster Crows) by August Hinrich, trans. by Jēkabs Zaķis (Jelgava: Jelgavas Teātra izd., 1936). L394

A comedy in three acts first published in Berlin in 1933 by the prestigious Drei Masken Verlag. Cover design not credited.

L397

Masās Elli Bakhorst laupitajs (The Robbing of Elli Bakhorst), anon. (Liepāja: "Mars" izd. commission with A. Zemītis, n.d.). L395

This 31-page example of sensational "street literature" was published in the port city of Liepājā. It exemplifies a type of lurid literature sold mainly at kiosks, thus often escaping the attention of the bibliographer or the deposit network of national libraries in many countries. The National Library of Latvia, however, has been diligent in gathering such elusive material from the 1920s to date. It is difficult to determine the role such literature played in the overall book economy and culture of Interwar Latvia because no studies documenting its impact appear to have been undertaken. Ten available titles are listed on the back cover of the title, where it is announced that every week a new title will appear. A similar example, *Tarzans*, a Riga imprint from Ģils izd. L396 capitalized on the enthusiasm for Tarzan and offered a series of three Tarzan titles, even giving credit to the author, Edgar Rice Burroughs. A third Riga example is from the *Princese Pahrgalwe* series. L397. A concluding title, also designed for kiosk sales published for Latvians in the USSR, is Alvils Ceplis' *Andra Vītola atmiņas* (Reminiscences of Andris Vītols). L398 Ceplis, a former Latvian Rifleman who chose to remain in the USSR and loyally support the regime, served on the board of the publisher Prometejs (Moscow). This fragile, 18-page

L398

292   Quite likely the Baroness Emma Orczy, author of sensational fiction.

L399

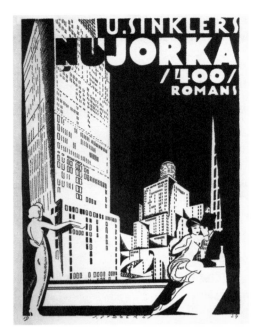

L400

L403

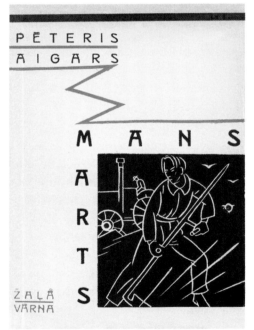

L404

title (1926) was one of the few published by Latvju izd. between 1924 and 1928. The National Library of Latvia holds five titles from 1925, three from 1926, and one from 1927.

Belles lettres from small publishers and self-publishers

Lapiņas: Dzejas (Leaves: Poems) by Voldemārs Birzgalis (Riga: Bohema, 1923). Design: Ansis Cīrulis. L399

Ņujorka 400 (New York 400) by Upton Sinclair, trans. by Jānis Grots (Riga: Saule, 1924). L400

A translation of *Metropolis* (1907), one of Sinclair's least successful novels. Design: Sigismunds Vidbergs.

Karjēra: Satirisks stasts (Career: A Satirical Story) by Andrejs Lankovskis (pseud. A. Lanka) (A. Viestura izd., 1929). Design: Aleksandrs Apsītis. L401

L401

Ners (Fool) by Ēriks Brikmanis (self-published, 1931). Design: Kārlis Padegs. L402

Tērauda ziedi (Steel Flowers) by Jānis Čavars (Latvijas Skolotāju kooperatīvs, 1932). Designer-illustrator: Pēteris Vanags. L403

The greater part of the edition was confiscated because of its politically inflammatory poems.[293]

Mans marts: Dzejas (My March: Poems) by Pēteris Aigars (Zaļās Vārnas izd., 1932). Design: Niklāvs Strunke. L404

Tilta pozicija (A Position on the Bridge) by Kārlis Fimbers (Kooperatīvs Jaunā Kultūra, 1933). Design: Pauls Šterns. L405

Bikts (Confession) by Ēriks Brikmanis (self-published, 1933). Design: Kārlis Padegs. L406

L402

Pārvērtība (Change) by Artur Brausewetter, trans. by Elita Dzenis (Grāmatu Zieds, 1937). Design: "B". L407

Mūzu vaimanas: Stāsti (Lamentation of the Muses: Stories) by Hilda Vīka (Erva, 1937). Design and illustrations: Hilda Vīka. L408

Exhibition catalogs

Exhibition catalogs published during the Interwar period fall into two general categories, the greater in number being those for art exhibitions, the other for trade and industry expositions.

Like any highly literate, industrialized country coming into its own, in those years there were also periodic exhibitions mounted in libraries, folklife centers, and social-welfare agencies with the latter organizations demonstrating techniques and materials designed to alleviate various medical or social conditions. Such exhibitions were often modest in size and mounted without catalogs.

Exhibition catalogs produced by private art associations or commercial galleries tended to be more elaborate in design, with covers featuring original graphics printed from stone, linoleum, or wood.

Museum exhibition catalogs were usually printed by letterpress with offset printed covers and half-tone illustrations. Examples of both are shown in the following illustrations.

293   Interview with Ilgonis Bērsons, Jan. 28, 2007.

L405

L406

L407

L408

Industry-related catalogs were generally sponsored by an industry association or the State with funds that allowed for color printing. Such catalogs looked similar to those printed in any European country of the period. The example shown illustrates a general exhibition of trade and folk culture with a design one might have seen on such a catalog in any Baltic State.

Near-comprehensive collections of art exhibition catalogs of the period are held by the Latvian National Museum of Art, the National Library of Latvia, the Library of the University of Latvia, the Library of the Academy of Art, and regional art and folk museums.

L409

Jēkabs Kazaks (dz. 1895 +1920.g): Peemiņas izstāde (Jēkabs Kazaks [born 1895 died 1920]: Memorial Exhibition), Rīgas mākslinieku grupa (Riga: City Art Museum, 1922). L409

This slender (5 leaves) memorial exhibition from March 26 to April 14, 1922, celebrated one of the key figures in the establishment of the modern tradition in Latvian art, despite his untimely death. 249 pieces covering the years 1915 to 1920—essentially Kazaks' entire oeuvre—was shown. Dace Lamberga has provided the most significant assessment of Kazaks in her monograph, *Jēkabs Kazaks* (Riga: Neputns, 2007).

Mākslinieku biedrība Sadarbs: II izstādes katalogs (Sadarbs Art Association: 2nd Exhibition Catalog) (Riga: City Art Museum, 1926). Cover design and typography: Jūlijs Madernieks. L410

Jūlijs Madernieks is the dominant presence in this show with 51 items on exhibition. Ludolfs Liberts is next in line, exhibiting 34 items. The exhibition features ten artists in all with what seems to be a gross imbalance in the quantity representing each artist. Two artists, Rudolfs Pelše and Kārlis Zāle, have but one item each.

L410

Mākslinieku biedrības Sadarbs III izstade (The Sadarbs Art Association's 3rd Exhibition) (Riga: City Art Museum, 1928). Design and typography: Jūlijs Madernieks. L411

This printer's color proof 22.25x17.5 cm shows the design for the 3rd biennial exhibition's poster and catalog. Because the catalog was published without color, this proof gives a sense of Madernieks' bold use of color.

Krievu grafikas izstādes katalogs (Russian Graphics Exhibition Catalog), sponsored by the Association for Furthering Connection with the Peoples of the Soviet Republics, held in the Central Market during November and December 1929. L412

This loan exhibition was quite likely a logistical (if not political) nightmare, given the year and existing cultural restrictions in the USSR and in Latvia. The works represented were by artists who were members of various Soviet art associations, including 4 Isskustva, Oktjabr, Rost, OMX,[294] Žar Cvet, OST,[295] AXP,[296] and ARMU.[297] The largest representation was of children's book illustrators from among the many organizations and is the concluding listing in the catalog—67 illustrators in all. An impressive list of "knowns" along with those who have not survived mentioned in the standard works or even recent studies attempting to track down "lost artists" of that generation.

L411

Katalogs 24. mākslas izstādei, no 18. jan. līdz 1. feb., 1931 (Catalog of the 24th Art Exhibition, Jan. 18—Feb. 1, 1931), sponsored by the Independent Artists Association, held in the Riga City Art Museum. Design: Jānis Ansons. L413

---

294   OMX = Obshchestvo Moskovskikh Khudozhnikov (Association of Moscow Artists).
295   OST = Obshchestvo khudozhnikov-stankovistov (Association of Easel-Painters).
296   AXP = Assotsiatsiia Khudozhnikov Revoliutsii (Association of Revolutionary Artists).
297   ARMU = Asotsiiatsiia revoliutsiïnoho mystetstva Ukraïny (Association of Revolutionary Art of Ukraine).

L412

L416

L418

L419

Radigars! Izstādes katalogs (Radigars [Create, Spirit]! Exhibition Catalog). L414

A 1933 exhibition to "sell, exchange, and loan" under the heading "Art for Everyone" and organized "Underneath the Linden Trees on Merķeļa iela". The artists exhibiting were relatively well known, with the greatest number of works (24) exhibited by Kārlis Padegs and the fewest (3) by Ernests Meļķis. Two artists exhibited as guests: Pāvils Štelmahers and Ilmārs Erlahs. Two artist "comrades", whose memory was evoked, were the graphic artist Voldemārs Zvaigzne and the painter Aleksandrs Eihe. Design: not credited.

Somu mākslas izstāde (Exhibition of Finnish Art, 1935) (Riga City Art Museum, 1935). Cover design: Sigismunds Vidbergs. L415

The 491 works exhibited range from painting to sculpture. The list of works is preceded by an essay on contemporary painting and sculpture and an essay on Finnish graphic art. The aesthetic conservatism of the Ulmanis regime undoubtedly contributed to the choice of conservative Finnish artists being shown in all categories.

Latvju mākslinieku biedribas darbu klāsts, 1936 (Works of the Latvian Art Association [for] 1936). Design: not credited. L416

Introductory texts by Jēkabs Bīne and Roberts Šterns followed by the work of 23 artists with one or two representative works illustrated with a biographical sketch and photo. No surprises here: representational works with an emphasis on "homeland" depictions. School book illustrations rather than studio work were shown by one artist, Elizabete Mednis.

1. Latvijas daiļamatniecības izstādes katalogs. 1937. gada 6.II.—7.III (1st Latvian Applied Art Exhibition Catalog: Feb. 6—Mar. 7, 1937), organized by the Latvian Chamber of Applied Art. Design: Vilis Krūmiņš. L417

Introductory essays on various mediums of distinctive, Latvian applied art followed by 80 half-tone plates of just about everything from armoire to mitten design. Objects that would likely bring a second look today include Romans Suta's design for a porcelain service. While it lacks the flair of his "Baltars"[298] design period, Suta's ability to create timeless, stylized folk figures shines through. Also Ansis Cīrulis' bedspread with 12 narrative panels illustrating country, village, and town life and Jānis Zibens' copper mask. Other items provide a record of period aesthetics.

Modernā Italijas peizāžu izstāde: Rīga, marts 1938—XVI g. (Exhibition of Modern Italian Landscape Painting). L418 Organized by the Italian Cultural Ministry in cooperation with the Italian and Latvian Foreign Offices and Ministries of Education. The only

---

298   "Baltars" was a porcelain workshop known throughout Europe (1924-1929), founded by a team of artists under the leadership of Romans Suta.

L413

L414

L415

L417

L420

L421

L422

"modern" element in the exhibition is in the cover and title page typography and image by "E. P." None of the Italian landscape painters identified with the "modern movement" is included.

25. mākslas izstāde (25th Art Exhibition), organized by the Zaļā Vārna Art Association (Jelgava, 1938). 24 artists exhibited; 8 works illustrated. Design: Jānis Plēpis. L419

Atjaunotās Latvijas 5 gadu sasniegumu skate: Vispārējās izstādes 1939. g. katalogs (A 5-Year Assessment of the Renewed Latvia: 1939 General Exhibition Catalog). Kārlis Freimanis was commissioned to design the catalog cover as well as the poster promoting the exhibition. L420

A major 16-day trade exhibition spread over the entire "Crafts Hall" in Riga, obviously designed to show how far Latvia had progressed under the leadership of Ulmanis. To counter negative opinion regarding the regime's cultural life, the show leads with sections on the National Theatre, the National Opera, and the Art Theatre and continues with sections on the Institute of History and press and book publishing. These are followed by the trade and industry sections, in which the reader is greeted with deserved boasting about the State Electronics Factory (VEF), where the Minox camera was developed in the late 1930s along with small and large appliances that became bywords for quality. Photos in this section show a group with a Latvian commercial bi-plane at Liepāja Airport and the assembly line (with three cars) at the Vairogs automobile plant.[299]

SPRS bērnu zīmējumu un bērnu grāmatu izstāde, kurai pievienoti Papaņina Ziemeļpola ekspedicijas un SPRS fotoattēli. No 1939. g. 19. jūlija—16. aug. (USSR Children's Drawing and Children's Book Exhibition [together with a display of photos from the Papanin Soviet North Pole expedition and the USSR]).[300] L421

---

299   For an informative and entertaining account of Latvia's automobile history, see Edvīns Liepiņš' *Rīgas auto: Riga and the automobile* (Riga: Baltika, 1997).

An exhibition mounted in the lobby of the Riga Art Theatre and sponsored by the Society for Cultural Relations with the USSR. Eduards Smiļģis, the long-time *régisseur* of the Riga Art Theatre, was also for a time the president of this decidedly Soviet-leaning society founded in 1929 with Rainis as its first president.

A few more periodicals from the 1920s and 1930s

The story of the Interwar periodical publishing—newspaper, journal, yearbook—is a study in itself with ample opportunity for demonstrating the vibrant cultural life that changed abruptly in the early summer of 1940. Provided here is a small sampling of periodicals complementing those titles already cited and shown in the preceding text.

Conjure the image of a country of little more than two and a half million people producing and consuming, in a two-decade period, periodicals and newspapers in the quantities and languages indicated: 1,408 Latvian, 49 Russian, 41 German, 20 French, 15 English, two Estonian, two Esperanto, two Spanish, and one Lithuanian. In addition, there were also titles implicitly advocating the replacement of the democratic government (or at least making it into a Soviet-friendly state). The quantity of titles precedes the language of publication: 389 Latvian, 87 Russian, and 23 Yiddish. Figures are approximate because there were undoubtedly newsletters and single-issue publications that eluded the bibliographers, librarians, and tax-and-deposit-copy enforcers assigned to tracking periodical literature. Proportionately, this gives a picture of a reading-hungry, democratic nation little different in its reading profile from Germany, the United Kingdom, or France at that time.

The diversity of themes and special interests of periodicals and newspapers in Latvia at that time was similar to that found in any industrialized country—news, business, religious, entertainment, political, general interest, children's and young people's interests, technical, professional. All topics were available. Added to this abundance and still not quantified in any study or represented in these press figures are the additional publications regularly available at the newspaper kiosks throughout the city, namely, periodicals and newspapers from the greater Baltic region, i.e., Sweden, Poland, Finland, Denmark, and the press of Latvia's two border neighbors, Estonia and Lithuania.

Throughout the text, reference has been made to the periodical press of the four languages with illustrations of design from a few specific titles. In the following brief section, a few additional journals with illustrations are provided with minimal background as a complement to what has gone before. However, comment here is confined to Latvian-language titles only and the progression is more or less chronological.

This presentation reflects an addition to the cross section and range in design already presented.

Latvju Grāmata (Latvian Book), ed. by Rūdolfs Egle. L422

Published monthly from the autumn of 1922 through 1923, when it began publishing bi-monthly to January 1931. Sober in appearance but rich in content, this book trade quarterly gives the most objective view of mainstream publishing. Its news of the publishing scene (domestic and foreign) and its "chronicle" section listing new books, with notes and reviews of many, provides the primary publishing record prior to the launch of the National Library of Latvia's *Valsts bibliotēkas biļetens* in 1927. *Latvju Grāmata* provided

300　The expeditions of 1931 and 1937.

L423

L424

readers with the scope, quantity, and type of publications issued by publishing houses in Riga and provincial towns. Coverage: Latvian-language publishing.

Teātra Vēstnesis (Theater News, 1920-1938), ed. by Kārlis Freinbergs et al. (from the 1926 edition of the Latvian National Theater).

With its cover design by the noted painter and set designer Ludolfs Liberts, this periodical kept the theatergoer informed not only of what was to come but provided background on performances and performers. L423 Later design by Vilis Valdmanis. L424

Aizkulises (Behind-the-Scenes), L425 edited by eight individuals, some returning on occasion over the nine years of its existence from 1925 to 1934. The Ulmanis regime, like most authoritarian regimes, was allergic to satirical periodicals. While this journal was not as famous as the satirical and vanguard forerunner *Ho-Ho*, L426 it was more durable than most and was exceeded in longevity only by *Svari* (1920-1931). L427 *Aizkulises* made a point of being impartial in its political satire and refrained from pandering to those in search of prurient fare (a rather large market in Latvia, judging from Raimonds Zalcmanis's overview[301] in which this genre is demonstrably visible). For the latter audience there was a host of titles such as the relatively short-lived *Lapsene* (The Wasp, 1922-1924), L428 *Senzacija* (Sensation, 1924-1925), and *Elegance* (Elegance, 1925-1926).

Atpūta (Leisure) was the most widely read weekly in Latvia from its inception in 1924 to its closure during the first Soviet occupation in June 1941. One of several publications of the highly successful Benjamiņš publishing enterprise, *Atpūta* was edited by Emīlija Benjamiņa, wife of the publishing tycoon Antons Benjamiņš. The photo-cover of an

301   *Latviešu satirs smejas: Ieskats Latvijas neatkarības gadu humoristiski satīriskās preses izdevumos* (Riga: Avots, 1994).

Mūsu Monte-Karlo aizceļošana.

Modernās sievietes tiesāšana — Mūsu Monte-Karlo gals
— Pulkveža Zeltiņa-Goldfelda traģedija — Dailes teatra
jubileja — Neatkarīgo izstādes slēgšana.

L425

L426

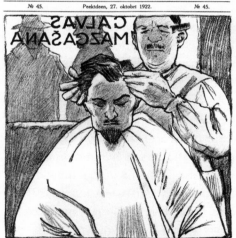

L427

Tris rozes.

L428

L429

L430

L432

L431

L433

early 1930s issue shows the publishing couple in the living room of their villa on Krišjāṇa Barona iela. L429 With an envied circulation reaching over 70,000 at its high point, *Atpūta* was likely read or browsed weekly by an audience that may have exceeded 200,000, considering shared copies. The socio-political viewpoint was conservative and mildly nationalistic; it provided what "the public wanted", yet in one sense provided "what the public needed" in the mind of its editor-in-chief.

Atpūta offered its readers news, humor, human interest, and fiction in original contributions and translations, and these were presented in a gentle effort to raise the general cultural level of the middle-class audience. The cover art was not demanding. Examples shown are typical. But one artist, Jūlijs Madernieks, contributed a number of covers and represented a high-water mark in the area of Latvian graphic design as he successfully worked toward a stylization of folk and national idioms. Madernieks was something of a William Morris-like figure for Latvia in his attempt to recover the strength of an earlier design tradition in materials as well as form. As Morris attempted to do for the late 19th century English home, Madernieks also put his ideas into practice in an exemplary manner through his decorative designs for the creation of rugs, furniture, wall hangings, and even mittens as well as designs for every print medium from sheet music to periodical and book design. The panel of illustrations shows a printers' proof for one of a number of stylized *Atpūta* covers by Madernieks L430 for January 1929 and the August 1930 cover by Aleksandrs Apsītis appealing to another sector of the readership, L431 a photographic cover

L434

L435

L436

for December 1938, L432 and the "Happy New Year" cover for December/January 1940/ 1941, L433 designed by Gunārs Vīndedzis, with its unmistakable indication of the Soviet take-over five and a half months earlier. By the time this issue appeared Emīlija Benjamiņa had already been dismissed and was but a few months from being deported. The newly installed editor Jānis Jēkabsons (Grants) presided over this last issue.

Nedēļa (The Week), published from 1922 to 1926, was a modest and not particularly successful competition to *Atpūta*. Without a large publishing firm in the background, it attracted neither major writers nor illustrators. Its circulation began at 3,000 and reached 10,000 at its highest point. Teodors Hermanovskis and Jānis Melderis shared editorial responsibilities with support from R. Aboms, Jānis Altbergs, and Lizete Skalbe. The content included stories, photo reportage, and health and beauty tips. The cover design for August 14, 1925, although signed only with the initials "C.R.", is likely that of Cilly Ruhtenberg. L434

Senzacija (Sensation), the "brain child" of 21-year-old Helmārs Rudzītis, lasted for 27 issues from September 1924 to May 1925, but not without a few problems. L435 Numbers 13, 15, 16, and 20 were confiscated by a decision of the public prosecutor, presumably because its editors, Nikolajs Džonsons, Rudzītis, and later Valdemārs Kārkliņš, were threatening public morals with racy content. But given the content of many short-lived Latvian humor magazines and imported titles on the kiosks, and even considering period standards, *Senzacija* was unlikely to have corroded the morals of even the most vulnerable teenage boys or their fathers. Issue No. 13 did provide a photo of "the most beautiful legs in Latvia" (from mid-thigh downward), but even titling of the articles generally promised more than delivered. A few examples from No. 20 with Oto Skulme's "Sunny Day" cover L436: "Women of our day", "Those who look for spice", "Passion", "Jester and dancer", "Treacherous pants", "Philosophy of love". Yet, possibly out of embarrassment or an imagined need for self-protection, a number of contributors hid behind initials, pseudonyms, or just left their pieces unsigned. Latvian contributors, in addition to the editors, included Gustavs

L439

Nr. 25   26. novembri 1925. g.
Numurs maksā 50 sant.

L437

L438

L440

L441

Krauja, Elmārs Hercenbergs, and Roberts Vizbulis along with translations from works by Paul Reboux, Marietta Shaginyan, and others. Sergejs Civinskis-Civis and Valdemārs Kārkliņš also contributed illustrations. Did *Senzacija* fulfill its promise of being "...devoted to very modern trends in literature and cinema...humor...news from all around the world... English-language lessons..." and something for "everybody"? At least its editors tried and it was, for a brief period, a sprightly antidote to the homespun content of *Atpūta*. But Rudzītis did not give up easily and within four weeks was bringing out a successor journal titled *Elegance* with its first issue on the newsstands by the first of June. (The last issue of *Senzacija* was the first of May.) *Elegance* was more subdued in tone, less provocative in its illustrative content, and managed to last for 38 issues before closing in February 1926. L437

Zeltene: Ilustrēts sieviešu žurnāls sabiedriski-ētiskai audzināšanai, literatūrai, veselības kopšanai, mājturībai un rokdarbiem (The Lass: An Illustrated Women's Journal for Social-ethical Education, Literature, Hygiene, Home Economics, and Needlework). The subtitle leaves little doubt as to what was offered in this monthly lasting from the autumn of 1926 until July 1940. The audience is identified in the first issue as "girls, wives, mothers" with a supplement for "young readers". Departments indicated by the subtitle were consistently presented month after month. Circulation figures were not given, but one can be reasonably sure that such a periodical had a wide readership beyond the number on the initial subscriber list. The cover art shown in the issues below was typical. The similar aesthetic sensibilities of Vilis Krūmiņš L438 and Zenta Kuple L439 made them ideal illustrators for such a periodical. Other cover artists included Aleksandrs Apsītis, Nikolajs Puzirevskis, L440, L441 Jēkabs Bīne, Reinholds Kasparsons, and Jānis Strauts. Beginning in January 1940 and continuing to the end in July of that year, only photographs were used on covers. But cover photography—usually photographs of well-known Latvian women, e.g., singers, actresses, and writers—was also used earlier from time to time. The article range remained fairly constant throughout the years: fashion, household hints, and Latvian cultural characteristics as reflected in national songs, national designs in folk costumes, and needlework. Latvian *belles lettres* appear throughout, mainly as selections from novels and short stories. Translations from other languages are infrequent but do appear. An ominous note appears in the final issue, No. 15 in July 1940, in which the editor, Oto Krolls, states that "due to the fact that the Red Army of the USSR has entered Latvia, there are new tasks and we must concentrate our great work... thus, instead of the four former magazines dealing with the themes of women's life, there will be one unifying magazine and *Zeltene* will cease its work." Krolls had a long career editing periodicals during the Interwar period. He escaped from Latvia via Germany, arriving in Chicago in 1950. Like many other exiled editors, he was soon editing Latvian émigré periodicals until his death in 1969.

L442

Zvans (The Bell) was yet another effort by an idealist, a political and socio-economic journal (according to its subtitle) lasting only from March to July 1930. The editor, Kārlis Krievs, with his traffic-engineering background seemed determined to enlighten his readers on Latvian and foreign political and social life along with domestic infrastructure problems. His concern for the rule of law in state affairs and strengthening relations with other democratic countries (including the USA) among other noble causes for that time apparently brought a small echo. He likely riled a few strong nationalists with an initial article titled "The 'cross' and misfortune of our language". But something more fundamental seemed to militate against continuation, as the journal ceased with a combined issue (4/5). Its design high point was Sigismunds Vidbergs' stylized bell cover—such a contrast between cover and text set in Latvian *Fraktur*. L442

Bohema: Žurnāls romantikai un mistikai (The Boheme: A Journal of the Romantic and the Mystical). Although an intriguing idea for a journal, this journal was poorly conceived and lasted only from autumn 1933 to May 1934. Like many a one-person periodical highlighting idiosyncratic interests (in this case local ethnography, folklore, and the occult), fiscal moments of truth came quickly. Without institutional backing and a team of like-minded individuals, demise came sooner rather than later. One would think that with his background and connections in the media and theater the editor Voldemārs Laursons should have been able to make it *work*. Judging from a single issue, however, the "all-over-the-map" content of issue No. 3 indicated an editorial approach that likely ensured circulation to a discouragingly small readership. A few article titles: "Beethoven's relation to the [Latvian] region of Kurzeme", "Jēkabs Bīne—master of nudes", "On the track of historic romance", "Protector of sepulchral life", and "In the dark vaults of a mortuary chapel". The illustrators were a mixed group led by Pauls Šterns, who created front and back cover linocuts. Nikolajs Puzirevskis contributed a drawing of "Old Berlin" (inside front cover) followed by illustrations from Sigismunds Vidbergs, Aleksandrs Junkers, Arvīds Gusārs, Kārlis Pakuls, Oļģerts Ābelīte, Jānis Ansons, and others. L443

L443

Mūsu Mājas Viesis (Our Home Visitor), published from December 1937 until March 1940. Jānis Blumbergs, an agronomist by training and a professional and experienced editor, had served in several governmental ministries and, as a loyal Ulmanis supporter, could be trusted to serve readers the "right" point of view in this popular (20,000 circulation) family publication. Blumbergs' responsibility was to present political life simplified—Latvian business success at home and abroad, life in foreign countries, and home and fashion features—all photographically illustrated. Eduards Dzenis designed the "sign of the times" cover. L444

L444

L445

L446

LATVIJAS MIERA UN BRĪVĪBAS SARGĀTĀJI

L447

Baltijas Apskats (Baltic Digest), with its eight issues a year (January 1935 to January 1937), was the promotional organ for the Baltic office of Wagons-Lits / Thomas Cook World Travel Service. Sections in the three Baltic languages as well as in English provided news notes on travel, with feature articles in English. Articles in the issue cited: "H. M. King George the Fifth"; "How to see Lithuania"; "The British royal residence: Windsor Castle"; "Tallinn, the capital of Estonia"; a centerfold on available Cook cruises; the success of the Lithuanian National Ballet abroad; Latvian literature prize winners in 1935: Aleksandrs Grīns, Vilis Plūdons, and Elza Stērste; and a photographic feature on the Ķemeri health resort in Latvia. L445

Tūrisma Apskats (Tourism Digest, 1936-1940). In comparison with the above periodical's purpose, the role of this journal was to promote tourism within Latvia. Again, its life was short—from 1937 to the summer of 1940, when its final issue was published under the guidance of the Soviet-installed "Minister of Tourism" Pēteris Blaus. The content of this last issue (shown together with one of the last issues published in a free Latvia) pretended that all was "just fine" but neglected to point out that while suggesting internal travel, the other Soviet "tourist agency" was loading Latvians onto modestly equipped railroad cars for trips to Siberia. L446 Although dated May/June 1940, this issue more likely appeared after the middle of July, for Blaus is in place as editor and a double-page spread carries a banner reading "Latvijas miera un brīvības sargātāji" (The protectors of Latvia's peace and freedom) and a smiling Latvian officer shaking hands with a Soviet officer among vignettes of laughing street dancers and other scenes of unlikely voluntary celebration. L447

Magazīna's editors, Žanis Šulcs and Rihards Zariņš, began in April 1934 with a manageable goal to deliver a weekly periodical of light fare on "literature, film, and the performing arts". The emphasis soon changed to "literature, politics, social issues, and art", a move likely brought about by Ulmanis' editorial watchdogs to whom such an editorial goal may have sounded a bit trivial. Thus, beginning in May (the Ulmanis coup took place on May 15) came a change of course to a more "purposeful editorial program". The editors kept the revised plan until July 1940, when the Soviets suspended publication. The issue shown marked Latvia's last merry Christmas in freedom for five decades. The cover artist is not credited. L448

L448

Senatne un Māksla (Antiquity and Art, 1936-1940) had the quality "feel" every editor-in-chief longs to place in the hands of a visitor. Cost of production was obviously of no concern and quite likely the contributors were paid, unlike contributors to other journals treating similar subjects. Francis Balodis was the republic's "senior archaeologist" and a friend of Ulmanis, who one might imagine may have said to Balodis one day, "What this country needs is a grand, scholarly journal that will show our ancient roots not only to our people but to the world." Such a statement or some variation of it was evidently followed with a blank check and the resources of the state's printing office standing ready. The journal, appearing first in the spring of 1936 and continuing through late spring 1940, was the combined effort of the state museum of history, the state art museum, and the state repository of folklore. The issue shown opens with a reproduction of an etching of Ulmanis in profile (protected with a tissue guard), followed by a typographically pleasing title page, which is followed by a superb color reproduction of Ludolfs Liberts' imaginary portrait of Visvaldis, the chieftain of the Selonian tribe ca. 1200 CE. This dramatic opening of a journal, depicting a contemporary "chief" followed by his "predecessor", leads the reader into well-illustrated articles on archaeological findings, architectural explorations, numismatics, and textile arts. Titling and pagination throughout are printed in the second color of the cover titling. This 168-page publication is a classic example of a scholarly journal serving the ideological needs of the state. Its analogs could be found in the same period in Germany, Italy, Japan, and the USSR, among other authoritarian regimes. But unlike its counterpart publications that more often than not contained articles with skewed findings to serve their respective authoritarian regimes, Senatne un Māksla maintained a scholarly integrity resulting in its articles being recognized and cited to this day. L449

L449

As indicated on its cover, *Dzimtenes Atskaņas* (Echos of our Native Land, 1939-1940) L450 was published a long way from home. But one wonders how many Latvians there were in a radius extending from its publishing office in Tientsin, North China, and waiting to read this professionally-designed and edited journal. At this late date it is difficult to know. But whatever the readership, it was not large enough to sustain or allow management of costs likely exceeding what can only be imagined as meager advertising revenue. The four advertisers in this second issue were an interesting lot: "United Engineering Works" of Tientsin (P. Eglīts, Mgr.), the Ayurveda Pharmacy on Woodrow Wilson Street in Tientsin, "La Femme de Demain" under the guidance of Mme. A. I. Thieme (Tientsin), and finally— if one were fit enough for the ride down to Bubbling Well Road in Shanghai, one could meet the fourth advertiser—Marija Ozoliņa, who was prepared to teach "Designing, cutting, and sewing" at her establishment named "Saule". The editor, P. P. Mirkšs, managed to keep his quarterly alive through four issues with "news from home", a nostalgia piece or two, and regular features about Chinese culture and places to see in the surrounding area. Contributions were in Latvian, English, and German; photos were included throughout. The impending geopolitical crisis was likely the prime factor in its closing, and the final number was dated October/December 1940.

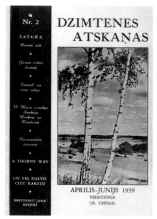

L450

Conclusion

Ending on a note of exile or diaspora reflects the uprootedness that was the theme through which countless Latvian lives continued to be tied to an ever-receding past, and all by means of the book, periodical, and particularly the newspaper. For decades, those Latvians surviving outside of their homeland maintained a connection to the past reflected in the documents of the Latvia's print culture. This is for the grandchildren of those Latvians, whose tie to the language and culture is often tenuous and thus in need of a reminder.

Evoking the story of the Interwar period could have been done with any number of mediums. Books and periodicals were chosen here because of ready availability. But whatever medium one chooses to convey life in a particular period—whether printed material in its variety, a sequence of locally produced films, a stack of phonograph discs, a display of clothing, or packaging design—almost any accumulation of a material culture's products can be used to interpret or at least evoke the life of a people in such a period as the two decades of our interest.

RUSSIAN-LANGUAGE PUBLISHING   PART 2

Introduction

Latvian print culture, particularly the look of Russian books and periodicals of the 1920s, was terra incognita from the beginning of my book-hunting life. Until a few years ago, only three Russian-language titles from the time of Latvia's first independence had ever stood on my shelves—and those, mainly by accident, having been found incidental to other book searching. I kept them because of their interesting authors and two had cover designs of interest.[1] But I did little to look further into what these books represented.

I was not alone in my lack of curiosity. As mentioned, even major exhibitions highlighting vanguard movements of the 1920s and 1930s and featuring Eastern European book cultures concentrated on countries with a readily identifiable graphic design vanguard such as the USSR, Poland, Hungary, etc.[2] Representative works from the Baltic countries were likely left out because of curatorial unfamiliarity with the region's publishing history, the languages, or both.

In 2003, when initiating this project, I began looking in bookshops in New York City, Berlin, and in the Baltic countries to see if there happened to be such a phenomenon as a distinctly "Baltic book look", possibly even an overlooked vanguard. At least I was sure to find representative examples of book design from that two-decade period. For starters, my search focused on Russian titles. That fortuitous choice led me to two Rigensians who provided me with a much-needed tutorial. Konstantin Beloglazov[3] put me on the right path by introducing me to an obsessive bibliographer, the late Iuriĭ Abyzov, and his extensive efforts, many of which are cited in footnotes in the following text.

Because of the need to experience the feel and "look" of locally produced Russica, Beloglazov and his colleague, the editor-collector Anatoliĭ Rakitianskiĭ, provided me with examples of books, periodicals, and sheet music from this short-lived but nonetheless fascinating era in Latvia's publishing history. These examples helped me to answer the underlying question: did Russian-language Latvian imprints look any different from Russian-language books (and periodicals) published in the USSR—mainly in the 1920s—and other centers to which Russian publishers and artists fled in the early 1920s, notably Berlin and Paris? Seeing what these two individuals laid before me was a prime impetus for looking further. After the introduction by Beloglazov and Rakitianskiĭ, followed by browsing sessions in several libraries and private collections, it was clear that a chapter devoted to this sector of publishing was merited. Herewith, a discursive account of selected Russian-language publishers, with a preliminary look at the intended audience's size and the potential market, as well as a few basic statistics on this minority language in Latvia and whatever reading needs it may have had.

1 The three titles: Erich Maria Remarque's *All Quiet on the Western Front* translated as *Na zapadnom fronte bez peremen* (Riga: Orient, n.d. [ca.1929]); **R97** Lion Feuchtwanger's *Jud Süss* translated as *Evrei Ziuss* (Riga: Orient, n.d. [ca.1929]); **R106** and *Like Gentlemen: with Russian Notes and Glossary*, compiled by I. Sharlov and edited by R. O. G. Urch (Riga: no publisher, 1921). This school book (printed at the "State Printing Office") hardly qualifies with its three and a half-page introduction in Russian and Russian glossary, yet the author also wrote *Latvia: Country and People* (London: George Allen and Unwin, 1938), among other titles.
2 *Paris-Moscou* (Paris, 1979); *Constructivisme in Poland 1923-1936. BLOK Praesens a.r.* (Essen: Museum Folkwang, 1973); *Wechselwirkungen: Ungarische Avantgarde in der Weimarer Republik* (Marburg: Jonas Verlag, 1986); *Standing in the Tempest: Painters of the Hungarian Avant-Garde 1908-1930* (Santa Barbara, CA: Santa Barbara Museum of Art, 1991); *Central European Avant-gardes: Exchange and Transformation, 1910-1930* (Los Angeles and Cambridge, MA: Los Angeles County Museum of Art and The MIT Press, 2002); and smaller exhibitions centered on an individual artist.
3 An art and rare book dealer and native Rigensian.

Around 1924, idealistic (and not so idealistic) publishing entrepreneurs, dreaming of being Russian-language publishers, began announcing their intentions to enter book publishing in Riga's Russian-language press.[4] It was apparent that a Russian-speaking and reading audience, admittedly modest, already existed, not only in Latvia, but also among the population of émigré Russian intellectuals and business people in Lithuania and Estonia. There was an additional, albeit small, Russian-language market among October Revolution refugees living in Warsaw, Berlin, Prague, and Paris—a population holding promise of some help to the balance sheet. The primary market in Riga consisted largely of just such émigré readers, in addition to those Russian residents who had made up a portion of the population of the region for more than two centuries. In his *Russia Abroad*, John Glad summarized the growth of Latvia's Russian population in a few sentences:[5]

"An estimated 231,000 Russians resided in Latvia before 1914; as a result of the Russian Civil War this historic population of Baltic Russians was augmented by 20,000 Russian refugees. On August 1, 1920, Soviet Russia signed a peace treaty with Latvia, and Russian cultural life in that country developed with considerable vigor. By 1930 12 percent (233,366) of the population consisted of ethnic Russians and 4.8 percent (93,479) were Jews, most of whom spoke Russian as their first language."

But to arrive at a potential readership one must factor in real as opposed to reported illiteracy, age, disposition toward reading, age levels, and other factors. It was not possible to find even a fragmentary, period "market study" of the potential Russian-reading community by any of the individuals or groups of would-be Russian publishers thinking of even small-scale enterprises. If ignorance of a market was no hindrance, printing and production capacity was certainly no impediment to any vision of potential market development. By the mid 1920s the printing capacity of Riga's printers was improving and expanding annually.

Riga also had a small but influential core population of artists and artisans that traveled widely and who were in touch with European trends. When at home in Riga, these individuals produced remarkable pottery, paintings, and even interesting book and periodical cover designs and illustrations, although mainly for Latvian- and Yiddish-language publishers. These artists—many in their late 20s and early 30s—provided a potential pool of remarkable creativity.

Nevertheless, despite the possibilities and the existing and potential talent, examples of competent design, discovered by me, were in the minority. One is tempted to speculate as to why a greater number of better-designed Russian-language books did not appear on the market, books similar to those one could find at that time among, for example, in Berlin and Paris.

If, indeed, titles from most publishers of Russica in Riga (with the exception of Zhizn' i Kul'tura) generally lacked head-turning appeal for the jaded 21st century eye, one might be initially tempted to put the blame indirectly on the content of the titles publishers often chose—content so ephemeral that skilled designers in many a country would have simply turned down commissions rather than become professionally tainted. However, designers and would-be designers in Latvia did not often have the luxury of choice because of existing financial conditions. Regrettably, much of the literature considered by publishers for translation and ultimate publication was predominantly popular, undemanding

---

4 See advertisements in *Segodnia*, *Narodnaia Gazeta*, etc., from 1924 onward.
5 *Russia Abroad: Writers, History, Politics* by John Glad (Tenafly, NJ: Hermitage and Birchbark Press, 1999), p. 195.

fiction by Anglo-American and European writers and a mix of lesser authors from the Imperial Russian era.

Some publishers took the inventive measure of putting a few Soviet writers in "pre-Revolution dress" by cutting politically tendentious passages and printing the text in pre-1917 orthography in an attempt to hoodwink those charged with implementing a governmental ban on publishing Soviet writers. For economic reasons, many fiction titles from Western Europe and the Anglo-American world were truncated, usually without the author's permission. Such compromised conditions were hardly ideal for tempting the handful of dedicated and gifted local designers into the Russian publishing scene, thus leaving much of the design work to typographers and ordinary designers.

Attempts by the young Latvian government to restrict importation and distribution of Soviet-published books may also have been a factor in limiting inspiring exposure to what was being published in the more cosmopolitan design centers of Leningrad and Moscow, at least during the NEP[6] period. Such a ban may have kept at least some of the potential local designers of Russian books unaware of the creativity and experimental design trends taking place in these centers. But that is a questionable argument given the general flow of books outside conventional channels clearly documented by what could be found in personal libraries in Riga and abroad, in libraries inherited by grandchildren of intellectuals living at that time.

By most accounts from contemporary informants,[7] a major contributing factor to design impoverishment was a lack of professional background among individuals who chose to go into Russian-language publishing—individuals inexperienced in the basics of publishing, including the ability to attract and guide competent designers. Contributing to this circumstance was, in all likelihood, the entrepreneurs' own limited sense of design. It is a matter of record that the majority of creative Russian book designers who had fled Moscow and Leningrad during the civil war of the early 1920s, with but few exceptions, headed for Berlin and Paris, among other points west.

The Riga designers and illustrators whose work might have made potential customers take a second glance in a Russian bookshop window were already working with Latvian-language or Yiddish-language publishers, if not busy in their own studios and printmaking workshops to feed a growing local demand for fine art. These designers may also have been reluctant to associate with many of the unprofessional individuals aspiring to become Russian-language publishers.

Nor was Latvian-Russian publishing a competitive market requiring distinctive, eye-catching graphics. By many accounts it was a captive market needing small press runs; 1,000 copies was the standard, with 3,000 copies for a projected best-seller. In the aggregate, Russian-language publishing in Latvia accounted for fewer than 1,000 titles in those two decades. In financial terms it was barely a break-even business.[8] Few books made a significant profit, thus a reluctance to pay professional designers.

One would have imagined greater, indirect outside artistic influences, for it is well documented that Riga's Russian musical, theater, and film life drew on the wider Russian cultural contribution of the time. Despite local government attempts, it was simply

6   New Economic Policy period, 1921-1929: a time in the young USSR when entrepreneurs and artists were allowed considerable freedom of expression.

7   Conversations with Iuriĭ Abyzov interpreted Konstantin Beloglazov and Anatoliĭ Rakitianskiĭ (2002-2004).

8   Iuriĭ Abyzov demonstrates these circumstances in his several publications cited elsewhere in this chapter.

R1

not possible to entirely seal the borders against cultural influences from the "east", particularly those coming between the end of the USSR's civil war in 1922 and Stalin's consolidation of power in 1928/1929. Books, periodicals, phono-recordings, sheet music, and the occasional poster did find their way through official barriers. Fragments of circumstantial evidence of a one-time cultural interchange still exist in locally discovered examples as already indicated, e.g., books and individual periodical issues with dated, period inscriptions found in shops and homes.[9]

There were a few licensed, Soviet-influenced periodicals—exclusively Latvian-language,[10] not Russian—that did echo the graphic dynamism seen in Moscow-Leningrad publications during that brief, relatively open era of the NEP years. But one must not be too harsh in judging the lack of any of these possible outside influences on local designers. A balanced assessment would have to credit Russian-Rigan book design in general, for their work on the whole was comparable to the design at the mid-level of the Latvian-language book market or that of any other industrialized country at that time.

When this inquiry was begun, there was, admittedly, anticipation of finding an extensive cache of overlooked design sophistication reflected in one book and periodical cover after the other throughout the shops and in library storage areas. Initial discovery of such work echoing movements beyond Latvian borders include the uncredited design for Avram Vysotskiĭ's *Tel Aviv: Palestinskiĭ roman*[11] R1 with its echo of the Devětsil[12] movement's book designs and the uncredited cover design for *Bliznetsy* (Twins),[13] Thomas Mann's story of incest. R2 A case might even be made for the latter example being the anonymous designer's conflation of designs seen on Russian and Polish constructivist books of the 1920s.

My hope continued that the utilitarian quality of book design found on shelf after shelf would ultimately give way to at least a reasonable number of well-designed books by unsung designers. Alas, there were but two designers who fit the category of "unsung" by present-day Anglo-European book design historians.

These notable exceptions deserving more than passing reference were men who took commissions from both Russian and Latvian publishers: the indefatigable Mihails Jo (i.e., Joffe), who raced among Russian, Latvian, and Yiddish-language publishers, producing a formidable number of cover illustrations, designs, and logos; and the equally versatile Raimunds Šiško.

In the introduction of this book mention was made of the discrete publishing cultures in Latvia that overlapped only moderately because of the general nature of ethnic German, Russian, Jewish, and Latvian societies being, for the most part, separate. There was, however, amicable interchange on various business levels, polite nods and greetings

9   Riga was anything but isolated. Given the waves of literary suppression through the decades, it is surprising that evidence of Riga as a crossroads can still be found in homes and bookshops—evidence reflecting Interwar intellectual vibrancy as one sees by finding such books as Erwin Piscator's *Das Politische Theater* (1929), Aleksandr Tairov's *Zapiski rezhissera* (1921), Nikolai Evreinov's *Teatr kak takovoi* (2nd ed., 1923), numerous Malik-Verlag books (although rarely with the Heartfield-designed book jackets present), and tattered issues of *L'Esprit Nouveau, Novyĭ Lef, Gebrauchsgraphik, Dźwignia, Linja,* and *Za Rulem.*

10   For example, *Kreisā Fronte, Signāls,* etc.

11   Published by Prosveshchenie and Grāmatu Draugs in 1933. Other titles by Vysotskiĭ published before his departure for Palestine were sought with discovery of *Subbota i voskresen'e* (Riga: Grāmatu Draugs, 1929) and *Zelenoe plamia: Palestinskiĭ roman* (Riga: Obshchedostupnaia biblioteka, 1935), the latter with other pagination and thus an unlikely "repackaging".

12   The most significant vanguard Czech design movement of the 1920s.

13   A translation of Mann's *Wälsungenblut* (München: Phantasus-Verlag, 1921), published in Riga by Kniga dlia vsiekh in 1932.

at the opera and at concerts, even inter-ethnic dating.[14] Nevertheless, Riga's cosmopolitan life of the time was little different from that found in most large and small urban centers with any extensive interaction among language minorities being the exception.

Riga's German- and Russian-speaking Jewish population had far greater association on a number of levels with other language groups, as the testimony of those interviewed has shown. The Latvian population interacted less so, particularly with the Russian-Jewish and Yiddish-speaking groups that will be seen later in the chapter on publishing for the Jewish community.

Substantive interchange in publishing circles having an effect on book design might have been fostered had there been an overarching, general publishers' association working for all language publishers. But such an association never quite coalesced even on an informal basis. With the exception of the Latvian-language publishers, other individual language groups were essentially too small for effective publisher associations.

Commentary on the way artists worked, from the beginning of the republic onward, indicates that the most capable designers generally worked on a freelance principle with the tendency to seek out (or be sought by) publishers with which the designers shared an affinity.[15]

Another observation, and certainly a factor in achieving positive design results, was the problem with which all but the largest publishers wrestled: the cost of quality paper. Moreover, in the early 1920s an uneven equipment mix existed in most of the print shops; new and antiquated printing equipment shared the same space. This situation, together with the lack of a well-developed, indigenous graphic design tradition, is reflected in the examples chosen to be shown here. In view of such constraints, one can only admire what was accomplished.

Latvia was certainly not lacking in artistic talent, as can be seen in a visit to the Latvian National Museum of Art. The Latvian region had a number of notable painters dating from the early 19th century down to the era discussed. Several of these major Russian and Latvian artists contributed distinctive graphic designs to a handful of books before the time of independence, as has been previously mentioned. But these few artist/designers did not constitute a fully developed tradition on which a young book publishing community, Russian or otherwise, could readily draw.

The relatively insular nature of ethnic populations and social constraints militated against the pooling of creative resources among the Latvians, Germans, Jews, Poles, Estonians, and Lithuanians as well as the Russians, who comprised the second largest language group after Latvians. Minorities were further divided along political and social lines, even within a given language group. The aggregate creative talent, while colorful and vibrant, was anything but unified when it came to working within the larger publishing sector. (The German population, once a major presence in publishing, rapidly dwindled with the establishment of the Republic in 1918.)

The Jewish population of nearly 100,000 at the beginning of the Republic was fragmented into three main groups: 1) the Yiddish-speaking, shtetl Jews who lived in the southeastern portion of the country with some pockets in the western provinces; 2) a largely Russian-speaking group of recently-arrived urbanized Jews fleeing a deteriorating Russia for Riga's business and professional opportunities; 3) a traditionally German-speaking

R2

---

14   Interview with Irra Schlossberg Gelin, New York, Oct. 2007.
15   Interviews with Jānis Borgs, Elfrīda Melbārzde, Konstantin Beloglazov, Oct. 2003.

Jewish population in the district of Courland (Kurland, Kurzeme), 40,000 of whom had been abruptly deported in April 1915 by a Tsarist edict but in many cases then drifted back as circumstances allowed.[16]

Given this non-Latvian-language setting, the obvious question arises: was there a commercially viable audience for Russian-language books? Being multilingual was the norm before and after independence among the intellectuals in the various language groups cited. It was for this mixed market that a few dozen hopeful, mostly inexperienced entrepreneurs took the initiative to publish Russian-language books, newspapers, and magazines.

The other, much smaller language minorities—Estonian, Lithuanian, Polish—did not figure appreciably in the book and print culture of Latvia at the time. Most reading individuals among the smaller minorities subscribed to newspapers in their own languages and relied on imported books, mainly popular literature available at some of the larger kiosks in sections of the cities and towns where language or national groups were concentrated.

It should be stated once again that since the late 19th century most Latvian intellectuals and leaders did read Russian papers and Russian literature as well as the German press and literature, despite there being a psychological distance from the literary cultures of both the Russian and German overlords.

Russian-language publishing in the Latvian-language region

Russian-language publishing in what is now Latvia in the period prior to independence began in earnest in the 1860s and 1870s, following a renewed Imperial Russian policy calling for the "Russification" of the Empire's Baltic provinces. Russian minor officials, soldiers, traders, and merchants had been moving in and out of the Baltic region since the time of Peter the Great; a few invariably found life pleasant in the region and settled. Those who were literate relied for intellectual stimulation on material brought from the Russian publishing centers rather than initiating local publishing efforts. By the late 19th century imperial plans called for school books to be produced specifically for the Russian-language schools then being built in the region. Coincident with this literacy effort was an increased distribution of St. Petersburg newspapers, journals, and popular fiction to regional shops and kiosks.

Indigenous Russian publishing carried out in Latvian-speaking regions in that early period remained primarily official government newspapers, e.g., *Kurlyandskiye gubernskiye vedomosti* (Courland Government Gazette, 1852-1915), or *Liflyandskiye gubernskiye vedomosti* (Livland Government Gazette, 1852-1865; 1868-1917) and *Liflyandskiye gubernskiye vedomosti* (Livland Government Gazette, 1831-1917). Mention should also be made of two papers for their revealing content and what their existence said about Russification efforts: the Russian nationalists' *Rizhskiĭ viestnik* (Riga Herald, 1869-1915) R3 and *Rishskiye epoarkhialnye vedomosti* (Riga Diocesan Gazette, 1888-1915).

Unquestionably, this Russification policy fueled the already rising Latvian nationalist and anti-Russian feelings that had begun surfacing as early as the 1850s in the areas ultimately to become Latvia and Estonia. There was also an allied effort for a time among

---

16   Commentators and contemporary diarists repeatedly point out that large numbers of Riga's Jewish population were German-speaking and -reading.

a handful of Latvian intellectuals led notably by the activist nationalist and scholar Krišjānis Valdemārs,[17] who saw the Imperial Russian nationalist movement as a possible force to aid Latvian nationalists in their efforts against a common enemy, the often exploitative German barons.[18]

The tempo of political and social events accelerated dramatically by the beginning of the 20th century, accompanied by upheaval more far-reaching than any russification policy. The Russian Empire was waning. Social democratic and Communist-inspired movements were rising, along with sporadic anarchic activity among Bakunists, inspired by smuggled issues of *Narodnoe Delo* (The People's Business, 1868-1870), which found their way into the Empire from Geneva via Riga and other ports.

R3

Following the January 9, 1905, uprising in St. Petersburg, important but lesser-publicized uprisings in the Latvian region continued to take place throughout the year. Like the crowds in St. Petersburg on "Bloody Sunday", Latvian and Jewish protesters, notably in the town of Tukums outside of Riga,[19] were fired upon by Tsarist troops with scores killed and more than 200 wounded. This was front-page news in the young Latvian press and the local Russian-language press that at the time numbered some half-dozen papers.[20] The Russian-reading population could also rely on the St. Petersburg and Moscow newspapers, making their appearance within the week in more than 75 Russian-language shops and kiosks in Riga.[21]

Russian-language publishing in Interwar Latvia

By the close of the second decade of the 20th century, Russian-language book publishing was in flux because of politically determined change brought on by change in the Russian-reading population of Latvia. Many Russians sympathizing with the October Revolution had either left for Moscow and Petrograd by 1919/1920 or retreated into an "inner exile". Those inclined toward political activism and who remained channeled their sympathies into clandestine and semi-clandestine activity. The pro-Soviet activists left kept a low profile most of the time. The Latvian government-in-formation made it clear that any printed agitation toward "Sovietization" of Latvia would not be tolerated. Latvians who had been living in Russia and Russian-Jewish entrepreneurs unsympathetic to the October Revolution were moving in large numbers to the now-independent Latvia in order to escape the horrors of civil war and the general upheaval that existed throughout much of revolutionary Russia.

17   Valdemārs was a major figure in Latvian public life as developer not only of national journalism but also founder of the first naval school and the influential but short-lived Latvian nationalist newspaper in St. Petersburg, *Pēterburgas Avīzes* (1862-1865). He is remembered today for his contribution to Latvian philology and folklore.

18   *The Baltic States: The Years of Independence*, by Georg von Rauch (London: C. Hurst, 1974), p. 9.

19   See *The Revolution in the Baltic Provinces of Russia: A Brief Account of the Activity of the Lettish Social Democratic Workers' Party*, by an Active Member (London: Independent Labour Party, 1907), p. 25.

20   See *Gazetniĭ mir: Adresnaya i spravochnaya kniga*. 2-oe izdanie. Ilia V. Volfson, ed. (St. Petersburg: self-published, 1912), columns 336-338.

21   Ibid.

R4

With Imperial Russia's entry into war and the subsequent Russian governmental retreat from the Baltic region beginning in 1915, sizeable portions of the Russian population left the Baltic and its industrial centers. Anatol Lieven summarizes the shift in population before and during the Bolshevik Revolution. He describes the flight of skilled and unskilled workers leaving Riga and other Baltic cities, followed by an influx of many refugees from Russia for whom reading and a print culture was, although not stated as such, a more important part of their lives because of their relatively higher level of education than that of their predecessors. Lieven states: "The educated sections of this new Russian emigration were a heterogeneous mixture, including both former White Russian officers and their families, and (in Latvia) large numbers of Russian-speaking Jews. Interwar Riga was the largest Russian émigré center after Paris."[22] Publishing circumstances would appear to be promising for this new population.[23]

Latvia's population constituencies in this period leading up to the transition from Empire outpost to independent country are easily shown with a few more statistics allowing one to speculate on the book publishing potential not only for the Russian-reading population but other language groups as well.

In the 1913 census the ethnic Russian population in Riga was 20%. The Latvian population was barely twice as great at 39.8%. The other populations: 13.9% German, 9.5% Polish, 7% Jewish, and 6.9% Lithuanian.[24] The implication of these numbers for publishing in what had been for generations one of Europe's most ethnically and intellectually diverse cities is even more telling when one realizes that a would-be publisher entering this fragmented book market needed entrepreneurial courage to address a total population of slightly more than 2,550,000 adults, including adult illiterates and children. In the mid 1920s illiteracy among Baltic-Russians (Russians living in Latvia for at least two generations) was 20.47%; among newly-arrived Russians illiteracy was 15.28%.[25] Obviously, publishing or distributing Russian-language books carried certain financial risks. In addition, any publisher with dreams of distributing Russian-language books from elsewhere met legal opposition for such books from at least one source. Laws were passed almost immediately with the founding of independent Latvia, and on February 24, 1920, it became illegal to import or sell publications by any agency of the Bolshevik regime. After 1922 the law was amended and extended to any works originating in the USSR.[26]

When newly arriving Russians looked for more serious reading than that available at kiosks in the early 1920s, there was but one main venue where serious book buyers could browse for new and antiquarian books: "Kymmel's", the best known Russian-language bookshop in Riga in the period before the Bolshevik Revolution and lasting into the mid 1920s. Kymmel issued catalogs—antiquarian and new—from the mid 19th century (1858) almost until the time of its closing. The cover of a Christmas and Stock Catalog from autumn 1890 is shown here. R4 The shop R5 was a continuation of a venture begun much

22 Anatol Lieven, *The Baltic Revolution: Estonia, Latvia, Lithuania and the Path to Independence.* 2nd ed. (New Haven: Yale Univ. Press, 1994), p. 182.

23 Lieven does not take into account the Russian population of Berlin and Germany, which at its high point in 1922/1923 approached 500,000, dropping to around 40,000 by 1933. See Marc Raeff, "Emigration—welche, wann, wo? Kontexte der russischen Emigration in Deutschland, 1920-1941", in *Russische Emigration in Deutschland 1918 bis 1941.* (Karl Schlögel, ed. Berlin: Akademie Verlag, 1995), p. 17.

24 Stephen D. Corrsin, "The Changing Composition of the City of Riga, 1867-1913", *Journal of Baltic Studies*, 13:1 (1982).

25 "Analfabet" in *Latviešu konversācijas vārdnīca*, vol. 1 (Riga: Gulbis, 1927), p. 466.

26 This law was amended in March 1928, allowing importation of a fixed number of Russian-language books and periodicals, presumably those not considered a threat to the state.

R5

R6

earlier by the noted Nikolaĭ N. Kymmel family.[27] In the beginning of the Republican years, Kymmel's was located on Zirgu iela. It served not only a general audience with books and periodicals from St. Petersburg and other Russian printing centers but also carried school books for Russian primary and secondary schools, a service continuing since Riga-born Nikolaĭ Kymmel purchased the Riga bookselling enterprise of E. Frantzen in 1842.[28]

For a note on what one was likely to see while walking in Riga's "Old Town" heading for Kymmel's bookshop in the early 1920s, a vivid description (although from a few years later) is that of American diplomat George F. Kennan, who was given his first diplomatic posting to Riga in 1925. In his memoirs written 40 years later, Kennan provided a succinct observation not only on life in Riga but also on Russian Riga a few years after the decade's beginning:

"Riga had the advantage of a variegated and highly cosmopolitan cultural life: newspapers and theatres in the Lettish, German, Russian, and Yiddish tongues and vigorous Lutheran, Roman Catholic, Russian Orthodox, and Jewish religious communities... In addition to its more serious cultural amenities, Riga had a vigorous night life, much in the Petersburg tradition: vodka, champagne, gypsies, sleighs or drozhki with hugely bundled coachmen waiting at the door, a certain amount of gaiety, R6 but even more of a nostalgic, despairing, shoot-the-works sentimentality—a mood—which had a tendency to prove highly irrelevant and unhelpful the next day. The nightclubs were, in fact, not

27   To this enterprise Nikolaĭ Kymmel added the Riga-St. Petersburg Steamship Company and co-founded Die Baltische Monatsschrift. His son assumed management of the book business as partner, continuing from the 1880s to 1921.
28   For a Kymmel family biographical sketch see *Deutschbaltisches Biographisches Lexikon* (Köln: Böhlau Verlag, 1970), p. 436.

R7

R8

the only relics of Tsardom in the sights and habits of the local scene. Riga was in many respects a minor edition of Petersburg. The old Petersburg was of course now dead, or largely dead... But Riga was still alive. It was one of those cases where the copy had survived the original."[29]

Kennan goes on to comment on climate and how Rigensians dealt with the Baltic's distinctive weather and its way of taking a toll on even the cheerier citizenry.

"The weather, for nine months of the year, was apt to be on the dreary side... Over the long rainy weekends, arguments about Russia, Marxism, capitalism, the peasant problem, etc., droned endlessly on... below us in the rain-drenched harbor could be heard the hooting of switch engines and the clanking of the strings of battered broad-gauged freight cars...But above all there was, as a relief from Riga in summer, that magnificent, seemingly endless stretch of seashore known as the Riga Strand. Here the Russian-type dachas[30] could be seen strung out for miles and miles along the dunes, among the great glistening Scotch pines... R7 I spent weekends there in June and July, bathing in the sea by day, bathing then later, in the nocturnal hours, in the magic and, to me, commandingly erotic twilight of the northern world in the weeks of the summer solstice—the twilight that has given the name to the 'white nights' of Petersburg."[31]

As to Russian-language print culture in the years from 1919 to 1923/1924—the period before Russian book publishing began in earnest—there were primarily short-lived newspapers[32] and journals and a few self-published efforts in the way of booklets and books. Among these, most all of which were lacking in any design distinctiveness, one might cite as examples Maks Shats-Anin's sketch of Latvian-Jewish history, *Temporalizm*,[33] and the *Russkiĭ Kalendar-spravochnik na 1921 god* (Russian Calendar Reference Book for 1921) published by the Russian Society in Latvia. A third undistinguished-in-appearance title is a booklet of contributions previously published in the newspaper *Novyĭ Put'* (New Way, 1921-1922). This third title, *Novoye v sovremennoi Russkoi poeziĭ: Pismo iz Moskvy* (The New in Contemporary Russian Poetry: Letter from Moscow, published in 1921), R8 was a 16-page critique of Russian poetry and commentary on art trends.[34] This fragile publication was the first book/pamphlet publication of a young and ultimately prolific Soviet literary critic, Viktor Pertsov, remembered today for his somewhat flawed biography of Mayakovsky.[35]

29 George F. Kennan's *Memoirs, 1925-1950* (Boston: Little, Brown, & Co., 1967), p. 29-31.

30 The structures sighted by Kennan were fishing huts that were architecturally different in design from what he presumed to be dachas although by the 1920s were sometimes used as dachas.

31 For a period glimpse of the "Riga Strand" see *Jūrmala: Nature and Cultural Heritage*, ed. by Rihards Pētersons, et al. (Riga: Neputns, 2004). This work also cites a Russian-language beach periodical, *Plyazh*, with its risqué cartoons, jokes, and very light reading, published from 1922 at least into 1926. Ten Latvian-language newspapers were known to have been published in the Jurmala region in those years.

32 *Segodnia* (1919-1940) was an exception for its longevity, discussed further at this chapter's end.

33 Subtitled *Opyt filosofii evreiskoi kultury (Experiment in Jewish Cultural Philosophy)*, first published in 1919 by Progress. Reprinted with photographs and editorial matter by Anatoliĭ Krapchin and Grigoriĭ Smirin (Riga: Muzei Evrei v Latviĭ, 2005).

34 Pertsov praises Osip Mandelstam, Fyodor Sologub, and Anna Akhmatova with balanced views of émigrés such as Ivan Bunin, Leonid Andreyev, and Alexseĭ Tolstoy—opinions that might not have fared well with censors at home in Moscow and likely brought him problems a decade later.

35 Mayakovsky. *Zhizn' i tvorchestvo*. 3rd ed. (Moscow: Khudozhestvennaya literatura, 1976), 3 vols.

This little pamphlet (along with the other two cited titles) could be counted among the incunabula[36] of Russian publishing in free Riga.

Design was likewise not a major consideration in another ephemeral-appearing compilation in those first years: a booklet of poems by the more established writer Ilja Ėrenburg. Ėrenburg, who was to become widely known as a peripatetic diarist and professional Soviet apologist, came to Riga in late March 1921 with a manuscript sheaf of 85 poems by literary luminaries-to-be[37] and, of course, by himself. On this stopover he was, among other things, looking for a publisher. In an exchange with Evgeniĭ Lyatzkiĭ, a publishing acquaintance in Stockholm, Ėrenburg was encouraged to seek out Kirill Bashkirov, an aspiring publisher who had recently arrived in Riga. This glimpse into the early days of Riga's Russian-language publishing is noted in a web article by Rashid Yangirov,[38] in which he tells us that Bashkirov, an economist, had a fleeting dream of being a publisher. It appears that he also had an equally short period in which he facilitated the printing of other people's manuscripts. The result of the Bashkirov-Ėrenburg connection was the publication of a selection of Ėrenburg's poems in a 31-page booklet titled *Razdumiya* (Meditation).[39] Either modesty or some other reason kept Bashkirov from adding the name Lira[40] to the title page, the name he had conceived for his planned publishing house, according to Yangirov.[41] This pamphlet is not much to look at even though some unknown calligrapher made an effort at giving the cover typography his best with what appears to be a flat-nib pen. R9

R9

R10

R11

R12

The relative visual austerity of the publications by Pertsov and Ėrenburg speaks subtly of the provisional state of Riga-Russian publishing in those first years of rebuilding. Ėrenburg did not stay long. His was just a brief visit like that of so many other intellectuals on their way from Moscow or Petrograd to Berlin or Paris.

It is puzzling that, with the usual ripples caused by an "Ėrenburg appearance" in a publishing center, his widely-popular *Trinadtsat' Trubok* (Thirteen Pipes, published in Berlin in 1923, R10 in Stockholm in 1925, R11 and in Kaunas in 1932) R12 was not published

36 My term for Russian-language books and booklets published between 1919 and 1922.

37 Marina Tsvetaeva, Osip Mandelstam, Sergei Esenin, Boris Pasternak.

38 In his letter written from the Grand Hotel to the Stockholm publisher Lyatskii, dated April 1, 1921, Ėrenburg asks about possibilities for publishing his collection of poems, *Razdumiya*. Lyatskiĭ, on his way to Berlin, turned down Ėrenburg but not before suggesting Kirill Bashkirov, according to Rashid Yangirov's website posted under his name on August 20, 2005.

39 Printed in 1921 by Dzintars, located at Elizabetes iela 22.

40 Not to be confused with Solomon Tager's publishing venture *Severnaia Lira*, which Iuriĭ Abyzov states published five titles between 1928 and 1929 and which also published Ėrenburg's *Ravvin i padshaya* but long after Ėrenburg had left for the brighter lights of Berlin and Paris.

41 In his web article "K istorii izdaniya Lebedinogo stana Mariny Tsvetaevoi" (posted Aug. 20, 2005) Rashid Yangirov goes into some detail on the Ėrenburg-Bashkirov-Lyatskiĭ connections.

in Riga in book form as it was elsewhere. Extracts in a Latvian translation, however, were serialized in 1923 in three periodicals: *Socialdemokrats* (The Social Democrat),[42] *Nedeļa* (The Week),[43] and *"Semgaleescha" literariskais peelikums* ("Zemgalietis" Literary Supplement).[44]

A greater impression in those early days on Riga-Russian publishing than Ėrenburg's, however, was made by another "passing meteor", an artist who also had no counterpart in subsequent years either in Riga-Russian book design or illustration. This artist, Vasyl Masjutyn, stopped over in Riga on his way from Petrograd to Berlin early in December 1920. Riga-born but reared and educated in Russia, he was returning briefly to the city of his birth shortly after the initial phase of rubble clearing had taken place and some semblance of government and rudimentary cultural life had returned.

To give some indication of his design ability already noticed in 1914, the 20-year-old art student graduate of the School of Painting, Sculpture, and Architecture in Moscow had been invited to participate in the prestigious Internationale Ausstellung für Buchgewerbe und Graphik in Leipzig together with such well-known Russian graphic artists as Ivan Bilibin, Boris Grigoriev, Evgeniĭ Lanceray, Dmitriĭ Mitrokhin, and Georgiĭ Narbut.[45] But despite this early recognition, Masjutyn decided to forego future local honor as well as the revolutionary excitement looming in a Russia heading into political and social uncertainty. The terror of the October Revolution and the subsequent civil war convinced him that better days and quite likely a calmer work environment lay beyond the borders of the still-to-be-formed Soviet Union, so he left. But in his brief Riga visit from December 1920 to December 1921, this energetic graphic artist contributed what was to be one of the brightest footnotes in two decades of Russian-language book design in Latvia. His book covers and illustrations are discussed to this day among present-day Riga book collectors.

In Waltraud Werner's detailed study and *catalogue raisonné* of Masjutyn's work, she begins by describing his time in Riga with this quote: "With enormous and valuable-in-content luggage, a Latvian passport in his pocket, Masjutyn finally reached Riga... despite the uncertain future, his stay in Riga was marked by enthusiasm and astonishing productivity."[46] For local book people paying some attention across language boundaries in that brief period, Masjutyn was something of a stellar attraction in the city's Russian artistic circle. Considering his Riga roots, it is unfortunate that he did not stay and inject his energy further into the book culture just beginning to form. But to Masjutyn, a future in Riga seemed almost as uncertain as in Petrograd; Berlin was waiting. Still, his stay provided a design and illustration standard only partially maintained when Rigan Russian-language publishing began in earnest some four years later.

Within two months of Masjutyn's arrival, a major show (216 pieces) of his work—etchings, wood engravings, lithographs, watercolors, drawings, and sculptures—was ex-

---

42 1923 (Nos. 70-75, 101-104, 130-132).

43 1923 (Nos. 45, 58, 59).

44 1923 (Nos. 1-3).

45 Unfortunately, examples of Masjutyn's work did not make their way into the lavish promotional work published in conjunction with the exhibition, cancelled because of the start of World War I. For examples of artists' work with whom Masjutyn was competing see *Der Moderne Buchschmuck in Russland*, ed. by Sergei Makowskiĭ, text by Nikolaĭ Radlow (St. Petersburg: General Commissar of the Russian Division, International Exhibition for Book Design and Graphics, Leipzig, 1914).

46 *Wassili Masjutin 1884-1955: Ein russischer Künstler, 1922-1955 in Berlin*. Waltraud Werner, ed. and comp. (Berlin: Verlag Willmuth Arenhövel, 2003), p. 27.

RUSLAN

R13

R14

R15

hibited in the Riga People's College from February 6-25, 1921.[47] And that was only the beginning. A few months later, nine illustrations for Pushkin's *Ruslan and Ludmila*, later published in Munich,[48] and other etchings and lithographs were included in a group show sponsored by the Russian Society of Latvia.[49] The following year, after Masjutyn had already left for Berlin, another group show of works by Russian artists, including seven by Masjutyn, was again held at the Latvian National University.[50] Only the cover of the second exhibition's catalog has a Masjutyn illustration, one of the Ruslan and Ludmila illustrations. R13

Although mainly a prize for postcard enthusiasts and determined Masjutyn collectors, his first project in Riga had been a five-piece linocut postcard series (175x145 mm) titled "Man and Woman". He followed this series with a book jacket for Augusts Baltpurviņš' *Starp diweem krasteem* (Between Two Shores, 1921) R14 and, according to Werner, the cover and 17 illustrations for his own *Rasskazy gluptsa* (Tales of a Fool),[51] which remained unpublished. Another Russian-language title to which Masjutyn contributed a cover design while in Riga was Mikhail Osorgin's *Iz malenkago domika* (From a Little House, 1921). R15

A respectable number of Masjutyn's Riga-Russian book designs and illustrations are not credited to Riga's book history, e.g., the Orchis Verlag edition of *Ruslan und Ludmila* with its already-cited illustrations. Even Masjutyn's best-known illustrated work, Alexandr Blok's *Dvenadtsat* (The Twelve; Berlin: Newa-Verlag, 1922) with its original cover graphics and illustrations R16, was created in Riga and sent by Masjutyn to Berlin

47   *V. Masjutina zimejumu, ofortu un akvareļu izstades katalogs 6.II–25.II, 1921* (Riga: Latvijas Tautas augstskola, 1921). 61 pp.

48   *Ruslan und Ludmila: Ein phantastisches Märchen*, by A. Pushkin (München: Orchis Verlag, 1922).

49   *Krievu makslenieku glezzu izstāde, sarikota no "Krievu biedrības Latvija"* (Riga: Krievu biedrības Latvija, 1921), 101 pp. Latvian and Russian text.

50   *Krievu mākslineeku glezzu un zīmejumu izstādes katalogs 14.V–14.VI, 1922* (Riga: Latvijas Tautas augstskolas mākslas salons, 1922), 41 pp.

51   Werner, ibid., No. 469, p. 121.

R16

R17

R18

for publication, first in a German translation in 1921 and the next year in Russian, also published in Berlin.[52] R17 The cover illustration is identical in both editions. The Latvian edition published in 1923 with its cover design by the remarkable cubist painter and book designer Jānis Liepiņš shows another approach. R18

To give one final note of credit to Masjutyn's "almost-Riga-Russian imprints", mention can be made of some 20 Russian-language titles published after his arriving in Berlin, works for which he had created illustrations or illustration concepts during his brief stay in what he termed the "freedom of Riga". These were the illustrations for the previously mentioned and later-celebrated work, Blok's *Die Zwolf*, as well as Tolstoy's *Die Kreutzersonate* (Berlin: Kiepenheuer, 1921) and titles by Bely, Gogol, Dostoevskiĭ, Lermontov, Pushkin, etc. Fifteen of the 22 works readied for publication in Riga with original art sent on to Berlin and published almost immediately on Masjutyn's arrival in Berlin in December 1921 were Russian classics published in the Russian language.[53]

Mention should also be made of Masjutyn's direct influence on other artists and would-be artists during his short stay. Probably the most noted Riga student from the small circle that gathered around him was the wood engraver of Russian background Nikolajs Puzirevskis, later chosen to illustrate the monumental *Latvju tautas daiņas* (Latvian Folk Songs), volumes 2-10 (Literatūra, 1928-1932), and Latvian translations of Knut Hamsun's *Mihlas wergi* (Slaves of Love, Freināts, 1928) and *Klaidoņu gaitas* (Vagabonds, Freināts, 1928) among many other works, not the least of which was a rambling history of slavery with its somber illustrations (illustrated in the Latvian-language chapter). As to Puzirevskis' contribution to Russian-language publishing, there are undoubtedly other examples, although this writer has yet to discover any other than the uncredited cover for his brother Dmitriĭ's self-published poems *Bez tebya* (Without You, 1927).[54] R19

A few statistics on Russian book market viability in Riga

With many of the early 1920s Russian-language publications being self-published or otherwise subsidized, once again, the question is raised of how there could be a viable market for the Russian book, given that the potential Russian-reading population of the newly independent Latvia in 1920 had stabilized at only 7.8% of the population.[55] (John Glad calculates approximately 250,000, rising to 10.5% by 1925.[56])

Between 1919 and 1934 Russian books accounted for only 8.7% of the total book market. Illiteracy among Great Russians living in Riga in 1925 was still more than 15.25%; for Baltic Russians illiteracy was nearly 20.5% and more than twice that in the Russian population of the largely agricultural province of Latgale.[57] An optimistic projection of potential Russian book buyers, given ages and literacy levels, was probably around 25,000, which accounts for the modest press runs of 1,000-3,000 copies per title once this sector of publishing began developing in the middle of the decade.

52   *Die Zwölf* (Berlin: Newa Verlag, 1921) and *Dvenadtsat* (Berlin: Newa Verlag, 1922).

53   Werner, ibid., pp. 122-23.

54   This speculative attribution deduced from a Riga city directory indicating a Nikolajs, Dmitriĭ, and Eliza Puzirevskis living at apt. 9, 12a Skolas iela, presumably with their father Vladimir, a physician, whose office was at apt. 5, 12 Skolas iela. Dmitriĭ is indicated as being employed as a doctor's assistant.

55   Plakans, Andrejs. *The Latvians: A Short History* (Stanford, CA: Hoover Institution Press, 1995), p. 158.

56   Glad, ibid., p. 195.

57   See article "Analphabet" in *Latviešu konversācijas vārdnīca*, vol. 1, p. 466.

Unfortunately, taking note of Russian publishing before 1925 was not a concern of the governmental offices charged with publishing matters, according to staff at the Latvian National Library.[58] But 80 years later we have a record, thanks to Iuriĭ Abyzov and his determined research of the Russian-language newspapers and journals of the period and the surviving Russian publishers' catalogs, often undated. He also spent months searching through the less-than-complete holdings of Russian-language Latvian imprints held in the National Library of Latvia, the National Literature and Music Museum, the Misiņš Academic Library of the University of Latvia (Misiņa bibliotēka, founded in 1885), and other institutional libraries. By doing so, he successfully pieced together a year-by-year picture in his *A isdavalos eto v Rige, 1918-1944: Istoriko-bibliograficheskiĭ ocherk* (Publications in Riga, 1918-1944: An Historical-bibliographic Essay).[59]

R19

Bibliographic researchers remain indebted to Abyzov for his *Russkoe pechatnoe slovo v Latviĭ, 1917-1944 gg: Bio-bibliographicheskiĭ spravochnik* (The Russian Printed Word in Latvia 1917-1944: Bio-bibliographic Reference Work)[60] in four volumes, a work listing in a somewhat unwieldy fashion "all publications in the Russian language published in Latvia" for the dates indicated.[61]

If one tabulates Abysov's calculations of production by individual publishers, a total of 865 Russian-language book titles appeared in the two decades of the Republic. John Glad in his *Russia Abroad*[62] estimates that "over the course of [those] two decades some 1,200 titles appeared", although he provides no source for his estimate. Alfrēds Bīlmanis, a government spokesman of that period, when summarizing the publishing sector of Latvia in 1928, stated that "over 1,500 books are published every year on all manner of subjects in different languages".[63]

According to Abyzov, of the 16 houses issuing Russian-language books in 1926, 14 were exclusively publishing in Russian,[64] the second year of the "great rush of dilettantes", as he terms them, who decided to establish Russian-language publishing houses. If economic success had been a criterion, it seems the majority was inexperienced as only three houses out of 12 had lists of four or more titles[65] and were still in the book publishing business in 1934, the year the Kārlis Ulmanis regime took control of the government and reduced by fiat the allowable number of Russian-language publishing houses.

Future researchers inquiring into Russian-language non-periodical publishing in Latvia between the wars, would do well to tabulate the titles in all categories that are cited in *Valsts bibliotēkas biļetens* (State Library Bulletin; hereafter VBB), an organ of the National Library of Latvia that began publication in 1927 with a conscientious listing of all titles (including pamphlets) in all languages, submitted by deposit law to the National Library of Latvia and other deposit libraries. Whenever provided in the deposited publications, the VBB bibliographical citations make note of the printing offices producing the

58 Interview with Dace Pamata, Nov. 2004.
59 (Moscow: Russkiĭ Put: Biblioteka-fond "Russkoe zarubezhe", 2006).
60 (Palo Alto: Stanford Slavic Studies, 1990-91).
61 Note Anatoliĭ Rakitianskiĭ's *Rizhskij bibliofil* (Riga: Bibliofil & Kollektsioner, 2003) and Abyzov's contribution
(pp. 165-170) commenting on 16 of the 50+ publishers identified in his four-volume work.
62 (Tenafly, NJ & Washington, DC: Hermitage and Birchbark Press, 1999), p. 196.
63 *Latvia in the Making, 1918-1928* (Riga: The Riga Times, 1928) by Alfrēds Bīlmanis, p. 53
64 Abyzov, Iuriĭ. *Russkoe pechatnoe slovo v Latvii 1917-1944 gg.: Bio-bibliographicheskiĭ spravochnik*, vol. 4, pp. 417-437.
65 These were M. Didkovskiĭ, Zhizn' i Kul'tura, and Mir. Of the remaining 12 still publishing a few titles, only
Grāmatu Draugs, N. D. Gudkov, and Obshchedostupnaia biblioteka had substantial lists previously.

R20

R21

titles and frequently give the size of edition, thus providing some indication of potential readership or at least a publisher's hopes.

It appears that titles in the *belles lettres* category were also generally published in editions of 1,000-3,000. Some popular fiction titles did reach an edition size of 4,000 as did select non-fiction titles, e.g., Aron Simanovich's *Rasputin i evrei* (Rasputin and the Jews), published by Istoricheskaiya biblioteka in 1928.

The publishers

Just what was published by some of the more prolific publishing houses such as Orient, Grāmatu Draugs, and Zhizn' i Kul'tura? Who were the individuals who entered into publishing, and a prime concern: What did the books look like?

It would be difficult to cite a characteristic Russian-language publishing house for the period because all were in some way the result of a personal dream (not necessarily altruistic) or were, as Abyzov once put it in conversation, a "sumasshedshaia ideia".[66]

Highlighting a few houses and the titles published should be all that is necessary for an opinion to be formed of the Russian-speaking population's reading interests. One further note for forming an impression is the Rigensian Petr Pil'skiĭ's most unflattering comment in *Chisla* (Paris) in 1931 on the literary culture of (Russian) Riga at the end of the first decade: "...no writers, no literary atmosphere, no literary publishing houses..."[67]

Oskar Strok

The publishing house of Oskar Strok was something of an anomaly within the circle of Russian-language publishing houses launched in the mid 1920s.[68] To begin, any contemporary interest probably derives less from the books he published but more likely from Strok's eccentricities and musical genius and the fact that his music, with its periodic revivals, remains in the memory of many even to this day. One need only scroll through current "YouTube" offerings of specific tunes to enjoy a bit of Strok musical nostalgia.

The "adventurer Strok", as Abyzov refers to him, was in fact more a musician than a book publisher, but whatever he may have lacked in publishing acumen was compensated by a bubbling self-confidence. Strok was a hard-to-miss man about town with his get-rich-quick schemes, such as starting a café called "Barberina" with live music on the week-ends or his efforts at securing financial backing for various "factories" by using his persuasive abilities, although what was manufactured, if anything, is not clear to present-day informants. What he manufactured is of little consequence, however, for the consensus among those asked was that his undertakings had nothing to do with books.

From the standpoint of book design, Strok began with a bold show of sophistication by arranging to publish Vicente Blasco Ibáñez's *Krov i Pesok* (Blood and Sand) with a cover design by the vanguard Moscow designer Natan Altman. R20 Strok rushed this title into

---

66   "Schnappsidee" or "crazy" idea.

67   Reported by Abyzov in *A izdavalos eto v Rige, 1918-1944*, p. 218.

68   According to Abyzov, publishers bringing out fewer Russian titles than Strok's nearly 40 titles and beginning in 1924 or earlier were: Progress (3 titles, 1920-1928), Presse (14 titles, 1924-1926), Riga (5 titles, 1924-1925), and Gulbis (4 titles, 1924-1940).

the shops while the film by the same name was still playing in Riga, during the spring of 1924.[69]

How Altman happened to design the cover is not
known. Also, it is not certain that the "printed in Riga"
statement in the Strok edition was a production fact or
a ruse to get around the proscription of imported USSR
titles. Strok's having "Riga – New York" printed on the
cover may have also been part of the ruse to deflect the
attention of local censors who might have questioned the
book's true source. The same translation of Ibáñez with
the same cover design appeared on the Moscow edition,
where Altman was living and working at the time.[70]

Moving into 1925 with the charismatic, ever-contro-
versial Alexandra Kollontai and her *Svobodnaja Ljubov'*
(Free Love, 1925),[71] R21 Strok separated a chapter from
her larger work *Liubov' pchel trudovykh* (Love Among the
Worker Bees, Moscow, 1923) for publication. It is surprising that Strok could bring out such a work in Latvia, given
the proscription against works published in the USSR and,
in this case, a work written by such a flaming revolutionary.[72] This Strok edition may also have been the first separate edition of the story to be published in the original
Russian. With this work, Strok was right in step with the
vanguard Malik-Verlag in Berlin, which also brought out
its translation[73] the same year. Stories of high living and
loving always sold well with the result that Strok added Ilja
Ėrenburg's *Liubov' Zhanny Nei* (The Love of Jeanny Ney)
R22 to his 1925 offerings,[74] translated and published in
Moscow the previous year with a similar uncredited cover

R22

R23

R24

R25

design, R23 in Czech in 1925,[75] and in German by Malik-Verlag[76] in 1926.[77] The suggestive
keyhole-view on the uncredited cover design of Strok's edition[78] gives an interesting design contrast to Karel Teige and Otokar Mrkvička's approach R24 or Wieland Herzfelde's
treatment. R25

69   The film was first produced in 1922 and starred Rudolf Valentino.

70   The Moscow imprint could not be found for comparison of typography at the time of this writing.

71   The cover design, possibly by Raimunds Šiško (see initials) has somewhat incongruous elements (high-heels and
a dress) for a proletarian love story. The style and palette are in keeping with Šiško's cover design for Verbitskaia's
Mat' i doch', done the same year. The artist's logo has also been read as "HR" for Hugo Rove.

72   By 1937 the book had been added to the Ulmanis regime's list of "forbidden books".

73   *Wege der Liebe* (Paths of Love) with cover design by John Heartfield and his brother, Wieland Herzfelde.

74   The editors of the journal *Elegance*, an example of Latvian "ero-satire", saw a circulation-enhancing opportunity
and began serializing Ėrenburg's mildly salacious novel *Zhenny Ney* with the November 26, 1925, issue.

75   *Láska Jeanny Neuillové* (The Love of Jeanny Ney) with cover design by Karel Teige and Otokar Mrkvička and
published by Komunistickě nakladatelství a knihkupectví.

76   Translated by Waldemar Jollos for the first edition in German, published by Rhein Verlag (Basel) as *Die Liebe der
Jeanne Ney*, then taken over by Malik-Verlag that same year. The second printing by Malik Verlag (1930) was given a
redesigned, photomontage dust wrapper with leftist journalist Maria Osten, i.e., Maria Gresshöner, as "model" (see
above). John Heartfield's brother Wieland Herzfelde was the photomonteur.

77   The Riga edition also met a fate similar to that of the Kollontai book, as it was added to the *Sēnalu literatūras
saraksts* (Trash Literature List) compiled by R. Lapsiņš (Riga: J. Roze, 1939).

78   Possibly designed by Liubov' Popova.

R26

R27

R28

R29

Strok's book publishing ventures continued only until 1927 and concentrated on popular fiction with titles such as Anastasia Verbitskaia's *Mat' ili doch'* (Mother or Daughter, 1925) R26 and its sensual cover design by Raimunds Šiško and Leonid Leonov's *Gibel' Egorushki* (The Death of Little Yegor, 1927) R27 with its cover design by the usually sentimental illustrator, Aleksandrs Apsītis, whose work shown here rises somewhat above the style for which he was known. Strok's list of authors was as respectable as the lists of his contemporaries with works by Yekaterina Breshko-Breshkovskaya, Gabriele D'Annunzio, Jack London, Rabindranath Tagore, Konstantin Fedin, and Claude Farrère, among others. Then there were those writers on his list (now lost to the memory of most), e.g., the English aeronautical adventurer Olivia Wadsley, author of the two-volume *Plamia* (The Flame, 1929), each having a different photomontage, regrettably with no credit for the designer.[79] R28, R29

Typical of the authors Strok published in translation were Pierre Benoit and his novel *Atlantide* (1926) and the widely popular Victor Margueritte, represented by his controversial *Kholostyachka* (Bachelor Girl, 1924).[80] R30 The cover of the American edition's fifth printing in February 1924 is shown here for contrast.[81] R31 The original French edition, *La Garçonne* (1922), caused such a ruckus that the archbishop of Paris condemned the book for obscenity, resulting in Margueritte having to return his Légion d'honneur medal.

In 1927, Strok's concluding year of publishing, he used Raimunds Šiško once again, this time for a cover for the internationally popular Bernhard Kellermann's *Ingeborg*[82] R32

79   Wadsley's stories were not only published in Russian translation by Orient (3 titles) but also by Atlantida (1), Grāmatu Draugs (2), and Mir (1).

80   Abyzov tells us Strok shortened this work without the author's permission. For further revelations about Strok see Abyzov's account in *A izdavalos eto v Rige, 1918-1944*, pp. 145-148.

81   First published in the United States by Alfred Knopf in July 1923, it was later licensed to Macaulay (New York) for a cheap edition, shown here.

82   Translator not credited.

R30

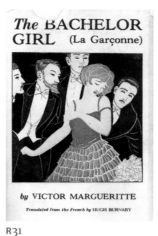

R31

R34

R32

R33

with its illustration a sharp contrast to the uncredited design of the Leningrad edition of 1925.[83] R33 Abyzov criticizes[84] Strok for his use of poor-quality paper, although an examination of the relative paper quality available to other Russian-language publishers common. Quality of paper often varied considerably within the output of a given title.

The financial problems Strok incurred in his book publishing were partially offset by his sheet music publishing efforts, to say nothing of the success he enjoyed with his own compositions and contributions to the "tango fever" in Latvia and Eastern Europe in those years. His most famous composition, "My Last Tango" (sometimes cited as "The Last Tango"), is still in the repertoire of piano bar musicians, at least in Riga.[85] R34 Some suggest the cover was designed by Sigismunds Vidbergs; others suggest Šiško.

Strok also envisioned himself as a publisher of periodicals, beginning in 1925 with *Zilais Žurnals* (Blue Journal), R35–R37 a slender effort with a few photos, mildly risqué drawings, anecdotes, caricatures, and film notes, but basically an advertising vehicle for himself. Raimunds Šiško was commissioned to design the covers for numbers two and three. With number three, the plan collapsed for what was to be a weekly. But Strok was

83   Published by Mysl in an edition of 6,000 copies. Translated from German by I. A. Frumson.
84   *A izdavalos eto v Rige, 1918-1944*, pp. 169-170.
85   *Moe Poslednee Tango / Mon Dernier Tango*, text and music by Oskar Strok (Riga: Commissionaire K. Reinhold, 1932).

R35

R36

R37

not deterred by such setbacks. He brought out a literary almanac called *Argus* (1925), with a bit of prose, verse, notes on the theatre, and promotion for his other publications. These publications (books and music) were already being touted in his somewhat longer-lived weekly, *Novaia Niva* (New Niva, 1926-1927),[86] a medium for promoting the 34 titles[87] he published before bankruptcy engulfed him.

Strok's efforts to make good on his offer in 1927 to *Novaia Niva* subscribers may have been among the causes of his being forced into bankruptcy. He had announced on the back cover of Leonov's *Gibel Egorushki*, for example, a heady list of bonus publications in addition to 52 numbers of Novaia Niva: "18 books by modern Russian writers, 18 books by foreign writers, 6 science fiction books, 6 'universally beneficial' books, 4 practical reference books, 24 pieces of sheet music (by both Russian and foreign composers)," one issue of *Elegantnyi Muzhchina* (Elegant Man) and one issue of *Damskiĭ Mir* (Ladies' World)[88] as well as a monthly calendar. As if this were not enough to encourage potential subscribers, as well as moving Strok a step closer to financial disaster, these subscribers were offered a 20-volume collected edition of Lev Tolstoy's writings with payment of no more than one additional lats or "one U.S. dollar for subscribers in other countries".

This grandiose promotional effort prompted Abyzov to comment that Strok was one to "promise the moon and neglect to deliver".[89]

With the end of his Russian book publishing dreams (but not his music publishing) and a brief stint in prison in 1931 (carelessness in financial matters), Strok found solace in his music and, presumably, royalties for the remainder of the Interwar era. In the 1939 Latvian telephone directory he is still listed as "komponists" (composer).[90]

Strok was to create some 300 compositions throughout his lifetime. For a graphic sample of his music publishing through Kazanova, his sheet music publishing house, note the panel of illustrations below. R38–R42

While the words for the songs are in Russian only, Strok contributed an introduction inside the front cover in English, with a concluding paragraph about his own music:

"In Harbin I was struck by the fact that everywhere I came across people who sang, played, and whistled my songs 'Blue Eyes' and 'Last Tango'. Gramophone records with these [songs] were distributed in thousands of pieces, and I wondered by which wind they had been brought to a far-distant country like Mandshuko."

From 1941 to 1942 Strok composed and arranged film music at Kasakhfilm Studios in Alma-Ata. He then moved on to work as an accompanist in the same city from 1944 to 1945 with the renowned singer and film star Klavdia Shulzhenko and her husband Vladimir Koralli and their jazz band. During this period he composed best-forgotten songs for the war effort, for example, "Driver of the Front", "Stalingrad Waltz", "Guard Division Number 8", and others.

Strok returned home to Riga in 1945, managed to find a piano, and began to rebuild his life, composing and playing until shortly before his death in 1975. One can only regret that he did not have time to leave us an account of his colorful life, although, given his propensities, it might have stretched our credulity.

---

86   52 numbers appeared in 1926 with a few supplements, followed by 32 issues in 1927 before collapse.
87   Possibly 36 titles (Abyzov gives two calculations).
88   Copies of these journals could not be located for verification of their existence.
89   *A izdavalso eto v Rige 1918-1944*, p. 80.
90   *Latvijas 1939. g. telefona abonentu saraksts*.

R38

R39

R42

R40

R41

R38   *Neue Bublitschki* (ca. 1930)

R39   *Zwei dunkle Augen schau'n mich an* (1930)

R40   *Zara Leander dzied Premjera* (ca. 1932)
Music and words for three songs sung by Zarah Leander in her movies. The "Premjera" refers to the first publication of her film music in Latvia; the lyrics are in German and Latvian.

R41   *12 Russkikh romansov, Russian Romances* (lyrics of twelve songs in Russian, 1937)
Cover design: Aleksandrs Apsītis

R42   *Russian Jazz* (1938)

R43

Today most, if not all, other Russian publishers' names from that era have faded from the general, collective memory. Few are likely to even recall Strok's Kazanova book-format scores of "Russian Jazz" and other popular music. But in November 2004, thanks to the impresario Vladimir Reshtov and his creative efforts and those of the Riga National Opera Company, Strok and his tango tunes were briefly brought back to life for the benefit of a new generation; in the spring of 2012, a film based on his life was under discussion.

Shortly before the mini Strok revival, I asked two or three acquaintances if they could tell me something about Strok. The answers were fairly uniform: "Oh, he was one of our 1930s composers... we still can hum parts of his tunes after we hear them again... I guess we heard them from our parents and their generation."

About this same time I found a CD of re-mastered[91] tunes from original 1930s Bel-laccord Electro phonodiscs with violin performances by Edvīns Krūmiņš; its lead tune was Strok's march "Jūrnieka dziesma" (Sailor's Song).

Literatūra

R44

Two individuals considerably less flamboyant than Oskar Strok (and somewhat more productive in the book department) were the founders of the publishing house Literatūra. Kārlis Rasiņš and Vasiliĭ Gadalin (pseudonym for Vasiliĭ Vladimirovich Vasilev) spent much of the time from the formation of their partnership in 1927 sitting at their desks publishing Russian books—more than 70 titles—in addition to publishing a respectable number of Latvian-language titles. According to Abyzov, little has surfaced in the way of documentation about the circumstances that brought Gadalin and Rasiņš together. Gadalin, a minor poet and journalist, came to Riga with his family in 1920 from Tallinn by way of Archangel. According to Abyzov, by 1922 he was working for the paper *Maiak* (Beacon), followed by a stint with the journal *Mir* (World) in 1923, *Russkaia Zhizn'* (Russian Life) in 1924, and the paper *Rizhskiĭ Kurier* (Riga Courier) from 1924 to 1926. These, among other editorial undertakings including participation in the establishment of the Russian-language publishing house Khronos, were but a prelude to his joining Rasiņš in the formation of Literatūra and becoming head of its Russian department.

Rasiņš, like Gadalin, was no newcomer to publishing and thus did not conform to Abyzov's characterization of the typical Russian publisher as dilettante. Rasiņš' first taste of publishing was working as a bookkeeper for the Riga newspaper *Brīvā Zeme* (Free Land) and later as manager of another paper, *Rīgas Ziņas* (Riga News).

Their Russian-language list emphasized serious fiction, including such writers of the time as Mikhail Bulgakov, Mikhail Zoschenko, and Valentin Kataev. To help with the cash flow, they chose Sergei Malashkin's *Luna s pravoi storony* (The Right Side of the Moon, 1928) with its "sure-to-sell" theme of free love and the book's central figure, Tanya, and her 26 husbands. R43 In addition, three pot-boilers by Edgar Wallace were added to their offerings in 1929 for continued fiscal health.[92]

The Literatūra list also carried the Russian émigré Aleksandr Kuprin and foreign writers such as Marcel Prévost. The Malashkin cover shown and the cover for Iuriĭ Galich's *Krasnyi khorovod* (Red Dance, 1929) R44 with its author-designed cover are indicative

---

91 Produced by Balss (ca. 2001) with liner notes by Atis Bērtiņš.
92 *Groznaia zaika* (Furry Rabbit), *Tainye sily* (Secret Forces), and *Ruki vverkh* (Hands Up!).

of the modest role of design among the priorities of the Literatūra publishing team.

Iuriĭ Galich (pseudonym of Georgiĭ Goncharenko, according to his daughter Natalia)[93] was born in Warsaw of a "russified German" mother and Russian father. Galich had a military education and rose to the rank of general in Aleksandr Kerensky's provisional government. He appears to have had a swashbuckling military career in those tumultuous years before retiring to a literary life in Riga in the spring of 1923. Although Galich was known as a poet and essayist in Tsarist Russia, in Interwar Latvia he was recognized for his earlier writing as well as fiction and non-fiction published during his Riga years. Galich designed a number of the covers for his own books. While not earth-shaking in their creativity, they are competently framed and uncluttered. Feliks Talberg included six Galich-designs in a contribution to *Rizhskiĭ bibliofil*.[94]

R45

A title from the Latvian side of their enterprise was a cultural calendar begun in 1936 with all the usual content of such annual publications. The 1937 volume R45 merits mention for the photo supplements, a bit of documentation for those interested in the development of art photography in the Interwar period.[95] Valdemārs Upītis contributed eleven photo images ranging from landscapes to a hotel interior in Ķemeri. Arturs Grapmanis provided conventional photo portraits of five performing artists. Galich's Latvian publishing undertaking was considerably more ambitious than the Russian publishing effort, having brought out multi-volume works on Latvian national folk poetry and Latvian history. The Latvian portion of the Literatūra operation continued until 1944, when Rasiņš fled to Sweden. In 1957 he left Sweden for Canada, where he continued in publishing, eventually returning to Sweden and dying in Göteborg in 1974.

Gadalin, unlike Rasiņš, stayed in Latvia and worked first as a plumber (he had many abilities besides editing and translating) in 1940/1941. From 1942 to 1944, he worked in an editorial capacity on the *Dvinskiĭ Vestnik* (Dvinsk Herald) and contributed to a few other papers and journals. In October 1944 it was reported[96] that he was "arrested and spent five years in prison and, when released, returned to Riga, where he died". The only problem with this information is the gap between 1949 and his death ten years later, during which time he must have been writing (or plumbing). It is also not clear which government or group arrested him. Perhaps it is sufficient to know that he survived.

M. M. Didkovskiĭ

The stern-visaged Maksim Mechislavovich Didkovskiĭ began his professional life as a military officer serving on the adjutant general staff in the Tsar's army. He came to Riga in 1920 as a representative to the Baltic States of a Ukrainian nationalist organization and the short-lived Ukrainian independent republic founded by Symon Petliura.[97] In 1921 Didkovskiĭ opened a bookshop specializing in monarchist literature. He had raised enough capital to begin publishing books under his own name.[98] His commendable

93   See *Baltiiskiĭ Archiv* v. 1 (Tallinn: Avenarius, 1996), pp. 265-276.

94   See his "Iu. I. Goncharenko-Galich" in *Rizhskiĭ Bibliofil*, ed. by Anatoliĭ Rakitianskiĭ (Riga: Bibliofil & Kollektsioner, 2003), pp. 63-75.

95   *Dailes Gada grāmata 1937. gadam* (Riga: Literatūra). Cover design by M. Grass.

96   A biographical sketch appeared in 2010 at www.russianresources.lt/archive/Gadalin/Gadalin_0.html.

97   When the Soviets took over Ukraine in 1921, Petliura was exiled to Paris, where he was later shot and killed by an agent of the Soviets.

98   See Rudīte Vīksne and Kārlis Kangers, *No NKVD līdz KGB: Politiskās prāvas Latvijā, 1940-1986* (Riga: Vēstures institūta apgāds, 1999), p. 167.

R46

R47

R48

R49

R50

aim was to reach the growing Russian-language mass market in Latvia. Because of his background, he included militaria among the monarchist and conservative history titles throughout his book list. But it was the popular Russian writers and their books of the previous generation as well as those of his own time, e.g., Iuriĭ Galich's *Zelenyi Mai* (Green May, 1929), R46 that were prominent on Didkovskiĭ's list throughout the 15 years of his publishing career. A few of the representative authors were Nikolaĭ Breshko-Breshkovskiĭ, Vera Krzhyzhanovskaia, Nadezhda Lappo-Danilevskaia, and Ol'ga Bebutova. While not names of authors coming readily to the minds of current-generation Russian literature readers, books by these authors were often in the baggage and on the shelves of many of the bourgeois Russian émigrés in Berlin, Paris, and scores of other cities in the first half of the 20th century. Despite Didkovskiĭ's seeming intellectual distance from a literary or design vanguard, he published a few titles that stand out for their design and, sometimes, content, e.g., *Afrodita i vakhanka* (Aphrodite and the Bacchante, 1930)[99] R47 with a cover design by Raimunds Šiško. This design could almost hold its own alongside that of the Czech avant-gardist Karel Teige and his design for Louis Delluc's *Filmová Dramata* (Prague, 1925)[100] R48 or any number of similar designs covering the more vanguard books published in Central European countries of that time.

Among other Didkovskiĭ titles with noteworthy Šiško covers, although not within the same style as *Afrodita i vakhanka*, is a Latvian translation of T. Penni's[101] *Skaistā svešniece: Romans no Indijas un Londonas dzīves* (The Beautiful Foreigner: A Novel of Indian and

99   Efforts to provide any details on the stated author, Evgenii S. Genin or Henin, have proved fruitless.
100   Published by Nakladatel Ladislav Kuncíř v Praze.
101   "T. Penni" appears to have eluded standard biographical dictionaries as well as having his/her titles acquired by libraries large and small in Western Europe and North America.

R51

R52

R53

London Life, 1934) by Georgs Jātnieks, R49 and Ivan Konoplin's[102] novel *Zhelieznoe kol'tso* (Iron Ring, 1928). R50 Iuriĭ Abyzov calculates that some 104 titles were published by Didkovskiĭ.

Although Abyzov gives 1935 as the closing date of Didkovskiĭ's publishing house, he goes on to record 21 additional titles with the Didkovskiĭ imprint, published between 1936 and 1939, including his *Vseobshchiĭ Kalendar* (General Calendar, 1937).[103] R51 This Ulmanis-regime output included an undistinguished eight-page children's book written and illustrated by Elena Kirshtein,[104] titled *Zain'ka-vavaka* (The Bunny-Vavaka, 1938), R52 which was soon followed that same year by two other titles for children, her *Nebylitsy* (Cock-and-bull Stories) and fairy tale *Kuvyrkalochka* (Somersault).

In 1939 Didkovskiĭ published a collection of 348 recipes (out of 1,500) from the much-beloved Imperial Russian cookbook of Elena Molokhovets titled *Podarok molodym khozyaikam* (Gift to Young Housewives). R53 The uncredited, mildly grotesque cover design is a sad addition to any selection of Riga-Russian book designs at the close of the era and is included primarily because of its rarity. Unfortunately, the designer took no inspiration from the memorable recipes in this culinary document.

Didkovskiĭ likely knew the importance of Molokhovets and her cookbook, which had enjoyed 21 Russian-language editions from the time of its Moscow appearance in 1861 down to the last edition, published shortly before the autumn of 1917.[105] Oskar Strok also

---

102   Could this be the "Ivan Konoplin" mentioned by Brian Boyd in his *Vladimir Nabokov: The Russian Years* (Princeton, 1990), p. 219, as being a GPU "plant" in the émigré Union of Russian Writers in Berlin in the early 1920s?
103   Published for the years 1932 to 1940.
104   No biographical information found.
105   See *Classic Russian Cooking: Elena Molokhovets' A Gift to Young Housewives*, translated, introduced, and annotated by Joyce Toomre (Bloomington: University of Indiana Press, 1992), p. 633.

R54

R55

published a 224-page compilation of recipes selected from Molokhovets in 1927.[106] R54 Quite likely better known than either the Didkovskiĭ or the Strok compilations is another cookery title (also 224 pages) edited by Nadezhda Bobrova and published in Riga by Praktiskā Bibliotēka in 1932.[107] According to Toomre,[108] Bobrova edited Molokhovets "down" to a quarter of the length of later editions published in the first two decades of the 20th century.

Among the five other titles Didkovskiĭ published in 1939 was a Russian-language edition of Edvarts Virza's classic prose poem *Straumēni* (The Straumēni Farmstead),[109] characterized by Andrups and Kalve[110] in its effort of "apprehending the eternal order of the universe... symbolized by the rhythm of work on the Latvian farmstead"—an order soon to be dashed by the first Soviet invasion and the subsequent 45 years of collectivization efforts. This may also have been the last book to have an illustrative contribution (chapter headings) designed by Raimunds Šiško before his farewell to Latvia.

Didkovskiĭ was arrested by the NKVD on August 6, 1940. He was tried and convicted because of his military service in the Tsar's army and sent into exile in Siberia. Broken in spirit and ill, he died in the Gulag labor camps in 1954.

As has been shown, inspired graphic design played a part in the cover illustration or internal typography of the work issued by several Russian-language book publishers. In some cases, it is comparable to the pre-1931 Russian-language books published in the USSR

106   *Podarok molodym khoziaikam ili sredstvo k umensheniiu raskhodov v domashnem khoziaistve*, Elena Molokhovets, Novoe izd. ispr. i dopoln. (Riga: O. D. Strok [1926]/1927), 224 [1] pp.

107   *Podarok molodym khoziaikam: Sostavleno po izvestnomu kulinarnomu trudu Eliny N. Ivanovny Molokhovets: Podarok molodym khoziaikam* (Riga: Praktiskā Bibliotēka, 1932), 224 [1] pp.

108   Toomre, ibid., p. 634.

109   Subtitled *Zhizn starogo latyshskogo khutora* and translated by V. Tretiakov.

110   *Latvian Literature: Essays*, by Jānis Andrups and Vitauts Kalve (Stockholm: Zelta Ābele, 1954), p 152.

R56

R57

R58

R59

R60

or in "Russian Berlin" in the early 1920s. Few designs from Riga were on the sophisticated level of work by leading USSR designers in the NEP period, or the best work of Russian émigré designers stopping in Berlin and producing covers for Avram Vishniac's Gelikon publishing house—as did Natan Altman and El Lissitzky—or Alekseĭ Remizov and his designs for Verlag Skythen. R55, R56 Remizov, like Masjutyn before him, had already passed through Riga before Russian-language publishing had found its feet there.

While highly professional work was being done by resident designers such as Mihail Jo, Raimunds Šiško, Sigismunds Vidbergs, and a few others, so many designers working in Russian-language publishing were content with undistinguished typography or graphic visual clichés and conventional Cyrillic calligraphy for cover typography, all too often showing little influence of the best of Riga-Russian book design or design currents in other European capitals. Thus it was not uncommon to see such efforts as the following examples typifying the day-to-day appearance by such houses as Logos, Grāmatu Draugs, Knizhnaia lavka pisatelei, and Kniga dlia vsiekh. R57–R60

For contrast, a few other publishers whose efforts to produce cover designs of greater interest than the four publishers just cited are shown here, beginning with Khronos.

R61

R62

R63

R64

R65

R66

R67

R68

R69

R61 *Molitvennik liubvi*
(The Prayerbook of Love, 1925)
by Alberic Cahuet
trans. by E. Russat
Cover design: [undecipherable
signature]

R62 *Devushka, kotoraia
puteshestvovala* (The Girl who
Traveled, 1925)
by Claude Farrère
trans. by S. Frants
Cover design: [unsigned]

R63 *Zhilets iz chetvertago etazha*
(The Boarder on the Fourth Floor,
1925) by Catherina Godwin
(pseud. of "Frau Dr. de Vargas")
trans. by I. Gutman
Cover design: Raimunds Šiško

R64 *Bratia Shellenberg*
(The Shellenberg Brothers, 1925)
by Bernhard Kellermann
trans. by L. and I. Efimov
Cover design: Heinrich Daiber

R65 *Velikiï Pandolfo*
(The Great Pandolfo, 1926)
by William John Locke
trans. by Tatiana Ivanova
Cover design: Raimunds Šiško

R66 *Mazgāpieris*
("Wash 'em Clean", 1926)
by Korneï Chukovskiï
Cover design: possibly Iuriï
Annenkov as he is cited as
illustrator

R67 *Krug v Treugolnike*
(Circle in the Triangle, 1926)
by Arthur Conan Doyle
trans. by Boris Arsenyev
Cover design: [unsigned]

R68 *Amok* (1926)
by Stefan Zweig
trans. by Daniil Gorfinkel'
Cover design: [unsigned]

R69 *Groznyi Prizrak: Okkultnyi
roman* (The Threatening Ghost:
A Novel of the Occult, 1926?)
by Vera I. Kryzhanovskaia
Cover design: Raimunds Šiško

Khronos

Khronos publishing house and its elusive publisher, Georg Leopoldovich Birkgan, managed to bring a bit of life to the graphics of his publishing venture (his second) through the choice of cover artists, notably Raimunds Šiško, and others who are unfortunately not credited. Even though this electrical engineer from Moscow had no previous experience in publishing, this did not deter him from coming west to Riga and founding his "Riga" imprint in 1924. But five titles later, in 1925, he was out of business or, more accurately, operating under a new name, Khronos. But even his Khronos venture was short-term, ending in 1926, although at least he managed to bring out nine titles under this imprint.[111]

R70

In some ways the content of the Khronos list epitomizes the tendency of Russian-language publishing in Riga, i.e., a concentration on ephemeral fiction. For this reason, all titles are cited here together with a representation of a number of the cover designs. We know more about Birkgan's cover illustrators than we do about him. But at least his modest Khronos production survives. Of the nine choices he gave Russian readers in 1925/1926, all but two were translations. R61–R69

Raimunds Šiško and his work for Didkovskiĭ and Birkgan deserves a paragraph not only for his book cover design, but also for his being a graphic artist of obvious importance during this period (shown here in a photo studio portrait). R70 His surviving posters for commerce and cultural events alone would certainly have won him recognition in international poster competitions of the era had they been shown, yet his book and poster design seem to have gone unnoticed by Western European and Anglo-American book and poster historians. He is, however, recognized with a brief biographical sketch in *Māksla un arhitektūra biogrāfijās*[112] and scattered references elsewhere.

Ilze Martinsone rescued Šiško with a few lines categorizing examples of his poster designs as Art Deco,[113] e.g., his 1937 poster for the Latvian Board of Trade's exhibition of office furniture, R71 the 9th Latvian Song Festival poster (1938), R72 and an undated poster for the joint stock company Gaita (Pace). R73 A fitting addition within Martinsone's definition of Art Deco design would surely be his book cover for Edgars Alberings' *Es lidoju* (I am Flying) R74 with its introduction by Rūdolfs Celms.[114] While there is a decidedly modernist style within the preceding examples of Šiško's work, one should avoid identifying a "Šiško style", whether poster or book cover design. Like any professional designer, Šiško worked at fitting the design to the need at hand with an appropriate image and "feel" rather than the superimposition of a signature style. A dramatic example of his flexibility, in light of the regime's preferred graphic clichés of folkcostumed maidens or conquering-hero-type males, is the commission given to Šiško by the quasi-governmental Latvian Labor Office: a "summer journey" poster with the design repeated for a travel guide cover,[115] R75 promoting vacation travel within Latvia, a concept with similar programs in regimes less authoritarian and more totalitarian, e.g., Germany, Japan and Spain.[116]

111   See pages 432 and 436 of vol. 4 of Abyzov's *Russkoe pechatnoe slovo v Latviĭ*.
112   See vol. 3, p. 152.
113   See her "Art Deco stils un latviešu māksla" (Art Deco style in Latvian art) in *Latvijas māksla starptautisko sakaru kontekstā* (Latvian Art in the Context of International Connections), ed. by Silvija Grosa (Riga: Neputns, 2000), p. 133-134.
114   Published in 1930 by Avioliteratūra, the same year in which this Latvian aviation pioneer was killed in a plane crash.
115   *Vasaras ceļojumi: Latvijas Darba kameras rokas grāmata strādnieku arodbiedrību tūrisma kopu darbībai* (Summer Journeys: Handbook of Activities for Trade Union Workers' Tourist Groups) compiled by Kārlis Vanags (Riga: Latvijas Darba kameras izd., 1937).
116   See Kenneth J. Ruoff's *Imperial Japan at its Zenith* (Ithaca: Cornell University Press, 2010), p. 7.

R71

R72

R73

R74

R75

R76

R77

However, in Šiško's best-known posters one sees more an echo of the late 1930s Italian Stile Futurista than the earlier decorative streamlining of the readily identifiable Art Deco design of the Paris Exposition des Arts Décoratifs of 1925. In addition to his book cover designs in the 1920s, Šiško also contributed a few drawings to *Segodnia* in 1926 and again in 1929.[117] In the 1930s he worked at the M.S. Kuzņecovs porcelain factory on Grēcinieku iela, presumably as a painter of porcelain as well as producing a few covers of note for Zhizn' i Kul'tura (shown below), and in 1937 he even produced three bottle label designs for the Aldaris beverage company. A surviving backdrop for a printing company's calendar (Jānis Mitrēvics' printing company, 1938) shows Šiško's skill at cartouche design. R76

One clear indication of Šiško's position in the graphic design world of the time was his being personally chosen by Vice Minister of the Interior Alfrēds Bērziņš to provide the cover and one internal illustration for the program of Latvia's first sound film, *Tautas dēls* (Son of the People, 1934). R77

117   See Abyzov's *Gazeta "Segodnia", 1919-1940*, vol. 2, p. 381.

As to Šiško's life, we know little more than that he was born in 1894 in Dashle-gar (now Sergokala), Dagestan. His being listed in the *Izceļojušo vācu tautības pilsoņu saraksts* (List of Émigré German Citizens)[118] would indicate a German heritage. At the beginning of the 1920s Šiško was working for the advertising company Kolokol and had at least one major interior design commission together with Eduards Pika for the restau-rant/music hall "Akvarium", once located on the first floor of the building on the south corner of Elizabetes iela and K. Barona iela. The previously mentioned index of German citizens relinquishing their Latvian citizenship indicates that Šiško, with his Riga-born wife, Karina, and son, Georgiĭ Viktor, left their apartment at Kaļķu iela 10 on December 7, 1939,[119] possibly to Germany and then later to South America. No date of death has been found as yet, nor indication of his taking up a post-WWII career.

R78

Zhizn' i Kul'tura

A major publisher with appealing books and some of the most interesting book cover de-signs of the period was the book publishing arm of *Segodnia*, the leading "free" Russian-language newspaper of the time. Zhizn' i Kul'tura (Life and Culture) was founded in 1929 and lasted until 1938. During that time, it published 96 titles with an emphasis on classic 19th century Russian writers, e.g., Dostoevskiĭ (12 volumes), Tolstoy (12 volumes), Lermon-tov and Pushkin (2 volumes each), and Turgenev (10 volumes), according to Abyzov.[120]

Interspersed among these sets of Russian classics were titles of a more popular nature with cover designs of decided interest. Among the popular authors were such 20th cen-tury figures as Panteleimon Romanov, whose candid NEP-period novel *Three Pairs of Silk Stockings* appeared in a Zhizn' i Kul'tura edition in 1930. This edition, *Tri pary shelkovykh chulok*, R78 was given its cover design by the painter, poster designer, and caricaturist Werner Linde and was an example of the infrequent phenomenon of a Baltic-German artist working outside his own linguistic-ethnic circle by taking a commission for a Rus-sian book cover design. An example of Linde's poster work can be seen in the travel poster shown promoting Riga's beach area Jūrmala. R79

R79

For comparison of Linde's design with contemporaneous editions of Romonov's work, note the Swedish edition[121] R80 and the American edition.[122] R81 Translations also appeared in French (1933), German (1932), R82 Yiddish (Warsaw, 1930), Polish (1932), and Dutch (1931).[123] R83 In addition to the Riga-Russian edition, there was also a Berlin-Russian edition (1931) and, perhaps most exotic, a New York-Russian edition (1952) by Chekhov, a publishing house established and funded by the US Central Intelligence Agency in New York City in 1951 with the express purpose of publishing non-Soviet authors.[124]

---

118   Subtitled: *Ziņas par personām, kas izceļojušas saskaņā ar līgumu par vācu tautības Latvijas pilsoņu pārvietošanu uz Vāciju* (Likumu krāj., 1939. g., 176) (Information on persons expatriated to Germany in conformity with the agreement on the displacement of Latvian citizens of German nationality. Latvian legal code, 1939. Code # 176), Oficiāls izdevums (Riga: Iekšlietu ministrijas administratīvais departaments, 1940).

119   *Izceļojušo vācu tautības pilsoņu saraksts*, ibid.

120   See Rakitianskiĭ, ibid., p. 165.

121   (Stockholm: Tiden, 1931), uncredited design.

122   (New York: Charles Scribner, 1931), uncredited design.

123   Designed by Fré Cohen, a versatile designer under-appreciated outside the Netherlands. This particular cover does not show her at her best.

124   Chekhov Publishing House was closed in 1956, with some records deposited in the Rare Book Division at the Columbia University Library.

R80

R81

R82

R83

In a design departure for Zhizn' i Kul'tura, the firm brought out a popular title, Arnoldi Fraccaroli's *Il Paradiso Delle Fanciulle: ovvero, American Girls* (1929). But instead of a Russian title for the book, the Italian portion of the title was dropped, the Russian transliteration of the author's name substituted, and the Austrian publisher's design modified the positioning of the title "American Girls".[125] R84, R85 Grāmatu Draugs also published this title in Latvian as *Amerikas meitenes* (American Girls, 1931; translated by V. Kārkliņš), according to its 1934/1935 catalog, using the same cover design as that of the Zhizn' i Kul'tura edition.

Once again, Raimunds Šiško, working for Zhizn' i Kul'tura, showed his understanding of printing processes and his deftness in combining lithographic and calligraphic skills. The following four titles with Šiško cover designs also give an indication of the popular fare in translation offered by this publisher: Maurice Dekobra's *Ulitsa nakrashennykh gub* (Street of Painted Lips, 1933) translated by Elena Kuznetsova-Pil'skaya,[126] R86 Pierre Benoit's *Korolevskiĭ fort* (Koenigsmark, 1933),[127] R87 Albéric Cahuet's *Ispanskaia Noch* (Spanish Night, 1934), R88 and Leo Perutz's *Sneg sviatogo Petra* (St. Peter's Snow, 1934) translated by Vladimir Zlatogorskiĭ.[128] R89

Two uncredited but nonetheless interesting designs for two titles published earlier: the cover for Valentine Williams' fictionalized World War I experiences, *5 iulia 1914 goda* (July 5, 1914), R90 and Dino Segre, i.e., Pitigrilli's *Vegetariantsy liubvi: Pozhiratel zhenshchin'* (Vegetarian Love: The Story of a Womanizer), R91 both published in 1931. Another striking, uncredited design appeared a year later, this time for a translation of Somerset Maugham's *The Painted Veil*,[129] the story set in China of the adulterous Kitty Fane, who gives her name to the titling (Kitti) for this translation. R92

Although not quite so sophisticated as the uncredited design for Segre's book or that of Maugham's *Kitti*, still worthy of showing is Mihails Jo's cover for the 1933 publication[130]

125 Designed by "Kora", Amonesta-Verlag (Wien-Berlin-Leipzig), 1930. The original publisher, August Amonesta, a publisher of "low-end" erotica of which this title was the first of six in a series titled "Mondänen Bücher", was later arrested during Austria's National Socialist period for his publishing emphases. Despite being an enthusiastic Nazi and not Jewish, he was still sent to Auschwitz, where he died in 1942. See *Österreichische Verlagsgeschichte, 1918-1938* comp. and ed. by Murray G. Hall (Wien: Böhlau, 1985), pp. 28-31.

126 Dekobra's *Rue des bouches-peintes* (Paris, 1925).

127 *Koenigsmark* (Paris, 1918), followed the next year by *L'Alantide*, marked the debut for this popular Interwar novelist in what was to become a highly successful career.

128 The Russian translation of Perutz's *St. Petri-Schnee* (Berlin: Zsolnay, 1933) had limited success because of timing. Hitler's suppression of books by Jewish authors in the first years of the National Socialist regime had a ripple effect, particularly in those countries with a sector of the population intellectually aligned with changes taking place in Germany. *St. Petri-Schnee*, for example, was reviewed in only one German journal of the time, *Die Literatur*, in December 1933.

129 First published by Heinemann (London) in 1925 and that same year in New York by Doran.

130 By Vladimir Zlatogorskiĭ.

R84

R85

R86

R87

R88

R89

R90

R91

R92

R93

R94

R95

of *Karera Marii Tul* (The Career of Maria Thul),[131] R93 written by Otto Zarek, a leading German theatre personality and critic of the time.

From 1935 to the end of the decade Zhizn' i Kul'tura modified its imprint to the Latvian form, Dzīve un Kultūra, as Abyzov tells us, "to keep within the Ulmanis edict on Russian publishing".[132] This was also the year in which Šiško appears to have concluded his book cover design work for this publisher with a cover for Robert Neumann's *Parokhod "Nadezhda"* (The Steamer "Nadezhda", 1934), R94 translated by Vladimir Zlatogorskiĭ, and a visual cliché for the cover of the first book by the ultimately prolific mystery and adventure writer Dennis Wheatley,[133] *Forbidden Territory*, titled as *V Sibir' za kladom* (To Siberia for Hidden Treasure, 1935) and translated by K. L. Verchovskaia. R95

Zhizn' i Kul'tura continued to bring Latvia's Russian readers still more well-known and popular writers, e.g., Vicki Baum, Robert Neumann, Gina Kaus, and others before succumbing during the first Soviet occupation to the same fate as its parent firm, Segodnia.

Orient

The Orient publishing house joined the Russian publishing scene in 1925 under the direction of Oto Petrovich Grobin (also Grobiņš) and Sergei Karachevtsev. In the course of its few years, this partnership managed to produce a number of worthy titles in translation as well as commission several cover designs of interest. A favorite cover design (uncredited) among Orient titles of the early years, is that created for Joseph Kessel's

131 A fictionalized account of the celebrated German actress of stage and film Elisabeth Bergner. First published as *Theater um Maria Thul* (Berlin: Zsolnay, 1932).
132 See his *A izdavalos zto v Rige* 1918-1944, p. 324.
133 It was Dennis Wheatley's *The Devil Rides Out* (1934), his best-known novel today, and the much later film version of the same title (London, 1968) that brought him considerable fame.

Liubov' aviatora (The Love of an Aviator), a translation of his *Equipage* (Crew, 1923) by M. Lerche published, as nearly as can be determined, for the first time in Russian in 1926. R96 The theme of this 118-page novel centers on a pilot whose wife is the lover of his friend, also a pilot. My hope at the outset—on viewing only the cover—had been that this title was a "lost work" of Kessel's, based on the life of the Russian-Estonian Liuba Galantschikoff, the first woman to fly to a height of 6,600 feet (November 21, 1912), in a single-winged Fokker no less![134] Alas, this was not the case, even though there were thin connections in the lives of Kessel and Galantschikoff. The designer of the *Liubov' aviatora* cover (signed E. M.) may have been Ēriks Mellups, an aviator of some military distinction and an artist, although the connection with this book has not been substantiated.[135]

R96

R97

A few years later, Grobin commissioned the Russian-born German designer, Heinrich Daiber, to design the cover R97 of Erich Maria Remarque's classic antiwar novel *Im Westen nichts Neues*, (Berlin, 1929, translated into English as *All Quiet on the Western Front*). To save time, Daiber appears to have "adapted" a poster design by the celebrated German poster maker Ludwig Hohlwein.[136] R98 In contrast to Daiber's design and decidedly less imaginative, the Latvian edition of Remarque's famed book, titled *Rietumu frontē bez pārmaiņām* (Grāmatu Draugs, 1929), was given a nondescript typographic cover. In further contrast, the Yiddish-language Riga edition was given an appropriately

R98

R99

dramatic design by M. Jo, i.e., Mihails Jo. R99[137] For other cover treatments of Remarque's all-time best-seller in its German first edition, R100 note how the designer of the first Japanese edition saved effort by simply lifting the German typographic design and providing a Japanese title translation. R101 The less-than-subtle design for the Lithuanian edition[138] R102 by Jonas Juozas Burba, known mainly for stylized, mildly Art Deco designs, in this instance used a hit-them-between-the-eyes realism. Burba's interpretation also provides an interesting contrast to Paul Wenck's sentimental style of illustration for the cover of the first American edition R103 or the somewhat uncertain design by Peet Aren for the Estonian edition.[139] R104

134 Various websites have provided information on her under various spellings of her family name. She lived in New York City for a time in the second half of the 1920s.

135 Mellups came to the United States after WWII and continued to work as an artist.

136 Daiber appropriated the central image of a soldier in front of a cross from Ludwig Hohlwein's Red Cross collection poster of 1914, with only a color change for the soldier's jacket and the cross. See *Ludwig Hohlwein, 1874-1949*, ed. V. Duvigneau et al. (Munich: Klinkhardt und Biermann, 1996), p. 189.

137 *Afn Mairon-front* (Riga: Grāmata priekš visiem, 1929). This translation was not cited in Thomas F. Schneider's otherwise impressive checklist, *Erich Maria Remarque "Im Westen nichts Neues": Bibliographie der Drucke* (Bramsche, Germany: Rasch Verlag, 1992).

138 *Vakarų fronte nieko naujo* (Kaunas: Sakalo, 1929).

139 *Läänerindel muutuseta*. Trans. G. Koch. (Tartu: Tapperi kirjastus, 1935).

R100

R101

R102

R103

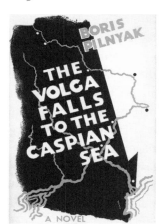

R104

R105

R106

R107

Orient once again turned to Daiber for design, commissioning him to illustrate the cover for Lion Feuchtwanger's *Evrei Zuss* (1929),[140] R105 the first Russian-language translation of his novel *Jud Süss* (The Jew Süss, Berlin, 1925). The story, based on the rise and fall of Josef Süss Oppenheimer, financial adviser to Duke Karl Alexander of Württemberg in the first half of the 18th century, brought Feuchtwanger's work to a new audience: a Yiddish-language Riga edition was also published the same year. Daiber created his own design for the Russian-language edition and initialed it. (Daiber had the honesty not to initial his design for the Remarque title.)

Daiber was quite productive at that time designing covers for two other Russian-language publishers, Nikolaĭ Gudkov[141] and Maksim Didkovskiĭ (six titles for Didkovskiĭ and two for Gudkov, as nearly as can be determined). Covers for these other works consist of singularly uninspired line drawings. Daiber continued as a book cover designer

140   Abyzov credits Šiško for the design and cites the 1929 edition as having 200 pages. The copy illustrated has the clear initials of Daiber and in addition has 201 pages plus six pages of advertising. Perhaps another edition appeared to which Abyzov refers, although it was not located in the collection of the National Library of Latvia.

141   Gudkov (located at Antonijas iela 11) edited and published school books as well as standard fare, e.g. Pushkin, Korolenko, Turgenev, Lermontov, Gogol, Dostoevskiĭ, and Edgar Wallace.

for nearly a decade, working for such publishers as the Riga German-language publisher, Allgemeiner Buchverlag and a commission for the Russian-language newspaper publisher *Novyĭ Golos* consisting of a cover for Boris Pilniak's *Volga vpadaet v Kaspiĭskoe more* (The Volga Descends to the Caspian Sea, 1930), R106 a design in sharp contrast to the cover for the first American edition.[142] R107 In that same year Daiber also produced an equally mediocre cover design for *Mir* and its edition of Brezhko-Brezhkovskiĭ's *Zhutkaia sila* (The Terrifying Force).

Regarding the short-lived children's periodical *Iunyĭ Chitatel* (Young Reader),[143] Daiber contributed more mediocre drawings to this well-meaning effort to provide adventure stories for Russian-reading children. His comrade-in-illustration on this journal was Nikolaĭ Puzirewski, whose woodcut illustrations were certainly several quality grades above Daiber's line drawings. R108

R108

Daiber likely carried out other commissions for Russian-language publishers yet to be identified, although, judging from the majority already examined, those worth mentioning are likely in the minority. Daiber emigrated from Riga to Posen in 1939, where he continued to work as a designer in an émigré advertising agency.[144]

Returning to the Grobin-Karachevtsev Orient venture, one can gain some insight into the publishing plan by simply browsing through the company's 1928 catalog. Offered here are 14 titles, staples of Russian-language publishing in Riga in this pre-Bern Convention[145] period. Other than pre-1917 Russian authors, the Orient list includes predictably popular translations from Western European languages with *Technika braka* (Techniques of Marriage), Theodoor Hendrik Van de Velde's best-seller on marriage and sexuality, published originally as *Het volkomen huwelijk* (The Complete Marriage).[146] The 1928 catalog commentary for this title consumes more than two pages.[147] Three of Karachevtsev's own works were listed in this same catalog: *1200 Anekdotov* (1200 Anecdotes), *Gvardiĭ Rotmistr* (Captain of the Guards) R109 with cover design by Sigismunds Vidbergs, and *Freilina Eya Velichestva* (Lady-in-waiting to her Royal Highness) by Anna Vyrubova. Other authors listed in the catalog included Paul Reboux with his peek behind the scenes at the "intimate life of Madame du Barry", the mystery writer Maurice Leblan and his *Vosem udarov* (Eight Strikes of the Clock), two books of humorous anecdotes compiled by Leblan, and works on military history. Only Vidbergs' design among this group has a particularly distinctive layout.

R109

At one point the partnership decided that publishing a few children's books in Latvian might be a good strategy for balance sheet improvement. Thus was launched the Orient *Jaunatnes literatūra* (Youth Literature) series (1-16), which was continued by the Kaija publishing company. One title in the series still carrying the Orient imprint but already published in Latvian is *Pasaciņas bērniem* (Fairy Tales for Children, undated) with its selections from the Brothers Grimm, illustrated with drawings by Aleksandrs Apsītis

142   Cover designed by "V.W." (New York: Cosmopolitan Book Co., 1931).
143   Launched with a special Christmas issue in December 1925. No. 1 begins in January and the periodical ends with No. 24 in December 1926.
144   *Baltiiskiĭ Arkhiv: Russkaia Kultura v Pribaltike*. Comp. by Iuriĭ Abyzov (Riga: Daugava, 1999), vol. 4, p. 279.
145   Prior to Latvia's becoming (in 1937) signatory to the Bern Convention on copyright, publishers, including Russian-language publishers, ignored the niceties of copyright, authors' general permission, and, even worse, condensing or cutting a text without any permission whatsoever.
146   (Leiden: Leidsche uitgeversmaatschappij, 1926).
147   The first English edition appeared the same year (London, Heinemann) with American editions appearing simultaneously in 1930, by Covici-Friede and Random House, apparently licensed from Heinemann as both appeared by the translator of the English edition, radical feminist, Stella Browne, and introductions by J. Johnston Abraham, who introduced the Heinemann edition.

R110

and an unsigned cover, presumably also by Apsītis.[148] R110 The book is a singularly unfortunate example of the type of graphic cover design common among many Latvian children's story compilations of the time, a design influenced by the worst of the sentimental Latvian-German graphic legacy for children.

As to the background of the Orient partners, Grobin and Karachevtsev: the latter assumed the role of comptroller of the publishing house, according to Boris Ravdin,[149] although Karachevtsev's background for such a task is not known. A line of biography in *No NKVD līdz KGB: Politiskās prāvas Latvijā, 1940-1986* (From NKVD to KGB: Political Litigation in Latvia, 1940-1986) indicates that Karachevtsev served under General Paulo Skoropadsky, the anti-Bolshevik puppet head of the German-occupied Ukrainian government in 1918. He had written for White Guard newspapers and compiled several booklets of anti-Bolshevik humor—all activities he would ultimately die regretting—but there is no indication that he acquired any training for his new fiscal responsibilities in publishing, other than some experience as a journalist.

The Latvian-born Grobin had gained some, but not enough, business skills by first working in what was little more than a Riga pawnshop. It is not known when Grobin encountered Karachevtsev, but by 1925 they had established a publishing partnership. Although their venture held together, more or less, for eight years, unspecified troubles developed in 1933, with Grobin out of the partnership by the end of that year, in bankruptcy (rumored to be the result of his pawnshop irregularities),[150] and sent to jail. By 1936 he was out of jail, although he presumably did not officially rejoin either Orient or his former partner, who published the last Orient title that same year.

During the months of the 1940 Soviet occupation, Grobin disappeared as did his former colleague, Karachevtsev, who was "taken from Latvia", that is, sent to Siberia, where he spent eight years in a labor camp for "publishing counter-revolutionary books". Death in deportation was the likely fate of both men.[151] Not even Karachevtsev's efforts to publish selected Soviet writers during his publishing days could save him. But his deportation should be no surprise, given the lack of sympathy the Soviet occupiers had in 1940 for someone with his CV of distinctively "anti-Soviet behavior".

The Orient legacy consisted of 67 Russian-language titles published between 1925 and 1936, according to Abyzov, and remained listed in the 1939 Latvian telephone directory at Ģertrūdes iela 49, the same address as the publisher Kaija, with its proprietor "A. Grobin". A lingering question: could this listing be for Anna Grobina, the wife of Oto, or else possibly Aleksejs Grobiņš, who in 1940 (according to the telephone directory) lived at Brīvības iela 34/36, the first address of Orient?[152] Through an interesting but clearly stated fictional account, Laima Muktupāvela indicates in her "biographical novel" *Mīla: Benjamiņa*[153] that Karachevtsev and Anna Grobin may have published "pornographic books" together, presumably in order to make ends meet. If so, editing was facilitated by the fact that Karachevtsev lived in the same apartment building as the Grobins during this period.

The Orient saga further supports the assertion that many Russian-language publishers began with a lack of experience and little was learned along the way.

148   Priced at 50 santims.
149   Three-way telephone interview with Konstantin Beloglazov and Boris Ravdin, Riga, Nov. 2005.
150   Interview with Anatoliĭ Rakitianskiĭ and Konstantin Beloglazov, Nov. 2005.
151   See Abyzov, v. 1, p. 405; v. 2, p. 160. Another source, Treijs, p. 448, indicates that Karachevtsev was "shot in 1942".
152   It is possible Oto Grobin's wife, Anna, had the Orient business transferred to her for legal reasons and thus continued the firm under her name.
153   (Riga: Daugava, 2005).

R112

Grāmatu Draugs

One could possibly expect finding design high points among Russian-language books from Grāmatu Draugs, if for no other reason than the founder of this publishing house, Helmārs Rudzītis, thought and worked like a professional.

Rudzītis was something of an anomaly in Russian-language publishing as he was not even a Russian and therefore in a category by himself. His Grāmatu Draugs (GD) was the principal Latvian-owned Latvian-language publishing house with a Russian list.[154] But Rudzītis clearly understood the potential reading interests of the ethnic Russian audience remaining in Latvia throughout the years of independence. Just as important, he perceived these interests among the recently arrived audience of middle-class Jewish business families whose tastes in many cases were not necessarily being met by other Russian publishers. For this latter readership, variety was the watchword. Among the 20th century writers essential for the shelves of the readers among the latter group were works by Stefan Zweig, Heinrich Mann, Liĭdia Seifullina, Romain Rolland, and Jaroslav Hašek (including Karel Vaněk's continuation volumes of the Good Soldier Švejk saga), among others.[155]

Mounted in a scrapbook of Grāmatu Draugs' advertisements and miscellaneous ephemera,[156] is a newspaper advertisement headed "Biblioteka Noveisheĭ Literatury" (Library of New Literature) and dated February 5, 1927, R111 listing forthcoming Russian-language translations of such diverse authors as Jack London, Henri Barbusse, Edgar Wallace, Hermann Sudermann, Karel Čapek, Bernhard Kellermann, and Gerhart Hauptmann along with editions of Ilja Ėrenburg, Mikhail Zoschenko, Petr Ivanov, Isaak Babel, Viktor Shlovskiĭ, and Valentin Kataev. If one subscribed to this series, the prize in advance was a translation of *Chelovek niotkuda* (The Man from Nowhere, 1927) R112 by the "popular American author Victor Bridges", whose translator was none other than the young, fervently nationalist publisher himself who, one would think, had better things to do than translate American mystery writers of the era. But mysteries meant sales and Rudzītis was

154 Other Latvian publishers occasionally publishing Russian-language titles were Gramatnitsa (two titles in 1934) and Gulbis (four titles between 1924 and 1940).

155 Irra Schlossberg Gellin interview (New York City), Jan. 2005.

156 The scrapbook, found in a Riga bookshop, contains assorted memos, newspaper clippings, book covers, and other memorabilia pertaining to Grāmatu Draugs, all dating from the late 1920s to 1940.

R113

a canny businessman. In contrast, he also published[157] *Korabl prikliuchenii* (Ship of Adventure, 1930) by the noted German theatre critic and dramaturge Felix Hollaender[158] with its modernist cover by Sigismunds Vidbergs, which was one of Vidbergs more effective cover designs. R113 In all, Rudzītis published nearly 180 Russian-language titles between 1927 and 1934 and one could hardly consider him parochial, considering the content of what he brought to Riga's Russian-reading public.

To get some sense of the ambition of Rudzītis and his publishing enterprise, one need only glance at the 1929/1930 Grāmatu Draugs catalog R114 for evidence of his effort to reach a varied audience. Eleven pages of this 46 page catalog are devoted to his Russian-language publishing, indicating it was anything but an adjunct to his Latvian-language program. Listed among the "currently in print" titles are works by authors cited previously or illustrated in the newspaper advertisement reproduced. In addition, three pages of the catalog promote titles by the ever-popular fiction and mystery-writing locomotive Edgar Wallace, who wrote some 170+ books, many widely translated into both Russian and Latvian and published in Riga. In this same catalog Rudzītis cites distribution of five titles from I. Glickman's Academia imprint, including Theodore Dreiser's *Jennie Gerhardt* (1929) R115 with its cover designed by the Russian-trained architect, Alexanders Kramarevs. The period influence of Kramarev's training shines through in the Tatlinesque Academia logo he designed for the work's cover. Glickman also published Dreiser's *Sister Carrie* the following year (1930), with a sentimental design, a gambit more likely to attract the bookshop browser than Kramarev's more cerebral approach to cover design.[159] R116 Also announced in this catalog is Grāmatu Draugs own two-volume compilation of "contemporary" writers, which included Dmitrii Merezhkovskii, Marina Tsvetaeva, and Ivan Bunin.

Of likely interest to researchers of Berlin-Riga publishing connections in those First Republic years was Rudzītis' role as distributor for Josef Samuelson and David Levit's Polyglotte (Berlin) publishing venture with several of their titles listed in this same catalog, e.g. Tat'iana Kuzminskaia's *Moia zhizn' doma i v Iasnoi Polianie* (My Life at Home and at Yasnaya Polyana, 1928), with an uncredited cover design. R117 According to Abyzov,[160] a total of ten titles of this imprint appeared in the 1928/1929 period. This connection brought such diverse Russian writers as Viktor Iretskii writing under the pseudonym I.Ya. Glikman, who, after deportation on the so-called "Philosophy Steamer" in November 1922 and arrival in Berlin, became part of the Aikhenvald Circle,[161] a group of intellectual exiles that included Vladimir Vladimirovich Nabokov's father, Vladimir Dmitrievich.

Other catalog inclusions: Sergei Mstislavskii, an anthropologist-anarchist exiled by the Soviets; Ivan Nikitin, a poet from another era; and Tat'iana Kuzminskaia, the sister of Lev Tolstoy's wife Sophia Andreevna Tolstoy. All were on Samuelson's and Levit's list and thus in the Rudzītis catalog.

As a close reader of *Segodnia*, Riga's leading Russian-language cultural newspaper, Rudzītis knew that articles in this paper by and about such writers as Aikhenvald, Krechetov, and Nabokov (then writing under the pseudonym V. Sirin) would give a sales boost to Nabokov's translations in Latvian as well as his editions in the original Russian.

---

157   GD may only have distributed this title or co-published it with M. M. Didkovskii, as Didkovskii's logo and address is given on the back cover.

158   Published by S. Fischer (Berlin, 1929) as *Das Schiff der Abenteuer*.

159   Cover design by Aleksandrs Apsītis.

160   See his *A izdavalos eto v Rige, 1918-1944*, pp. 186 and 211.

161   For further discussion of this group see Lesley Chamberlain's *The Philosophy Steamer: Lenin and the Exile of the Intelligentsia* (London: Atlantic Books, 2006).

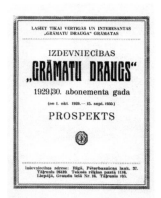

R114

R115

R116

R117

R118

R119

R120

R121

One could only wish Rudzītis had taken greater advantage of the Latvian artists and illustrators available to him for the design of his Russian list. But he was fiscally conservative, with the result that his Russian-language titles were rather dreary in their monochrome cloth bindings. If published with dust wrappers, even the wrappers usually carried little more than a straightforward typographic layout with the "GD" logo on matte, finished, colored paper. With the opportunity for an original, even a derived, design afforded by Fedor Gladkov's *Tsement* (1929), Rudzītis stayed with his signature style, which in this case was singularly appropriate for the book's theme in color choices for paper and titling. R118 Other translations chose variations of the John Heartfield design for the German edition *Zement*.[162] R119 The Estonian designer Paul Liivak gave Juhan Vanatoa's translation of *Tsement*[163] a creative variation incorporating the statue of the antithesis of the "real Soviet man".[164] R120 The uncredited Japanese designer for *Semento* took a different direction by attempting to bring the hero alive through a photographic adjustment of the statue design.[165] R121

162 (Berlin: Verlag für Literatur und Politik, Wien u. Berlin, 1927).
163 (Pärnu: Oma, 1930).
164 The "real Soviet man" depicted in the films and fiction of the time was more likely to be a maimed and otherwise broken victim of war and revolution.
165 Translated by Tsuji Tsunehiko (Tokyo: Nansou Shoin, 1928).

R122

R123

R124

R125

There were, of course, notable exceptions among the often dreary Grāmatu Draugs cover designs. One example was the inviting but uncredited cover design for one of Lidiĭa Seifullina's farm life stories, this one with the less-than-inviting title *Peregnoi* (Humus, 1928). R122 One might speculate that Rudzītis wished to spare design costs for his Russian titles so he could spend more on attractive designs for Latvian titles.

A work of major importance and a bold undertaking for Grāmatu Draugs was the publication of *Civi-s: Karikaturen-Karrikatury* (Civi-s: Caricatures, 1930) R123, R124 by Sergejs Civinskis-Civis, cover artist and compiler of its biting satirical caricatures. This remarkably prolific contributor of caricatures to Russian- as well as Latvian-language publications, e.g., *Segodnia* (1920-1940), *Sikspārnis* (1922-1926), *Svari* (1920-1931), also produced book cover illustrations, posters, and sheet music covers such as that for *Tsyganka* (1931) with its libretto and score by the popular Riga composer Mark Maryanovsky. R125 Civinskis-Civis produced two other compilations of satirical caricatures. The first was a Latvian-language caricature album titled *Augstais 100: Deputatu šarži* (100 Leaders: Friendly Satirization of the Deputies, 1929) with a cover designed by the author and depicting members of the Latvian parliament. R126–R128 The final compilation, and probably his most important contribution to the history of 20th century satire, was his *Geroi nashego vremeni* (Heroes of our Time).[166] R129 His *Civi-s Karikaturen-Karrikaturi*, with its introduction by literary critic Petr Pil'skiĭ, is a general compilation of cartoons and caricatures lampooning totalitarian regimes, local leaders, and European political leaders of the time. Civinskis-Civis' *Geroi nashego vremeni* collection was centered on thuggish types attracted to the Soviet and Nazi regimes. Predictably, *Geroi nashego vremeni* was withdrawn from bookstores and libraries in 1935 by the publishing watchdogs of the Ulmanis regime. One can assume that by doing so the government wished to avoid reprisals from either of the two regimes so sharply caricatured.

166   (Riga: Rota, 1933).

R126

R127

R128

Civinskis-Civis moved to the United States in 1934 and worked in advertising and contributed to various periodicals.[167] After a year he returned to Riga, did some sports reporting, contributed to Riga's Russian-language periodical *Dlia Vas* (For You, 1933-1940), and, to some degree, picked up his former life. Given the nature of the new regime in Latvia, it was necessary for him to keep a low profile, although he had at least two exhibitions of work during this period. One of his exhibition posters (undated, likely from the early 1930s) is shown here. R130

Civinskis-Civis, like others of his creative contemporaries such as the futurist Giacomo Balla, had a fascination for mechanical speed—planes and automobiles. Civinskis-Civis entered and graduated from the Imperial Russian military aviation school in Gatchina (1916) and then attended flight school in Odessa (1917). He flew for the Russian Imperial Air Force and for an even briefer period with the Bolshevik-commandeered air force, from which he deserted almost immediately. He was an auto racing enthusiast and driver as well as a competitive wrestler—and this, all before settling down to become a caricaturist in the new Latvia. With a biography that included fleeing the Bolshevik regime and his repeated negative depictions of it, he was an obvious target for the regime to come. When the Soviets marched into Latvia in July 1940, he was arrested along with other like-minded individuals, taken to Moscow, thrown into Lubianka Prison, and shot on July 30, 1941.

Although exhibitions of Civinskis-Civis' work were held in Riga in 1923, 1927, and 1931, he was all but forgotten in the post-WWII years until his remarkable contribution was referred to in a poorly conceived and produced booklet published in conjunction with an exhibition at the Persemuseum in Amsterdam in 1982.[168] He and his timeless caricatures deserve better.

R129

R130

167   The advertising firm and periodicals to which he contributed have yet to be discovered.
168   *Tekenen tegen de overmacht: de strijd van S. A. Civinski (1895-1940)*, comp. by Martin van den Heuvel. Half of its 36 pages consist of the compiler's essay on Baltic history followed by an appreciation of Civinskis by Isaak Kaplan and a biographical sketch by Koos van Weringh. It contains no bibliography selected or otherwise of Civinskis' work nor any word on his New York period. Interspersed are seven caricatures.

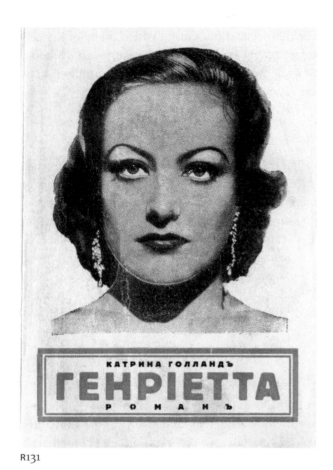

R131

R132

R133

R134

R135

Rudzītis was a consummate publishing entrepreneur and obviously calculated his audience. Unlike his Russian publishing competitors, it is generally known that Rudzītis managed to make money with his Russian list as he did with nearly all his imaginative publishing ventures, with the possible exception of a short-lived venture into Estonian and Lithuanian publishing.[169]

Filin

Rudolf (Ruvim) Rubinshteyn's Filin (Owl) publishing house, which he directed from 1929 to 1938, published some 23 titles, including the popular Swiss-German author Katrina Holland and her *Genrietta* (1933).[170] R131 Filin was more of a sideline than primary activity, for Rubinshteyn was also editor of the cultural weekly *Dlia Vas* (For You), R132 a weekly that began publication in December 1933 with a partial intent to diminish the influence of *Segodnia*. By 1939 it had become pro-Soviet and was closed by the government in August 1940.

169   Interview with Jānis Krēsliņš (New York City), July 2005.
170   Katrin Holland, i.e., Katrin H. Lamon, a Swiss-German/American writer of 40-plus mysteries, spy novels, and romances, wrote under various pseudonyms including Martha Albrand, a name perpetuated in the US Pen Club's Martha Albrand Award for an American author's first non-fiction book.

Rubinshteyn survived the first Soviet occupation, during which many of his colleagues were either deported or shot. Ultimately, his being Jewish resulted in his being shot by an SS detail near his Mežaparks home on the outskirts of Riga on July 1, 1941, shortly after the German army entered Latvia.

Renaissance

Avram Perelman was another publisher contributing modestly to Riga's Russian-language literary culture with his firm Renaissance. It brought out some 23 titles over four years of publishing, from 1929 to 1932. Perelman, like others of his contemporaries, saw opportunity in cheap editions of popular literature in translation, e.g., E. Phillips Oppenheim, Pitigrilli (pseudonym of Dino Segre), Hermann Sudermann, Edgar Wallace, and H. G. Wells. Renaissance titles were no drearier in appearance than those of its competitors. The design of Perelman's books appears to have been mostly in-house. His choice of cover for Edgar Wallace's *Liubov Syshchika* (1932) R133 illustrates the result when design is left to an amateur. The quality of the cover design for Upton Sinclair's *Provokator* (1930) R134 is no different.

Obshchedostupnaia Biblioteka

Beniamin-Leib Shereshevskiĭ was certainly more than a passing actor on the publishing scene despite being a relative latecomer with the launch of Obshchedostupnaia Biblioteka (Everyone's Library) publishing house. Even though he chose an inauspicious year to begin (1929), he managed to stay afloat through 1931. But his output diminished each year from 1931 onward until he closed his doors in 1935. The final and only title of his last year was Avram Vysotskiĭ's *Zelenoe plamia: Palestinskiĭ roman* (Green Flame: A Novel of Palestine, 1931). This was his 52nd title, including reprints of popular titles.

In the interest of making financial ends meet, Shereshevskiĭ also had to publish many a popular author such as Edgar Wallace[171] and the widely popular American writer Fanny Hurst, some of whose causes paralleled those of Shereshevskiĭ.[172] An author or two with name recognition, such as Giovanni Boccaccio, R135 was also likely to boost sales. Abyzov tells us[173] that Shereshevskiĭ had hoped to bring out Yiddish-language translations of a number of Wallace's mystery stories, a project that failed to materialize. Abyzov also speaks of his publishing religious Judaica but does not indicate the language.

Abyzov does mention that Shereshevskiĭ published Russian-language pamphlets on abortion, birth control, and masturbation and prominently displayed them in his shop window. In keeping with these interests was his publication in 1930 of a Russian-language edition of Theodoor Hendrik van de Velde's best-seller *Het volkome huwelijk* (The Complete Marriage, 1926), titled *Erotika v brake* (Erotica in Marriage, 1930).

The anticipated quick sales of such subjects, however, failed to provide a proper accumulation of capital for his firm or prepare for any future losses he might have sustained by publishing more serious works in his first year, e.g., Petr Pil'skiĭ's *Roman s teatrom* (My Love Affair with the Theater, 1929) and two of the titles in Arnold Zweig's anti-war trilogy,

---

171 At least twelve Wallace titles were published under Shereshevskiĭ's imprint.
172 Hurst, like Shereshevskiĭ, had a publicly-expressed interest in sex education.
173 See his *A izdavalos eto v Rige, 1918-1944*, p. 204.

R136

R137

R138

Tragedia untera Grishi (Der Streit um den Sergeanten Grischa [The Case of Sergeant Grischa], 1929) R136 with its striking, uncredited cover design and *Grisha v zapadne: Prodolzhenie i konets romana "Tragediĭa untera Grishi"* (Grisha Trapped: The Sequel and Conclusion of "The Case of Sergeant Grisha"). R137 Zweig's work had had immediate success on publication and translation into other languages and was therefore not considered a likely financial risk.

Among other authors published by Shereshevskiĭ over the next few years were the 19th century Russian humorist and satirist Nikolaĭ Leĭkin; the contemporary novelist of proletarian themes Leonid Grabar; and Pavel Loginov-Lesniak, another Soviet writer, although, given the government's proscription of Soviet writers, the outside observer is left guessing as to the gradations of "permissibility" that allowed publication of some writers while banning others. The renowned American mystery writer of the time S.S. Van Dine,[174] i.e., Willard Huntington Wright, included elements in his works that likely appealed to Shereshevskiĭ for their non-stereotypical presentation of minorities, a literary practice uncommon for the time. In this same year (1930) Shereshevskiĭ also published Sinclair Lewis's *The Job* (1917) in translation as *Dve liubvi Uny* (Una's Two Loves). R138 The book's theme of a woman, Una Golden, striking out into the traditional man's world—this time into commercial real estate—contained a subplot of problematic romance and divorce. This selection may have been a reflection of what appears to have been the publisher's concern for women's social pressures in industrialized countries.

Other writers in translation indicative of the publisher's seriousness and appearing in 1930, the year of his last substantial list, were Karl Friedrich Nowak's *Versailles* and Hermann Sudermann's *Der tolle Professor* (The Mad Professor) translated into Russian as *Shalnoĭ Professor*.

As indicated earlier, the offerings of Shereshevskiĭ were too modest for comment and reflected the plight—money problems—of most Russian-language publishers by the end of their one, relatively free decade of publishing.

A number of very small publishers brought out but two or three titles per annum, mainly in the period from 1924 to 1935. Fortunately for future historians, Abyzov tracks down as many of these as possible, including religious publishers such as the local Russian Orthodox Church office that produced titles to augment books coming from outside Latvia. Other examples were the Lutheran organizations determined to publish locally.

Yet another such publisher, Probuzhdenie (Awakening), published three titles in 1930, according to Abyzov, and two works not tabulated by Abyzov in 1929, by the widely translated Canadian Protestant evangelist Oswald J. Smith. Translated were two of his devotions-with-a-plan-for-action books, *The Revival We Need* and *From Death to Life*, the latter in an edition of 5,000 copies, a sizeable edition for any Russian-language title at that time.

The story of idealistic publishers using their own savings or salaries to bring out one or two titles is a story that can be summed up in one word: disappointment. Abyzov tells of no such small publishers who brought out a title of any lasting importance.

174   The one Van Dine title translated, *Zloĭ geniĭ Niu Ĭorka* from among the four mysteries Van Dine had published by the date of publication (1930), does not correspond to any readily identifiable English-language titles, making it difficult to identify the translation.

Latvian publishers with Russian-language printing services

A note on Russian-language printing services for large and small Latvian publishers: a few of the larger Latvian publishing houses maintained their own printing plants and had on-staff compositors able to set type in both Latvian and Russian. This was true of the largest Latvian-language publishing house at the time, Valters un Rapa,[175] which, according to Abyzov, published only eight Russian titles between 1927 and 1940.[176] (Abyzov must have been referring to *belles lettres*, for even the 1926/1927 Valters un Rapa catalog listed a dozen school books in Russian, and its catalog No. 44 for 1928/1929 is devoted solely to Russian books, both published or distributed by Valters un Rapa.) With the loss of Valters un Rapa records during World War II and the vague nature of the descriptions in their Russian-language catalogs, it is difficult to make a distinction between what they published and what they distributed for others. For instance, on the back page of the previously cited *Iunyĭ Chitatel*, No. 1, December 1925, Valters un Rapa purchased an entire page, advertising books for children and young people with short titles, sometimes an author but no indication as to the place of imprint, date, or publisher, thus of little help in determining if they were all Valters un Rapa titles. But Valters un Rapa were presumably distributing some Russian-language children's books published in other Baltic countries because of the relative ease of trade in those years. It is likely that *Azbuka* (ABC),[177] a collaborative effort by Zinaida Dormidontova and the artist Aleksandr Grinev, two Russians with Estonian ties, R139 would have been among those available, as this title was found in two different Latvian antiquarian bookshops in the late 1990s with Riga-owner inscriptions from the period. The Valters un Rapa advertisement mentioned, however, did not include this title, and the list was dominated by titles in the public domain, including Russian translations of "Little Red Riding Hood", "Robinson Crusoe", five titles by the 19th century American writer James Fennimore Cooper, and a few 19th century Russian-authored children's books. For obvious reasons, none of the well-known Soviet writers for children of the time were included and even relatively non-political picture books were not listed. A few classic titles for young people, e.g., works by Turgenev, Chekhov, and Pushkin, were added. Concluding the list were treats for the precocious young explorer such as four titles by Swedish explorer-adventurer Sven Hedin but, again, no bibliographical information indicating the publisher or date. One Valters un Rapa children's title "organized" for the Russian-language market was *Dietvora: Sbornik angliĭskikh razskazov* (Kiddies: A Compilation of English Stories, 1930),[178] a repackaging of four stories selected from an English storybook collections with the original English illustrators' work but no credits given to either authors or illustrators. Even the cover illustration had a Russian text covering the artist's signature. R140

Continuing with this digression to give an idea of the market: the number of Russian-language schools in Latvia at the time was 231 primary and 14 secondary schools for "Great Russians" with nearly 20,000 pupils combined, and 34 primary and three secondary schools for "White Russians" with approximately 2,500 pupils total.[179] Although

R139

R140

---

175 Interview with Jānis Rapa (Riga), Oct. 2004.

176 The Valters un Rapa printing plant was located at Brīvības iela 129/133.

177 (Reval: Varrak, 1921).

178 Translated by E. Lezevits. This title carries the printer's name "Riti" on the title page and on the verso of the title page under the phrase "Glavnyi Sklad" (Main Depot): "Valters un Rapa".

179 Zalcmanis, ibid., p. 39.

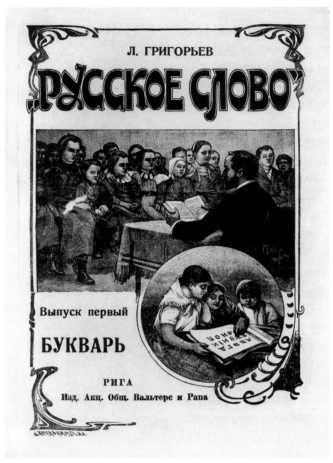

Л. ГРИГОРЬЕВ

„РУССКОЕ СЛОВО"

Выпуск первый

БУКВАРЬ

РИГА
Изд. Акц. Общ. Вальтерс и Рапа

R141

Valters un Rapa was not the only printer-publisher of textbooks for Russian schools, the firm likely had a tidy revenue from school books, although definitely not much was spent on graphic design, judging from the archaic design and illustrations of a primary school book published in 1936. R141

The chief competitor for Valters un Rapa in Latvian-language publishing in those years, Jānis Roze, apparently did not publish Russian-language works, if the bibliography in the latter's recent company history is an indication.[180] Yet Roze, like Valters un Rapa, apparently maintained a Russian-language print shop with a range of text and display Cyrillic typefaces, judging from its 1931 type specimen catalog, offering both type and decorative-cut availability. This catalog contained nine pages of Cyrillic type styles and sizes in cursive and text faces, including a 36-point size display typeface. An explanation for the Roze print shop having Cyrillic typesetting capacity is hinted at in an article by Gunta Jaunmuktāne,[181] in which she mentions that during World War I Jānis Roze bought a print shop from an "emigrating German". It would not be surprising for this purchase to have included a number of cases of Cyrillic type and cuts, because the larger German printing houses were known for their "full-service", judging from their period advertisements.[182] Jaunmuktāne also mentions that in 1923 Roze bought Dāvid Golts' establishment with all its equipment. The Golts' shop was reputedly large and well equipped and would likely have had several text fonts of Cyrillic type, although this has yet to be corroborated from examples of Russian-language printing commissions Golts may have had.

The printing houses commissioned to produce Russian books and job printing for the smaller publishing houses, seemed to offer little more than two or three standard Cyrillic text typefaces, varying only in point size, judging from more than 120 titles examined from 17 Russian-language publishers.

Among the Russian print shops or shops with Russian composition capability:
"Apt i I'urevich", later "D. Apt", but both located at Parka iela 1a; "Atmoda", L. Kalēju iela 56; "Dzintars", Elizabetes iela 22; "Globus", Elizabetes iela 22; "Grāmatu Draugs," Pēterbaznīcas laukums 25-27; "Izdevējs", Elizabetes iela 83/85; "E. Levin", Dzirnavu iela 33; "M. Makhtenberi'a", Marijas iela 8; "A. Nitiavskaya", Merķeļa iela 6; "Riti", Dzirnavu iela 57; "Rota", Dzirnavu iela 57; "Salamandra", L. Kalēju iela 43; "Star", Jumaras iela 15; "Vārds", L. Peldu iela 24; "Viktoria", Dzirnavu iela 33; and "Zieds", Jumaras iela 15. Undoubtedly there were more.

180 *Grāmata par grāmatnieku Jāni Rozi* (Riga: 1999), pp. 151-183.
181 See "Grāmatizdevējs Jānis Roze" in *Varavīksne* (Riga, 1996), pp. 57-75.
182 Berthold Typefoundry (Berlin) opened an office in Riga in 1918 and carried a line of Cyrillic type for regional clients.

One of the largest of these printing enterprises and likely the most versatile in its capability was Salamandra, a company that was also a leading book and periodical publisher.[183] Founded in pre-1917 Russia, Salamandra moved its printing-publishing operation from St. Petersburg to Riga using capital from Denmark as well as Latvia, according to Rihards Treijs in his *Latvijas republikas prese, 1918-1940*,[184] to reestablish its operation. This plant was capable of printing books in relatively large editions (5,000+ copies) as well as producing fine-quality, four-color work for book illustration and providing complete photolithographic services for other publishers. The firm's color printing services were used extensively for producing tipped-on color illustrations, a relatively common need in Latvia among both book and periodical publishers in the 1920s who wished to brighten their publications.

R142

Four of Salamandra's well-known periodicals were the conservative daily newspaper *Slovo* (The Word, 1925-1929), the literary and art monthly *Perezvony* (Chimes, 1925-1929), the weekly general periodical *Novyĭ Dom*, and the previously mentioned children's periodical *Iunyĭ Chitatel* (Young Reader, 1925-1926). In addition, there was Salamandra's paperback library *Deshevaia Biblioteka* (Inexpensive Library), which was just as indicated, offering reprints of earlier popular literature priced at 60 santims, and, not to be forgotten, the firm's profitable textbook publishing program for the Russian-language schools. According to Treijs, Salamandra's printing and publishing capital source was the exiled Russian Nationalist Insurance Society, thus giving the firm significant financial resources.[185]

Salamandra initially attempted to crush the lively *Segodnia* newspaper with its own newspaper, the conservative and somewhat stodgy *Slovo*. But despite its power and its less sophisticated level of reportage, it was no match for *Segodnia*. In addition, Salamandra's financial fortunes took a turn for the worse as the result of an earthquake half a world away. The great Kanto earthquake in Tokyo-Yokohama in September 1923 brought insurance claims from scores of businesses and private persons toward the close of 1924, and continuing until 1929. With such a drain on its resources, Salamandra was forced to suspend its periodical and book publishing operation.

R143

Russian-language newspapers and journals

Russian-language periodical and newspaper publishing in Latvia merits its own detailed chapter, but here comment will be made on only a sample of some 23 general journal and newspaper titles. In addition to these, there were more than 80 short- and long-lived Russian-language titles of the hard left and pro-Soviet factions.

R144

Dlia Vas

Dlia Vas (For You), R142–R144 begun in 1933 "with the hope of ousting the widely read and respected *Segodnia*",[186] according to the media historian Inta Brikše, featured popular themes and such regular fare as the "Mata d'Or" gossip column on Parisian life but

183   John Glad cites it as being the "largest" Russian publishing house in Riga in his *Russia Abroad*, p. 196.

184   Treijs, ibid., p. 441.

185   Treijs, ibid., pp. 441-442.

186   See Inta Brikše's contribution "Journalism in independent Latvia during the 1920s and 1930s" in *Towards a Civic Society: The Baltic Media's Long Road to Freedom; Perspectives on History, Ethnicity, and Journalism*, ed. by Svennik Høyer, Epp Lauk, and Peeter Vihalemm (Tartu: Baltic Association for Media Research / Nota. Baltica, Ltd., 1993), p. 150.

R145

R146

R147

R148

by 1939 had "turned into a vehicle of pro-USSR propaganda".[187] It was not a distinguished contribution to Russian-language publishing by any measure.

Perezvony

Perezvony (Chimes, 1925-1929) was a solidly produced monthly featuring a cover design (unchanged from issue to issue except for color) by the renowned Lithuanian artist Mstislav Dobuzhinsky and frequently appeared with tipped-in color plates. R145–R147 The literary department was edited by Boris Zaitsev, who left Paris to come to Riga, maintaining his wider émigré community connections and publishing authors among them, e.g., Ivan Bunin, Sasha Cherny, Aleksandr Kuprin, Alekseĭ Remizov, and Marina Tsvetaeva. The journal also brought the art of such émigrés as Iuriĭ Annenkov, Boris Grigoriev, Simon Lissim, Nikolaĭ Roerich, and others to its readership. But even with its impressive stable of contributors, the monthly's publisher, Salamandra, could not counter the financial collapse of 1929.

With few exceptions, such as *Nord-Ost*, the design of Russian-language periodicals and newspapers appears in so many cases to have been a task given over to print shop compositors. The cover and internal design of the social democratic annual *Kalendar Rabochego* 1934 (Worker's Calendar)[188] R148 is typical of such non-descript design.

In contrast, Romans Suta's cover design for the first issues of *Nord-Ost*,[189] R149–R150 the title page and publisher's signet by Isaak Sherman, R151 and the internal typography were decidedly several design gradients above the no-nonsense but drab design of *Kalendar Rabochego*. Even more dramatic design and format changes for *Nord-Ost* were to come.

Nord-Ost

Nord-Ost (Northeast) announced itself as a journal for Riga's young Russian poets. It was clear from the first issues that its direction was politically on the left and in support of the USSR, even though it was ostensibly designed to foster cultural exchange and understanding between ethnic Russian-Latvians and ethnic Latvians. If there was any question about ideological allegiance, one need only skim the poems and prose by such figures as philosopher-poet Pāvils Vīlips or the committed Marxist and sometime-member of parliament Andrejs Kurcijs as well as the politically-erratic-but-never-dull Austra Ozoliņa-Krauze. There were also reminiscences from time to time such as Aleksandrs Čaks' account of his first visit with Vladimir Mayakovsky. In general, the contributions were broadly

---

187 Ibid., p. 150.
188 Published for the years 1933 and 1934 by Osvobozhdenie Truda, Maskavas iela 140.
189 Edited by Aleksandr Magilnitskiĭ with Semen Pevzner, Lev Zaks, and artist Isaak Sherman, and others.

R151

R149

R150

R152

cultural and even included art reproductions (of poor quality) by well-known figures such as Marta Skulme,[190] Romans Suta, and lesser-known Latvian artists, some all but forgotten.[191] *Nord-Ost* was one example of a publishing effort in which intellectuals, holding varied ideological views, joined together to produce a journal without apparent major disagreements hampering the effort.

A few individuals contributing poems to *Nord-Ost* were Boris Veinberg, Leonid Kavetskiĭ, Semen Pevzner, Lev Zaks, and the journal's own editor-in-chief Aleksandr Magilnitskiĭ.[192] The journal also included essays, reviews, and literary critical articles by authors such as A. Čaks, A. Kurcijs, V. Kaverin, Isaak Sherman, Vera Babst, "G. [or possibly Lydia] Tabak", Boris Pasternak (likely reprinted from another source but not credited as such), Moses Michel Kitai, and Marietta Shaginyan (a reprint), who even exceeded Austra Ozoliņa-Krauze in her eccentricity in politics and literary output.

A major design and format change for *Nord-Ost* came about in February 1932 with issue No. 7 appearing in an expanded format (38.4x28.3 cm), with Niklāvs Strunke as the journal's cover artist. His woodcut illustration for the issue's cover R152 was a stark proletarian image unlike the flowing, poetic style of much of Strunke's other work of the period. By the time the 11th issue appeared, Samuils Haskins had signed on as cover artist and a

R153

190   A recent and highly informative monograph on Marta Liepiņa-Skulme compiled by Gundega Cēbere and Laima Slava includes contributions by art historians Ruta Čaupova and Ojārs Ābols as well as Džemma Skulme, the artist's daughter, and a superb English translation by Līva Ozola (Riga: Neputns, 2009).

191   No. 2 (1931) reproduces Romans Suta's "Natiurmort", the portrait of his mother, two George Grosz caricatures illustrating a review essay on him by K. Romanov, a Rēzekne street scene by Francisks Varslavāns, caricatures by K. Ozols, a linocut by Pauls Šterns, and concluding with a page of "world caricatures" reprinted from *Ulk*, *Monde*, and *Berlin am Morgen*. No. 5 (1931) shows three of Marta Skulme's sculptures, two of Romans Suta's wash drawings, and a linocut titled "Demonstration" by Kārlis Bušs. In No. 2 (7) for 1932, following the untypically crude cover by Niklāvs Strunke, is a woodcut illustration by Frans Masereel and three unsigned linocuts.

192   Magilnitskiĭ provides an account of the journal in "Pret fašismu un karu" (Against fascism and war) in *Cīņas balsis* (Riga: Latvijas Valsts izdevniecība, 1959), pp. 397-407.

R154

R155

R156

second color appeared in the cover art.[193] R153 Haskins, a prolific caricaturist, who often contributed striking designs to left-oriented and Communist periodicals,[194] R154 illustrated covers for *Nord-Ost* from 1931 until ceasing publication in December 1932, after 20 issues.

With the advent of the Ulmanis regime in 1934, Haskins fled to the Soviet Union, where he continued to work as a designer, in addition to working in Moscow for the Latvian-language publishing house Prometejs. He apparently served in the Soviet Army, according to Laime Reihmane,[195] and thus did not experience a tragic end as did so many of his Latvian communist colleagues working in the USSR. He survived, returned to Riga in 1946, and remained an active caricaturist and poster designer throughout the second Soviet era until his death in 1974, even managing to have a one-man exhibition of his work in Moscow in 1970.[196]

Kino

The founding editors of *Kino*, the first bilingual (Russian and Latvian) film magazine to last longer than one issue,[197] with its covers designed by Sergejs Civinskis-Civis, R155, R156 likely envisioned a bright publishing future serving Latvian- and Russian-language populations. First appearing in mid December 1926, this bilingual journal aspired to become a "weekly journal of literature and art". But its life was cut short, apparently by the realities of production and the editorial demands of having different content for both of its language sections. One would have imagined that its chief financial officer or at least one of its backers, possibly a business manager at the printing-publishing house Salamandra, could have quickly calculated that such a plan was doomed, given the general economic problems of the time. But its six issues give a glimpse into what its editors thought might interest the anticipated readership and, for us, some idea of the "film topics of the time". Although the content in the two languages differs, in the first issue both the Latvian and Russian portions lead with a Rainis interview, presumably hoping this literary hero's thoughts on contemporary film and, in particular, Hollywood films might bring subscribers. Other contributors: Jānis Sudrabkalns wrote on "The loveliest art", Roberts Kroders (creator of the script for the first Latvian sound film)[198] contributed a few paragraphs on the new medium, "Dr. Orientācijs" (i.e., Valdis Grēviņš) contributed a "Film director's notebook", and there are even poems by both Aspazija and Pāvils Rozītis. The issue concluded, as did subsequent issues, with a "Hronika" section edited by Jānis Gūters that, as the title implies, gave domestic and foreign film news notes to keep local film-goers aware of world film trends.

193   No. 3 (8) has a striking caricature in red and black, depicting Hitler and Mussolini as balloons with their strings being held by a cartoon capitalist.
194   Such contributions were mainly to leftist Latvian-language periodicals such as *Informators* (Oct.-Dec. 1932), *Tribīne* (1931-1933), etc.
195   Interview with Laime Reihmane, Oct. 2010.
196   *Samuel Khaskins vystavka* (Moscow, 1970).
197   *Ekrāns*, edited by A. Antens in Latvian and Russian, appears to have lasted for but one issue—Nov. 1, 1924—but despite its short life, it lays claim to being Latvia's first film magazine. An all-Russian language journal called *Kino-Rampa*, R157 edited and published by V. I. Romanovskiĭ, appeared briefly (autumn 1925), and provides insight into the type of entertainment available with its week-by-week schedule of offerings at the National Opera, National Theater, Art Theater, and Russian, German, and Jewish theaters as well as the 14 movie houses and their sensationally titled silent films, mostly comedies.
198   "Tautas dēls" (Son of the People, 1934).

In addition to the Rainis interview, the first issue's Russian section featured an article by Valentin Turkin titled "Film and other arts" and an article written under the pseudonym "Operator" titled "Objections to film work in Soviet Russia". Another bashful writer hiding behind "Chap Lin" contributed a feuilleton in nearly each issue, and a portion of the autobiography of the Berlin film star Willi Fritsch was serialized in several issues. Other issues had film stars and film critics contributing such memorable pieces as Olga Chekhova's "How I become a hero", Norma Shearer's "Care of face color", and Artur Landsberger's "Jealousy does not lead". Such give-the-public-what-they-want fare was little different from that found in other contemporary film magazines from Paris to Tokyo.

While speaking of film magazines in Latvia (there were few in any language in those years), after the journal folded, another *Kino* appeared, but only in the Latvian language.[199] This second *Kino* appeared at the beginning of 1929 and had a slightly longer life or at least more issues—50 issues in 1929—and managed to reach a double number in 1930 before ceasing publication in November of that year. Then in 1932 another editor-entrepreneur, presumably with money to lose, initiated yet another bilingual film magazine, this time in Latvian and German. The publishers of this journal, *Kino un Teātra Ziņas*, managed to bring out nine issues before collapsing just before Christmas of the same year.

R157

The left Russian-language press in Latvia

Moving away from specialized-audience periodicals to general periodicals, albeit of interest largely to the politically left sector of the population, there is little to show in the way of interesting design. The utilitarian approach dominates. These Russian-language periodicals of the political left, like the Russian or bilingual film magazines, also had lives like the proverbial mayfly.

Because of the clearly stated concern of the government for publications of any sort that would destabilize the fragile democracy, periodicals advocating or even hinting at a violent overthrow of the "new order" were certainly suspect. While general registration for Social Democratic organs was allowed, Latvian Communist Party periodical publications had to be fully registered and were otherwise controlled, whether published in Russian or in Latvian. After May 1934, when the Ulmanis government took control, all such publications were banned. Despite the ban, 12 such publications had sufficiently audacious editors and backers to begin publication in 1934 and continue until the German army's occupation of Latvia in the summer of 1941. With the exception of two periodicals, *Vpered* (Go Forward) and *Na Bor'bu* (To Arms), both of which began in 1933 before the ban and continued until 1936, most other left-oriented Russian-language periodicals appearing between 1920 until shortly before 1934 ceased publication after a year or so. Only two, *Bolshevik* (1921-1931) and *Pravda Molodezhi* (Truth for Youth, 1922-1931), lasted for any length of time; both were organs of the Latvian Communist Party and printed by the Communist-Party-operated Russian-language print shop "Spartak".

The printing and distribution history of these controlled or outright banned periodicals—some 56 Russian-language titles alone between 1920 and 1940—can be found in a

199 Other film/movie magazines in the Latvian language were as short-lived as the bilingual magazines, e.g. *Filma un Skatuve* (Jun. 1930 – Apr. 1932), *Filma un Teātris* (Sept. 1932 – Feb. 1933), and *Filmu Apskats* (just four issues from Oct. 20 to Nov. 17, 1934).

R158

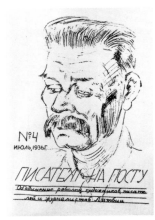

R159

number of sources.[200] For editorial information on the underground or banned Latvian periodicals of the era, one need only consult volume two of *Latviešu periodika*, titled "Revolucionārā un padomju periodika, 1920-1940" (Revolutionary and Soviet Periodicals, 1920-1940).[201] The adventure of the hurried production of an issue in one printery, the inevitable moves among print shops, the switching in "mid-stream" from available metal type to a Latvian version of a multilith and even a hectograph—all are told in detail in *Cīņas balsis* (Voices of Struggle).[202]

Underground publications such as *Pisatel' na Postu* (Writer on Guard), the underground publication of the Association of Latvian Revolutionary Writers, Artists, and Journalists (1935-1936),[203] R158, R159 is typical in its appearance of "near-print" composition, hand-drawn cover typography, and illustrations. *Bolshevik*[204] is typographically little different from the nearly 60 such banned publications appearing between 1920 and 1940. It is clear that there were few dramatic, revolutionary illustrations in the stock illustration "cut cases" of these Russian-language printers, although there were a number of local graphic artists who might have contributed a little eye-catching proletarian-style linocut illustration to at least the covers of these publications. But if one is continually hiding the evidence of one's printing operation or running from the authorities, it is content, not appearance, that matters.

The general interest Russian-language press

Although Rihards Treijs lists some 22 Russian-language periodicals and newspapers in Latvia not sustained by the politically left, only seven could be counted as "general interest". Among those lasting for any length of time, and among these seven, only four had a circulation of 3,000 or more.[205]

Treijs goes on to state[206] that after Ulmanis came to power the decision was made that there would be one "Jewish-Russian" newspaper, *Segodnia*; one "Russian" newspaper, *Gazeta dlia vsech* (Newspaper for Everyone, 1936-1940); one "illustrated Russian" periodical, *Dlia Vas*; and the Russian-Orthodox oriented journal *Vera i Zhizn'* (Faith and Life, 1923-1940).

There was hope that somewhere in six years of browsing in Riga's antiquarian shops a stack of Russian-language satirical papers would be discovered, titles on the order of the scores of publications Raimonds Zalcmanis explores in his *Latviešu satirs smejas: Ieskats Latvijas neatkarības gadu humoristiski satīriskās preses izdevumos* (The Latvian Satyr is Laughing: An Insight into the Satirical Press During the Years of Latvia's Independence).[207] Evidently, when Russian-readers longed for satire, they leafed through available Latvian

200   An article by B. Ozola "LKP nelegālās tipogrāfijas Rīgā" in *Pa vēsturisko notikumu pēdām* (Riga: Zvaigzne, 1972); Samuel Levitan's dissertation *Latvijas nelegālā komunistiskā prese cīņā par padomju varu (1920-1940)* (Riga: Latvian State University, 1967).

201   Edited by Ā. Brempele, et al. (Riga: Zinātne, 1976).

202   Compiled by Jūlijs Ķipers (Riga: Latvijas Valsts izdevniecība, 1959).

203   Only five issues published in an edition ranging from 200 to 500 copies.

204   An erratic publishing schedule is to be expected from a banned paper, but an attempt at being a fortnightly while maintaining an edition size ranging from 1,000 to 6,000 copies was a major logistic accomplishment, to say nothing of the editor's excitement brought on by unrelenting surveillance.

205   Those with a circulation of 3,000 or more: *Dlia vas* (Riga, Dec. 1933-Aug. 1940) [ca. 3-5,000], *Segodnia* (Riga, Sept. 1919-Jun. 1940) [ca. 40-50,000+], *Segodnia vetscherom* (Riga, Dec. 1924-Jun. 1940) [ca. 40,000], *Slovo* (Riga, Nov. 1925-May 1929) [ca. 10,000]. See Treijs, *Latvijas republikas prese, 1918-1940*, pp. 493-496.

206   Ibid., p. 447.

207   (Riga: Avots, 1994).

publications or browsed among old issues of *Novyĭ Satirikon*,[208] brought to Riga by those who fled Russia during the Revolution of 1917.

What such readers might have chanced upon at some point were a few special, Russian-language issues published by the Latvian satirical journal *Satīrs*, e.g., *Reorganizovannyi Satir* (Reorganized Satyr, February 1931), R160 the one-issue forerunner, at least in its year of appearance, of the periodical *Satirikon*, which appeared in Paris two months later by a reconstituted team from the St. Petersburg journal of the same name and closed in 1918. A connection is probable. The illustrated Riga title was published in a mix of languages: its first five pages in Russian, followed by two pages in Yiddish, followed in turn by 12 pages in Russian. The text and caricature portion concludes with 13 pages of advertising in Russian, German, Latvian, and Yiddish. The National Library of Latvia also holds a 1932 *Satir* title in Yiddish; this issue was not examined, although a scan of its cover illustration shows the "A.S." artist's initials.

R160

Was the cover artist "A.Š." possibly Abram Šur?[209] The "A.B." signing internal caricatures may be signed in Cyrillic and thus be "A.V.", as in A. Veinbergs, who was on the *Satīrs* editorial staff at the time. "A.B." signed two internal illustrations and five appear to be signed by "A.Š." Contributors to the text left their pieces unsigned or used initials.

The *Segodnia* legend

Segodnia (Today) is a special case in the history of Russian-language newspaper publishing. Celebrated in its day, much mourned at its untimely death, *Segodnia* (1919-1940)[209] R161 was not only the intellectual life blood for much of the Russian-reading community outside the USSR but also an influence on other exile Russian newspapers and periodicals wherever it was read. This vital role has been reiterated by diarists of the period and surviving readers who provided this writer with wistful accounts of its importance to them as teenagers growing up in exile.

R161

From the paper's somewhat shaky beginnings in September 1919 by Yakov Brams, the surgeon Boris Poliak, and its editor-in-chief Mikhail Mil'rud[211] to its forced closure in 1940, *Segodnia* and later *Segodnia Vetscherom* (This Evening) R162 and *Ponedelnik* (Monday) were the Russian-language newspapers of choice of Latvia's Russian-reading community.

From its earliest, difficult years during the reconstruction immediately after World War I, *Segodnia* attracted some of the most gifted reporters and feuilletonists as well as theatre, literary, and music critics writing in Russian outside what was to become the Soviet Union. To a great degree the attraction for this talent was the newspaper's second editor-in-chief, Maksim Ganfman. Ganfman's more than 70 contributions[212] to the paper not only give insight into Russian cultural life in Latvia but also offer a picture of the heady intellectual life in the country at that time.

Ganfman established a news reporting system with multilingual correspondents throughout Latvia and other European countries, thus giving the paper a decided advantage over other Russian-language papers in Latvia. While some later commentators

---

208   Published in St. Petersburg from 1913-1918 by a circle of artists and writers who had been the mainstays of M. Kornfeld's *Satirikon* published from 1908-1914.

209   A graphic designer working on Yiddish-language publications.

210   *Gazeta "Segodnia" 1919-1940*, vol. 1-2, ed. by Iuriĭ Abyzov (Riga: Latviiskaya Natsional'naja biblioteka, 2001).

211   Mil'rud's associate editors, also Russian refugees, were Boris Khariton and Petr Pil'skiĭ.

212   See *Gazeta "Segodnia" 1919-1940*, vol. 2, p. 355.

R162

referred to it as a "Russian-Jewish" paper, it had a much wider audience than that because, according to Oskar Grosberg, it was read by Germans, Latvians, Estonians, Lithuanians, and Poles.[213] From the beginning, Ganfman fostered the work of Latvian writers by publishing in translation such leading—and in some cases relatively young—writers as Vilis Plūdons, Jānis Poruks, Andrejs Pumpurs, Rainis, Kārlis Skalbe, and Edvarts Virza.[214] As for publishing Soviet and émigré writers, an editorial stance of relative neutrality was maintained, for the newspaper published writings and reviews by major writers holding various ideological positions.[215]

Among *Segodnia's* problems were local detractors. John Glad characterizes one of these controversies in his *Russia Abroad: Writers, History, Politics:*[216]

"Since the paper's staff was largely Jewish, as were many of its readers, coverage of Jewish topics was especially thorough, a situation which alienated some of the ethnic Russians. A former Petersburg journalist, Leonard Korol'-Purashevich, founded *Rizhskiĭ kur'er* (Riga Courier, 1921-1924), evidently with Polish funding, and then *Vechernee vremya* (Evening News, 1924-1925), using these publications to attack *Segodnia* as 'non-Russian'. In 1933, he created *Zavtra* (Tomorrow) to counter *Segodnia*... Korol'-Purashevich left for Germany in 1939, but Iuriĭ Rzhevsky published the weekly *Gazeta dlya vsekh* (Newspaper for Everyone, 1936-1940), also stressing that it was a truly 'Russian', not a Jewish publication."

213   See p. 61, *Die Presse Lettlands* (Riga: Baltischer Verlag, 1927).
214   See Treijs, *Latvijas republikas prese*, 1918-1940, p. 440.
215   For example, Y. Aikhenvald, M. Aldanov, M. Bulgakov, I. Bunin, S. Esenin, I. Érenburg, M. Gorky, N. Gumilev,
V. Mayakovsky, V. Nabokov, and Y. Zamyatin, among others. See volume two of Abyzov's index to *Segodnia* cited previously.
216   Glad, ibid., p. 195-196.

Though *Segodnia* had published Soviet writers from time to time, this offered no insurance against what was to come. The paper was despised and surely envied in the Kremlin for its enthusiastic world-wide readership. Thus, in June 1940, when the Soviet government ordered its shock troops and political apparat to occupy Latvia on the heels of the Hitler-Stalin Pact, many *Segodnia* staff were rounded up over the next weeks and months for deportation to Siberia or "disappeared", which often meant shot.[217] From Treijs we learn the fate of the editorial staff members.[218] Mil'rud died in Camp Karaganda, likely in 1942. Khariton was deported at the same time and met a similar death around 1941. Israel Teitelboim was shot in Astrakhan Prison in 1942. The fate of *Segodnia's* long-time staff cartoonist Sergejs Civinskis-Civis was previously mentioned. The prolific contributor Petr Pil'skiĭ[219] suffered a heart attack when the NKVD came to arrest him in the summer of 1940 and died a few months later at his home.[220]

These are but a few of many personal tragedies. Individual acts of cultural barbarism, not the last to be visited on the intellectual communities of Riga and of Latvia by their "liberators", were but a portent of what was to come in those initial months of the Soviet occupation before the German troops arrived in July 1941. Massive attacks were carried out on the Jewish population by the SS apparat as well as selected assassinations or imprisonment of Latvian intellectuals. The story of the second "liberation" and the cost to the Jewish population is recounted in numerous memoirs. Bibliographical details regarding several of these accounts are provided in the chapter on publishing for the Jewish community.

A Russian-language publishing history has yet to be written for the Interwar era. A bibliographical starting point has been established by Abyzov through his previously cited works and his complete listing of all articles published in *Segodnia* from its inception in 1919 to its closure in 1940.[221]

There is also much publishing history of the era to be found in *Kniga o russkom evreistve, 1917-1967* (Books on Russian Jewry, 1917-1968), compiled by Jacob Frumkin, Grigoriĭ Aronson, and Alekseĭ Gol'denveĭser.[222]

But telling the full story of Russian-language publishing in Latvia remains hampered by two phases of destruction. First, the confiscation and subsequent burning or pulping of Russian books and editorial paper files (along with Latvian, Jewish, and German publications) at the time of Latvia's first Soviet occupation from July 1940 to June 1941. This action was repeated in the late 1940s and early 1950s, according to Beloglazov.[223] In another alleged case in the 1990s, surviving Russian-language newspaper and periodical archives stored for decades were lost when the storage facilities housing them were purchased and the extensive files (often unique) relegated to the dumpster by the new owners of the storage area.[224] But despite this destruction the National Library of Latvia and other research libraries in Riga collectively maintain a substantial portion of what was published in book, periodical, and ephemeral form during the Interwar period.

---

217 Yakov Brams and Boris Poliak contrived a way to leave the country for the USSR, according to Abyzov.
218 Ibid., p. 447.
219 Pil'skiĭ contributed some 420 essays and reviews to *Segodnia* from 1920 to 1940.
220 See Glad, ibid., p. 198.
221 *Gazeta "Segodnia", 1919-1940*, 2 vols. (Riga: Latviiskaya Natsional'naja biblioteka, 2001).
222 (New York: Union of Russian Jews, 1968).
223 Interview with Konstantin Beloglazov, Jan. 2007.
224 Eyewitness accounts by individuals wishing to remain anonymous observed this facility being emptied within a 72-hour period and the contents "hauled away".

Conclusion

Looking back at Russian-language book publication in Latvia, one can say it was something of a Wild West Show. The legacy: less than 1,000 "products" of good, bad, and indifferent quality were produced by largely amateur publishing adventurers, a few professionals such as Kārlis Rasiņš and Helmārs Rudzītis, and the professionals behind the Zhizn' i Kul'tura imprint.

As to the design of most of these books and the periodicals, again there was competent, professional design by such individuals as Raimunds Šiško, Mihail Jo, and the few titles Vasyl Masjutyn managed to create in his months in Riga.

Regrettably, the professionally designed and typographically successful designs tended to be outnumbered by uninspired ones, whether book or periodical. Most of the Russian-language publishers rushed into the business without an appropriate management background or previous experience in design or typography. Graphic design as an important part of selling books appeared to have crossed the minds of only a few of the nearly 40 Russian-language publishers who entered the Latvian scene in that period. At least these publishers with their enthusiasm and often limited experience knew their audience—captive, eager readers looking mainly for "escape" literature. Content mattered more than cover graphics or even illustration, judging from the modest number of Russian titles published with illustrations.

One can only wish that somewhere, in some unlikely (or even likely) place, a tell-all memoir by one of the Russian publishers of that era is waiting for discovery.

Meanwhile, we have the bibliographical legacy of Iuriĭ Abyzov, the bibliographical efforts of Anatoliĭ Rakitianskiĭ and his periodic publication *Rizhskiĭ bibliofil*,[225] and the work of a few others.

225   Volumes for years published as of spring 2011: 2003 and 2010.

PUBLISHING IN THE JEWISH COMMUNITY PART 3

Introduction

The phrase "Jewish Riga" once evoked images of a diminutive St. Petersburg. There was also "Riga the science city" with its inventors and scientists known from Moscow to London and Paris to New York. In the decades before World War II the entire Baltic region enjoyed the path-breaking medical fame and staff expertise of the Bikur-Holim Hospital, established in 1870, as well as those physicians of other Riga medical centers. The Yiddish edition of this hospital's 1938 annual report is shown here. Y1

Y1

Looking today at a roster of Latvian-Jewish personalities either born or living and working in the country before the summer and autumn horrors of 1941/42, one can well imagine what Latvian life might have been like from the late 19th century through the 1930s. Here is a much abbreviated list of Jewish Rigensians whose names are known to many Europeans and Anglo-Americans: Isaiah Berlin,[1] Leo Blech, Sergei Eisenstein, Philippe Halsman, Solomon Mikhoels, and Mark Rothko. Others include portrait sculptor Naum Aronson, Jewish history scholar Simon Dubnow, pioneer neurosurgeon Vladimir Mintz,[2] painter and book illustrator Abel Pan, painter and children's book illustrator Feodor Rojankovsky, pioneer physio-chemist and endocrinologist Lina Stern, composer and publisher Oscar Strok, molecular-spectroscopy pioneer Joseph Eiduss, film director Friedrich Ermler, philologist Nehemiah Pereferkovich, Yiddish lexicographer and prime force in YIVO's founding Max Weinreich,[3] and leading Israeli composer/conductor Marc Lavry. Renowned present-day performing artists whose lives began in Riga include Mischa Maisky, Inez Galant, Inna Davidova, and Julia Gurvitch.

But what changed Latvian-Jewish life in Latvia forever? Ābrams Kleckins answers with a succinct view of the demographic history of Latvian Jewry and its untimely end:

"[The] community… existed… for more than 400 years. During the 20th century the number… decreased by more than 12 times… Out of approximately 73 thousand Jews who stayed in Latvia occupied by the Nazis, less than 300 survived on its territory, and about 800 in the concentration camps of Europe… the 1941 deportation of [Jewish] 'class enemies' sent to Siberia by Stalin's order… about 5,000 people…'only' one-third perished."[4]

Several publications in Western languages give us a sense of Latvian Jewry's tortured history, yet also its remarkable contribution to the region in the German, Tsarist, and Republican periods, often mixing years of heartache with progress and accomplishments.

---

1 Isaiah Berlin was only twelve when the family left Riga for London in 1921.

2 Mintz's medical acumen altered history by his saving Lenin's life in August 1918 following Fanny Kaplan's assassination attempt.

3 The Yidisher Wisnshaftlekher institut founded in Vilna in 1925 was moved to New York City in 1940.

4 See Gunta Branta, ed. *Sava krāsa varavīksnē* (One's Own Color in the Rainbow) (Riga: AGB, 1997), p. 232. Compare Kleckins' statistics with those of other writers, e.g. Frank Gordon and his online postings.

One recent work on the subject is *Outstanding Jewish Personalities in Latvia* by Grigoriĭ Smirin, Pēteris Apinis, and Maija Šetlere.[5] The illustrated profile portion of this work with its mini-biographies is prefaced by a well-researched essay by Apinis. A complementary volume, Aleksandrs Feigmanis' *Latvian Jewish Intelligentsia Victims of the Holocaust*, includes brief biographical sketches and photos of 77 personalities in Latvian, English, Russian and French.[6] Then there is the burgeoning online effort of a number of individuals and organizations, not the least of which is "Jews of Latvia, a Project: Names and Fates 1941-1945" providing basic and sobering data.

Marģers Vestermanis, founding director of the Latvian Jewish Museum in Riga, is known in the post-Soviet period for his walking tours of Jewish Riga. His guide, *Fragments of the Jewish History of Riga*,[7] with its summary of culture, personalities, and institutions, is indispensable for those wishing a brief, stirring overview.

The most extensive work undertaken—by Latvian and Estonian Jews in Israel—during the Soviet era, when access to archives was still restricted, is *The Jews in Latvia*,[8] written under the editorial supervision of Mendel Bobe,[9] Shneour Levenberg, Yitzhak Maor, and Ze'ev Michaeli.[10]

We have Harro von Hirschheydt, a German antiquarian bookseller, to thank for reprinting *Geschichte der Juden in Riga bis zur Begründung der Rigischen Hebräergemeinde im J. 1842* (History of the Jews in Riga Until the Founding of the Riga Hebrew Community in the Year 1842) by Anton Buchholtz (Riga: N. Kymmel, 1899).[11]

While being grateful for reprints, we should also mention Maks Shats-Anin's *Evrei v Latviĭ* (Jews in Latvia; Riga: Oze, 1924), included as a portion of conference proceedings commemorating Shats-Anin in June 1997,[12] coordinated by Ruta Shats-Mariash and Aleksandr Posev, with Grigoriĭ Smirin's editorial direction.

A recent scholarly work, *History of Latvian Jews* by Josifs Šteimanis is a most useful summary background, thanks to the translation by Helena Belova and the editing and incorporation of other material by Edward Anders.[13]

Although Andrew Ezergailis' *The Holocaust in Latvia, 1941-1944*[14] has another focus, his chapters and chapter sections on Latvian Jewry before 1941 are essential reading for his insight and concise presentation of historical detail.

After having skimmed through two or three of these works and one or two memoirs of Riga Jewry such as Max Michelson's moving biography *City of Life, City of Death:*

5   (Riga: Nacionālais apgāds, 2003).

6   (Riga: Privately published, 2006).

7   (Riga: Museum and Documentation Centre of the Latvian Society of Jewish Culture, 1991).

8   (Tel Aviv: Association of Latvian and Esthonian [sic] Jews in Israel, 1971).

9   Bobe has drawn from his previous research published in *Perakim be-toldot Yahadut Latvijah* (1651-1918) (Chapters in the History of Latvian Jewry) (Tel Aviv: Reshafim, 1965) and expanded in a Yiddish-language edition, *Yidn in Letland* (Jews in Latvia) (Tel Aviv: Reshafim, 1972).

10   Other contributors: M. Laserson, A. Godin, B. Sieff, M. Amir, S. Lipschitz, M. Beth, E. Amitan-Wilensky, and M. Kaufman.

11   (Wedemark – OT Elze, Germany: Verlag Harro von Hirschheydt, 1996).

12   *Maks Shats-Anin: Zhizn, nasledie, sud'ba* (Riga: Rizhskaya Evreiskaya obshchina, Muzei i dokumentatsionnyi tsentr "Evrei v Latviĭ", Fond "Shamir" im. M Dubina, 1998).

13   Edward Anders further translated, revised, and essentially created a new work by incorporating Helena Belova's English translation from the Russian edition and adding a bibliography and index. Dr. Anders also included the hitherto generally unavailable "The Jews of Latvia 1919-1940", an anonymous memorandum submitted to the United States Department of State ca. 1942, introduced by Andrew Ezergailis (Boulder: East European Monographs, distributed by Columbia University Press, 2002).

14   (Riga and Washington, DC: Historical Institute of Latvia and US Holocaust Memorial Museum, 1996).

Memories of Riga[15] or Frank Gordon's *Latvians and Jews Between Germany and Russia*,[16] it is possible to make a rudimentary mental reconstruction of what once was and of what has been lost.

Publishing in the Jewish community

Generalizations about the language orientation of Latvian Jewry carry some qualifications. As indicated in the chapter on Russian publishing, Jewish business families fleeing revolutionary Russia brought with them their Russian language and often a conversational knowledge of German. The Jewish population of the western region of Latvia (Kurzeme) generally had a German-language orientation and, if engaged in business, a working knowledge of spoken Yiddish.[17] In the communities of Latvia that were once part of the Pale of Settlement, i.e., the southeastern region, Yiddish was the primary language. A knowledge of Latvian within the Jewish community depended largely on the level of need and was predominantly conversational spoken Latvian, in keeping with business or professional necessity. Historically, the use of Hebrew in Latvian lands was confined almost solely to religious use and depended on the nature of an individual's involvement in the life of the religious community. With the arrival of Zionist proselytization efforts in Latvia, particularly in the 1920s, the appearance of Hebrew instructional programs gave yet another aspect to this multifaceted language phenomenon of the Jewish community. Publishing in Hebrew in the Interwar period was limited primarily to religious works or publications directed to Palestine-recruitment efforts.

The Latvian setting for Yiddish-language publishing

For almost two decades, Yiddish-language print culture was an important element in much of Latvian-Jewish secular culture. Yiddish was the language of instruction in 48% of the nearly 100 Jewish schools in Latvia before the Ulmanis coup of May 1934, which more than 80% of Jewish children attended.[18] Prior to the coup, Yiddish-language-only schools in Latvia established by the Central Yiddish School Organization throughout Eastern Europe in 1920 had some 6,000 registered students.[19]

Latvian Jewry at the time was as diverse as any sizeable population of Jewry in almost any country then or now. Primary language, religious adherence, religious sectarianism, socioeconomic status—the differences implied by all these categories were reflected in the Latvian Jewish population of the 1920s and 1930s. Marģers Vestermanis characterizes one element, language adherence:

15   (Boulder: University Press of Colorado, 2001). Clara Michelsons, a family member living in Western Europe, where she wrote in German and French, is known to the present older generation for *Jüdisches Kind aus dem Osten* (A Jewish Child from the East) (Berlin, 1936), a collection of stories giving the feel of Jewish life in Riga and St. Petersburg during the era, followed by a Yiddish edition, *Di Idishe Neshome* (The Jewish Soul) (Riga: Bilike Bikher, 1937).

16   Revised edition (Stockholm: Memento – Daugavas Vanagi, 2001).

17   Dribins, L. "Ebreji Latvijā". *Mazākumtautības Latvijā*. Vēsture un tagadne (Riga: LU Filozofijas un socioloģijas institūts, 2007), p. 210.

18   See Anette Reinsch's "Jews in Latvian literature and society in the 1920s and 1930s" in *The Ethnic Dimension in Politics and Culture in the Baltic Countries, 1920-1945*, edited by Baiba Metuzāle-Kangere (Huddinge: Södertörns Högskola, 2004), p. 176. Reinsch goes on to cite that Hebrew was the language of instruction in 31% of these schools, German in 14%, and Russian in only 7%.

19   See Dovid Katz, *Words on Fire: The Unfinished Story of Yiddish* (New York City: Basic Books, 2004), p. 286.

Y2

"There was a great variety of traditions and cultures... Originally the simple Kurland 'Mitnaggedim', under strong German cultural influence, dominated. In 1881 half of Riga Jews considered their spoken language to be German. A leaning to German culture lasted among many Riga Jews, especially the prosperous ones, up to the tragic end of the community... Hasidim from some neighboring provinces, who spoke mainly Yiddish, also arrived in Riga. At the end of the 19th century the Russian language propagated by the aristocracy formed one more layer above the German and Yiddish cultures... During the 1920s and 1930s the youth learned the Latvian language in the schools... This language became more familiar...and for many it was the second language after 'mame loshn'."[20]

Max Michelson confirmed, speaking of his grandmother, whose family lived in Kurzeme:

"[She] was influenced by German culture and was very outspoken in her admiration of everything German... Cultural alignment with Germany (as opposed to Russia) was typical of the Jews... connected through service to the Baltic German gentry."[21]

Speaking and reading German came as a matter of necessity. The children of numerous Riga Jewish families sent their sons and daughters to German schools, as testified by a number of informants commenting on their own childhoods as well as that of their parents.[22]

One survivor, Irra Schlossberg Gelin, maintained that her childhood and teenage years were very much like that of others in her Jewish German- and Russian-speaking, upper middle-class circle. In a 1931 photograph of Schlossberg and her father she is wearing a locally designed and manufactured fur coat—a gift for her 16th birthday. She looks confident about the future.[23] Y2

In the course of our conversation, I asked Schlossberg about "dating". Her response: "Oh, we didn't date then... we only went out with groups of girls, but we did go to the gala events that Jewish organizations sponsored every spring and autumn... At those, we danced with boys." To elaborate further on the similarities of life to other young women of her circle she stated quite candidly that "my friends and I waited impatiently for our 17th birthdays and finishing the first stage of our school... The next step was leaving Riga for Geneva or Paris to perfect our 'school French' and our manners and have a few supervised dates... But we waited until we were 18 and in London to improve our English and begin dating more frequently... But there were drawbacks to the latter... English men, even the Jewish boys, seemed to have such bad teeth."

Curious about what she and her friends read from their early teens until leaving Riga for school abroad, I asked if she could recall the names of papers or journals and the writers read before and during her gymnasium years. She was quick to respond: "I read a lot of the literature older girls read in those years: Georg Hermann's[24] books, my mother's Marlitt books,[25] and sometimes I even picked up the Russian adventure stories my brother

20   Vestermanis, ibid., p. 4.
21   See Michelson, ibid., p. 11.
22   Interviews with Irra Schlossberg Gelin, Luta Bagg Vishniac, Judith Bagg Neumann, Marina Hoff, and Mara Vishniac Kohn on various dates, 1999-2006.
23   Extended interview with Irra Schlossberg Gelin in New York City, 2004 and 2005.
24   Georg Hermann Borchardt, whose book *Jettchen Gebert* (1906), a tragic love story of mid 19th century middle-class Jewish life in Berlin, was mentioned as having been "read and reread".
25   Eugenie Marlitt (pseudonym of Eugenie John) was one of the most widely read authors of popular novels for women in late 19th century Germany. Ten of Marlitt's novels were offered in the 1928 catalog of the Academia Buchhandlung und Verlag in Riga (Aspazijas bulvāris 4) along with scores of other German authors and German translations of the works of foreign authors.

Efraim[26] read. There were also stories and even articles of interest in the newspapers my parents subscribed to such as *Segodnia* and the *Rigasche Rundschau*. My father also bought French illustrated magazines at kiosks from time to time such as *L'Illustration*. Of course we subscribed to the Latvian-language *Ilustrēts Žurnāls* and *Atpūta*. I'm sure there were other magazines in the house such as the Zionist propaganda my brother read in German... newsletters and papers the militant Zhabotinskyists published...My brother was determined to go to Palestine... It's so long ago... more than a lifetime it seems."

I asked about Schlossberg's family's religious affiliation, to which she quickly responded: "Oh, we were only culturally Jewish... we celebrated the holidays and all that but it wasn't as serious for us as you might think... I can't even remember if the synagogue we attended on high holy days sent us a newsletter or regular announcements as they do here in America... Remember, our family was like so many hundreds of other Jewish families in the business world, émigrés from various parts of the Russian Empire. My mother's parents, the Sandomirskys, were successful flour milling business people from the Crimea."

Y3

Schlossberg Gelin continued her family Y3 story: "My father, Mecieslav (Meier) Schlossberg,[27] was sent to Riga from Poland by an uncle to work in one of his textile (linen) factories, which employed some 3,000 workers, if I remember correctly. He met my mother, Anna Sandomirsky, and they were married in 1911 and lived for a time in a villa he had built in Sassenhof (today Zasulauks) Y4

Y4

on the other side of the Daugava River. This home was on the extensive property of the textile factory, which can be dimly seen in the background of the winter photo showing our ice skating pond in front. The villa was demolished during the summer of 1915 and the family moved to Elizabetes iela 31, a more fashionable address in Riga proper. This meant quite a different life for us, as my mother was quite sociable... ladies-only luncheons became a regular feature in our home. Y5 I still have a photo from one of those luncheons and in it you can see from right to left Cecilia Bagg, mother of Luta Bagg, Roman Vishniac's first wife. I don't remember the next person, but sitting next to her is Eugenia Rolovich, who also came to New York City in the late 1930s. She's sitting next to my mother, Anna. I don't remember the woman next to her. But sitting next to her is Maria Glück (Mrs. Felix Glück), who came around the same time to New York City, possibly 1939, as nearly as I can recall. I don't know the last woman in that row."

I queried Mrs. Gelin further on the similarities of her "book life" to those of her friends. Once again, she responded: "There was little difference in the type or quantity

---

26   Efraim changed his name to Erick Sandor and lived an adventurous and successful life in business and as a philanthropist. See *A Memoir of Erick Sandor né Efraim (Efri) Schlossberg*, 1998, unpublished, 35 pp.
27   Mecieslav Schlossberg's parents, Uri and Sofia Schlossberg, were from Lodz, Poland.

Y5

[of books and periodicals] in the homes of my friends or read by their parents compared with what my parents read. Boys' reading was somewhat different... and the boys tended to be more interested in what was happening in Palestine, in Germany, and other countries. I do remember my brother sometimes showing me issues of magazines he'd picked up from organizations promoting Palestine. The Jewish National Fund office in Riga produced a lot of material, as I recall, and its publications were often picked up by my brother. Y6, Y7 The events of those times seemed to determine boys' reading more than it did mine or that of my girlfriends."[28]

For daily news, her parents (and several thousand in similar circumstances) subscribed to the leading German-language daily, *Rigasche Rundschau*, edited by the liberal lawyer/politician Paul Schiemann. Mrs. Gelin commented that the Schlossberg family and German-speaking Latvian-Jewish families in general began dropping their subscriptions "when the paper turned [to the political] right just before the Ulmanis coup in 1934 and began taking on a tone and view sympathetic with National Socialist papers in Germany". Mrs. Gelin recalled that for a very brief period the liberal daily *Europa-Ost*, published in Libau (Liepāja, 1933-1934), provided an editorial alternative. Founded and edited by Fritz Lachmann, the paper was published from January to December 1934 and then ceased publication.[29]

Another sector of Latvian-Jewish life was the anything-but-homogenous Zionist movement in Latvia, which was a major contributor to the print culture in the Interwar period.[30] Zionism spread throughout Jewish communities in Eastern and Western Europe with Hovrei Zionist groups already established in the 1880s in Riga, Libau (Liepāja), and Dvinsk (Daugavpils), among other cities.[31] Wherever there was Zionist influence, the study

---

28   Interview with Irra Schlossberg Gelin, May 2004.
29   See Bernard Press, *Judenmord in Lettland, 1941-45* (Berlin: Bernard Press-Selbstverlag, 1988), p. 14.
30   For a detailed study of Zionist activity in Latvia see Boris Volkovich, *Sionistskoe dvizhenie v Latvii, 1918-1940*, 2nd ed.
(Daugavpils: Saule, 2012), 2 volumes.
31   *The Jews in Latvia*, p. 11.

Y6   Y7

of Hebrew became more than phrases and verses learned with varying degrees of fluency in homes and congregations by those following a religious tradition. With increasing Zionist activity in Riga and other larger Latvian population centers, Jewish schools and after-school Zionist programs provided encouragement for Latvian Jewish youth to prepare for life in Palestine. Local Zionist newsletters and periodicals fostered learning about Palestine in general as well as encouraging readers to learn to speak and read Hebrew.

Marģers Vestermanis maintains that "the majority of Riga Jews sympathized with Zionism and actively supported it" and that in the two decades between the wars "all the Zionist political movements [in Latvia] were represented".[32] Much of this activity and the accompanying publishing efforts were curtailed when the Ulmanis regime came to power. Ulmanis allowed three Jewish organizations to continue:[33] the Revisionists' Trumpeldor, Agudat Israel,[34] and Hashomer Hatziar (renamed Olim). Their respective publications continued, but somewhat erratically.

Yiddish speakers in Latvia in general and in Riga in particular provided a ready audience among the middle and lower socioeconomic strata as well as a segment of the intellectual Jewish population, as attested by Vestermanis:

"According to the 1925 Census, 85% of the Jews in Latvia considered their mother tongue to be Yiddish. Yiddish was the language taught in the majority of primary schools. Local Yiddish publishers issued literature as well as dozens of newspapers… and it sounded from the stage of the Jewish Theater."[35]

Stop for a moment to think of the relative size of this small country with a Jewish population, according to the first census to be taken in the new republic in 1920, of only

32   Vestermanis, ibid., p. 23.

33   Ibid., p. 23.

34   This international Jewish organization's Latvian edition, *Achdut*, begun in 1927, was published in three languages: Yiddish, Russian, and German. The organization's and journal's purpose was to promote adherence to "rabbinic law" in daily life. Its conservatism was the likely reason for its being allowed to continue throughout the Ulmanis regime.

35   Vestermanis, ibid., p. 5.

79,368 and no more than 95,474 in 1925.[36] The increase was the result of refugee return, emigration from the USSR, and an increased birthrate stemming from settled conditions.

Would-be publishers needed to take the following factors and statistics into consideration: 1) number of individuals 12 years of age and under; 2) number of illiterates in 1925 (6.61% in Riga, 19.52% in the province of Latgale, and similarly high percentages in other provinces for an overall illiteracy-in-Yiddish average of 12.34%[37]); 3) the sizeable but difficult-to-determine number of literate small-business and trades people who worked so hard each day that sleep likely came before skimming a daily Yiddish newspaper.

One can imagine that the potential readership and thus the potential market for Yiddish-language publishing were slightly more than break-even undertakings. Edition sizes of Yiddish books cited in *Valsts bibliotēkas biļetens* (VBB) from its inception in 1927 indicate a range from 500 to 3,000 copies, often with higher numbers for fiction.

A few examples include such titles as Lion Feuchtwanger's *Yud Zis* (Jew Süss), Part 1 (published by Bikher far Alemen, 1928; translated by Mark Razumny), produced in a relatively small edition of 4,000 copies. Jaroslav Hašek's *Der braver soldat Shvayk in der Velt-milkhome* (The Good Soldier Schweik in the World War; translated by Zelig Kalmanovitsh) was also published by Bikher far Alemen that year in an edition of 3,000 copies. Y8 For interest's sake, a 15-page pamphlet reporting on and promoting the Birobidzhan colony, *Far Birobidzshan* (Riga: Rekord, 1928), was published at 2,000 copies and Nehemiah Pereferkovich's *Hebreyizmen in Idish* (Hebrewisms in Yiddish; Riga: Globus, 1929) in an edition of 1,500 copies. Smaller editions were the norm.

As the center of Jewish cultural life in Latvia between the wars, Riga was not much different in language makeup than other European Jewish population centers. The largest city often had the largest Jewish population. Such Jewish populations were invariably diverse in language, politics, and religious practice.

Yiddish-speaking Latvian Jewry was aggressively publishing in its language while "assimilationists" used either Russian or German, sending their children to schools according to the favored language in the home or on the parental educational agenda.

Parents who favored using Hebrew in the home were supported in their language maintenance efforts through the two Riga Hebrew schools and, of course, the social and political associations, e.g., Zionist organizations, where Hebrew was the language of choice.

Secular Jews sent their children to schools according to family, cultural, and language traditions. Language choice was also fostered through "some forty synagogues and minyanim" in Riga alone, the congregants of which determined the language of worship and fellowship.[38]

Additional associative groups that furthered specific language use in activity through their publications were youth and sport associations, e.g., the Maccabi sports organization and the Jewish Boy Scouts.[39] In addition, there were a number of welfare societies, medical clinics, and Bikur-Holim Hospital, all of which employed this practice.

The Jewish theater with performances primarily in Yiddish was celebrated outside the country as was its artists' organization. But the theater was by no means limited in the language of performance nor to a presumed language of the audience addressed, which

---

36   Cited from Andrew Ezergailis, *The Holocaust in Latvia, 1941-1944* (Riga and Washington, DC: Historical Institute of Latvia and the United States Holocaust Memorial Museum, 1996), p. 58.

37   *Latviešu konversācijas vārdnīca*, vol. 1 (Riga: Gulbis, 1927), p. 466.

38   See *Jews in Latvia...*, p. 220.

39   Ibid., p. 194.

was, for the most part, multilingual. A document of the theater illustrating this point is the poster announcing the first stop of the Moscow Habima Theater performing in Hebrew on its famed first (and only) "world tour" in 1926.[40]

Art exhibitions of individual artists as well as group shows were a frequent part of Jewish cultural life in Riga and other centers. A group show opened in November 1919 at the Jewish National University's gallery on Tērbatas iela curated by Mihails Jo—the catalog cover Y9 designer— with eight Latvian residents exhibiting,[41] including Jo and four artists from other countries.[42]

The Jewish art era closed, along with everything else, in a final group show organized and sponsored by the Jewish Education Association. Opening in January 1939 and billed as an international graphic art exhibition, it showed 252 works with more than 40 artists from outside the country. The catalog with Aleksandrs Junkers' cover design Y10 was not published in Yiddish or Russian but in Latvian. Given the period and constraints imposed by the regime, the exhibition's purpose was most likely to enlighten the Latvian viewer on the universality of Jewish art. Also, a multilingual catalog would have considerably raised the cost. An aside on content: eight of the artists giving a city of residence indicate Riga, five of whom are cited in *Māksla un arhitektūra biogrāfijās*:[43] Leja Aronova, Bernhard Dannenhirsh, Isak Friedlander,[44] Samuils Haskins,[45] and Mihails Jo. How and when the works on exhibition were returned to their non-Latvian owners has yet to be clarified.[46]

Y8

Y9

Y10

Y11

Another Jewish-audience publication not published in Yiddish and further indicating language diversity in the Jewish community was the yearbook of the Baltische Yacht Klub, a Jewish club on the Lielupe River. The club is known to have published at least one non-newsletter publication, namely, its twelve-page yearbook *Die Heul-Boje* (The Whistling Buoy).[47] Y11 This not-so-serious publication in German and Russian poked gentle fun at a few Jewish organizations as well as prominent members of the club, e.g., Dr. Vladimir Mintz and Jacob Hoff, among others.[48] Then there was the Jewish tennis club "Ritek".

40 The next stop was Berlin (with a different poster) and the final stop was New York, where the cast had second thoughts about returning and stayed to enrich the already lively New York Yiddish theater.

41 Only two of the local exhibiting artists have been included in *Māksla un arhitektūra biogrāfijās*, Jo and David Skolnik, but not Skolnik's wife, Elena Skolnik-Lipschitz (19 works), Aron Lipschitz, Nikolaī Arenstam, Teodor Brenson, Wilhelm Hirschberg, or an artist named Wulfsons.

42 *Ebreju mākslineeku izstāde: katalogs*, comp. by Mihaels Jo (Riga: [the association of Jewish artists], 1919).

43 (Riga: 1995-2003).

44 Friedlander moved to New York in 1929 but arranged for loan of his works from local collections.

45 Haskins had fled to Moscow in 1935 and likely arranged for three linocuts to be locally loaned.

46 See *Žīdu grafiķu izstāde* (Riga: Žīdu izglītības biedrība, 1939).

47 Probably appeared in 1934 as a one-time yearbook, because no other issues have been discovered.

48 While it is difficult to identify some members with only a family name given, it may be of some interest to list those for whom no more than an initial or title is given with a family name: Rechtsanwalt Rubinstein, L. Stender, B. Löwenstein, D. Löwenstein, N. Blindreich, Dr. Feiertag, B. Minsker, G. Minsker, L. Wolpe, M. Schiemann-Schimansky, M[artin] Chait, Dr. Kamenetzky, Morris Binsker, Jāzeps Zābaksons.

According to Marġers Vestermanis, many such organizations at some point published a newsletter, yearbook, or membership directory—some bilingual, others monolingual, depending on the dominant language spoken within the membership.

With the foregoing in mind, it is hoped that the following commentary will give some hint of the dominant language of the Latvian-Jewish community, despite the use of other languages for various social, business, and political purposes.

Searching for Yiddish-language remnants

Late November is ideal for book hunting in Riga's antiquarian shops. Days are often rainy, cold, and poetically gray. Bookshops are warm. Customers are looking for Christmas gifts; no one—almost no one—is looking for 1920s and 1930s Yiddica.

A long-time Riga acquaintance did warn me in the spring of 2002 as I began my search: "It's hopeless. What survived the Nazi era, didn't survive in any quantity in the Soviet Era. What may have survived the Soviet era, didn't survive the attic cleanouts of 1992/93. Don't waste your time."

Grigoriĭ Smirin, then director of Latvia's Jewish Museum, corroborated this loss and added that organized withdrawal from public libraries, bookshops, and even private collections of "Jewish books", i.e., Yiddica, Hebraica, and books in other languages on Jewish subjects with an intended Jewish audience, was systematic during the Nazi occupation. Works of considerable intrinsic value were shipped to Germany for sale or "research use" by various government propaganda offices.[49]

Having long thrived on discouraging words, I set out for Riga again in November 2002 and headed through the wet streets for the five antiquarian shops I had visited during the previous spring. Once again, I asked my question. The negative responses were variations on earlier comments.

There was one likely shop, "Vēsture" (meaning simply 'history') on Čaka iela. Y12 When first visited, I noticed the owner's emphasis on hard-to-classify printed matter. An abundance of periodicals and ephemera flowed through three rooms. The shop's warmth was a welcome contrast to the weather outside. I began looking along a wide and deep ledge running the length of the store on which were piled Latvian magazines published during the first seven decades of the 20th century. Mixed in an order that I could not immediately determine was everything from "kalendāri" (yearbooks and almanacs) for a variety of audiences to seemingly endless numbers of periodicals in various languages: *Baltische Monatsschrift* (Baltic Monthly) from the World War I era with headlines evoking the once dominant German presence; a scattering of *Ondo de Daugava* (organ of the Latvian Esperanto Society) from the mid 1920s; issues of *Rigasche Rundschau* (largest circulation German daily paper from the late 19th century through the 1930s) in somewhat tattered bundles; Soviet era Russian magazines from the post-WWII era in great and colorful abundance such as *Znanie-Sila* (Knowledge is Power), *Sovetskaya Zhenshchina* (Soviet Woman), *Kul'tura i Zhizn'* (Culture and Life), and *Ogonyok* (Sparkle); scattered issues of Latvian periodicals from the Soviet occupation from July 1940 to July 1941, e.g., *Radio Vilnis* (Radio Wave); and a revival of an earlier periodical with its original title,

---

49   Conversation with G. Smirin, Mar. 2006. Smirin commented that the operation was coordinated from the Nazi-commandeered Jewish Community Center on the Skolas iela. The building once again houses the Jewish Community Center and the Jewish Museum of Latvia.

Y12

Y13

Darba Sieviete (Working Woman), which certainly fit the ideological titling protocols of the occupiers. There were also stacks of other Latvian periodicals such as the venerable *Atpūta* (Leisure). At a conservative guess, 100 or more other titles called out for buyers.

Then there were bound volumes to be attacked, volumes that hid their content behind untitled spines and were mostly stacked flat rather than arranged vertically on shelves. My first reward was opening a bound volume (sans spine titling) and finding the *Baltischer Emigrant* (Libau, 1923), a Yiddish paper with its purpose implied in the title.[50] Y13

Next, a volume from the only year of Dr. M. Brender's short-lived effort at publishing a weekly Yiddish-language picture magazine, *Yidishe ilustrirte tsaytung* (Yiddish Illustrated Newspaper, Berlin, 1924).[51] While not Latvian Yiddica, resisting acquisition was not possible and, on browsing through it, a few Riga connections in the advertisements were noted. This particular "remnant" surely must have made its way to Riga readers in its era rather than later, a small indication of the cross-boundary periodical culture of a Yiddish-reading audience.

With the *Ilustrirte* added to my pile and lesser material moved aside, a copy of Icik Morein's *Dos Naye Letland* (The New Latvia; Riga: Livonia, 1934) Y14 surfaced, just waiting, or so it seemed. I was slightly acquainted with Morein's work from reading and listening to admiring comments about him from an elderly acquaintance. Morein's main journalistic contribution in those years was to allay the apprehensions of the Western European business community about the commercial climate in Kārlis Ulmanis's "new Latvia".[52] This was no small public relations challenge, because Ulmanis had by fiat nationalized most major and minor smaller businesses, including the factory that produced

50 Not cited in Rihards Treijs' *Latvijas republikas prese, 1918-1940* (Riga: Zvaigzne, 1996), Oskar Grosberg's *Die Presse Lettlands* (Riga: Baltischer Verlag, 1927), or other obvious sources.

51 Dr. Brender's major life effort.

52 Ulmanis ruled Latvia as both prime minister (from 1934) and president from 1936 until the first Soviet occupation.

Y14

much-loved "Laima" chocolate.[53] To this day, through all seasons, "Laima" releases its inviting aroma for the length of a few blocks along the No. 11 tram line running north along Miera iela.

Morein served in the late 1920s and into the 1930s as reporting liaison between the Foreign Ministry and the Yiddish press. He had studied law at the University of Latvia in the first years of the new republic and, on graduation, began work as a journalist, writing articles about Latvia in Yiddish, Hebrew, German, and Arabic. Aside from my newly found title *Dos Naye Letland*, which I later learned had also been published in French, Latvian, and German editions, much of Morein's other writing remains buried in the daily and weekly press of the languages cited. From 1926 to 1930 he taught Latvian at the Tushia (Resourcefulness) Jewish school in Kielce, Poland. During that time, he wrote and published his first promotional work on Latvia and its economic prospects, a work serving as a basis for subsequent writings, including the work cited.[54] On returning to Riga, Morein was involved in the establishment of the independent daily paper *Ovnt-post* (Evening Post, 1932-1934) and traveled to promote Latvia as far afield as Athens and Jerusalem. He managed to live through the first days of Soviet terror of 1940/41 but, according to Gregoriĭ Smirin, he is believed to have died in the "second terror", when the SS continued what the Soviets had begun.

After finding this unexpected trove at "Vēsture", I was determined to look at every pamphlet in this shop's new location with brighter lights and improved arrangement. On a subsequent wintry day, the only item of Yiddica waiting on the shelves was a ten-year summary of the Jewish Education Administration activity from 1919 to 1929. Hunting in this shop was over for the time being.

---

53   Laima's founders, the Marc Moshevitz family, were properly compensated, according to Frank Gordon's web posting, "The Good Years" on the Centropa.org website, 6.13.05. The family took its money, left for Palestine, and founded "Elite—the largest chocolate factory in the Middle East", which exists to this day.

54   *Letland: ir kultur, ekonomik, melukhe ordnung, politik, gezelshaftlekhkeyt, kurartn* (Riga: Letlendishn Oysern-ministeryum, 1929).

Y15

Y16

The next day I confidently returned to the "Jumava" shop on Riharda Vāgnera iela[55] where I had spent time in previous years browsing and buying Letonika and visiting with the manager of the German Department, Ari Kamenkowitsch, and his wife, Taisa, the shop's manager. Mr. Kamenkowitsch greeted me cheerily, disappeared into his back room, and reappeared holding the type of "find" for which I had hoped: *Žīdu kalendārs "Hamazkir"*[56] (Jewish Calendar "Hamazkir") for 1937, published by the Yiddish-language publisher Bilike Bikher at Marijas iela 6 and apparently the first year of this calendar's publication. Y15 Records indicate the calendar was published again in 1938 and 1939 under the same title but by Logos, a Yiddish-language publisher that took over Bilike Bikher and remained at the same address. Bilike Bikher published at least thirty non-textbook[57] titles since its founding in approximately 1928, not including Russian-language titles published mainly in the early years. Among other Yiddish-language publishers of *belles lettres* (and non-fiction) was Bikher far Alemen, known to have published at least fourteen titles.

Yet another publisher, Grāmata priekš visiem, appears to have published only about a half dozen titles but was the publisher of Yiddish-language translations by the colorful author-translator-editor-collector Mark Razumny, including his 1929 translation of Erich Maria Remarque's *All Quiet on the Western Front* and Lion Feuchtwanger's *Pep, Y. L. Vetshiks Amerikaner Liderbukh* (Y. L. Wetcheek's American Songbook) published in 1930. Yudel Mark's translation of Thomas Mann's *Tonio Kröger* into Yiddish also appeared that same year.[58] Y16 Razumny was one of the few Rigensian Jewish writers of the time known outside Latvia as a poet, novelist, and essayist writing in Yiddish.

55   Moved to Dzirnavu iela in November 2008.
56   "Hamazkir" (i.e., "ha-Mazkir") is possibly named in memory of the great 19th century bibliographer Moritz Steinschneider's bibliographical journal of that name.
57   The textbooks published by Bilike Bikher for the Yiddish-language schools appear to have been limited to grades one through five and published mainly in the years 1935 to 1937.
58   Published by Bikher far Aleman.

Y17

Y18

Y19

Y20

Y21

Subsequent trips to the "Jumava" shop,[59] Y17 with its orderly and inviting interior, netted mainly non-fiction Yiddica. Design in this publishing category invariably tended to be utilitarian, mainly reports by Jewish schools, professional and fraternal organizations, and Zionist publications. Titles of a report or promotional nature sometimes carried an in-house photographic design or a stylized image reflecting the content. Two typical examples: a publication by Zhizn' i kul'tura promoting the city of Tel Aviv and its salubrious climate (*Jewish Port, Tel-Aviv*) from 1937 Y18 and a report by the Jewish sports association "Hakoah"[60] from 1938. Y19 The Hakoah title was professionally designed by that always-available artist for Jewish causes, the energetic Mihails Jo. But the mass of non-fiction report-type Yiddica of those years was conventional in typography and design, as shown in the following display of representative titles: G. Freids' 29-page mildly Zionist tract on Palestinian life; Y20 a thirty-year report, from 1906 to 1936, of the trade school of the Jewish education administration of Latvia.[61] Y21

---

59 From 1991 to 2009, a regular stop for antiquarian books.

60 Jewish Sports Association "Hakoah", established: spring 1924, closed down: November 1940.

61 Opening with a photo of the school building at Kazaku iela 2 (now Abrenes iela), the first 28 pages of this 48-page pamphlet are illustrated with photos of founders, leaders, and students at work in shops. The concluding 20 pages consist of advertising, much of which is in Latvian.

Turning to the design elements anticipated in this search, one always hopes for remarkable examples of non-fiction book cover design from the period just waiting for discovery. If one does take the time to make a comparative quest by looking through a few piles of non-fiction German, Latvian, and Russian production of those years and then looks at the non-fiction Yiddish production, a modest case could be made for a Riga-Yiddish avantgarde. But the quantity does not compare favorably with that of the Yiddish-language book design vanguard existing contemporaneously in Warsaw, Minsk, and Odessa before 1930.

Marc Gerc

If, however, there were to be a design competition for avantgarde non-fiction in Yiddish published in Latvia, pride-of-place would probably go to a 25-year history of the Yiddish-language press in Latvia[62] Y22 by Marc Gertz-Movshovits, i.e., Marc Gerc, with its cover design signed "A. Šur", who was likely Abram Shur, an architect working in Riga who, according to Grigoriĭ Smirin,[63] seems to have "left" his apartment after August 4, 1941, and "probably moved to the Ghetto, already under construction at that time and where he was probably killed". The author of this work, born Gershon Movshovits, is the "story". We are indebted to Menahem Beth for his account[64] of

Y22

this Kaunas-born journalist-bibliographer and, at times, political radical. Gerc's invaluable, contemporary document gives us an enthusiast's history of many of those newspapers and periodicals now lost to memory and the individuals behind the endeavors, beginning with the *Natsayonal-Tsaytung* (National Newspaper, 1905-07) and *Di Idishe Shtime* (The Yiddish Voice, 1910) and continuing his account to 1933. A recent and indispensable bibliographically detailed account of Latvia's Yiddish press from 1919-1940 is Boris Ravdin's inquiry.[65]

One hesitates to speak of Gerc as ideologically unstable, but in the course of his journalistic career he seems to have traveled a road from ardent communist to equally ardent participant in the orthodox Bund Israels (or Agudas Jisroel). During the Soviet takeover of Riga from January to December 1919, Gerc was a regular contributor to the Yiddish-language *Der Roiter Emes* (The Red Truth), a paper providing its readers with a daily dose of "class war" propaganda.

62   *25 yor idishe prese in Letland* (Riga: Idishe Literatn Farayn in Letland "Alef", 1933).
63   Letter from Grigoriĭ Smirin, June 2006.
64   See pp. 310-311 of the work cited for background on Movshovits.
65   "Materialy k ukazately evreiskoi pechati Latviĭ, 1919-1940" in *Baltiiskiĭ Arkhiv: Russkaya kul'tura v Pribaltike*, vol. 6
(Riga: Daugava, 2000), pp. 324-380.

When the Soviet-backed administration was forced out of Riga, Gerc seemed to calm down somewhat in his politics and by 1920 he had begun to contribute to the Yiddish-language daily *Dos Folk* (The People, 1920-1927). During this period Beth reports that Gerc also "...took a hand in editing humorous publications, children's books, etc.",[66] though copies of the latter have yet to be located. Gerc moved on from *Dos Folk* in 1925 and, according to Beth, became part of the group encouraging Y. Brams and B. Poliak, the publishers of *Segodnia*, to launch (in January 1927) a Yiddish-language daily that became *Frimorgn* (Morning, 1926-1934). Y23 Yet, Gerc's lasting contribution was as unofficial historian of Latvia's Yiddish press in that time. His end, like that of so many other Jewish-Latvian intellectuals, was tumultuous, but *unlike* others, he survived. He fled to the USSR in 1940 with the first Soviet occupation, living there until returning to Riga in 1945. During that first year back in Riga, he ran afoul of Latvia's new Soviet occupiers, was arrested, and was sent to Siberia. He managed to live through that ordeal, returning to Riga in 1956 and dying two years later. During these periods and wanderings he continued writing and published a number of biographical and autobiographical works.

Jacob Zhagorsky

Beth makes a passing reference to an individual honored as a forerunner to Gerc's work on Yiddish-language bibliography: "[Zhagorsky] a bespectacled man with a tiny little beard..., the unwearying collector of printed Yiddish in Lettland [Latvia]". Gerc acknowledges that it was Zhagorsky, a born Rigensian, to whom we can be grateful for gathering much of what Gerc used in his history. Zhagorsky was also a philanthropist-organizer to whom many Riga Jews of that era can be grateful for his participation in founding the city's Hacedek maternity hospital Y24 and the Hachnassat Kallah Society that provided poor Jewish brides-to-be with dowries as well as supporting the Aleph Society of Yiddish Writers, the publisher of Gerc's Yiddish-press history. As to the fate of Zhagorsky and his collection, he presumably perished in Riga's Ghetto with his collection scattered or destroyed after his arrest.

Maks Shats-Anin and the Arbeterhaym Farlag

Maks Shats-Anin was a remarkable survivor. No matter the political winds, Shats-Anin "came through". He even lived into the middle of the second Soviet occupation of Latvia, which is the reason so many elderly Latvians have some memory of him today.

The energetic and ideology-driven Shats-Anin could hardly be ignored in any regime. Born in 1885 in Jaunjelgava, a late 19th century commercial center, he went off to law school in St. Petersburg and began turning "left". He never looked back. Shats-Anin certainly never looked "right" either, dying an unreconstructed Marxist-Leninist in 1975 in Riga. We will never know if he ever had misgivings about the direction he followed because he left no published, confessional autobiography. He did leave behind a sizeable body of pamphlets, books, and contributions to periodicals and newspapers that leave no doubt as to where he stood ideologically.[67] Fluent in Yiddish, Russian, Latvian, and German, he

---

66 See *Jews in Latvia*, p. 311.

67 A 24-page bibliography of writings by and about him, *Profesors Maksis Šacs-Anins 1885-1975: Bibliogrāfiskais rādītājs* (Riga: Self-published, 1997), was compiled and published by Grigoriï Smirin, Aleksandrs Losevs, and Ruta Shats-Mariash. This work also contains a list of his 17 pseudonyms.

Y23

Y24

translated selections of Maksim Gorky's writings into German while still a young man. He studied in Bern, completing his doctorate in Riga in 1910 with a dissertation titled *Zur Nationalitätenfrage* (On the Question of Nationalities). In 1915, he was evacuated to Petrograd and began contributing to the journal *Vestnik Trudovoi Pomoshchi* (Messenger to Assist Labor). Later he moved to Moscow, but in 1917 he went to Kiev, where he wrote for the weekly newspaper *Evreiskiĭ proletariĭ* (Jewish Proletariat). It is there, while being tortured during a prison ordeal, that he was blinded and lost almost all of his sight.[68] In 1919 Shats-Anin returned to Latvia with his wife and daughter[69] to become a full-time agitator for "the revolution" by directing (1919-1923) the legal affairs for what is assumed by many to have been a Soviet-subsidized front organization, the Arbeterhaym, with offices at Tērbatas iela 13/15.[70] During this time, he had a brief prison stay in 1921, having been arrested for political agitation with comrade and fellow author Leons Paegle.

What Shats-Anin's Arbeterhaym program and other efforts did to create instability during the new republic's founding years remains a matter for speculation. As a Marxist, Soviet-oriented umbrella organization, the Arbeterhaym audaciously carried out, at least for a time, its propaganda agenda in the guise of a "folk high school" with courses in bookbinding, key making, Russian for Latvian speakers, Latvian for Russian and Yiddish speakers, and journalism (for aspiring revolutionaries)—all courses loaded with Marxist theory, except for bookbinding and key making.

The publishing arm, also termed Arbeterhaym, claimed to be the first Marxist-Yiddish publisher in the Latvian lands. Despite its short life as an organization and

---

68   In an interview with Ruta Shats-Mariash in October 2006, who indicated that his diminished eyesight was nearly gone by the mid 1920s.

69   Judīte Shats-Anin Baga was a highly visible figure in design and arts administration in Soviet Latvia. Her younger sister, Ruta, was a parliamentarian and lawyer in the late Soviet period and the post-1991 era of independence.

70   According to Marģers Vestermanis, these quarters also housed "a large library..reading-hall.. music studios" and the Jewish People's University with Shats-Anin as rector. See *The Jews in Riga*, p. 23.

Y25

Y26

Y27

Y28

publishing operation, it managed to bring out several collections of essays, poems, and polemical writings beginning with *Baginen, A Samelbukh* (Dawn: A Collection) in the spring of 1920 stating Arbeterhaym's publishing intent and direction.[71] Y25

Included among the first *belles lettres* titles in the program was a book of poems by Moyshe Lifshits titled *A ber tantst* (The Bear Dances, 1922) Y26 with a strong linocut-illustrated cover by M. Jo. According to Shats-Anin's daughter, Ruta,[72] Vladimir Mayakovsky encouraged her father to "broaden the publishing program... even include some compilations of love poems". So, in 1922 Arbeterhaym published in Russian—not Yiddish—Mayakovsky's *Liubliu* (I Love), Y27 which appeared in Moscow the same year with the same cover design, although with terracotta rules, as No. 1 in the *MAF* poetry series.[73] The title was soon confiscated, but the order was later revoked. Most important from the standpoint of Arbeterhaym's publishing and other activities was its yearbook,[74] for which M. Jo not only designed the cover but also its stylized calligraphic titling and prominently displayed Arbeterhaym logo. Y28 The yearbook provided an account of Arbeterhaym's work and plans and its role as the Latvian coordinating arm of the Kiev-centered KulturLige and its program within that framework.[75] The contributions to the

71   No publisher is given for this 24-page pamphlet, but its unsigned editorial by Shats-Anin on the direction of Arbeterhaym points to Shats-Anin as editor. Articles signed by him in two different forms of his name: "Fear of power", "The Jewish socialist association". Mark Donskoi contributed "The national problem and the Jewish proletariat". Other contributions: "The struggle for our national school" by Aron Vorobaichik and two articles by M. Jo titled "Letter of an artist: art and bread" and "Several words about our theater". A contribution on the direction of Latvian political parties has unclear initials (possibly M. P.). The content concludes with an unsigned article (likely by Shats-Anin) on the Arbeterhaym organization.

72   *Grāmata par tēvu* (A Book about a Father) by Ruta Shats-Mariash (Riga: Self-published, 1995), p. 98.

73   Published in Moscow by Vkhutemas for the Mezhdunarodnaya Assotsiatsiia Futuristov (MAF). Both Moscow and Riga editions are indicated as the second edition.

74   *A Yor Arbeterhaym* (Riga: Arbeterhaym, 1921?), 58 pp.

75   Conversation with Hillel Kazovsky (Jerusalem), June 2006.

Y30

Y29

Y31

yearbook were primarily those of Shats-Anin, M. Jo, and Mark G. Donskoi.[76] In July of that same year, another collection of essays, titled *Kultur und Arbeit* (Culture and Work), Y29 was published as well as a collection conceived as an annual, *Afn Shvel* (On the Threshold, 1921) Y30 with cover design by M. Jo and contributions by Shats-Anin and Shmuel-Yitskhok Kozinits, among others. In 1922, Arbeterhaym's official last year in publishing, the *Sambatyen*[77] almanac of "Jewish literature and art" appeared with contributions by Shats-Anin, Dovid Hofshteyn, Moyshe Lifshits, Israel Joshua Singer, Lipe Reznik, "Der Nister" i.e., Pinkhas Kaganovitsh, and Moshe Gross-Tsimerman, among others, and again with cover design and illustrations by M. Jo. Y31 But publications continued to surface in other guises, such as broadsides, and, for a period in 1923, 40 issues of a newspaper titled *Naye Tsayt* (New Time) appeared before the government shut it down.[78]

While serving as president of the Jewish People's University from 1920 to 1929, Shats-Anin also served as legal advisor to the USSR embassy in Latvia (beginning in 1925). All the while he was writing, lecturing, and working hard for his cause, the cause further east. The writings—many in Yiddish, some in Russian, some with interesting cover designs, such as the above, and others quite drab—all issued from his fertile mind with impressive regularity. Mention of a few titles from the 1920s shows something of the range of his interests: *Fun Roym tsu tsayt: Gedanken tsu a kulturfilozofye* (From Rome to the Present: Thoughts Toward a Cultural Philosophy, 1922), *Di Idn in Letland* (The Jews of Latvia, 1924), *Kunst w forgefil fun der makht* (Art as a Fore-shadowing of Power, 1924), *Sotsial'naia oppozitsiïa v istoriï evreev* (Social Dissent in Jewish History, 1927), and *Gezelshaftlekhe*

---

76 Not to be confused with the film director Mark Donskoi.
77 "Sambatyen" is one of several spellings for a river in ancient Jewish tradition, which some consider mythical.
78 Bobe, ibid., p. 58, while Ravdin cites it as appearing during the year 1923, p. 360.

Y32

Y33

Y34

bavegungen ba Yidn far 1917 (Jewish Social Movements before 1917, 1930). Y32 The cover design of this last work seems to play on El Lissitzky's aggressive "red wedge" in his legendary poster of 1919.[79] The symbolic design and the work's title convey what awaits the reader without the cover even being opened. Like the best of effective poster or book jacket design, the prospective reader's eye was likely caught by the way its design stood out from among the ordinary-looking titles on display in the Daile un Darbs bookshop, a regular destination for "left" readers in those years. We can only speculate as to the designer's identity. M. Jo is a reasonable guess, given his general sympathy with Shats-Anin's ideological aims and his earlier involvement with Arbeterhaym. Less obvious is the designer for Shats-Anin's *Krizis fun der burzshuazer kultur* (Crisis of the Bourgeois Culture, 1932, no publisher cited). Y33 A possible designer might have been Ernests Kālis. The political sympathies of the two are in order and the circumstance of the Kālis design two years earlier for the previously-shown *Romantika autobusā* L293 with its symbolic wedge help support such a speculation. During this period of prolific writing, Shats-Anin also took an interest in Stalin's idea of establishing a Jewish colony in the Soviet Far East and published a small monograph on this relatively unsuccessful experiment in Birobidzhan.[80]

During the Ulmanis regime Shats-Anin had no choice but to live inconspicuously until the first Soviet occupation, when his political fortune briefly resumed until he and his family evacuated to Kazan before the subsequent German occupation. According to his younger daughter, Shats-Anin came back to Riga with his family in 1945, where he continued his writing and fervent support of the Soviet occupiers, although he was not always appreciated by them.[81] His legacy is described in detail in his daughter's autobiographical account.[82]

Juda Julius Frīdmanis, i.e., Friedman

The third non-fiction work selected for comment is a promotional piece Y35–Y36 by the designer and advertising agent Juda Julius Friedman, who during the 1930s maintained offices and residence at Ģertrūdes iela 14.

Friedman's clients appear to have been relatively sophisticated, judging from the appearance of several of his advertising pieces held by the National Library of Latvia as well as his own fourteen-page studio prospectus that includes several examples of how his firm took design needs and formed them into a finished work.[83]

Friedman survived both the first Soviet occupation and the Nazi occupation and lived in Riga until his death, continuing as a designer and author of two conventional, regime-serving book-length works on printing and graphic design techniques. *Nabor afish* (Poster Composition) (Moscow: Iskusstvo, 1955) is as uninspired in its text as is the design of the posters Friedman chose for illustrations. For this and the later work[84] the examples used for illustration show nothing of the graphic élan of his 1930s typography and design.

79   "Hit the 'Whites' with the red wedge!"
80   *Biro-bidzshan: nokhtn-haynt-morgn* (Birobidzhan: Yesterday—Today—Tomorrow) (Warsaw: Iberboy, 1933). Some of Shats-Anins' articles published in the *Naierd* magazine, in Riga 1930-1934. Y34 (Cover design: B. Dannenhirsh.)
81   Interview with Ruta Shats-Mariash, Mar. 2006.
82   *Byl', iav' i mechta: Kniga ob ottse* (Riga: BOTA, 1995).
83   Published for Friedman by Livonia in 1934. The content gives information on services, examples of design, and considerable insight into this Yiddish-language hand-set type operation.
84   *Mana pieredze ielūgumu, programmu un afišu salikuma veidošanā* (My Experience in Typographic Composition in the Making of Invitations, Programs, and Posters) (Riga: Latvijas Valsts izdevniecība, 1961).

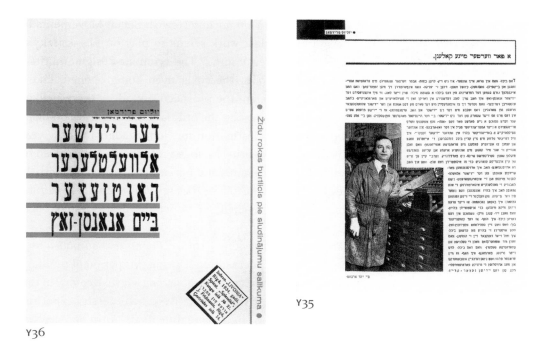

Y35

Y36

Instead, all examples are typical of what one associates today with late Stalinist typography and imagery. The bilingual Latvian-Russian examples of graphics shown in *Nabor afish* may or may not be Friedman's own work as no credits are given. Both monographs are "safe" in their avoidance of reference to the vanguards of the past or in showing any hint of Friedman's remarkable designs of the 1930s. He even promotes folk design elements considered desirable to employ in poster design, a style at odds with his 1930s work. His second title recounts his experience producing posters and other ephemera.

Yiddish-language non-fiction

Yiddish-language non-fiction pamphlets issuing from a variety of social, political, and cultural organizations were as varied and elusive as one can imagine. Deposit of such material in the National Library of Latvia and in other national research libraries was on the honor system. Unfortunately, such a relaxed approach left the present-day bibliographer with a major task of tracking those items that may have fallen out of the national bibliographic network. Any latter-day attempt to create a national bibliography of Yiddica for those years means not only being attentive to the *Valsts bibliotēkas biļetens* but also searching the holdings of institutions *outside* of Latvia that happened—through gift or chance—to acquire these fragile traces of a vanished life. One can gain some idea of the tantalizing range of pamphlet content by a few titles from 1928 and 1929:

II Izstāde [Neatkariga] 31.111-30 VI 1929 (Žīdu Mākslinieku Biedrība-Yidisher Kinstler Farain in Letland, 1929), 13 pp. (in Latvian, Yiddish, Russian). Edition size unknown.

Arbeter Lider (Borochov-jungt in Lettland, 1928), 8 pp. Edition size unknown.

Far Biro-bidzhan (Osek, 1928), 15 pp. Edition size unknown.

Vos vil der Linke Arbetershaft un dos horepashne pavertum? Valplatform (Latvju Kultura, 1928), 16 pp. Edition size unknown.

Y37

Y38

In addition to these titles (cited from *Valsts bibliotēkas biļetens* and not available for illustration), the following display of pamphlet items gives an idea of the varied design, particularly of non-fiction:

Evreiskiĭ Kalendar na 1920-1921 g. (Jewish Calendar for 1920/1921) (Riga: Malbish-Arumim, 1920), 32 pp. Printer: E. Lewin. Y37

Derefnungs Rede Tsum Grindungs Kongress (Opening speech by Vladimir Zhabo-tinsky on the founding of "Betar" in Riga [the Revisionists' Association, later the underground organization "Irgun" in Palestine]) (Riga: N.Z.O., 1923), 16 pp. Y38

Shereshevsky's Luakh "Hamazkir", 1928/29 (Shereshevsky's Calendar "Hamazkir") ed. by Beniamin Shereshevsky (Riga: Bukhandlung un fabric-lager fun taleysim, 1928), 32 pp. Printer: Vārds. Y39

Der Bafrayer Almanakh (The Liberators' Almanac) (Riga: Latvian Jewish National Liberators' Association, 1931), 66 pp. Printer: Riti (in Yiddish and Latvian). Y40

Arbeter Jugnt in Sotsialistishn kamf (Worker Youth in the Socialist Struggle) (Riga: Arbeter Jugnt, 1933), 27 pp. Printer: Splendid. Y41

Marks Lebt! (Marx Lives!) ed. by Z. Fleišmans (Riga: privately published, 1933), a celebratory pamphlet on the 50th anniversary of Marx's death. Y42

Z. Žabotinskis karaliskās komisijas priekšā [Introduction to the Royal Commission Palestine Report, 1937] by Ze'ev (Vladimir) Zhabotinsky (Riga: Bilike Bikher, 1937), 64 pp. Printer: Star. Y43

Shlomo Ben Josef (memorial pamphlet for a Volhynian Zionist who died in Rozhpina, Palestine) (Riga: Logos, 1939), 39 pp. Printer: Zieds. Y44

B-bas "Keren-Hajesod" (Pamata-Fonds) Latvijā biedru sanāksmes par Palestīnas uzbūvi 1938. 23. oktobrī protokols (Protocols of the meeting of the "Keren-Hajesod" Latvian Association for the Rebuilding of Palestine, October 23, 1938) (Riga: Keren-Hajesod, 1939), 78 pp. Printer: Splendid. Y45

Y39

Y41

Y40

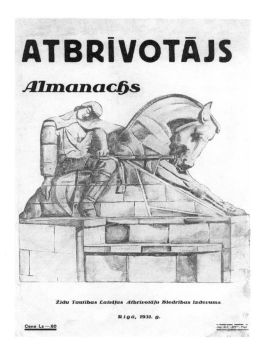

Y42

Y43

Y44

Y45

Yiddish-language *belles lettres*

So much for Yiddish-language non-fiction examples. But "where had all the Yiddish fiction gone?" This was a recurring question in looking through the shelves of the five antiquarian shops frequented twice yearly from 2003 onward. The pessimistic dealers and other informants were unfortunately correct in their assessment. Even though I didn't stop asking or looking, another approach was needed.

Y46

"When all else fails, try the national library," chided a colleague of many years. So, on a snowy March day in 2005, I went to see Dace Pamata at the National Library of Latvia. This remarkable librarian has had more than two decades to store the library's titles in manifold categories in her seemingly unfailing memory. I described my search for Yiddica and outlined my needs, namely, fiction with interesting covers. She responded, "Come back tomorrow after lunch."

Waiting on my return the next day was the substance of Yiddish bibliographical dreams: translations of major literary works with illustrated or typographically interesting covers and non-fiction much more interesting than that which I had found in the bookshops. To be sure, there were also non-fiction works with uninteresting design in the categories already discovered.[85]

M. Jo, i.e., Mihails Jo[ffe]

On the top of the pile, however, was a title that I had pursued unsuccessfully through e-mail queries to Jerusalem and St. Petersburg, New York and Buenos Aires: Erich Maria Remarque's *Afn Mairon-front*[86] (published in English as *All Quiet on the Western Front*) with a cover illustration by M. Jo. R99 The book needs little comment. Remarque is universally known by several generations of readers for this widely translated—into some 50 languages—classic anti-war novel. But Jo merits further comment here. A few of his designs and illustrations have been cited previously. His many talents found continuing outlets within the Riga Jewish community, creating book cover designs and illustrations for publishers, set and costume designs for the Riga Jewish theater,[87] or painting Jewish themes for the local and wider middle-European art audience.

The first exhibition of Jewish artists to be held in the "new Latvia" at the Jewish People's University from October to December 1920 not only had a catalog[88] Y9 and a poster[89] Y46 designed by Jo, but also contained more than 70 works by him.[90] A solo exhibition of

85   Beginning in 1926, locally published Yiddica was deposited by law in the National Library of Latvia (LNB), Misiņa Library, and the University of Latvia Library. Compliance was left to the publisher. Loss through years of turmoil is admitted by staff at all institutions. One LNB card catalog drawer of about 700 cards, each reflecting a title, exists with Yiddish bibliographical entries transliterated into Cyrillic and arranged alphabetically. Interfiled one finds all Yiddish titles held, regardless of place of imprint, thus Warsaw, Odessa, Kaunas (Kovno), New York City, etc., entries are interfiled with Latvia imprints. The *Valsts bibliotēkas biļetens* cited Yiddish titles deposited each year in the LNB. But searching for titles requires a month-by-month leafing through the *Biļetens* looking among titles in other languages as no union list of Yiddish-language Latvian imprints exists as yet.

86   (Riga: Grāmata priekš visiem, 1929?), a publisher located at Brīvības iela 7.

87   The Paul Mandelstam- and Edmund Trompowsky-designed building built in 1913 is still standing at Skolas iela 6, although it was "totally reconstructed in 1926", according to Marģers Vestermanis, who also informs us that the Moscow Jewish theater "Habima" began its Europe-USA tour here in 1926.

88   Courtesy Latvian State Museum Library.

89   Courtesy National Library of Latvia.

90   Other artists included (some identified only by last name): Nikolaï Arenstam, Teodor Brenson, Wulfson, Wilhelm Hirschberg, Aron Lipschitz, (Paul) Mandelstam, Elena Skolnik-Lipschitz, David Skolnik, (Leonid) Pasternak, (Abel) Pan, and (Hermann) Struck.

LATVIJAS
STRĀDNIEKU TEĀTRIS

Y47

Y49

Y50

Y48

Jo's paintings was mounted in 1931 at the "Altberga Mākslas salons" at K. Barona iela 4. As the catalog indicates in its 82 entries, Jo's work was not limited to Jewish subjects. While Jewish subjects and views of Jewish Warsaw, Vilna, and Lodz are listed, as well as general views of Paris and Riga, also included are details from his set designs, book illustrations, and interiors. One particularly intriguing item is titled *Ebreju alfabets* (Hebrew Alphabet), but a search for this typographic curiosity has been unsuccessful. Much of Jo's work was taken to Israel by a relative after his death and at this writing is still privately held.[91] His illustrations for Yiddish-language newspapers and periodicals of that time have yet to be documented, to say nothing of his contributions to Latvian-language publications.

Jo's book cover designs for publications in all of Latvia's languages have yet to be comprehensively cited in a checklist. Only a few book covers have been scattered through the three principal chapters of this text with one additional representative work shown here, his cover for the fifth-year progress report of the *Latvijas Strādnieku teātris* (Latvian Workers' Theater) Y47 published in 1932.

No bibliography has been compiled of Jo's extensive writings—theater criticism for the papers of his day, not the least of which were his contributions to the Yiddish-language paper *Dos Folk*. Jo is reported to have illustrated picture books for children and found time to write a monograph on Isaac Levitan, the noted Russian landscape painter of the previous generation.[92] No copy has been located.

There was a respectable number of works of poetry in the titles brought from the Yiddish-language stacks, not all of which were Latvian imprints. Most of the volumes

91 *Korni* (Moscow-Kiev), a journal of Jewish culture, devotes pages 59-98 of No. 27 (2005) to memories of a number of individuals (including relatives) who knew Jo, e.g., Vladimir Gens, Ilona Jakobinets-Shneerson, and Moisei Berchenko. Few contributions provide hard facts or specific dates. Grainy black and white illustrations of paintings are included, giving some indication of his land- and cityscape style. One of his most dramatic surviving paintings, *Kol Nidre*, is shown. The painting is believed to be in a "private collection somewhere in New Jersey, USA", according to a relative.
92 *Isak Levitan* (Riga: 1927).

lacked a distinctive design and the majority had conventional typographic covers. But what they lacked in design appeal was compensated by the emotions they evoked. Several of these now largely forgotten authors were either deported during the first Soviet occupation of Latvia or, if they survived, lost their lives at the hands of the Nazi occupiers. (Of the nearly 100,000 Jews living in Latvia during the Interwar period, only 76 managed to flee to Palestine during the turmoil of 1940/1941, according to Schneour Levenberg.[93] Levenberg also points out that for the entire period from 1919 to 1941 only 4,547 Latvian Jews resettled in Palestine.)

A number of translations were among the books on the pile laid before me. Lion Feuchtwanger was represented by several titles, three of which showed the prevailing Western European rectilinear, typographic cover designs; one gave a nod toward asymmetrical typography and the then-fashionable vanguard use of red. Part Four of Feuchtwanger's *Yud Zis* (Jud Süss) fit the rectilinear category and the use of red.[94] Y48 Another title in the pile was *Pep: Y. L. Vetshiks Amerikaner liderbukh* (Y. L. Wetcheek's American Songbook), Y49 appearing in Riga in 1930.[95] Bikher far Alemen was the publisher. The cover designer is not credited, but the design certainly falls into the vanguard tradition. Note the cover design contrast with the first German edition[96] with an illustrative treatment by the set designer Caspar Neher. Y50 Max Brod's *Di froy fun undzer beynkshaft* (The Woman of our Dreams)[97] is an example of a designed, calligraphic treatment of Yiddish typography with the added element of an image, both designed by M. Jo. Y51

Following along with a typography-but-no-image cover design example is a recent book shop discovery with content of considerable literary-historical interest: *Jidn un Lotvišn* (Jews and Latvians).[98] Y52 The presumed compiler K. Tolmans, about whom no further information was found, provides an introduction titled in translation "Jewish-Latvian literature: a literary-critical introduction". Tolmans then follows with Yiddish-language translations of Latvian texts by well-known Latvian writers of the first quarter of the 20th century: Apsīšu Jēkabs' "The Jew has Arrived!"; Anna Brigadere's "Three Dressmakers"; Rūdolfs Blaumanis' "Crazy Isaac"; Jānis Poruks' "The Eternal Jew"; Ernests Birznieks-Upītis' "The Little Polecat"; Mārtiņš Liepa's "Motke"; Jānis Jaunsudrabiņš' "Joske's Wife", "The [Male] Dressmakers", "Sheep Buyer", and "Ripka's Marriage"; Ādolfs Erss' "The Amazing Garjāņi [Family]" and "Kakis"; Edvards Vulfs' "The Unknown Jew"; and Jānis Ezeriņš' "Dowry Money".

Mark Razumny

An indigenous example of Yiddish *belles lettres* with an illustrated cover of more than passing interest is M. Jo's design for Mark Razumny's collection of stories titled *Hintergeslekh: Dertseylungen* (Backstreets: The Stories).[99] Y53

Y51

Y52

Y53

93 See p. 11, "Introduction" in *The Jews in Latvia*.
94 (Riga: Bikher far Alemen, 1928), printed by Globus, presumably in an edition of 4,000 in keeping with the size of the printing of Part One the previous year.
95 Two years after its first publication in Berlin (1928) in book form and four years after these poems first appeared anonymously in the *Berliner Tageblatt* in 1924.
96 (Potsdam: Gustav Kiepenheuer, 1928).
97 (Riga: Bikher far Alemen, 1928). Zelig Kalmanovich translated this title from the German edition, *Die Frau, nach der man sich sehnt* (The Woman for Whom One Longs) (Wien: Zsolnay, 1927).
98 (Riga: Logos, 1938), p. 203, [204-208]. Translated from Latvian by H. Etkins. Edition: 1,000.
99 (Riga: Bikher far Alemen, 1929). Edition: 1,000.

Y54

Razumny had worked with his friend M. Jo on the paper *Dos Folk* in its earliest days and eventually left with Jo, Moses Michel Kitai, and others. But he continued, as did others, with newly initiated newspapers. While working at *Dos Folk*, Jo and Kitai collaborated in publishing two satirical "reviews": "Gomens Mamzer" (Gomens' Bastard)[100] and "Die Elfte Make" (The Eleventh Plague) alluding to the "ten plagues" visited on the Egyptians during the time of Israelite captivity.[101] According to Smirin,[102] a number of the staff of *Dos Folk* left the paper in early winter of 1922 and in December published a one-time newspaper, *Gele Prese* (Yellow Press), criticizing *Dos Folk*'s editorial management.

In addition to his writing for various papers, Razumny remained productive as a novelist, translator, and travel writer. His first novel, *Aranea di shpin* (Spider-Woman, 1924), Y54 is a story of "love and death", as one might guess from the image in Jo's[103] cover design. His last work of fiction published in Riga before the end of the Republic was a collection of stories of Jewish life in the 16th century called *Idishe melukhe: Historishe novele fun Idishn leben in XVI yorhundert* (Jewish World: An Historical Novel of 16th Century Jewish Life).[104] Razumny survived the Holocaust by fleeing to the USSR, returning to Riga in 1946. According to Grigoriĭ Smirin,[105] from 1946 to 1948 Razumny regularly contributed to *Eynikeyt* (Unity, Moscow), a government controlled Yiddish-language publication. But in 1950 he was repressed for a decade by the Stalinist regime. With the thaw in the early 1960s, he was once again able to continue writing as well as contributing to another government-sponsored Yiddish-language journal, *Sovetish Heymland* (Soviet Homeland, Moscow), all while living and working out of his one-room Riga apartment on Blaumaṇa iela.

With cane in hand, Razumny was a readily recognizable figure around Riga and frequented the theater, concerts, movies, and the one antiquarian bookshop at that time (on the corner of Dzirnavu iela and what is now Brīvības iela) until his death in 1988.[106] A revival of interest in his writing before his death resulted in two collections of his stories being translated into Russian and published in Moscow and two collections being re-published in Yiddish, also in Moscow. One collection of stories was translated into Russian and published by the Liesma publishing house in Riga in 1981.[107]

A note on Yiddish-language children's books

In searching through libraries and bookshops, it was somewhat disappointing not to find Yiddish-language children's books, those ephemeral documents used by any group wishing to perpetuate something of its culture into the next generation. Zionist young people's publications have been mentioned but, other than an encounter with two picture books, this genre did not seem to be high on the introduction list of the Yiddish-reading community or perhaps high on the list of those charged with saving such material that had been produced. One exception was the sub-genre of school books, of which there were many graded examples for the Yiddish and Hebrew school systems. But examples of these were

100   Published March 11, 1922.
101   Published for Pesach in 1922.
102   Interview with Marina Hoff (Stockholm), May 2006.
103   (Riga: Farlag Oazis). Edition: 1,000.
104   (Riga: Farlag Logos, 1939).
105   See his biographical sketch on Razumny in *Outstanding Jewish Personalities in Latvia*, p. 40.
106   Interview with Ari Kamenkowitsch (Riga), Mar. 2006.
107   *Razgovor s portretom: malen'kie novelly, basni* (Conversation with a Portrait: Little Stories, Fables).

Y55

Y56

also not to be found, except for one splendid title in the National Library of Latvia of *Sefer Heshbon Le-mathilim* (Arithmetic Book for Beginners, 1938) by Sch. Safer and based on the system of M. Sosteh. Unfortunately, the quaint illustrations are not credited, although they may have been the work of M. Sosteh.[108] Y55

One example I found in a bookshop was a Yiddish-language translation from Russian of Korneĭ Chukovskiĭ's celebrated and widely translated *Krokodil: Poeme far kleyn kinder* (Crocodile: Poems for Little Children; translated by S. L. Samuelson) with the original illustrations by "Re-mi", i.e. Nikolaĭ Remizov.[109] Y56 The other title, moving from a known author to the unknown, was a collection of self-published poems by M. J. Bliach, *Far kleyn un greser kinder* (For Small and Bigger Children) published in Dvinsk (Daugavpils), also in 1929.[110] There is still hope that other children's book titles may surface, such as those alluded to by M. Kitai and M. Jo.

The Yiddish press: a few additional comments

Latvia's Yiddish-reading population in the 1920s and 1930s had a lively and varied periodical and newspaper culture. Book reviews in the newspapers and periodicals, as in any literate society, fed the demand for Yiddish books, both original works as well as Yiddish-language translations.

---

108   Approved by the Latvian Ministry of Education for publication by Logos (a publisher of Yiddish and Hebrew books), distributed by Bernard Shereshevski and printed by Saflender at Kungu iela 21. Nothing further could be found on either "Sch. Safer" or "M. Sosteh".

109   Published by Undzer tsukunft (1929), located at Aspazijas bulvāris 7, and printed by Globus at Elizabetes iela 22. This classic of Russian children's literature was first published as a book in Petrograd by Petrosovet in 1919, having first appeared in 1917 in the annual literary supplement of *Niva*.

110   Printed by Sh. Z. Klumel.

Any picture of this Yiddish print world would be incomplete without at least some reference to the newspapers that held the community and its various factions together (somewhat) and prevented at least a few publishers from going bankrupt by promoting their respective publications through reviews and providing the usual vehicle for advertising. For details and some history of this press, one can turn to several sources.

One of the many commendable undertakings by the Soros Foundation in Latvia was its support for Rihards Treijs' compilation *Latvijas republikas prese, 1918-1940*[111] containing a thirteen-page chapter called "Ebreju prese" (The Hebrew Press) on the history of this phenomenon and the personalities involved. Treijs appended a table giving dates, frequency, editors, and other information for the 40 titles identified.

What is not included in Treijs' table of titles are some twenty left-wing Yiddish-language titles and one Hebrew-language title. For these publications one must turn to the volume titled "Revolucionārā un padomju periodika" (Revolutionary and Soviet Periodicals)[112] of the four-volume set *Latviešu periodika*.[113] For commentary and further information on this latter category, one should also consult Maks Shats-Anin's "Ebreju revolucionārā prese Latvijā" (The Jewish Revolutionary Press of Latvia).[114]

There are bibliographical fragments in the publications of the Interwar era, e.g., Oskar Grosberg's *Die Presse Lettlands* (Latvia's Press), in which he gives a brief comment on "Die jüdische Presse" mentioning the beginnings in 1907 with the *Natsyonal Tsaytung* (National Newspaper) and another short-lived Jewish newspaper called *Di Idishe Shtime* (The Yiddish Voice). Grosberg points out that the competition to these small, few-page efforts was to be found in the larger and much more sophisticated dailies and weeklies from the Jewish centers of Warsaw, St. Petersburg, Odessa, Vilna, and other cities, although by the time trains carrying these papers reached Riga the news in these papers was more a record than "news".

New periodical titles in German and Yiddish multiplied during the Interwar period, starting from modest beginnings and, surprisingly, developing individual voices within the numerous factions of such a relatively small population.

The influx from Russia during and following the Bolshevik Revolution and what the subsequent civil war precipitated (mentioned at the beginning of Part 2: Russian-language publishing in Latvia) was a sizeable increase in the numbers of Russian-Jews who read mostly in Russian, with some Yiddish and German. In July 1919 several leading intellectuals, including Marc Gerc, founded with funds from Jakob Hoff *Di Idishe Folksshtime* (Yiddish People's Voice) with an unassuming start—four pages and an initial press run of 500 copies. While lasting for only three months, it did not fold because it had tried to include something for "everyone": socialists, Zionist factions, and other parties. It ceased publication largely because the problems facing this paper (and most Rigensians) were brought about by one upheaval piled upon another. The resulting chaos can be attributed to an attack in the autumn of 1919 by an anti-Bolshevik force of Baltic Germans, Russian POWs, and others commanded by Pavel Bermondt-Avaloff. Andrejs Plakans and others considered Bermondt-Avaloff "a brazen military adventurist",[115] and it was clear to the

111 (Riga: Zvaigzne, 1996).
112 Pp. 273-280.
113 (Riga: Zinātne, 1976-1989).
114 See Jūlijs Ķipers' *Cīņas balsis* (Riga: Latvijas Valsts izd., 1959), pp. 451-464.
115 Plakans, Andrejs, *The Latvians: A Short History* (Stanford: Hoover Institution Press, 1995), p. 119.

young Latvian government that he had a malign intent. A conscripted Latvian force suc-cessfully drove him and his sizeable but rag-tag army out of the country. Order and some degree of quiet returned, but among the casualties was *Di Idishe Folksshtime*.

In May 1920 two highly successful and generous businessmen, Jakob Hoff[116] and Abram Gilelevich Becker,[117] financed the first major Yiddish-language paper, *Dos Folk* (The People), which managed to last until July 1927. It reached a circulation of 6,000 at its highest point despite a somewhat zig-zag ideological course, first supporting one cause and then changing just as quickly to another. As Marc Gerc referred to it, "Left-wing to-day, Right-wing tomorrow, Zionist and pro-Hebrew today, Yiddishist and Socialist soon after, an Orthodox paper today, and Free-thinking tomorrow".[118] But this comment came after Gerc, one of the original *Dos Folk* editors, had become disaffected and left the paper. Dr. Jacob Hellman and other founding editors lost interest almost immediately and left the paper, later returning for a year before leaving again.[119] All of this gives some hint of the revolving-door nature of Yiddish newspaper life in Riga in the 1920s.

The paper, however, had its stars such as the Riga-born but compulsively peripatetic Moses Michel Kitai who, in his wandering, invariably contributed to the local Yiddish press whether in Vilna, Odessa, or Moscow. Unfortunately, he stayed with *Dos Folk* for only a few years, beginning in 1921 when he worked with M. Jo. All the while Kitai contributed to other Yiddish-language papers, e.g., *Der Veg* (The Way, 1922-1923) followed by *Undzer Veg* (Our Way, 1923-1924). When Kitai and Jo both left *Dos Folk* at about the same time, they moved on to another Yiddish newspaper, *Frimorgn* (Early Morning), discussed below.[120] *Dos Folk* was given credit by one commentator who stated that its "chief merit was.. creation of a Yiddish reading public".[121] A more modest claim was its being one of several mediums for nurturing a Yiddish-reading public.

Dos Folk and two other smaller circulation Yiddish-language papers were given credit by this same commentator for preparing the way for *Frimorgn*, which began publi-cation in January 1926 and continued until May 1934. This daily paper achieved consider-able influence. It was able to attract gifted and experienced reporters, essayists, and crit-ics; it was also the creation of the publishers of the celebrated *Segodnia*. Keeping largely to an independent line of reporting, unlike the colorful *Dos Folk*, its strength was main-tained by its publishers' ability to attract and maintain, among others, such well-known writers as novelist, children's book author, and poet David Bergelson and Simon Dub-now, the prolific scholar and historian of Eastern European Jewry who died in the Riga

---

116   Hoff, born in Viljandi, Estonia, was a self-made businessman in the truest sense. He left school at age 15, built business after business, including two short-line railroads, and ultimately became a generous donor to civic causes as well as Jewish cultural and religious efforts. He supported not only his synagogue, the Peitach congregation, but also various ventures such as *Dos Folk*. (Details drawn from "Die Familie Hoff in Riga" by Eva Pulvermacher Hoff, a two-page, unpublished, typescript published in 1979).

117   According to Grigoriĭ Smirin, Becker (born in Jēkabpils) became a highly successful importer and exporter of grain and seed and, like Hoff, was a generous supporter of Jewish cultural institutions. Interview with Smirin, Riga, Jan. 2007.

118   Quoted from Menahem Beth in his "Men and Deeds" in *The Jews of Latvia*, p. 310.

119   Bobe, p. 57.

120   When the government closed *Frimorgn* in 1934, Kitai moved to the more favorable Yiddish-publishing and intellectual center, Warsaw. While working there as an editor of *Literarishe Bleter* (1924-1939), he continued work on a compendium of bio-critical essays on Jewish artists and writers he had known throughout his wanderings, including his time in Riga. This important contemporary account, *Undzer Shrayber un Kinstler*, was published while he was in Warsaw (Yidishe Universal-bibliothek, 1938). WWII brought more wandering, this time all the way to Samarkand, where he died in a hospital, all but forgotten. (For more details, see Menahem Beth's "Men and Deeds" in *The Jews in Latvia*, pp. 308-309).

121   See Mendel Bobe's account, "Four hundred years of the Jews in Latvia" in *The Jews in Latvia*, p. 57.

Y57

Y58

Y59

Y60

Ghetto having fled his Berlin home for the presumed safety of Riga. *Dos Folk*'s popularity may also owe something to its physical appearance; its publishers made use of up-to-date printing technology and, according to Grosberg in his essay cited earlier, "advances in American page-layout".

Between the founding of *Dos Folk* and *Frimorgn*'s suspension in May 1934, nearly 40 Yiddish-language newspapers bloomed and faded, a few lasting no more than one or two issues. Some were directed to a particular audience, e.g., the satirical paper *Ashmedai* (Satan, 1922-1929?) Y57, Y58 and the equally satirical *Kol boj: Ilustrirte zhurnal far satire humor un literatur* (And Everything Else: Illustrated Journal of Satirical Humor and Literature, 1927) Y59 or *Dos Idishe folk* (The Jewish People, 1926), a Zionist paper. Then there were the general papers published in smaller cities, e.g., *Di Zemgaler shtime* (The Zemgale Voice, Jelgava, 1931) and *Libauer folksblat* (The Libau People's Paper, Liepāja, 1931-1934), to mention a few.

From a design standpoint, there was little variation in the layout of the Yiddish press, although some effort at stylization of the banner titling can be seen in the example of *Jungvarg* (Young People) shown here.[122] Y60

As to periodicals, the cost of production coupled with uncertainties about potential audience size kept publisher-entrepreneurs away from this assured method of losing investment capital in the short term. Those readers who longed for illustrated weeklies or monthlies could choose from imported Russian-, German-, and French-language titles from Western Europe, readily available at kiosks and some of the larger bookshops.[123]

Idishe Bilder

There was one bold but short-lived exception: *Idishe Bilder* (Jewish Pictures), a venture of the *Segodnia* publishers Brams and Poliak, the only entrepreneurs in town with the capital and staff to consider such an undertaking. The weekly appeared from May 28, 1937, to September 22, 1939.[124] Circulation figures are not given but it must have been in excess of the 3,000-4,000 copies typical of the majority of Yiddish-language periodicals in Latvia. *Idishe Bilder* announced an ambitious distribution network listing cities from Stockholm to Bucharest, Danzig to Istanbul, and Amsterdam to New York City among many others. Akiva Zimmerman stated that it was "one of the most impressive of the pre-war Jewish weeklies (presumably anywhere), an achievement enhanced by the very fact of its appearing under the restrictive rule of Kārlis Ulmanis".[125] The initial managing editor, A. Baramas,[126] was succeeded a year later by the philologist and Yiddishist Zelig Kalmanovitch. Once again, Mark Razumny became involved as a regular contributor as well as literary editor. The paper's founders and editors worked at bringing the world to Yiddish-reading Jewry; the very first issue's cover story on India's Jews is but one example.

---

122 The banner text, "The First of May lives; the unity of the world's workers lives", was a daring declaration by any organization on the eve of the Ulmanis coup. It appears to be the only issue published, although many other publications were issued by the publisher, the Latvian Jewish Central School Organization. N. Šteimanis was the editor.

123 Interviews with Irra Schlossberg Gelin (New York), May 2004, and Judith Neumann (Stockholm), Mar. 2002.

124 Treijs, ibid., p. 461.

125 "[Jewish pictures before the holocaust: the weekly 'Idishe Bilder' of Riga, 1937-1939]" by Akiva Zimmerman, *Kesher* (Tel Aviv), No. 24, Nov. 1998.

126 Baramas seems to have slipped from memory or at least publications by him seem to have eluded most of the likely libraries.

Y61

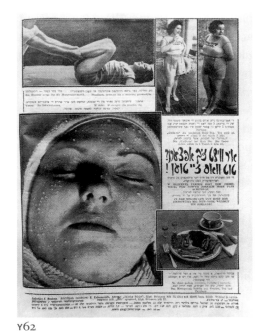

Y62

The role of photography in this undertaking was considerable and was the result of an editorial decision to have reporting photographers throughout the world, in addition to correspondents. Every issue made use of photography, invariably with a cover photo tied to a lead article. Internally, the use of photomontage was common, although it was not particularly sophisticated or noteworthy. The content of the first issue gives some idea of the paper's scope. In addition to the India article, this same issue also featured Scandinavian Jewry, the dramatic architecture of an expanding Tel Aviv, and the birthday celebration of the young Archduke Otto von Habsburg, who later in life became a staunch supporter of Israel.[127]

In addition to a regular literary section that highlighted young as well as mature Yiddish writers, the serialized novel—a feature certain to ensure sales—was begun with the first issue. The first issue even published two novellas: one by the prolific poet, feuilletonist, and novelist Zusman Segalovitch; the other by Efrayim Kaganovsky, about whom I have learned nothing other than that he died in Paris. The paper also included a regular humor section edited by Yosef Tunkel, who spent his life and considerable energy editing compilations of jokes, humorous stories, and children's stories and moving from country to country after his stint with *Idishe Bilder*.[128] He gained some fame in Yiddish-speaking circles as the translator of the classic 19th century German humorist Wilhelm Busch. Tunkel's translation of *Max und Moritz* reached at least two editions in Poland during the Interwar period.[129]

In their mission to educate provincial readers to contemporary world Jewry, the editors of *Idishe Bilder* published articles on "personalities", e.g., Simon Dubnow, Leon Blum,

---

127   Interview with Tom Freudenheim (New York City), Dec. 2007.

128   In the autumn of 1939, when the paper ceased publication, Tunkel headed for a vacation in Belgium. Then, attempting to flee ahead of the Wehrmacht, he fled to France, was caught, and interned. He then escaped and found his way to New York City, where he lived out his life writing for Jewish publications, notably *The Forward*.

129   *Notl un Motl: zeks shtifer-mayseh'lakh*, 2nd ed. (Warsaw: Brider Levin-Epshtayn un Shutfim, 1928).

the film actress Sylvia Sidney (think back to 1936 and Alfred Hitchcock's *Sabotage*), Albert Einstein, a platoon of Soviet commissars who happened to be Jewish, and the gifted all-purpose diplomat Meir Wallach-Finkelstein, i.e., Maxim Litvinov, known primarily to Americans as the USSR ambassador (1941 to 1943) to the US during World War II. These were but a few. Then there were thumbnail sketches of remote or lesser-known communities of Jews such as the "Black Jews" of Harlem, North African Jews, Jews of China, and so on.

Y63

The quality of the paper on which it was printed declined over the periodical's brief life, though toward the end it appeared on good quality newsprint. What did not deteriorate was the scope of reportage. The issue shown here, No. 37 (Sept. 1938), in two panels, gives an impression of the diversity of reporting: the front cover with a photograph of the Association of WWI Sephardic Jewish Veterans in a joint memorial meeting with the French Garibaldi Veterans' Association at the "Grave of the Unknown Soldier" in Paris; Y61 the back cover carries a brief item and photos citing the opportunities for weight loss and getting fit at Rose Dor's "Milk Farm" in Irvington-on-Hudson, several miles north of New York City. Y62 An additional feature in this issue was an illustrated article on Irving Berlin and his celebrated position in American popular music.

When threatening political clouds had accumulated on the horizon by the first weeks of 1939, the paper began a series about possible countries to which Jews might flee in order to avoid the inevitable. Among the possible places noted for refuge were the Belgian Congo, Bolivia, British Guiana, and Haiti as well as such ports as Dar-es-Salaam and Panama City. This series also generally implied what was likely to happen to those Latvian Jews choosing to remain in Latvia. Yet, in the final issue of 1939 the editors "expressed hope that the closure of the magazine would be temporary only", according to Akiva Zimmerman.[130] Until their respective final issues *Segodnia*, *Idishe Bilder*, and *Frimorgn* were published from the famed Alfrēds Birkhāns-designed building at Dzirnavu iela 57.

Y64

As already indicated, Yiddish-language pictorial magazines directed to a general audience were few and far between throughout the European communities where there was a literate, Yiddish-reading audience. It is not known if issues of *Dos Hayrats-glik* (Married Bliss) (Warsaw, 1925-?), *Oyfgang* (Rising) (Sighet, Romania, 1933-1936), or any other such illustrated Yiddish periodicals from Central Europe made their way by subscription to Riga or were at least carried back by travelers. Certainly, there was an abundance of Latvian-language picture and satirical magazines available at corner kiosks and on the newspaper wagons set up where pedestrian traffic was assured.

By the end of 1940, with the Soviet occupation in control of all publishing in Latvia, Yiddish-language periodical publishing had come to an end, that is, except for the effort by the apparat of the first Soviet occupation to engage the Yiddish-reading population with both a newspaper titled *Kamf* (Struggle)[131] Y63 and a journal called *Oyfboy* (Construction, as in the process of "building-up"),[132] subtitled a "political-literary monthly". Y64 Neither title was cited by Flīgere et al.,[133] thus making it difficult to determine the concluding dates, but assuredly both were abruptly stopped when the Soviets withdrew and turned the country over to the National Socialists. The *Kamf* issue shown is dated January 12, 1941, and numbered as the 2nd year, No. 11. Despite advertisements for theater, ballet, and

130 Zimmerman, ibid., p. 8e.
131 Published by the Riga Committee "Kamf" from September 1940 to the spring of 1941.
132 Published from October 1940 to the spring of 1941.
133 See *Latviešu periodika*, vol. 4.

lectures, implying that life was going forward normally, the content is what one could expect from an occupying force's propaganda machine.[134] The issue shown of *Oyfboy* contains articles with such telling titles as M. Andri's "Jews in Latvia", H. Bloshteyn's "A hymn to Stalin", S. Friedland's "About Soviet Yiddish", Abraham I. Kairov's "The children's collective and the role of the teacher",[135] M. M. Kitai's "Yitschak Yoel Linetski",[136] and M. Shats-Anin's "Mayakovsky in Riga", among other articles. The existence of these two Yiddish-language periodicals with their heavy propaganda strikes a somber note as prelude to an even darker conclusion to Yiddish-language publishing in Latvia.

Conclusion

When a vibrant society comes to a sudden end, or a *phased tragedy*, in the case of the Latvian-Jewish community, there is little to say. Its destruction was no less horrible than the much more familiar annihilation of Jewish communities throughout Central Europe. But the Riga Holocaust remains in the world's eyes as little more than an historical footnote, except in publications specifically concerned with Latvian Jewry.

When one walks around Riga now at the beginning of the 21st century, it takes a great effort to conjure pleasant images of Riga and the provinces with a visible, energetic Jewish population. The dark and the terror come more quickly to mind. Chasing away the haunting images of Soviet political police rounding up Jewish and Latvian intellectuals in the spring of 1940 for summary execution or deportation is as disturbing as are the images in the subsequent years when SS troops[137] rounded up thousands of Jews in the 1940s for ultimate destruction in the Riga Ghetto, Šmerlis Cemetery, Biķernieki Forest, Rumbula Forest, Salaspils, and any number of other "killing fields" sequestered in the outlying melancholy-inspiring wooded areas.

So, one might well ask whether Latvia or Riga deserves to have a vital Jewish community live again? If, for some reason, the answer is "yes", should it develop similarly to that of the new Jewish community in Berlin? That particular community of émigrés from Russia, other European countries, and, increasingly, from Israel—all coming together to form a new community—certainly cannot replicate the German-Jewish community that was destroyed. The question once again is whether a Latvian-Jewish community should even be fostered in the "New Latvia", in the "New Riga"?

Whatever is allowed, or simply happens, still cannot resurrect that distinctive liveliness and style of the Latvian-Jewish community of the 1920s and 1930s, welded by a dynamic print culture and then suddenly, in little more than two years, brutally obliterated.

Our only way to experience something of the atmosphere of that lost community today is through what one is able to read into those surviving printed fragments of poetry, fiction, sheet music, and posters that now rest in libraries, museums, and archives.

---

134   This "machine" was well-oiled in that Yiddish-language publishing had been a part of the overall Soviet publishing program from the beginning of the 1920s, with Yiddica of Soviet origin undoubtedly finding its way into Latvia throughout the Interwar era. See David Schneer's "Who owns the means of cultural production? The Soviet Yiddish publishing industry of the 1920s" in *Book History*, vol. 6, ed. by Ezra Greenspan and Jonathan Rose (University Park, PA: Pennsylvania State University Press, 2003), pp. 197-226.

135   Kairov rose within the USSR's education hierarchy to become Minister of Education after World War II.

136   A brief biographical account of this colorful 19th century Yiddish writer, translator, and sometime-entertainer who was born in 1839 and died in 1915.

137   In many cases the SS troops worked with the complicity of Latvians, both in and out of uniform.

GERMAN-LANGUAGE PUBLISHING   PART 4

Introduction

After spending a few days walking around Riga and reading street names (beginning in the Old Town with Riharda Vāgnera iela)[1] or searching through a recent telephone book, skimming from almost any point or just beginning with "A" (note Alberts Akermanis), one soon senses a shadowy but lingering German presence in many Latvian place and street names and family names.[2] Even lurking in many Latvian words[3] that have long since rubbed off obvious German edges, a core, Latvianized morpheme still remains after 65 years since the last episode of German dominance (the good and the bad German episodes lasted from the 13th to the mid 20th century).

From the standpoint of book culture, much good German residue is in the work and print legacy of the early authors and translators: Mancelius,[4] Fürecker,[5] Glück,[6] Stender,[7] and Merkel,[8] to mention but five of many Baltic-Germans who left their collective mark on Latvian literature, education, and publishing. In a diffuse way, the German cultural contribution continued down into the years of the 1920s and 1930s. But the real Baltic-German culture and the place of publishing in its centuries-long saga took place long before Latvia's independence and the period between World Wars I and II.

The first books and the first periodical publications—newspapers, journals, and year-books—printed in the Latvian region were in German, although the first known book to be printed in the Latvian language, *Catechismus Catholicorum*, was printed by Jesuits in Vilnius in 1585. Not to be outdone, the German Lutheran administration saw to it that a Lutheran catechism was produced (in Königsberg) the following year.[9] In Riga, Nikolai Mollyn established the first printing house in what is now Latvia and produced the *Kirchenordnung der Stadt Riga und Rigasches Gesangbuch* (Rules Governing Church Life of the City of Riga and the Riga Hymn Book) in 1588.[10]

In the beginning,[11] or at least by the mid 17th century, German pastors and teachers in the Latvian lands had produced a number of texts for German-language church services and instructional material for the German schools serving the small but industrious population of this Baltic outpost. Alongside their German-language publishing efforts, the more gifted and concerned pastors and teachers among the population set to work translating catechisms, portions of the Bible, hymnals, and school books into the Latvian

---

1   Aptiekas iela (Apotheke=pharmacy), Fazānu iela (Fasan=pheasant), Herdera laukums (Herder Square, as in Johann Gottfried von Herder), Kastaņu iela (Kastanien=chestnut), etc.

2   Braunšveigs, Ekšteins, Freivalds, Lauterbachs, Stefenhāgens, etc.

3   Ābols (Apfel=apple), blūze (Bluse=blouse), cukurs (Zucker=sugar), flauta (Flöte=flute), lasīt (lesen=to read), papīrs (this may have come directly from papyrus, but more likely from the German Papier).

4   Georgius Mancelius produced, among other things, a major Latvian dictionary.

5   Christophor Fürecker was a writer and translator of hymns and also had a profound influence on the development of Latvian lyrical writing, both religious and secular.

6   Ernst Glück was the first translator of the Bible into Latvian.

7   Gotthard Friedrich Stender is given credit for providing a secular basis for Latvian literature. Stender also created a German-Latvian/Latvian-German dictionary.

8   Through his journalistic efforts, Garlieb Merkel worked for the abolition of serfdom of the Latvians.

9   *Das Lettische Buch*, ed. by Ziedonis Krastiņš, Edgars Ķiploks, Miķelis Goppers (Riga: Zelta Ābele, 1942), p. 12.

10   See *Geschichte der Buchdruckerkunst in Riga 1588-1888* by Arend Buchholtz (Riga: Müllerische Buchdruckerei, 1890), p. 43.

11   The beginnings of German influence in the region of what is now Latvia could be dated from the time when the Augustinian monk Father Meinhard arrived from Schleswig-Holstein in approximately 1184 and began missionary efforts among the Liv population along the Daugava River in present-day Ikšķile, some 70 km southeast of Riga. His efforts, while disappointing from the standpoint of establishing a continuing congregation of Christian believers, resulted in the building of a church, completed in 1186.

language. A number of these intellectuals fostered and then, in notable cases, worked side-by-side with Latvian intellectuals to bring about a range of religious works that prepared the way for the codification of the Latvian spoken language and, in time, a printed Latvian literature.

Concurrent with religious publishing in the early years, a modest amount of secular German publishing, together with a steady importation of German books, was bringing about an insular German book culture in the Baltic region with some similarity to British colonial book culture in 19th century India or its imperial sphere of influence in the Levant and other areas.

Printing and publishing activity by the German community continued in the Latvian lands at a small but consistent pace for more than three centuries until the early 20th century, despite intervals of Imperial Russian, Imperial Swedish, and then once again Imperial Russian influences.[12]

It should also be stated that by the turn of the 20th century German influences had begun to manifest themselves subtly in the developing Latvian printing/publishing scene—"Teutonic influences", one might say. These influences were evident in organizational style, not only in publishing and printing but also in banking, education, welfare organizations, and the arts.

These positive contributions were historically sandwiched between a less than civilized beginning, involving routine attacks on rebellious tribes by several waves of German invaders during the 11th and 12th centuries and, centuries later, closing on the darkest of notes with the occupation of Latvia by the Hitler regime (mid 1941 to mid 1945).

During the two centuries before the early 19th century and the rise of the Latvian literary movements, the secular, locally produced German publications were predominantly almanacs, yearbooks, and directories. The German-speaking and -reading populations of the Latvian and Estonian region of the Russian Empire relied to a large degree on the importation of *belles lettres*. This is not to say, however, that there were only a few Baltic writers producing a provincial literature. On the contrary, there were many, and their lives and works have been delineated in such monumental works as Carola Gottzmann's and Petra Hörner's three-volume *Lexicon der deutschsprachigen Literatur des Baltikums und St. Petersburgs: Vom Mittelalter bis zur Gegenwart* (Lexikon of the German-language Literature of the Baltic and St. Petersburg from the Middle Ages to the Present)[13] and Gero von Wilpert's *Deutschbaltische Literaturgeschichte* (German-Baltic Literary History),[14] among others.

So much of what these Baltic-German writers created was confined to publication in the locally published newspapers and periodicals. Few of these writers living out at least the earlier part of their writing lives in the Baltic became known beyond the area. Notable exceptions were Werner Bergengruen, Gertrud von den Brincken, and Siegfried von Vegesack.

From their beginnings in the late 19th century, Baltic-German newspapers and other periodical publications are generally conceded to have played a major role in the maintenance of this culture within a culture. Certainly, the Baltic-German press of the era is the starting place for researchers and the curious to gain some feel for this historical

---

12   See the initial chapters of Arnolds Spekke's *History of Latvia* (Stockholm: M. Goppers, 1957) for a general discussion of these imperial powers and their relationship to the German presence in the region.
13   (Berlin: Walter de Gruyter, 2007).
14   (München: C. H. Beck, 2005).

culture. Until its decline in the Interwar period, the press remained the prime source for insight into the closing era of the Baltic-German phenomenon.

In short, the story of German-language publishing after Latvia's independence in 1918 is but a mildly interesting footnote to the larger story of regional publishing history. The contribution of German-language publishing to the Baltic region in general and to Latvian cultural history in specific took place in the previous years and is implied in the content of numerous articles in the *Latviešu konversācijas vārdnīca* (Latvian Conversational Encyclopedia)[15] or, for example, the early compilation by the Baltic-German literary historian Ulrich Ernst Zimmermann and his *Versuch einer Geschichte der lettischen Literatur* (Attempt at a History of Latvian Literature).[16]

Nevertheless, given that so much space has been devoted to Interwar publishing in the other languages, it would be inappropriate to ignore publishing in the fourth language of Latvia, even though the local German publishing sector was on the wane by the early 1920s, with an accompanying dependence on imported books by the residual German community. Given the political changes and general upheaval in the Baltic-German community, it is not surprising that in Latvia's first two decades only 2,141 German books were published in all categories—*belles lettres*, calendars, directories, non-fiction, and reference.[17]

German-Latvian interaction in the 1920s and 1930s

With the beginning of the Republic and the Interwar period, whatever smoldering societal divisions existed between Baltic-Germans and Latvians were now aggravated further as land-holding Baltic-Germans watched with dismay while laws were being passed in the new Latvian parliament to divide their large estates. Any hopes and dreams that they harbored to be once again economically in charge were shattered following the turmoil of the period from 1918 to 1920.

For a brief but excellent background summary of this transition and the understandable tensions created between Germans (on and off the land) and the newly enfranchised Latvians, one must consult Raimonds Cerūzis' *Vācu faktors Latvijā (1918-1939): Politiskie un starpnacionālie aspekti* (The German Factor in Latvia [1918-1939]: Political and Interethnic Aspects)[18] with its exceptional English-language summary. The beginning chapters of Andrejs Plakans' *The Latvians*[19] are also essential reading. For readers wishing a magisterial account of all that went before, there is no substitute for Arnolds Spekke's *History of Latvia*, modestly subtitled "an outline",[20] and his view of what Germans did to and for Latvians. For those wishing another approach, there is the more journalistic but nonetheless valuable account by Alfrēds Bīlmanis in *A History of Latvia*.[21]

Risking oversimplification, one might say that at government and personal levels in the new Latvia, Baltic-Germans tended to feel superior to ethnic Latvians, although they might not have admitted to such feelings. Sensing this, many ethnic Latvians were in

15 Edited by A. Švābe, 21 volumes (Riga: Gulbis, 1927-1940).

16 (Mitau: Steffenhagen & Sohn, 1812).

17 See table of Latvian and German title production in *Das Lettische Buch* (Riga: Zelta Ābele, 1942), p. 139.

18 (Riga: LU Akadēmiskais apgāds, 2004).

19 (Stanford, CA: Hoover Institution Press, 1995).

20 Ibid.

21 (Princeton, NJ: Princeton University Press, 1951). While both Spekke and Bīlmanis provide bibliographies, Spekke gives a full account of his sources and a much more detailed index.

D1

D2

varying degrees quietly resentful of these Germans. Within those general feelings there were, of course, extremes both negative and positive to be observed within government and in businesses large and small.

An exemplary positive political figure was Paul Schiemann, the 20th century Baltic-German leader prior to World War II, who worked tirelessly to promote "a new German Ostpolitik—one based on cooperation with the Latvians, rather than... occupation of their country".[22] A curious, related, and general phenomenon illustrating Latvian-German relations and cited in Elizabete Melbārzde's "Notes towards my memoir"[23] of the painter Kārlis Melbārzdis: she comments that among the Latvian population there were a few individuals who identified with, or wanted to be identified with, German culture and thus Germanized their Latvian names along with affecting German styles in clothing and other domestic preferences. One of the most prominent of these was Vilhelms Purvītis, Latvia's major landscape painter of the first quarter of the 20th century, who, when it suited him, took to using the German form of his name, Wilhelm Purwit, and who on occasion chose to "dress German".

Baltic-German society in Latvia

Almost immediately after the signing of the accords in 1920 that curtailed what had once been a major German presence in the Baltic, many Germans began leaving for East Prussia and other regions of Germany. Some, with far-sightedness, given what would transpire in Latvia and Germany within two decades, left for South America, Canada, and Australia. The story of this gradually increasing emigration from Latvia has been told and retold in scores of readily available reminiscences and scholarly studies.

Yet despite this emigration, many Baltic-Germans stayed behind in Latvia for business reasons or because the Baltic region had been "home" for generations and, like British colonists throughout Africa, thoughts of leaving for an unknown life in another country or even returning to Germany were too daunting. The diminishing German population still maintained those distinctive features readily associated with German culture: choral societies, German-language schools, trade associations, and religious organizations connected mainly to the Lutheran Church in Latvia, etc. Art exhibitions of German artists continued as before, of which an exhibition in 1932 of Werner Linde's work together with Oto Pladers, i.e., Otto Pladder, is but one example. D1 The catalog was designed by another Baltic-German, Vilis (i.e. Wilhelm) Krūmiņš. Maintaining a general welfare structure was perceived as a necessity to ensure care for its members as a hedge against possible uncertainties within the larger Latvian society. A poster for the Baltic-German benefit society's lottery of 1923 reflects this concern. Note that the designer, Erich Heinrich Balthasar von Campenhausen, denominated the lottery's monetary goal in rubles, still a legitimate medium of exchange at that time and a carry-over from the previous regime. D2

Those Baltic-Germans who chose to remain continued to read as before. In the following few pages, what they read and the "look" of what they read will be characterized with a few representative examples—representative because the generally tedious sameness in both book and periodical design makes brevity a more considerate approach.

22 See John Hiden's chapter "Paul Schiemann on Reconciling 'Nation' and 'State'" in *The Ethnic Dimension in Politics and Culture in the Baltic Countries 1920-1945*, ed. Baiba Metuzāle-Kangere (Stockholm: Almqvist & Wiksell, 2004), p. 10.
23 In the process of compilation and editing by Elizabete Melbārzde.

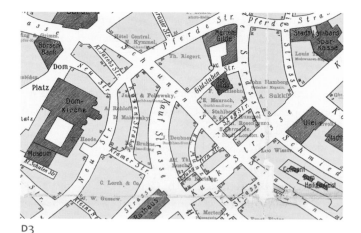

D3

D4

D5

But by 1921 printing and publishing in German had become an ever-diminishing factor in the overall publishing sector of the country. The German population of Riga in 1913 had dropped to 68,831 from almost twice that for all of Latvia in the late 19th century; by 1920 the German population in Riga had dropped still further to 29,533.[24] By 1925, however, this segment of the Riga population had increased through post-conflict stabilization to 43,792, rising to an overall German population in Latvia of 70,964.[25] The number of resident German printers and publishers providing for this reduced market had dropped considerably from the late 19th century to no more than three or four. The primary printer/publishers—those with their own printing operations—were Jonck & Poliewsky with its large retail shop at Kaufstrasse 3 (today Tirgoņu iela) and E. Bruhns with a retail book and art shop at Tirgoņu iela 15. D3, D4, D5 A few German printers, such as J. Grünberg at Grosse Schmiedestrasse 50 (today Kalēju iela) and R. Ruetz & Co. at Domplatz 5 (today Doma laukums) as well as several Latvian printing houses maintaining compositors with multilingual competence and type racks of German Fraktur type, provided for the printing needs of German associations and those commercial directory publishers producing one or two titles per year.

24 *Rīgas iedzīvotāju dabīgā kustība, 1911-1930* (Riga: 1932), p. 80.
25 *Otra tautas skaitīšana Latvijā 1925. gada 10. februārī*. 2. burtnīca (Riga: 1925), p. 84.

D6

D7

D8

During the 1920s and 1930s, it was far more economical to import German books for the dwindling population. It remained for Jonck & Poliewsky, E. Bruhns, and Academia Buchhandlung und Verlag at Aspazijas bulvāris 4 as well as a few small importers to keep this population supplied with recreational reading from German publishers. But unfortunately, the international financial crisis of the time took its toll on the venerable Jonck & Poliewsky, which fell into bankruptcy and was out of business by the end of 1931.

One gets a sense of reading interests in the German community by browsing through the Academia Buchhandlung catalog of 1928. D6, D7, D8 Readily seen from its contents are the variety and tastes in popular literature and the classics of German and other literatures. In all likelihood, what one sees in this catalog was imported; there is no indication of the titles being local imprints. If imported from Germany, no comment is needed about the design of these imports. If one is familiar with the look of German trade publishing of the

D9

D10

D11

era, one can readily conjure the stodgy design of bindings and wrappers in which most of these books arrived for display in the Academia Buchhandlung shop windows.

The locally published *belles lettres* were mostly as lackluster in design as those titles being imported from Germany, whether self-published on commission with houses such as Valters un Rapa or published by one of the few German-language publishers. A selection of typical book cover designs illustrates this point. One example is the nostalgia-evoking *Deutsches Leben im alten St. Petersburg* (German Life in Old St. Petersburg)[26] with a cover design by "HR". D9 A sample of local design provided by Heinrich Daiber, introduced in the Latvian and Russian chapters, has given a modest but uninspired cover to Leonid Grabar's *Gestalten: Roman aus dem heutigen Russland* (Figures: A novel of present-day Russia).[27] D10 Another title from the same publisher (likely the same year although undated) and also a translation from Russian was Leo Larsky's *Die Frau am Scheidewege: Russland von Heute!* (Women at a Turning Point: Russia Today!). D11 The title page, however, carries another subtitle: *Aufzeichnungen einer Frauenärztin* (Notes of a Woman Doctor).[28] The uncredited design carries the feel of Heinrich Daiber's other work. From the same year, yet another title with content that might have led the anonymous designer to reach a little higher or farther into the future: *Aeropolis: Roman aus dem Jahre 1952* (Aeropolis: A Novel from the Year 1952).[29] D12

D12

26   Compiled by Heinrich Pantenius and Oskar Grosberg (Riga: R. Ruetz, 1930).

27   (Riga: Allgemeiner Buchverlag, 1929).

28   Leo Solomonovich Leibowitz usually signed his work "L. Larsky". This work was first published (Orient, 1928) in Riga in Russian as *Zhenshchina no pereput*.

29   By Ladislaus Palasti and Friedrich Ernyei, translated from Hungarian by Maurus Mezei (Riga: Riga am Sonntag, 1929). Volume 11 in the *Fiction library* of the *Riga am Sonntag* German-language weekly.

In der Romanbibliothek der „Riga am Sonntag" sind bisher
erschienen:

Band I. Liesbet Dill: „Rose Ferrons erste Liebe und Ehe".
166 Seiten. Mit Bildnis der Autorin. (Vergriffen.)
Band II. A. von Hahn: „Das Gespenst im Schlosspark". Kri-
minalroman. 128 Seiten. (Vergriffen.)
Band III. Paul Wild: „Die Schuld des Vaters". Roman aus
der Gegenwart. 141 Seiten. (Vergriffen.)
Band IV. Max von Weissenthurn: „Treu bis in den Tod".
185 Seiten. (Vergriffen.)
Band V. Elisabeth Ney: „Die Liebe der Brigitta Holler-
mann". 158 Seiten. (Vergriffen.)
Band VI. Walter Erbse: „Der Gast der Lilian Svendson".
Werner Krueger: „Verräterische Schatten". Kri-
minalroman. 145 Seiten. (Vergriffen.)
Band VII. Ernst Klein: „Wenn Frauen kämpfen". Sensa-
tionsroman aus dem Leben einer Aristokratin, die sich in
den Netzen einer Agentin der „Tscheka" verstrickt.
Band VIII. Siegfried Bergengruen: „Gegen den Strom".
140 Seiten. (Vergriffen.)
Band IX. Lola Stein: „Herzen im Kreis". (Vergriffen.)
Band X. Kopernikulus: „Das Lächeln im Spiegel". 163 Seiten. (Vergriffen.)
Band XI. Ladislaus Palasti und Friedrich Ernyei: „Aeropolis". Spannender Zukunftsroman aus dem Jahre 1952.
Band XII. Erika Forst: „Die Gouvernante zu Ross". 141 Seiten. (Vergriffen.)
Band XIII. Gert Rothberg: „Frau Danielas Liebeswirren".
150 Seiten. (Vergriffen.)
Band XIV. Oskar Grosberg: „Strypin". Roman aus dem
kaiserlichen Petersburg. 4.—6. Auflage. 148 Seiten. (Vergriffen.)

Band XV. Paul Wild: „Doktor Hella Welling auf der An-
klagebank". 136 Seiten. (Vergriffen.)
Band XVI. Fritz Gantzer: „Narren der Liebe". 174 Seiten.
(Vergriffen.)
Band XVII. Liesbet Dill: „Dein Leben gehört nicht Dir!...".
172 Seiten. (Vergriffen.)
Band XVIII. Oleg Berting: „Der Mann, der sich selbst ver-
lor". 200 Seiten. (Beide Auflagen vergriffen.)
Band XIX. Alfred Schirokauer: „Finstere Vergangenheit".
180 Seiten. (Vergriffen.)
Band XX. Wanda Baronesse Bönninghausen Budberg: „Wenn
Frauen lieben..." 216 Seiten (Doppelband). Mit Bildnis
und Faksimile der Verfasserin.
Band XXI. Gert Rothberg: „Das kleine Blumenmädchen".
152 Seiten. (Vergriffen.)
Band XXII. Karl G. Kupffer: „Livländische Liebe". Ein Roman aus versinkender Zeit. Mit Bildnis und Faksimile
des Verfassers. 164 Seiten. 3. Auflage.
Band XXIII. Elisabeth Goercke: „Nach den Sternen". Gedicht-
sammlung. Mit Bildnis und Faksimile der Verfasserin.
Band XXIV. Hanns Marschall: „Flucht in die Heimat."
164 Seiten.
Band XXV. Friedrich Lange: „Inferno". Ein Eheroman.
120 Seiten.

Alle Romane, soweit nicht vergriffen,
stehen den Lesern der „Riga am Sonntag" zum Preise von 60 bezw. 70 Sant.
zur Verfügung.

D13

Romanbibliothek der „Riga am Sonntag"

Band VIII.

Siegfried Bergengruen:

Gegen den Strom

Roman

Ausgabe der „Riga am Sonntag"
1929

D14

A side venture of the publisher of the German-language weekly *Riga am Sonntag: Illustrierte Zeitung für Politik, Unterhaltung und Kunst* (Riga on Sunday: Illustrated Newspaper for Politics, Entertainment, and Art)[30] was its *Romanbibliothek der "Riga am Sonntag"* (Fiction Library of "Riga on Sunday"), an inexpensive series selling for between 60 and 70 santimes that had reached 29 titles by 1931. A hint of the series content can be seen in the first 25 titles listed inside the back cover of Friedrich Lange's *Inferno: Ein Ehero-man* (Inferno: A Novel of Marriage, 1931). D13

The series reflected a degree of loyalty to the local Baltic-German circle of writers by including Bergengruen (N.B.: Siegfried, not Werner[31]), Baroness Bönninghausen Budberg (i.e., Moura Zakrevskaya), Lotty Burchard-Nauck, Oskar Grosberg, and Elisar von Kupffer, among others. Several titles, mainly those by local authors, were enhanced with a frontispiece portrait of the author. One example of such a practice can be seen in *Gegen den Strom* (Against the Current, 1929) by Siegfried Bergengruen, pseud. Quidam, in which a portrait sketch appears.[32] D14, D15

D15

Any investment in design for this series was limited to typography similar to the above or that of the cover for Lotty Burchard-Nauck's *Trude Schoenhaus und ihre Liebe: Eine Lebensgeschichte aus dem Baltenlande* (Trude Schoenhaus and her Love: A Life Story from the Baltic, 1932). D16

The closing of the newspaper in 1934 brought an end to what appeared to be a successful publishing venture, given that so many of the first 20 titles were indicated as out-of-print by 1930.

30   Published from December 18, 1927, to September 23, 1934.
31   In contrast to his little-known brother Siegfried, Werner Bergengruen was a widely popular Riga-born author published throughout German-speaking countries.
32   A second edition was published in Berlin by Eden-Verlag in 1934.

D16

D17

D18

The German press in Latvia

The wide availability at kiosks throughout the cities, towns, and villages of German-language newspapers, periodicals, and yearbooks direct from Königsberg and publishing centers further west gave the German-reading public some sense of cultural continuity during this period of transition, even though they were now classed as a minority, albeit a minority with a voice with political parties and representation in parliament.

Some 41 newspapers and journals started and stopped between 1919 and 1940, some lasting a year or less. Many served a professional or business audience, as a glance through one bibliography shows.[33] A few such titles serving specialized audiences and with more than two years of publishing life include: *Arbeitsrecht* (Labor Law, 1926-1934), *Gewerkschaftliche Monatsschrift für Staatsbeamte* (Union Monthly for Civil Servants,

33 *Latviešu periodika*, vol. 3, pp. 731-733.

1926-1934), *Journal der Lettländischen Pharmazeuten* (Journal of Latvian Pharmacists, 1925-1940), and *Lettländische Landwirtschaftliche Marktzeitung* (Latvian Agricultural Business Newspaper, 1929-1932).

Maintaining a sufficiently large or dedicated audience to pay the printing bills seemed to be an impediment to continued publication for such ephemeral offerings as *Heirats-Zeitung* (Marriage Newspaper, 1924-1925) and *Liebe, Ehe und Flirt* (Love, Marriage, and Flirtation, 1925) D17 and even the more purposeful papers such as *Lettländische Schachzeitung* (Latvian Chess Newspaper, 1924-1925) and *Rigaer Kino Woche* (Riga Movie Week, 1929). With occasional notes on new publications, the review sections of the specialized newspapers and periodicals assumed a modest role in fostering reading. Surprisingly, the *Rigasche Rundschau* (Riga Review, 1867-1915 and 1919-1939) was published six days a week. D18 This was the major, German-language paper for much of the German-speaking community outside of Germany in Eastern Europe, but it seems not to have maintained any consistent review section. The circulation in Latvia of *Rigasche Rundschau*, however, would have made it an ideal vehicle for this role, given that in 1931 its circulation was as high as 20,000, although dropping to 12,000-15,000 in 1937.[34] If a random leafing through 1920s and 1930s issues provides any indication, reviewing new books was simply not an editorial priority. In fact, one must look through many issues to find a single book review or publisher's advertisement. But to the paper's credit, novels by mainly Baltic-German authors were serialized. One could have imagined that this paper's long-time editor-in-chief, Paul Schiemann, would have seen fit to dedicate at least some space in each issue for book reviews, perhaps works that might have furthered his democratic goals for the larger Baltic-German community.

Parenthetically, Schiemann, as a Baltic-German leader, was concerned not only with his own ethnic community; his vision was much wider. To again quote John Hiden:[35] "Schiemann's innate liberalism and personality made him an early advocate of the right of Latvians to decide their own destiny." In light of Schiemann's leadership of the Baltic-German community during the first 15 years of the Interwar period, a further assertion from Hiden that Schiemann "believed that the twin assault late in the 19th century on Baltic Deutschtum—from russification and from the 'national awakening' of Latvians and Estonians—could only be survived by the German minority if they worked alongside the indigenous majority peoples to bring democratic reform to the Baltic provinces".[36]

Was there a politically dissenting voice countering the views in the largely conservative German press? Yes, but not a very loud or very long one; at least the two standard bibliographic works referred to previously do not explore the area. One such short-lived newspaper was the *Rigaer Tageszeitung für Volkstum und Sozialismus* (Riga Daily Paper for Community and Socialism), which began in 1934 and ended that same year after 68 issues, according to the holdings in the National Library of Latvia. The image on the poster (possibly by Ernests Kālis) encouraging readers in three languages implies a desired working-class readership. D19

It is difficult to determine the range of the Latvian-German press at that time. Surprisingly, no comprehensive, interpretive press bibliography exists. The brief citations in

34 Rihards Treijs, *Latvijas republikas prese, 1918-1940* (Riga: Zvaigzne, 1996), p. 490.
35 "Paul Schiemann on reconciling 'Nation' and 'State'" in *Ethnic Dimension in Politics and Culture in the Baltic Countries, 1920-1945*, ed. Baiba Metuzāle-Kangere (Stockholm: Almqvist & Wiksell, 2004), p. 9.
36 Ibid., pp. 9-10.

D19

D20

Latviešu periodika[37] provide a starting point, together with Grosberg's listing[38] that gives an additional 14 major and minor German-language newspapers and periodicals not included in the aforementioned bibliography. But much remains to be done in tracking down the elusive short-lived newsletters and journals of both formal and informal associations.

Yearbooks

An important yearbook for the Baltic-German community and lasting nearly the length of the Interwar period, initiated by Jonck & Poliewsky,[39] is *Jahrbuch und Kalender des Deutschtums in Lettland* (Yearbook and Calendar of the German Community in Latvia).[40] D20 In addition to advertisements for everything from pianos to perfume, the 1925 yearbook carries ads for 15 publishers in Germany, including Julius Hoffmann (Stuttgart), Vandenhoeck & Ruprecht (Göttingen), B. G. Teubner (Leipzig), Verlag Moritz Diesterweg (Frankfurt am Main), Velhagen & Klasing (Bielefeld), Drei Masken Verlag (München), F. Bruckmann (München), Otto Quitzow Verlag (Lübeck), C. Ed. Müller's Verlag (Halle/Saale), Grethlein & Co. (Leipzig/Zürich), and Chr. Belser, A. G. Verlags-Buchhandlung (Stuttgart). The implication being that any books from the advertising publishers could be found in the stock of Jonck & Poliewsky or ordered through them.

The 1925 yearbook's content gives additional insight into the cultural life of the German population with Paul Schiemann's lead article reflecting on the previous year's political activity. Following this is another Schiemann article dealing with the economic

---

37   *Latviešu periodika*, vol. 3, pp. 731-733.

38   *Die Presse Lettlands mit einem geschichtlichen Rückblick*, by Oskar Grosberg (Riga: Baltischer Verlag, 1927), pp. 119-120.

39   Continued by Verlag der Buchhandlung G. Löffler, following the bankruptcy of Jonck & Poliewsky.

40   Title variations published from 1924 to 1931 for the Zentrale deutsch-baltischer Arbeit beim Ausschuss der deutsch-baltischen Parteien. The cover illustration was possibly designed by Albert Gebhardt.

welfare levels of the German population. The yearbook continues with reports on various aspects of cultural life—church, welfare, schools (there were nine German secondary schools and one institution of higher learning, the Herder Institute)—as well as reports on German life in Latvia's neighbors, Estonia and Lithuania. Contributions to inspire the readership are part of the factual mix, e.g., "The state of contemporary Protestantism",[41] "Beethoven's Baltic connection", "Kant and the Balts", poems to bring various degrees of cheer, and a bit of prose—a novella—from the prolific early 19th century Baltic-German writer Willibald Alexis, i.e., Georg Wilhelm Heinrich Haring.[42]

Of interest is the yearbook's report on organizations, including those in the education sector. This section gives credence to common assertions by contemporary Latvian informants that the Baltic-German community was exceptionally well organized in contrast to other population sectors. This organizational characteristic was also reflected in parliamentary life, where the Baltic-German factions were few[43] and often voted as a bloc, thus having an influence out of proportion to the 3.7% of the population they represented.[44] One might also add that this seemingly insignificant portion of the population accounted for nearly 20% of the representation in the professions, including education.

This yearbook's section headed "Books and Periodicals" is limited to three pages with nearly a third of the space confined to "two new Baltic novels" by Baltic-Germans whose work was of sufficient quality in treating themes of "the happy early years in the Baltic" to find publishers in Germany. Two authors, Theophile von Bodisco and Valerian Hugo Tornius, are not included in the candor of the reviewer's lead sentence, in which he states: "Authorial talent is not richly seeded among us Balts, as one unfortunately knows." Both of the reviewed authors were widely read in German-speaking countries of the time because of what was for many German readers the romantic land- and cityscapes of the "distant Baltic". This Baltic setting was particularly characteristic of Bodisco's works set in her home country, Estonia, as is the work reviewed here, *Dorothee und ihr Dichter* (Dorothee and her Poet). The author, in this case, happened to be the famed high-level civil servant and dramatist August von Kotzebue of Reval (now Tallinn), whose dramas had a way with the early 19th century adolescent heart, and thus was an appropriate character to cast as a leading figure in a romantic novel. The Rigensian Valerian Tornius and his *Elisa: Die Geschichte einer schönen Seele* (Elisa: The Story of a Beautiful Soul; Leiden: O. Quitzow, 1925) probably fits in style and content that portion of Tornius's oeuvre known for its titillation of readers with themes of the love lives of the Baltic nobility. Tornius tended to redeem himself with relatively serious writings on literary and musical figures, e.g., Goethe and Mozart. The reviewer follows along with a brief review of a work by another widely read Baltic author, Anna Katterfeld, commenting on her *In Treue Fest* (In Abiding Loyalty; Halle, 1924), an historical novel of Kurland in "Tsarist times".

Three other titles in the review section are cited here not only to show the diversity of audience to which the yearbook is addressed, but also to demonstrate the seriousness of the readership. One is Monika Hunnius' *Mein Weg zur Kunst* (My Path to Art; Heilbronn, 1925). Another title, and clearly a subject of interest to the recently dis-

---

41 Lutheranism was the primary religion among the Baltic-Germans.
42 His collected writings were published in 1874 in 20 volumes.
43 Five political parties and their leaders are cited: Deutsch-Baltische Demokratische Partei (led by the aforementioned Paul Schiemann), the most influential of the parties, followed by the Deutsch-Baltische Fortschrittliche Partei, Deutsch-Baltische Einigungspartei, Deutsch-Baltische Reformpartei, and the Deutsch-Baltische Volkspartei.
44 See Cerūzis, ibid., p. 272.

enfranchised Baltic land barons, is Hamilkar Baron von Fölkersahm's *Die Entwick- lung der Agrarverfassung Livlands und Kurlands und die Umwäl-zung der Agrarverhält-nise in der Republik Lettland* (The Development of the Agricultural Law of Livland and Courland and the Overthrow of the Agricultural State of Affairs in the Republic of Latvia; Greifswald, 1923). The section concludes with Baron Frederick Wolff's *Inventar Baltischer Baudenkmäler* (Inventory of Baltic Architectural Monuments), a long-in-the-making study of the architectural heritage (mainly of Baltic-German heritage) illustrated throughout with drawings and photographs.

Six periodicals are announced in the periodical review section,[45] including one for young people. None is cited in the German section of *Latviešu periodika*.

As indicated earlier, directories, yearbooks, and almanacs published by and for German organizations comprised the greater percentage of locally produced German-language publishing in Latvia. As could be expected, given its aesthetically oriented audience, an annual such as the *Jahrbuch der Bildenden Kunst* (Yearbook of Fine Art)[46] rose above the commonplace in design and typography D21, unlike the largely typographic, utilitarian design of medical, business, and association directories. The cover designer, Kurt Bätge,[47] also designed posters D22 and other advertising graphics. But he was known more for having practiced architecture and civil engineering in Riga in partnership with Alfred Karr, also a prominent figure in Riga's

D21

Baltic-German community. Together they designed and built a number of well-known buildings in Riga, including the "Aina" movie theater. Their apartment buildings were known for echoing the functionalist style of the era.

The yearbook's publisher, the Architekten-Verein zu Riga (Riga Association of Architects), had sufficient wherewithal to produce a yearbook that was a visual contribution as well as an important record of the arts of the new republic and the region. The illustrated lead article deals with the sculptural quality of Lithuanian wayside crosses and is followed by two articles on the architecture of Reval (Tallinn). This section of text is followed by extensive reproductions of work by nearly 30 Riga artists[48] and

---

45 *Für baltische Jungen und Mädel* (Der Deutsche Gemeindeverband, 1923-1926), monthly; *Herdflammen*; *Baltisches Haus- und Jugendblatt*, fortnightly (Reval, 1924-1928); *Baltische Blätter für allgemein-kulturelle Fragen* (Deutsch-Baltischer Lehrerverband, 1923-1925), bi-monthly; *Deutscher Bote für Stadt und Land*, weekly; *Evangelisch-lutherisches Kirchenblatt für die deutschen Gemeinden Lettlands*, weekly; *Baltische Blätter* combined with the *Baltische Nachrichten*, fortnightly.

46 This volume marked the resumption of the yearbook that had ceased publication in its seventh volume in 1913 and resumed with volume eight in 1926, which appears to have been the last volume published.

47 Other spellings of his name: Kurts Betge, Kurt Baetge.

48 The list includes Erich Freiherr von Campenhausen, Elizabeta Kaehlbrandt-Zanelli, Vilhelms Purvītis, Friedrich Albert Leekney, Martha Hellmann, Kārlis Kurle, Anna von Römer-Soltan, Jānis Kuga, Kārlis Miesnieks, Jānis Jaunsudrabiņš, Indriķis Zeberiņš, Jānis Ansons, Oto Pladers, etc. (Note: Spelling of names follows that of the yearbook's editors for ethnic Germans. Germanicized Latvian names are spelled according to Latvian orthography. Dates are provided in the index.)

D22

D23

D24

D25

D26

23 architects.[49] All illustrations are in black-and-white. This section is followed by an article on Latvian art porcelain that, with the exception of two color plates, shows in black-and-white the work of the three multi-talented Baltars porcelain studio artists: Romans Suta, Aleksandra Beļcova, and Sigismunds Vidbergs.

This issue of the yearbook is an example of co-production with a Russian publisher-printer, the color reproductions being the work of the firm Salamandra, cited in the Russian-language publishing chapter.

Using yearbooks and calendars to make the point that Baltic-German book design remained locked in a conservative idiom might seem questionable, due to the small sample presented here. But having systematically browsed among German-language titles in the National Library of Latvia, the Misiņš Library, *belles lettres* titles, and nearly 50 yearbooks and almanacs designed, printed, and published in Latvia (mainly Riga) between 1919 and 1941, this writer is confident that what has been shown represents a reasonable range of the typography and illustration (or lack thereof) found in Latvian-German publishing.

The following five titles—three yearbooks, an anniversary volume, and a school book—only further support the contention of a conservative "look" that is undeniably "Germanic" and easily identifiable as belonging to the overall image of general German publishing for the middle-class throughout the German-speaking countries in the Interwar period.

Baltischer Kalender 1920 (Riga: E. Bruhns). D23 The longest, sustained Baltic-German publication of its type, beginning in 1884 and continuing—with a World War I gap and then a name change to *Heimat Kalender*—until it ceased publication with the 1940 volume. The yearbook is illustrated throughout (including covers) by the Baltic-German painter and illustrator Theodor Doebner, known for his somber West-Latvian landscapes.

Baltischer Almanach 1931 (Riga: Jonck & Poliewsky). D24 As the name implies, this is primarily a ready reference for calendar-related events ranging from name days, times of sunrise and sunset, conversion tables, postal information, bus line schedules, train distances and ticket prices, a Latvian-German glossary, a Jewish calendar of holidays, a perpetual calendar, a directory of Baltic-German associations, an address list of the 15 German schools in Riga, a few short stories, and, among other contributions, a photo reportage on the German community of 1930 with images by H. Schinke.

49 Including Paul Campe, Alexandrs Birznieks, Alexander Schmaehling, L. Laserson, Pauls Kundziņš, Eugen Laube, Alexander Trofimoff, Paul Mandelstamm, Nikolai Herzberg, Kārlis Fridrihs Skujiņš, and Wilhelm Bockslaff. (Dates and Latvianized spellings for German names are provided in the index.)

Libauscher Haus-Kalender 1934 (Libau: G. D. Meyer). D25 This appears to be the annual's final number, according to National Library of Latvia records. Cover designer: Frederic Fiebig.

1907-1932, 25 Jahre Rigaer Sängerhort (Riga: E. Plates, 1932). D26 This Riga singing group, with its motto "Pure in song, true in word, steadfast in harmony", lasted at least until 1936 and possibly even longer (the official notice of its liquidation did not appear until 1939). Cover design not credited.

Baltische Fibel (Baltic Primer), ed. by Edith Adolphi, illustrations by Th. Kraus (Riga: E. Bruhns, 1930). D27 One of numerous school books published by Bruhns and other publishers for the German school system. While the content is distinctively Baltic-German, there is a decided tie to a larger German culture through references to "persons, places, things".

D27

Afterword

To expand this chapter quantitatively would add little to the overall impression of design and content of Baltic-German books. This somewhat isolated German-speaking community could quite easily maintain its time-honored institutions rooted in the past and shielded from the revolutionary movements in literature and art (and book design) taking place in major centers of Weimar Germany nearly 800 miles to the west.

Authors who remained wrote nostalgia-laden works that often depicted the "world that once was". Looking forward was not a prime concern, let alone integrating fully into this new republic of which they were citizens. Skim once again through the titles being offered in the pages of the Academia Buchhandlung reproduced at the beginning of this chapter. Escape literature dominates. Although it is unwise to speculate about reading preferences, it is highly unlikely that a display suddenly appearing in a Riga shop of modernist-in-design books on contemporary social problems or themes would have found many readers among this particular population. This may explain the absence on the Academia Buchhandlung's import list of any representation from such Berlin publishers as Gustav Kiepenheuer, the Cassirers, Wieland Herzfelde,[50] Ernst Rowohlt, and Julius Berthold Salter,[51] among many others known for vanguard literature or non-fiction presenting political alternatives to a conservative view. However, titles from these publishers would likely have had some takers among intellectuals of the German-reading Latvian, Russian, and Jewish population. This is not to belittle the remaining German population, but the book buyers among them were mainly contented, successful businessmen and their wives, professionals, craftsmen, tradesmen—a population looking more for literary diversion, when not in their clubs or association meeting rooms, and not very different from individuals with middle-class ambitions to be found in most industrialized countries.

The day's newspapers usually came first. Of course, books had a place on their shelves as reminders of their "Germanness". But whenever there was a moment for more relaxed reading, more often than not it was as an escape, a means to avoid thinking about what might be their future, if the accounts of present-day informants looking back

50   Malik-Verlag.
51   Verlag der Schmiede.

D28

at their parents' and grandparents' lives provide an accurate reflection.

For many Baltic-Germans there was undoubtedly a glimmer of hope that their uncertain future in Latvia might become certain, if the growing strength of the German Reich under Hitler were to bring back German hegemony in the Baltic.

The story, however, had another ending with a second German exodus, this time in 1939. Still, some Germans remained only to sample uncertainty of another sort with the first Soviet occupation beginning in July 1940, which was followed a year later by the arrival of the German army and the Nazi apparat. This brought terror for the Jewish population that had remained, guilt for many remaining Germans, and opportunity for complicity for those relieved at the arrival of the Nazi occupiers.

In conclusion, if one wishes to evoke something of the extent of German culture once existing in Latvia, take tram No. 11 along Miera iela to the former Grosser Friedhof (Lielie kapi),[52] once the main cemetery of Riga. This was the final resting place for the remains of many Baltic-Germans as well as Latvians living in the greater Riga area and dying there before the conclusion of World War II. Although at the war's end the retreating Soviet Army carted off many thousands of tombstones to be used in road construction and repair in the Soviet Union, many markers remain, scattered among the mausolea still standing, and offer a silent testimony to an all-but-forgotten culture with-in a culture. D28

When one attempts to characterize a brief period in a country's life with nothing more than an assemblage of visual printed images, it is probably better to provide more white spaces for extrapolation than rambling, fact-filled captions attached to the images. Most likely, readers will bring to bear what is known from their own readings of 20th century book culture. Also, the prime benefit of such an approach is to stimulate the reader to dig through the texts that further explicate the era under examination.

Between the two World Wars, Latvia was a laboratory for democracy, including such basic institutions as book publishing and the periodical press. For the majority-language speaking Latvians it allowed such an outpouring of emotion and cultural expression—an opportunity for the first time to exhibit something that was culturally and linguistically unique. This was also a time for Latvians to take up cultural spears against a few detractor-critics living in larger countries with much longer and more developed histories in literature and art than those of this small but culturally energetic country.

One must keep in mind throughout this extended reflection that this largely agricultural society had at the 1930 mid-point slightly over 90% male literacy above ten years of age and nearly 83.5% female literacy. When broken down by the dominant populations whose publishing has been under discussion, the literacy picture looked like this:[53] Latvians, 89.99%; Baltic-Russians (those living for generations in Latvia), 64.67%; Jews, 88.9%; Germans, 97.66%.

---

52 Established in 1772 and extending over nearly 55 acres.
53 *Latvju mazā enciklopēdija*. Ed. by Alfrēds Bīlmanis (Riga: Grāmatu Draugs, 1930).

1   Aizliegto grāmatu un brošūru saraksts Nr. 3
(List of Banned Books and Booklets, No. 3, 1941)

2   Liste des aus den lettischen Volksbüchereien und Antiquariaten zurückzustellenden Schrifttums /
No latviešu tautas bibliotēkām un antikvāriātiem izņemamo grāmatu saraksts
(List of Books that Have to Remove from the Latvian Public Libraries and Antique Shops, 1941)

3   No apgrozības izņemamo grāmatu un brošūru saraksts Nr. 5
(List of Books and Booklets to be Taken of the Trading, No. 5, 1947)

4   Apvienotais novecojušo izdevumu saraksts (1–7), kas nav lietojami Latvijas PSR sabiedriskajās bibliotēkās un grāmatu tirdzniecības tīklā, un Novecojušo izdevumu saraksts Nr. 8
(Combined List of Outdated Publications (1–7), Taken of the Use in Public Latvian SSR Libraries and Bookshops, and the List of Outdated Publications, No. 8, 1951)

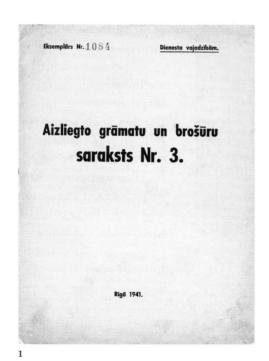

1

2

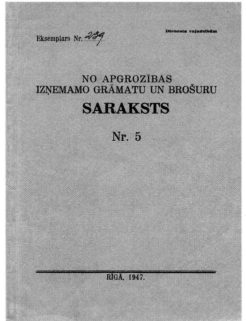

3

4

Books and ethnic communities in Latvia after 1940

Between the two world wars, Latvia was a sovereign and independent nation, a parliamentary republic, and a member of the League of Nations. Its constitution (*Satversme*), adopted in 1922, guaranteed personal liberty and ethnic minority rights. Latvia had a multi-party system until 1934, when, similar to other Eastern European nations, an authoritative regime took over. This regime was anti-democratic, but not repressive. Until 1934, Russian communities existed alongside Latvian communities, Jewish communities alongside German communities. Each ethnic group had its own social organizations and press. But the autonomy of these communities was restricted after the coup in 1934, when they were subjected to national policy and the authoritative regime strove to Latvianize ethnic communities.

The 1890 Russian press and censorship law was in effect in Latvia until 1924. The "Temporary regulations regarding the commerce of press materials, libraries, and reading rooms" were adopted in 1921. But from February 12, 1924, until May 15, 1934, Latvia had a Press Law that ensured freedom of the press. Confiscation of books took place according to the Criminal Law. Lists of banned books were published in the newspaper *Valdības Vēstnesis* and thus were accessible to the public. Even though the Press Law was formally in effect until February 14, 1938, when the second Press Law was passed, in reality the publication and distribution of books and periodicals after May 1934 was controlled by order of the Ministry of the Interior. The 1938 Press Law regulated much more strictly those who were allowed to publish books and periodicals and the laws they needed to observe in their work.

The Department of the Press and Societies within the Ministry of the Interior monitored compliance with the Press Law. Approximately 500 publications (including 95 books, 242 periodical issues, and 160 leaflets[1]) were confiscated in Latvia up until the year 1934. Among these works were those the government considered subversive, called for the violent overthrow of the government or "fomented rebellion or disloyal activities" (the case with the almanac *Signāls*, 1933), expressed disrespect towards religion, or incited hatred between segments of the population, ethnic groups, or social classes (as was the case with the leftist youth journal *Jaunā Gvarde* [1928] and its subsequent publications).

Approximately 60 newspapers representing various political parties were closed after the coup in May 1934. A total of 50 Latvian-language publications were closed, among them the newspaper *Socialdemokrats* and the journal *Domas* as well as *Aizkulises* and *Intīmā Rīga*. German, Russian, and Jewish publications were also closed, such as the German newspaper *Rigaer Tageszeitung*, the Russian *Golos naroda* and *Za kulisami*, the Yiddish-language newspaper *Frimorgn*, and other publications that promoted a left political view or the views of one particular political party.

329 books[2] were banned from distribution between 1934 and 1940. These were mainly books with a socialist bend, including previously published books such as Linards Laicens' and Leons Paegle's *Panama*; Linards Laicens' *Mebelīgā Rīga un pielikumi*, *Attaisnotie*, and *69 dienas*; Indriķis Lēmanis' *Mašīnas* and *Māte*; Ādolfs Talcis' *Dumpīgā grāmata*; Andrejs

---

1   Paeglis, J. *Kas bija liegts pirmās republikas lasītājiem?* (Riga: Zinātne, 1996), p. 33.
2   Paeglis, J., p. 34.

Kurcijs' *Cilvēciskie lopi, Ēzelis, mūks, Eiropa,* and *Dzīvības vārtos*; Jānis Plaudis' *Panama galvā*; and others. Other publications were deemed Communist propaganda (Z. Fleišmanis' booklet *Marks lebt*) or sympathetic to the revolution (Sergei Malashkin's *Luna s pravoj storoni*) and thus banned. Anti-Semitic publications were also banned.

According to a research on censorship by Jānis Paeglis, a total of 424 books (1.6% of the total number of books published between the two world wars) were confiscated, taken out of circulation, or banned from distribution during the period between 1920 and 1940. The publishing houses that suffered most were Kultūras Balss (22 books confiscated or banned), Daile un Darbs (17), and Nākotnes Kultūra (9); the authors that suffered the most were Linards Laicens (14 works), Leons Paegle (9), Fricis Menders (8), Kārlis Dziļleja (8), Andrejs Kurcijs (5), and Indriķis Lēmanis (3). Publications were closed for a variety of reasons, including interpretations of international relations that could harm Latvian foreign policy, opposition to the national economic or social or political policy, criticism of national policy, Communist or Nazi propaganda, subversive sentiments, and incitement to disobey laws.

Simultaneously, the Commission for Literature Harmful to Youth (*Jaunatnei kaitīgās literatūras komisija*, established in 1928) compiled lists of literature deemed full of "trash and filth", however, this description did not apply to publications that contained political interpretations. Two lists of banned books compiled by Roberts Lapsiņš, director of the Department of the Press, were published in the late 1930s: "List of banned books, booklets, and other materials printed in Latvia" (1939) and "List of third-rate literature" (1939).

World War II played a fateful role not only in the history of Latvia as a nation, but also for books and book publishing. The Baltic States, including Latvia, experienced three periods of occupation during World War II. Each of these occupying regimes attempted to not only control publishing policy, but also cracked down on existing collections of books in libraries and other repositories of books.

Regarding foreign policy, throughout the 1930s Latvia had been forced to maneuver between two large powers that threatened the peace in Europe: Nazi Germany and the Soviet Union. The non-aggression treaties Latvia had signed with the Soviet Union (in 1932) and Germany (in 1939) provided only an illusory sense of peace. The political situation quickly changed after the signing by Adolf Hitler and Joseph Stalin of a non-aggression treaty on August 23, 1939. The secret supplemental protocol of this treaty, known as the Molotov-Ribbentrop Pact, which divided Eastern Europe into German and Soviet spheres of influence, determined that Latvia would be in the Soviet Union's zone of interest. The treaty allowed Nazi Germany to destroy Poland and thereby begin World War II. On October 5 the Soviet Union forced Latvia to sign a treaty of mutual assistance; supplemental protocols of this treaty called for the establishment of Soviet Red Army bases on Latvian soil, which in effect pulled Latvia into the Soviet Union's sphere of interest and began the gradual destruction of Latvia's independence.

The Red Army occupied Latvia on June 17, 1940. A little over a year later, in July 1941, Nazi Germany occupied Latvia. These two occupations *de facto* destroyed the independent nation of Latvia. The Soviet Union annexed Latvia in August 1940, and in July 1941 Latvia became a General Region (*Generalbezirk*) of the Reichskommissariat-Ostland (RKO). Although the Soviet occupation did create an illusory People's Government in 1940 and the German occupation established a Latvian self-government in March 1942, both institutions operated under the direction of the respective occupying nation and only minimally influenced political and social processes in Latvia. The Soviet Union entered and occupied Latvia for a second time in 1944-1945. This second Soviet occupation lasted over 45 years, and Latvia regained its independence only in 1991.

World War II and the occupations of Latvia changed the historical composition of Latvia's population. In the lead-up to World War II, Germany signed an agreement with Latvia on October 30, 1939, regarding the resettlement of ethnic Germans (*Umsiedlung*, in which the Germans were expected to renounce their Latvian citizenship). A similar agreement signed with the Soviet Union on January 10, 1941, allowed Germans still in Soviet-occupied territories to resettle in the spring of that year (*Nachumsiedlung*). Approximately 54,000 Baltic-Germans left Latvia during the 1939-1941 period of resettlement. German schools and organizations were closed near the end of 1939. The last issue of the *Rigasche Rundschau* newspaper was published on December 13, 1939. The German community in Latvia ceased to exist. By 1939 more than 4500 Jews had also left Latvia for Palestine.

Repressions during the year of Soviet occupation affected the Latvian, Jewish, and Russian communities alike. Politicians and public figures from the communities were arrested and deported. The largest deportation took place just two weeks before the German occupation, on June 14, 1941. In 1941 a total of 11,598 Latvians, 1789 Russians, 761 Jews, and 42 Germans were deported. (41,084 Latvians, 772 Russians, and 4 Germans were deported in a later wave of deportations in 1949.)

The Nazi German occupation proved tragic for Latvia's Jewish population. Approximately 70,000 Latvian Jews were exterminated during World War II. By 1945 only around a thousand Jews who had stayed in the German-occupied territory of Latvia remained alive. Approximately 14,000 Jews who had followed the Red Army to Russia in 1941 returned to Latvia after the war.[3]

In 1944 approximately 140,000 citizens, mainly Latvians, fled to the West in fear of repeated repressions by the Soviet regime. Those who remained in Latvia were affected by continued repressions from 1944 onward until the 1950s.

Both the German and Soviet occupations not only created an apparatus of repression to serve their purposes, but also created systems to control information with the goal of not only controlling the public press and newly printed books but also existing collections in public libraries.

A decision by the Soviet Union in August 1940 abolished the Department of the Press and Societies and set up in its place the Main Administration for Literary and Publishing Affairs (abbreviated as Glavlit, or GLP in Latvian), modelled after the same structure in the Soviet Union's government. Glavlit was in charge of censorship for all publications. On August 10, 1940, all previous periodical licenses were rescinded and a total of 30 newspapers and journals were allowed to circulate. Of all the former periodicals, only the journal *Atpūta* continued to circulate until June 1941. On August 19, 1940, all Latvian newspaper correspondents abroad were suspended as were foreign correspondents in Latvia. During the second half of 1940 all printing and publishing houses were nationalized and the National Board of Publishing and Polygraphy (*Valsts Apgādu un poligrāfisko uzņēmumu pārvalde*, or VAPP) was established. All publications came under the scrutiny of Glavlit; permission from Glavlit was required for all publications and books as well as for business publications, business cards, and public speeches.

---

3   See Dribins, L., "Ebreji Latvijā" in *Mazākumtautības Latvijā. Vēsture un tagadne*, edited by L. Dribins (Riga: LU Filozofijas un socioloģijas institūts, 2007), p. 223.

Although in 1940 the Soviet regime, in its effort to counter the previous political system, used the slogan "in support of freedom of speech" and declared that previously banned books were again freely available, it simultaneously began a campaign against books that praised or showed the former era in a favorable light. Control of libraries and clearing them of publications deemed harmful to the new regime was also one of the functions of Glavlit. Four lists of banned books were compiled in the span of only one year. These lists included 4586 book titles intended to be taken out of circulation immediately. A fifth list with another 100 or so titles was never published. These lists of banned books were secret and meant only for use by censors during library inspections. Reports by the Nazi occupying forces claimed that 749,540 books had been confiscated during the first Soviet occupation, but this number is only an estimate.

Nationalized publishing business were not automatically returned to their owners during the Nazi occupation. Instead, owners were required to receive concessions anew as well as a separate license for each individual publication. At first the German military board controlled publishing in Latvia; later, when the civilian administration was established, this task was taken over by the *Amt für Verlagswesen* (Office of Publications). By the end of 1941, five publishers—merged in the Latvju grāmata publishing house—were allowed to operate. By 1943 the number of publishers had grown to 35. Kārlis Rasiņš' publishing house Literatūra reopened, as did Miķelis Goppers' Zelta Ābele and Helmārs Rudzītis' publishing business; others, such as T. O. Šteinbergs, Otto Krolls, and Ernests Ūdris, also began publishing businesses.

The Nazi occupation continued the work begun by Glavlit of destroying books. It removed books from circulation according to the *Liste aus den lettischen Völksbücherein und Antiquariaten zurückstellen Schriftums* (1941), proposed by *Propagandastaffel Lettland* and compiled by the *Direktion für Kunst- und Kultur-Angelegenheit Lettland*. Works by Latvian authors representing both the political right and left were banned. All travel guides to Riga and Latvia were removed from libraries as well books in French and English published after 1933 and their translations into Latvian, Russian, or German. All works by Jewish authors were destroyed. The majority of works on the list, however, were by Russian authors, both those published in the Soviet Union and in Riga.

In 1944 the Soviet regime and its institutions returned to Latvia, including the Glavlit employees, who renewed their supervision of printing presses and newspaper editorial offices. The first "cleansings" of libraries, which took place before the end of the war, were barbaric. Glavlit employees searched bookshelves, throwing out books on the basis of their titles alone because, as their reports stated, the harmfulness of a book is determined by the fact that "they do not arouse the need to be read from the first to the last page". The first injunction to remove books from book stores and libraries (according to List No. 1, called the "Latvian SSR list of harmful books to be removed") was issued on November 20, 1944. This list was secret and could only be distributed to Glavlit staff and contract employees. A section of closed stacks was created at the two largest libraries in Riga, where two copies of each "harmful" book could be held; access to these closed stacks was restricted to a small group of individuals with special permits. The first list of banned books contained 3573 titles; a note added to some authors' names stated that "all works are to be removed". Prohibited works included books that reflected political life during the time of the Republic of Latvia, literature of a nationalistic nature, school books, and mass literature. Already by the end of the year in 1944 authorities had removed 7653 books from Riga city libraries, 2506 books from school libraries, and around 5000 books from institutional libraries. Any books associated with "Fascist agitation" were removed without hesitation, regardless of whether they were on the list. So many books in the German, Russian, and Latin languages were removed that in their reports censors wrote that "quantities cannot be described in the number of books, but rather in tons and cubic meters". During the first months of this campaign, Glavlit attempted to burn all the removed books, but when this became too difficult, the books were instead sent to paper factories. A second list of banned books was already being compiled during the first book removal campaign; List No. 2 contained approximately 1000 titles. A third list, with approximately 600 titles, was compiled in 1945.

Libraries were not the only institutions to be affected by Glavlit; antiquarian book-sellers and people selling books at markets were also affected. Glavlit employees participated in arrests carried out by the Ministry of State Security (MGB) and confiscated home libraries.

Lists of banned books were compiled one after another. After the publication of list No. 4 (in 1946, containing 296 titles), Glavlit complained to the Council of Ministers that it lacked the resources to "destroy 5,500,000 removed books". List No. 5 was published in 1947 and contained 914 titles. List No. 6 was published in 1948 and contained 521 titles. List No. 7 was published in 1948 and contained 488 titles. List No. 8 was published in 1951 and contained 433 titles. The "Combined list of outdated publications, 1-7; 8", containing a total of 7118 titles, was published in 1951. This was followed in 1954 by lists No. 9 and No. 10, which contained not only older publications but now also books that had been published recently, in the Soviet era. The confiscation of books continued by special Glavlit order until the 1980s.

As the political situation in the Soviet Union became more open in the second half of the 1950s, some (albeit not very many) of the books placed in closed stacks were returned to public libraries, but this number was negligible. The closed stacks at the national libraries were opened only in 1991, when Latvia regained its independence. The majority of the books that had been destroyed "by the ton and cubic meter", ground into pulp for paper, or burned were the body of literature and periodicals published in Latvia in the 1920s and 1930s: Latvian, Russian, Yiddish, Hebrew, German, and other publications expressing a variety of worldviews and providing evidence of the country's era of democracy, when several ethnic communities had existed side by side in Latvia.

It is impossible to determine the total number of books destroyed in Latvia from 1940 onward. Various authors, using data provided by repressive institutions as well as other sources, have suggested figures ranging from 3,632,137[4] books destroyed between the years of 1944 and 1960 to 17,383,778[5] books destroyed during the entire era of Soviet occupation.

It is true, however, that not all of the books on the lists were destroyed, nor were all of the books actually removed from libraries eventually destroyed. Some of these books, containing library stamps, found their way into personal libraries, which were not subject to state control. There are, of course, stories of librarians saving banned books from destruction, but the number of these saved books cannot compare to the unimaginable numbers of books destroyed.

4   See Briedis, R. "Karš ar grāmatām. Desmit saraksti (1944-1960)" in *Karogs*, No. 5 (1997), p. 196.
5   See Strods, H. *Politiskā cenzūra Latvijā 1940-1990*. 1. daļa (Riga: Jumava, 2010), p. 180.

The German community in Latvia ceased to exist in 1939. Latvia's Jewish population was destroyed in 1941. World War II destroyed the state of Latvia, and the Soviet occupation controlled all public information until the late 1980s and tried to subject it to its own ideology. But books continued to be important for Latvians and Latvian culture. Already in the 1940s Latvian exiles established publishing houses in the countries to which they had fled or emigrated—Western Europe and later the United States, Canada, and Australia—while publishers and artists in Latvia preserved the tradition of publishing books in an ideologically transformed Soviet land. But that is another story, requiring another study.

Checklist of frequently consulted reference works

The footnotes in the text carry the primary references supporting a given statement. Those references are not listed here:

A izdavalos eto v Rige 1918-1944. Iuriĭ Abyzov, compiler and ed. (Moscow: Biblioteka-Fond "Russkoe Zarubezhe" Russkiĭ put, 2006), 416 pp. An invaluable, year-by-year commentary and compilation of Russian-language book and periodical publishing in Riga. Some photographs, title pages, and covers are reproduced, but of poor quality.

A Wayfarer in Estonia, Latvia, and Lithuania. By E. C. Davies (New York: Robert M. McBride & Co., 1937). The chapters on Latvia are a sensitive and informed account of Latvian life and the setting mid-point in the 1930s; highly recommended for gaining a feel for the Baltics in general in the period between World Wars I and II.

Baltiĭskiĭ Arkhiv, VI: Russkaia kul'tura v Pribaltike. Iuriĭ Abyzov, Boris Ravdin, Zhanna Zeit, compilers (Riga: Daugava, 2000), 404 pp. Of primary interest is Ravdin's chapter titled "Materialy k ukazateliu Evreĭskoĭ pechati Latviĭ, 1919-1940", pp. 324-370. An exhaustive study and bibliography of the Jewish press in Latvia for the period indicated.

Eesti kunsti ja arhitektuuri biograafiline leksikon. Mart-Ivo Eller, ed. (Tallinn: Eesti Entsüklopeediakirjastus, 1996), 622 pp. The standard single-volume biographical reference work for 19th and 20th century Estonian architects and artists. All articles are signed and conclude with additional biographical sources.

Es viņu pazīstu. Žanis Unāms, ed. (Riga: Biogrāfiskā arhīva apgāds, 1939), 562 pp. A biographical dictionary primarily of ethnic Latvians living and dead but with emphasis on figures of some public importance during the interwar period.

Futur Antērieur: L'avantgarde et le livre Yiddish (1914-1939). Nathalie Hazan-Brunet, editor-in-chief with Ada Ackerman (Paris: Skira-Flammarion and Musée d'art et d'histoire du Judaïsme, 2009), 271 pp. Although attention to Yiddish-language publishing in Latvia is limited, the context is of great interest.

Gazeta "Segodnia" 1919-1940. Iuriĭ Abyzov, compiler, 2 vols. (Riga: Latviĭskaia Natsional'naja biblioteka, 2001). A compilation of all article titles and contributors to the leading non-Soviet Russian-language newspaper published in the interwar period. Indexes allow access by author and author pseudonym. Although lacking a subject index, the chronological arrangement by issue allows one to find the subjects desired.

Grāmata par grāmatu. Jānis Grīnbergs, ed. (Riga: J. Roze, 1925), 149 pp. With eight unnumbered leaves of advertising for typographic and printing services. The first and only major compilation on printing and publishing history in Latvia's Interwar period.

Historical Dictionary of Latvia. Andrejs Plakans, compiler (Lanham, MD: Scarecrow Press, 1997), 193 pp. Although I did not have access to the additional 118 pages of the second edition, one can only assume it is an improvement over this first edition, in which one can look repeatedly only to be surprised at what is *not* found, either subject or individual.

The Jews in Latvia. M. Bobe, S. Levenberg, I. Maor, Z. Michaeli, compilers (Tel Aviv: Association of Latvian and Estonian Jews in Israel, 1971), 384 pp. A useful "labor of love" worthy of a revised edition.

Latvian Jewish Intelligentsia—Victims of the Holocaust. Aleksandrs Feigmanis, compiler with the assistance of Gregoriĭ Smirin (Riga: publisher not given, 2006), 120 pp. Text in English, Latvian, Russian, and French. Brief biographical sketches with photo portraits where available.

Latvian Literature: Essays. By Jānis Andrups and Vitauts Kalve, introduction by Arnolds Spekke (Stockholm: M. Goppers, Zelta Ābele, 1954). A basic introduction to Latvian literature by two of the major literary historians in exile. To my knowledge, this is the first and only extensive monograph on the history of Latvian literature in English.

Latviešu literatūras hronika sastatījumā ar notikumiem pasaulē un Latvijā, 1888-1944. Raimonds Briedis, compiler (Riga: Valters un Rapa, 2006), 284 pp. An illustrated (with book covers) cultural comparison "timeline" guide with separate biographical appendices for Latvian and world writers. A second volume continues the concept from 1945 to 2005.

Latviešu literatūras vēsture. Viktors Hausmanis, research director. Vol. 2, 1918-1945 (Riga: Zvaigzne ABC for the Institute of Literature, Folklore, and Art of the Latvian Academy of Sciences, 1999), 448 pp. Some portraits and a few book covers of titles mentioned.

Latviešu, vācu un krievu grāmatrūpniecības vārdnīca. Ansis Auziņš, compiler (Riga: Latvju Grāmata, 1942), 518 pp. 12 leaves of illustrations, some in color, some tipped-in. An invaluable Latvian-, German-, and Russian-language technical dictionary of the book trade, printing, and allied fields.

Latvijas māksla, 1915-1940. Jānis Siliņš (Stockholm: Daugava, 1993), 320 pp. Vol. 3, the concluding volume, is an indispensable history of Latvian art by the leading art historian of his generation. Written in exile and thus free of tendentious text, the three volumes also have English summaries.

Latvijas telefona abonentu saraksts 1939. g. (Riga: Pasta un telegrafa departaments, 1939), varying pagination.

Latviešu periodika. Various editors. 4 volumes in 5 parts. (Riga: Zinātne and Latvian Academic Library, 1977-1995), v.p. An extraordinary bibliographical enterprise begun in the Soviet era and continued into the second period of independence. Volume 1, covering the period 1768-1919, was edited by K. Egle, V. Lūkina, A. Brempele, and V. Jauģiets. Volume 2 is confined to the "Revolutionary and Soviet Periodicals" published during the first period of independence (1920-1940) and was edited by Ā. Brempele, Ē. Flīgere, and V. Lūkina. Volume 1 gives brief biographical information for Russian and German serials at the conclusion of the detailed Latvian-language serials section. Volume 2 provides comparably detailed information for the Russian and Yiddish serials that conformed to the party-determined editorial guidelines, i.e. Social Democratic titles were *not* included. Volume 3 covers all non-revolutionary serials of the Interwar period— 1,408 titles—and cites with brief notes the Russian, German, French, and other language titles published during the period. The editors of volume 3 were Ā. Brempele, Ē. Flīgere, D. Ivule, L. Lāce, and M. Lazdiņa. Volume 3 is in two parts, the second part being a detailed summary giving access to the previous volumes by editor, title, and place of publication together with chronological access. The second part of volume 3 was edited by the same team as the first part. The concluding volume (4) covers the serials of the period 1940-1945 and was edited by Ē. Flēgere and J. Paeglis. Two thirds of this volume is devoted to summary indices to the earlier volumes as well as providing the above-mentioned access points to its own content. This reference work is indispensable to any research into Latvian literary endeavor and is complemented by Rihards Treijs' work for the Latvian press (see below) and Boris Ravdin's work, also cited below.

Latvijas republikas prese, 1918-1940. Rihards Treijs, compiler (Riga: Zvaigzne ABC, 1996), 524 pp. A most useful discursive reference. Some portraits and other illustrations.

Latviešu satīrs smejas: Ieskats Latvijas neatkarības gadu humoristiski satīriskās preses izdevumos. Raimonds Zalcmanis, ed. (Riga: Avots, 1994), 183 pp. Brief biographical data in an appendix. Illustrated throughout with banner pages and cartoons.

Latviešu rakstniecība biogrāfijās. Anita Rožkalne, project director (Riga: Zinātne, 2003), 739 pp. An essential bio-bibliographical dictionary of Latvian writers from Latvian literature's beginnings to the present century. Articles are signed and illustrated with portraits when available. Sources are given for the majority of entries.

Latvju rakstniecība portrejās. Alberts Prande, compiler (Riga: Leta, 1926), 515 pp. The first major bio-historical reference work to be produced in the Interwar period and designed to codify Latvia's literary and publishing history. Because the first half of the work is organized according to distinct phases of Latvian cultural development from 1530 to the 1920s, the user is given a useful, illustrated overview along with biographical details about writers not easily found elsewhere. The editorial approach is casual by comparison with the previously cited work, but it is no less helpful. Reproductions of title pages, handwriting examples, and portraits of authors, editors, and publishers make it a pleasant work in which to browse. Subject, author, and works, i.e., books, journals, and newspaper, indexes are provided.

Lexikon deutschbaltischer bildender Künstler 20. Jahrhundert. Kuno and Margarete Hagen, compilers and eds. (Köln: Vlg. Wissenschaft und Politik Berend v. Nottbeck, 1983), 152 pp. Useful, but numerous individuals seem to have eluded the compilers.

Māksla un arhitektūra biogrāfijās. Andris Vilsons, ed. Vol. 1, A-Kal (Riga: Latvijas Enciklopēdija, 1995), 239 pp.; Vol. 2, Kal-Rum (1996), 239 pp.; Anita Vanaga, ed. Vol. 3, R-V (Riga: A/S Preses Nams, 2000), 255 pp.; Vol. 4, V-Ž (Riga: A/S Preses Nams, 2003), 303 pp. A major and indispensable reference work for the visual arts historian. Beginning with volume three, color is added and paper quality and binding are greatly improved. Most importantly, the content benefits from an additional number of researchers added to the compilation staff. Supplement "A-U" appended to volume four.

Oblozhka: Graficheskoe litso epokhi revoliutsionnogo natiska, 1917-1937. Vladimir Krichevskiĭ, compiler (Moscow: Samolet Design Studio, 2002), 240 pp. Although numerous such works (including others by Krichevskiĭ) have been produced in the past few years, this continues to be a useful overview of period book cover design and is of particular utility because designers' life dates are provided.

Outstanding Jewish Personalities in Latvia. Gregoriĭ Smirin, compiler (Riga: Nacionālais apgāds, 2003), 128 pp. Illustrated with photos. While the work provides valuable information on those included, clearly defined criteria for inclusion would have improved the work's usefulness. The introduction, "A Latvian story about outstanding Latvian Jewish personalities" by Pēteris Apinis, greatly enhances the work's value.

Rīgas arhitektūras meistari, 1850-1940. Jānis Krastiņš, compiler (Riga: Jumava, 2002), 360 pp. An excellent, well-indexed, and illustrated reference work with English translation by Sanita Supe and Regīna Jozauska accompanying the Latvian text.

Rossiyskaya evreiskaya entsiclopediya. (Moscow, 1995-2007). The online form has been consulted. The name index has been edited and translated by Josef and Vitaly Charny.

Saules akmens: Latviešu bērnu literatūras gadu gaita. Jāzeps Osmanis (Riga: Liesma, 1977). The most comprehensive study of Latvian children's literature published to date. Although written under the constraints of the Soviet era and all that implies, it remains of prime importance for any inquiry into this sector of publishing.

Teātris un kino biogrāfijās. Māra Niedra, editorial director, Vol. 1, A-J (Riga: Preses nams, 1999), 462 pp.; Vol. 2, K-N (Riga: Pils, 2002), 460 pp. A well-produced, well-illustrated reference with all biographical entries signed. At the time of this writing, financial difficulties have prevented the completion of the projected third volume.

Index of Persons

Index of Publishers

James H. Fraser

Publishing and Book Design
in Latvia 1919–1940: a Re-discovery

Editor: Raimonds Briedis
Editorial Coordinator: Guna Zelmene
Design: Anta Pence
Translator and Proof-reader: Amanda Jātniece

This edition contains reproductions from books and periodicals from the private archive of James H. Fraser, and collections of: National Library of Latvia, Misins Library (Academic Library of the University of Latvia), archive of Art Academy of Latvia, Library of the Latvian Academy of Culture, as well as reproductions from books and periodicals in private libraries.

The book contains photos by Mārcis Lapiņš (L15, L18), Meria Michelson Lewentstein (R7), Roman Vishniac (R6), Raimonds Briedis (L37, Y12, Y17, D28), as well as pictures by unidentified authors included in periodicals and private collections. Enquiries regarding author's rights should be addressed to Copyright and Communication Consulting Agency / Latvian Authors Association.

Publishers:

Neputns

Neputns
Tērbatas iela 49/51–8, LV-1011, Rīga, Latvia
www.neputns.lv

in collaboration with the
Latvian Academy of Culture

Printed at Jelgavas tipogrāfija

ISBN 978-9934-512-18-6